Wuthering Heights

A Kaplan SAT Score-Raising Classic

Look for more Kaplan SAT Novels:

The Ring of McAllister: *A Score-Raising Mystery Featuring 1,046 Must-Know SAT Vocabulary Words*

Frankenstein:
A Kaplan SAT Score-Raising Classic
Tales of Edgar Allan Poe:
A Kaplan SAT Score-Raising Classic

Coming in May 2005

Dr. Jekyll and Mr. Hyde:
A Kaplan SAT Score-Raising Classic

Coming in August 2005

Scarlet Letter:
A Kaplan SAT Score-Raising Classic

Wuthering Heights

A Kaplan SAT Score-Raising Classic

By Emily Brontë

Simon & Schuster
New York ❖ London ❖ Sydney ❖ Toronto

Kaplan Publishing
Published by Simon & Schuster, Inc.
1230 Avenue of the Americas
New York, NY 10020

For bulk sales to schools, colleges, and universities, please contact: Order Department, Simon & Schuster, Inc. 100 Front Street, Riverside, NJ 08075. Phone: 1-800-223-2336. Fax: 1-800-943-9831.

For information regarding special discounts for other bulk purchases, please contact Simon & Schuster Special Sales at 1-800-456-6798 or business@simonandschuster.com

Kaplan® is a registered trademark of Kaplan, Inc.

Cover Design: Cheung Tai
Cover Illustration: Greg Copeland
Interior Page Design and Production: Lori DeGeorge
Editor: Beth Grupper

Manufactured in the United States of America

December 2004

10 9 8 7 6 5 4 3 2 1

Library of Congress Cataloging-in-Publication Data is available.

ISBN: 0-7432-6199-2

❧ How To Use This Book ❧

Not only is Emily Brontë's classic novel, *Wuthering Heights*, filled with turbulent tales of love and haunting beauty—it's also filled with SAT words! Now Kaplan makes it as easy as 1-2-3 for you to learn these vocabulary words as you read the story.

On the right-hand pages you will find the story of *Wuthering Heights* with selected words **bolded** throughout. These bolded words are frequently found on the SAT. On the left-hand pages Kaplan defines these SAT words, as well as gives you the part of speech, pronunciation, and synonyms for each word—everything you need to know to improve your vocabulary and to ace the SAT.

Some of the most challenging vocabulary words found in *Wuthering Heights* aren't likely to appear on the SAT, but we thought you might want to learn those, too. That's why we've underlined them throughout the text and added their definitions to a glossary at the end of the book. After all—you never know where they might pop up next!

So what are you waiting for? Start reading!

MISANTHROPIST (mihz <u>aan</u> throh pihst) *n.*
  person who hates human beings
    Synonyms: cynic, loner, curmudgeon
DESOLATION (deh suh <u>lay</u> shuhn) *n.*
  barren wasteland; sadness, loneliness
    Synonyms: bleakness, devastation, ruin; despair
RESOLUTION (reh suh <u>loo</u> shuhn) *n.*
  a firm decision
    Synonyms: determination, will, explanation
PERSEVERANCE (pehr suh <u>veer</u> ihns) *n.*
  resolve, determination
    Synonyms: persistence, tenacity, pertinacity,
    steadfastness
SOLICIT (suh <u>lih</u> siht) *v.* **-ing,-ed.**
  to petition persistently
    Synonyms: entice, tempt, request, entreat
WINCE (wihns) *v.* **-ing,-ed.**
  to flinch, to shrink away from pain or fear
    Synonyms: cringe, recoil, grimace, cower
HINDER (<u>hihn</u> duhr) *v.* **-ing,-ed.**
  to prevent action; to delay or impede
    Synonyms: restrain; hamper, inhibit, obstruct
SENTIMENT (<u>sehn</u> tuh muhnt) *n.*
  an attitude, thought, or judgment prompted by
  feeling; a romantic or nostalgic feeling
    Synonyms: idea; emotion
MANIFEST (<u>maan</u> uh fehst) *v.* **-ing,-ed.**
  to make evident or certain by display
    Synonyms: exhibit, showcase, expose

Chapter 1

1801—

I have just returned from a visit to my landlord—the solitary neighbour that I shall be troubled with. This is certainly a beautiful country! In all England, I do not believe that I could have fixed on a situation so completely removed from the stir of society. A perfect **misanthropist's** heaven, and Mr. Heathcliff and I are such a suitable pair to divide the **desolation** between us. A <u>capital</u> fellow! He little imagined how my heart warmed towards him when I beheld his black eyes withdraw so suspiciously under their brows, as I rode up, and when his fingers sheltered themselves, with a jealous **resolution**, still further in his waistcoat, as I announced my name.

"Mr. Heathcliff!" I said.

A nod was the answer.

"Mr. Lockwood, your new tenant, sir. I do myself the honour of calling as soon as possible after my arrival, to express the hope that I have not inconvenienced you by my **perseverance** in **soliciting** the occupation of Thrushcross Grange. I heard yesterday you had had some thoughts—"

"Thrushcross Grange is my own, sir," he interrupted, **wincing**. "I should not allow any one to inconvenience me, if I could **hinder** it—walk in!"

The "walk in" was uttered with closed teeth, and expressed the **sentiment**, "Go to the deuce." Even the gate over which he leant **manifested** no sympathizing movement to the words, and I think that circumstance determined me to accept the invitation; I felt interested in a man who seemed more exaggeratedly reserved than myself.

SINEWY (<u>sihn</u> yoo wee) *adj.*
  lean and muscular
    Synonyms: brawny, strapping, hefty, hardy
SOLILOQUIZE (suh <u>lih</u> luh kwiez) *v.* **-ing,-ed.**
  to talk to oneself; to make a literary or dramatic speech
    Synonyms: express, verbalize; dramatize
CONJECTURE (kuhn <u>jehk</u> shuhr) *v.* **-ing,-ed.**
  to infer, predict, guess
    Synonyms: postulate, hypothesize, suppose, surmise
PIOUS (<u>pie</u> uhs) *adj.*
  dedicated, devout, extremely religious
    Synonyms: observant, reverent, sanctimonious
EJACULATION (ih <u>jaak</u> yuh lay shuhn) *n.*
  a sudden exclamation
    Synonyms: chatter, vociferation, expletive
PROVINCIAL (pruh <u>vihn</u> shuhl) *adj.*
  rustic, unsophisticated, limited in scope
    Synonyms: uncouth, unpolished, unrefined,
    countrified, parochial
TUMULT (<u>tuh</u> muhlt) *n.*
  state of confusion, agitation
    Synonyms: disturbance, turmoil, din, commotion
STUNTED (<u>stuhn</u> tehd) *adj.*
  having arrested growth or development
    Synonyms: little, petite, dwarfish, undersized, runty
GAUNT (gawnt) *adj.*
  thin and bony
    Synonyms: lean, spare, skinny, scrawny, lank
LAVISH (<u>laa</u> vihsh) *v.* **-ing,-ed.**
  to shower with abundance or extravagance; to waste
  or spend excessively
    Synonyms: cram, overflow, saturate, teem; squander
SURLY (<u>suhr</u> lee) *adj.*
  rude and bad-tempered
    Synonyms: gruff, testy, grumpy

When he saw my horse's breast fairly pushing the barrier, he did put out his hand to unchain it, and then suddenly preceded me up the causeway, calling, as we entered the court—"Joseph, take Mr. Lockwood's horse, and bring up some wine."

"Here we have the whole establishment of domestics, I suppose," was the reflection suggested by this compound order. "No wonder the grass grows up between the flags, and cattle are the only hedge-cutters."

Joseph was an elderly, nay an old man: very old, perhaps, though <u>hale</u> and **sinewy**. "The Lord help us!" he **soliloquized** in an undertone of <u>peevish</u> displeasure, while relieving me of my horse, looking, meantime, in my face so sourly that I charitably **conjectured** he must have need of divine aid to digest his dinner, and his **pious ejaculation** had no reference to my unexpected <u>advent</u>.

Wuthering Heights is the name of Mr. Heathcliff's dwelling. "Wuthering" being a significant **provincial** adjective, descriptive of the atmospheric **tumult** to which its station is exposed in stormy weather. Pure, bracing ventilation they must have up there at all times, indeed; one may guess the power of the north wind blowing over the edge, by the excessive slant of a few **stunted** firs at the end of the house; and by a range of **gaunt** thorns all stretching their limbs one way, as if craving alms of the sun. Happily, the architect had foresight to build it strong; the narrow windows are deeply set in the wall, and the corners defended with large jutting stones.

Before passing the threshold, I paused to admire a quantity of grotesque carving **lavished** over the front, and especially about the principal door; above which, among a wilderness of crumbling <u>griffins</u> and shameless little boys, I detected the date "1500," and the name "Hareton Earnshaw." I would have made a few comments, and requested a short history of the place from the **surly** owner, but his attitude at the door appeared to demand my speedy entrance, or complete departure, and I had no

PRE-EMINENTLY or PREEMINENTLY
(pree <u>ehm</u> uh nuhnt lee) *adv.*
 to an outstanding degree, with superiority
  Synonyms: notably, prominently, importantly,
  illustriously, supremely

INTERSPERSE (ihn tuhr <u>spuhrs</u>) *v.* **-ing,-ed.**
 to distribute among, mix with
  Synonyms: commingle, scatter, infuse

DISPOSE (dih <u>spohz</u>) *v.* **-ing,-ed.**
 to put in place; to settle a matter
  Synonyms: organize, position; determine, adapt

LURK (luhrk) *v.* **-ing,-ed.**
 to hide, to lie hidden or unsuspected; to prowl, sneak
  Synonyms: conceal; stalk, creep, skulk, slink

REPOSE (rih <u>pohz</u>) *v.* **-ing,-ed.**
 to relax or rest; to lie dead
  Synonyms: sleep, slumber; pass on

COUNTENANCE (<u>kown</u> tuh nuhns) *n.*
 appearance, facial expression
  Synonyms: face, features, visage

STALWART (<u>stahl</u> wuhrt) *adj.*
 stout, physically sturdy, and strong; resolute
  Synonyms: husky, muscular; steadfast, tenacious

desire to aggravate his impatience previous to inspecting the <u>penetralium</u>.

One step brought us into the family sitting-room, without any introductory lobby or passage: they call it here "the house" **pre-eminently**. It includes kitchen and parlour, generally; but I believe at Wuthering Heights the kitchen is forced to retreat altogether into another quarter: at least I distinguished a chatter of tongues, and a clatter of culinary utensils, deep within; and I observed no signs of roasting, boiling, or baking, about the huge fire-place nor any glitter of copper saucepans and tin cullenders on the walls. One end, indeed, reflected splendidly both light and heat from ranks of immense pewter dishes, **interspersed** with silver jugs and tankards, towering row after row, on a vast oak dresser, to the very roof. The latter had never been underdrawn: its entire anatomy lay bare to an inquiring eye, except where a frame of wood laden with oatcakes and clusters of legs of beef, mutton, and ham, concealed it. Above the chimney were <u>sundry</u> villainous old guns, and a couple of horse-pistols: and, by way of ornament, three gaudily-painted canisters **disposed** along its ledge. The floor was of smooth white stone; the chairs, high-backed, primitive structures, painted green: one or two heavy black ones **lurking** in the shade. In an arch under the dresser, **reposed** a huge, liver-coloured bitch pointer, surrounded by a swarm of squealing puppies; and other dogs haunted other recesses.

The apartment and furniture would have been nothing extraordinary as belonging to a homely, northern farmer, with a stubborn **countenance**, and **stalwart** limbs set out to advantage in knee-breeches and <u>gaiters</u>. Such an individual seated in his arm-chair, his mug of ale frothing on the round table before him, is to be seen in any circuit of five or six miles among these hills, if you go at the right time after dinner. But Mr. Heathcliff forms a singular contrast to his <u>abode</u> and style of living. He is a dark-skinned gypsy in aspect, in dress and manners a gentleman: that is, as much a gentleman as many a

SLOVENLY (<u>slah</u> vuhn lee) *adj.*
 untidy, messy
  Synonyms: negligent, slipshod, sloppy, unkempt
AMISS (uh <u>mihs</u>) *adj.*
 out of place
  Synonyms: astray, awry, lost, wrong
NEGLIGENCE (<u>nehg</u> lih jehnts) *n.*
 carelessness, inattention
  Synonyms: indifference, casualness, disinterest
MOROSE (muh <u>rohs</u>) (maw <u>rohs</u>) *adj.*
 gloomy, sullen, surly
  Synonyms: glum, dour, saturnine
AVERSION (uh <u>vuhr</u> zhuhn) *n.*
 intense dislike
  Synonyms: antagonism, antipathy, abhorrence,
  repulsion, repugnance
MANIFESTATION (maan uh fehs <u>tay</u> shuhn) *n.*
 a clear appearance or certain display
  Synonyms: expression, exhibition, indication
IMPERTINENCE (ihm <u>puhr</u> tuh nuhnts) *n.*
 rudeness, audacity
  Synonyms: boldness, gall, impropriety
BESTOW (bih <u>stoh</u>) *v.* **-ing,-ed.**
 to give as a gift; to apply or devote, as in time or effort
  Synonyms: endow, confer, present; allocate, dedicate
OVERLIBERALLY (oh vuhr <u>lihb</u> uh ruh lee)
(oh vuhr <u>lihb</u> ruh lee) *adv.*
 extremely generously, too lavishly
  Synonyms: bounteously, munificently
ACTUATE (<u>aak</u> chuh wayt) (<u>aak</u> shuh wayt) *v.* **-ing,-ed.**
 to put into mechanical action; to move into action
  Synonyms: activate; stimulate, motivate, inspire
CONSTITUTION (kahn stih <u>too</u> shuhn) *n.*
 the physical structure or health of something or
 someone; the sum of components, composition
  Synonyms: disposition, nature, stature; formation,
  design, architecture, make-up
DISPOSITION (dihs puh <u>zih</u> shuhn) *n.*
 mood or temperament
  Synonyms: behavior, tendency, inclination, nature

country squire: rather **slovenly**, perhaps, yet not looking **amiss** with his **negligence**, because he has an erect and handsome figure; and rather **morose**. Possibly, some people might suspect him of a degree of underbred pride; I have a sympathetic chord within that tells me it is nothing of the sort: I know, by instinct, his reserve springs from an **aversion** to showy displays of feeling—to **manifestations** of mutual kindliness. He'll love and hate equally under cover, and esteem it a species of **impertinence** to be loved or hated again. No, I'm running on too fast; I **bestow** my own attributes **overliberally** on him. Mr. Heathcliff may have entirely dissimilar reasons for keeping his hand out of the way when he meets a would-be acquaintance, to those which **actuate** me. Let me hope my **constitution** is almost peculiar: my dear mother used to say I should never have a comfortable home; and only last summer I proved myself perfectly unworthy of one.

While enjoying a month of fine weather at the seacoast, I was thrown into the company of a most fascinating creature: a real goddess in my eyes, as long as she took no notice of me. I "never told my love" vocally; still, if looks have language, the merest idiot might have guessed I was over head and ears: she understood me at last, and looked a return—the sweetest of all imaginable looks. And what did I do? I confess it with shame—shrunk icily into myself, like a snail; at every glance retired colder and farther; till finally the poor innocent was led to doubt her own senses, and, overwhelmed with confusion at her supposed mistake, persuaded her mamma to <u>decamp</u>. By this curious turn of **disposition** I have gained the reputation of deliberate heartlessness; how undeserved, I alone can appreciate.

I took a seat at the end of the hearthstone opposite that towards which my landlord advanced, and filled up an interval of silence by attempting to caress the canine mother, who had left her nursery, and was sneaking wolfishly to the back of my legs, her lip curled up, and her

PROVOKE (proh <u>vohk</u>) *v.* **-ing,-ed.**
   to cause a response, e.g., anger or disagreement
      Synonyms: aggravate, stimulate, vex, incite

INTIMATION (ihn tuh <u>may</u> shuhn) *n.*
   clue, suggestion
      Synonyms: implication, allusion, insinuation

ASCEND (uh <u>sehnd</u>) *v.* **-ing,-ed.**
   to rise to another level or climb; to move upward
      Synonyms: elevate, escalate, mount; hoist, lift

TACIT (<u>taa</u> siht) *adj.*
   silently understood or implied
      Synonyms: implicit, unspoken

INDULGE (ihn <u>duhlj</u>) *v.* **-ing,-ed.**
   to give in to a craving or desire
      Synonyms: humor, gratify, allow, pamper

PARRY (<u>paa</u> ree) *v.* **-ing,-ied.**
   to ward off or evade, especially by a quick-witted
   answer
      Synonyms: avoid, repel

CONSTRAIN (kuhn <u>strayn</u>) *v.* **-ing,-ed.**
   to force or compel; to restrain or confine
      Synonyms: control; restrict, curb

VEXATIOUS (vehk <u>say</u> shuhs) *adj.*
   irritating, annoying; confusing, puzzling
      Synonyms: bothersome, distressing; troublesome

TEMPEST (<u>tehm</u> pehst) *n.*
   rage or fury; a storm
      Synonyms: tumult, turbulence, torrent; inclemency

white teeth watering for a snatch. My caress **provoked** a long, <u>guttural</u> snarl.

"You'd better let the dog alone," growled Mr. Heathcliff in unison, checking fiercer demonstrations with a punch of his foot. "She's not accustomed to be spoiled—not kept for a pet." Then, striding to a side door, he shouted again, "Joseph!"

Joseph mumbled indistinctly in the depths of the cellar, but gave no **intimation** of **ascending**; so his master dived down to him, leaving me *vis-à-vis* the <u>ruffianly</u> bitch and a pair of grim shaggy sheep-dogs, who shared with her a jealous guardianship over all my movements. Not anxious to come in contact with their fangs, I sat still; but, imagining they would scarcely understand **tacit** insults, I unfortunately **indulged** in winking and making faces at the trio, and some turn of my <u>physiognomy</u> so irritated madam, that she suddenly broke into a fury and leapt on my knees. I flung her back, and hastened to <u>interpose</u> the table between us. This proceeding roused the whole hive: half-a-dozen four-footed fiends, of various sizes and ages, issued from hidden dens to the common centre. I felt my heels and coat-laps peculiar subjects of assault; and **parrying** off the larger combatants as effectually as I could with the poker, I was **constrained** to demand, aloud, assistance from some of the household in re-establishing peace.

Mr. Heathcliff and his man climbed the cellar steps with **vexatious** <u>phlegm</u>. I don't think they moved one second faster than usual, though the hearth was an absolute **tempest** of worrying and yelping. Happily, an inhabitant of the kitchen made more <u>despatch</u>: a lusty dame, with tucked-up gown, bare arms, and fire-flushed cheeks, rushed into the midst of us flourishing a frying-pan: and used that weapon, and her tongue, to such purpose, that the storm subsided magically, and she only remained, heaving like a sea after a high wind, when her master entered on the scene.

MEDDLE (<u>meh</u> duhl) *v.* **-ing,-ed.**
to interfere in others' affairs, to impose
Synonyms: interlope, tamper, snoop, encroach

VIGILANT (<u>vih</u> juh lehnt) *adj.*
attentive, watchful
Synonyms: alert, aware, careful, wary, guarded

COUNTENANCE (<u>kown</u> tuh nuhns) *n.*
appearance, facial expression
Synonyms: face, features, visage

LOATH (lohth) *adj.*
reluctant and unwilling
Synonyms: averse, opposed, uneager

PRUDENTIAL (proo <u>dehn</u> chuhl) *adj.*
careful, cautious, having good judgment
Synonyms: circumspect, politic, pragmatic,
judicious, sensible

LACONIC (luh <u>kah</u> nihk) *adj.*
using few words
Synonyms: terse, concise, pithy, succinct

DISCOURSE (<u>dihs</u> kohrs) *n.*
the verbal interchange of ideas; a formal, orderly, and
extended expression of thought
Synonyms: dialogue, conversation; speech

"What the devil is the matter?" he asked, eyeing me in a manner that I could ill endure after this inhospitable treatment.

"What the devil, indeed!" I muttered. "The herd of possessed swine could have had no worse spirits in them than those animals of yours, sir. You might as well leave a stranger with a brood of tigers!"

"They won't **meddle** with persons who touch nothing," he remarked, putting the bottle before me, and restoring the displaced table. "The dogs do right to be **vigilant**. Take a glass of wine?"

"No, thank you."

"Not bitten, are you?"

"If I had been, I would have set my <u>signet</u> on the biter." Heathcliff's **countenance** relaxed into a grin.

"Come, come," he said, "you are flurried, Mr. Lockwood. Here, take a little wine. Guests are so exceedingly rare in this house that I and my dogs, I am willing to own, hardly know how to receive them. Your health, sir!"

I bowed and returned the pledge, beginning to perceive that it would be foolish to sit sulking for the misbehaviour of a pack of <u>curs</u>. Besides, I felt **loath** to yield the fellow further amusement at my expense; since the humour took that turn. He—probably swayed by **prudential** consideration of the folly of offending a good tenant—relaxed a little in the **laconic** style of chipping off his pronouns and auxiliary verbs, and introduced what he supposed would be a subject of interest to me—a **discourse** on the advantages and disadvantages of my present place of retirement. I found him very intelligent on the topics we touched; and before I went home, I was encouraged so far as to volunteer another visit tomorrow. He evidently wished no repetition of my intrusion. I shall go, notwithstanding. It is astonishing how sociable I feel myself compared with him.

INFERNAL (ihn <u>fuhr</u> nuhl) *adj.*
  devilish; relating to the dead or hell
    Synonyms: fiendish, awful, malicious; damned, accursed

EJACULATE (ih <u>jaak</u> yuh layt) *v.* **-ing,-ed.**
  to exclaim suddenly
    Synonyms: blurt, shout, declare
PERPETUAL (puhr <u>peht</u> chyoo uhl) *adj.*
  endless, lasting
    Synonyms: continuous, constant, ceaseless, eternal,
    perennial
CHURLISH (<u>chuhrl</u> ihsh) *adj.*
  rude and uncultured
    Synonyms: vulgar, boorish, surly, impolite, lowbred
RESOLVE (rih <u>sahlv</u>) *v.* **-ing,-ed.**
  to determine or to make a firm decision about
    Synonyms: solve, decide
VEHEMENTLY (<u>vee</u> huh muhnt lee) *adv.*
  strongly, urgently
    Synonyms: intensely, passionately, ardently

Chapter 2

Yesterday afternoon set in misty and cold. I had half a mind to spend it by my study fire, instead of wading through <u>heath</u> and mud to Wuthering Heights. On coming up from dinner however (N.B.—I dine between twelve and one o'clock; the housekeeper, a matronly lady, taken as a fixture along with the house, could not, or would not, comprehend my request that I might be served at five), on mounting the stairs with this lazy intention, and stepping into the room, I saw a servant-girl on her knees surrounded by brushes and <u>coalscuttles</u>, and raising an **infernal** dust as she extinguished the flames with heaps of cinders. This spectacle drove me back immediately; I took my hat, and, after a four miles' walk arrived at Heathcliff's garden gate just in time to escape the first feathery flakes of a snow shower.

On that bleak hill-top the earth was hard with a black frost, and the air made me shiver through every limb. Being unable to remove the chain, I jumped over, and, running up the flagged causeway bordered with straggling gooseberry bushes, knocked vainly for admittance, till my knuckles tingled and the dogs howled.

"Wretched inmates!" I **ejaculated** mentally. "You deserve **perpetual** isolation from your species for your **churlish** inhospitality. At least, I would not keep my door barred in the day-time. I don't care—I will get in!" So **resolved**, I grasped the latch and shook it **vehemently**. Vinegar-faced Joseph projected his head from a round window of the barn.

"What are ye for?" he shouted. "T' maister's down i' t' fowld. Go round by th' end o' t' laith, if ye went to spake to him."

"Is there nobody inside to open the door?" I hallooed, responsively.

DEIGN (dayn) *v.* **-ing,-ed.**
  to do something beneath one's dignity; to stoop
    Synonyms: condescend; patronize
AMIABLE (<u>ay</u> mee uh buhl) *adj.*
  friendly, pleasant, likable
    Synonyms: affable, convivial, amicable, agreeable
REPELLINGLY (rih <u>pehl</u> lihng lee) *adv.*
  repulsively, with disgust, offensively
    Synonyms: nauseatingly, revoltingly
OBSCURE (uhb <u>skyoor</u>) *adj.*
  dim, unclear; not well known
    Synonyms: dark, faint; remote, minor

"There's nobbut t' missis; and shoo'll not oppen't an ye mak yer flaysome dins till neeght."

"Why? Cannot you tell her who I am, eh, Joseph?"

"Nor-ne me! I'll hae no hend wi't," muttered the head, vanishing.

The snow began to drive thickly. I seized the handle to <u>essay</u> another trial when a young man without coat, and shouldering a pitchfork, appeared in the yard behind. He hailed me to follow him, and, after marching through a washhouse, and a paved area containing a coal-shed, pump, and pigeon-cot, we at length arrived in the huge, warm cheerful apartment, where I was formerly received. It glowed delightfully in the radiance of an immense fire, compounded of coal, peat, and wood; and near the table, laid for a plentiful evening meal, I was pleased to observe the "missis," an individual whose existence I had never previously suspected. I bowed and waited, thinking she would bid me take a seat. She looked at me, leaning back in her chair, and remained motionless and mute.

"Rough weather!" I remarked. "I'm afraid, Mrs. Heathcliff, the door must bear the consequence of your servants' leisure attendance: I had hard work to make them hear me."

She never opened her mouth. I stared—she stared also: at any rate, she kept her eyes on me in a cool, regardless manner, exceedingly embarrassing and disagreeable.

"Sit down," said the young man gruffly. "He'll be in soon."

I obeyed; and <u>hemmed</u>, and called the villain Juno, who **deigned**, at this second interview, to move the extreme tip of her tail, in token of owning my acquaintance.

"A beautiful animal!" I commented again. "Do you intend parting with the little ones, madam?"

"They are not mine," said the **amiable** hostess, more **repellingly** than Heathcliff himself could have replied.

"Ah, your favourites are among these?" I continued, turning to an **obscure** cushion full of something like cats.

17

COUNTENANCE (<u>kown</u> tuh nuhns) *n.*
appearance, facial expression
Synonyms: face, features, visage

SUSCEPTIBLE (suh <u>sehp</u> tuh buhl) *adj.*
vulnerable, unprotected
Synonyms: sensitive, impressionable, prone, subject

SENTIMENT (<u>sehn</u> tuh muhnt) *n.*
an attitude, thought, or judgment prompted by
feeling; a romantic or nostalgic feeling
Synonyms: idea; emotion

EVINCE (ih <u>vihns</u>) *v.* **-ing,-ed.**
to show clearly or display
Synonyms: express, exhibit, demonstrate, manifest

MISER (<u>mie</u> zuhr) *n.*
an extremely stingy and greedy person
Synonyms: cheapskate, scrooge, misanthrope

CORRUGATE (<u>kohr</u> uh gayt) *v.* **-ing,-ed.**
to become wrinkled or folded
Synonyms: crumple, furrow

"A strange choice of favourites!" she observed scornfully.

Unluckily, it was a heap of dead rabbits. I <u>hemmed</u> once more, and drew closer to the hearth, repeating my comment on the wildness of the evening.

"You should not have come out," she said, rising and reaching from the chimney-piece two of the painted canisters.

Her position before was sheltered from the light; now, I had a distinct view of her whole figure and **countenance**. She was slender, and apparently scarcely past girlhood: an admirable form, and the most exquisite little face that I have ever had the pleasure of beholding; small features, very fair, flaxen ringlets, or rather golden, hanging loose on her delicate neck; and eyes, had they been agreeable in expression, that would have been irresistible. Fortunately for my **susceptible** heart, the only **sentiment** they **evinced** hovered between scorn and a kind of desperation, singularly unnatural to be detected there. The canisters were almost out of her reach; I made a motion to aid her, she turned upon me as a **miser** might turn if anyone attempted to assist him in counting his gold.

"I don't want your help," she snapped. "I can get them for myself."

"I beg your pardon!" I hastened to reply.

"Were you asked to tea?" she demanded, tying an apron over her neat black frock, and standing with a spoonful of the leaf poised over the pot.

"I shall be glad to have a cup," I answered.

"Were you asked?" she repeated.

"No," I said, half smiling. "You are the proper person to ask me."

She flung the tea back, spoon and all, and resumed her chair in a pet; her forehead **corrugated**, and her red under-lip pushed out, like a child's ready to cry.

Meanwhile, the young man had slung on to his person a decidedly shabby upper garment, and, erecting himself before the blaze, looked down on me from the corner of

UNAVENGED (uhn uh <u>vehnjd</u>) *adj.*
not yet retaliated, having not had revenge for an injury or crime
Synonyms: unpunished, unpaid

DEVOID (dih <u>voyd</u>) *adj.*
being without, lacking
Synonyms: destitute, empty, vacant, null, bare

ENCROACH (ehn <u>crohch</u>) *v.* **-ing,-ed.**
to intrude gradually
Synonyms: infringe, invade, trespass, overstep

HAUGHTY (<u>haw</u> tee) (<u>hah</u> tee) *adj.*
arrogant and condescending
Synonyms: proud, disdainful, supercilious, scornful, vainglorious

ASSIDUITY (uh sih <u>dyoo</u> ih tee) *n.*
diligence, persistent attention, perseverance
Synonyms: steadfastness, effort, commitment

ABSTAIN (uhb <u>stayn</u>) *v.* **-ing,-ed.**
to forgo an activity or action
Synonyms: forbear, refrain

SAGACITY (suh <u>gaa</u> sih tee) *n.*
shrewdness, intelligence
Synonyms: perspicacity, wisdom, knowledge

his eyes, for all the world as if there were some mortal feud **unavenged** between us. I began to doubt whether he were a servant or not: his dress and speech were both rude, entirely **devoid** of the superiority observable in Mr. and Mrs. Heathcliff; his thick, brown curls were rough and uncultivated, his whiskers **encroached** bearishly over his cheeks, and his hands were embrowned like those of a common labourer. Still his bearing was free, almost **haughty**, and he showed none of a domestic's **assiduity** in attending on the lady of the house. In the absence of clear proofs of his condition, I deemed it best to **abstain** from noticing his curious conduct; and, five minutes afterwards, the entrance of Heathcliff relieved me, in some measure, from my uncomfortable state.

"You see, sir, I am come, according to promise!" I exclaimed, assuming the cheerful. "And I fear I shall be weather-bound for half an hour, if you can afford me shelter during that space."

"Half-an-hour?" he said, shaking the white flakes from his clothes. "I wonder you should select the thick of a snowstorm to ramble about in. Do you know that you run a risk of being lost in the marshes? People familiar with these moors often miss their road on such evenings; and I can tell you there is no chance of a change at present."

"Perhaps I can get a guide among your lads, and he might stay at the Grange till morning—could you spare me one?"

"No, I could not."

"Oh, indeed! Well, then, I must trust to my own **sagacity**."

"Umph!"

"Are you going to make th' tea?" demanded he of the shabby coat, shining his ferocious gaze from me to the young lady.

"Is *he* to have any?" she asked, appealing to Heathcliff.

"Get it ready, will you?" was the answer, uttered so savagely that I started. The tone in which the words were said

INCLINED (ihn <u>kliend</u>) *adj.*
   predisposed, having a certain tendency
      Synonyms: likely, prone
RUSTIC (<u>ruh</u> stihk) 1. *adj.* 2. *n.*
   1. simple and unsophisticated; typical of country life
      Synonyms: unrefined, crude; bucolic, pastoral
   2. a rural person with a simplistic character
      Synonyms: bumpkin, hick, clod, countryman
AUSTERE (aw <u>steer</u>) *adj.*
   stern, strict, unadorned
      Synonyms: dour, bare, ascetic
PREVAIL (prih <u>vayl</u>) *v.* **-ing,-ed.**
   to succeed lastingly; to overcome
      Synonyms: persist, endure; dominate, triumph
DISPEL (dihs <u>pehl</u>) *v.* **-ling,-led.**
   to drive out or scatter
      Synonyms: disband, disperse
TACITURN (<u>taa</u> sih tuhrn) *adj.*
   uncommunicative, not inclined to speak much
      Synonyms: reticent, reserved, secretive, tight-lipped
COUNTENANCE (<u>kown</u> tuh nuhns) *n.* *(See page 18.)*
EXILE (<u>ehg</u> ziel) (<u>ehk</u> siel) *n.*
   the state or period of time where one is forced or
   volunteers to live outside of their country or in isolation
      Synonyms: banishment, displacement, ostracism
AMIABLE (<u>ay</u> mee uh buhl) *adj.* *(See page 16.)*
DIABOLICAL (die uh <u>bah</u> lih kuhl) *adj.*
   characteristic of the devil
      Synonyms: fiendish, wicked, evil
INTIMATE (<u>ihn</u> tuh mayt) *v.* **-ing,-ed.**
   to hint or suggest obscurely
      Synonyms: implicate, allude, insinuate
DISPARITY (dih <u>spaar</u> ih tee) *n.*
   contrast, dissimilarity
      Synonyms: discrepancy, contradiction, divergence,
      incongruity, incompatibility
SOLACE (<u>sah</u> lihs) *n.*
   comfort in distress, consolation
      Synonyms: succor, balm, cheer, condolence

revealed a genuine bad nature. I no longer felt **inclined** to call Heathcliff a <u>capital</u> fellow. When the preparations were finished, he invited me with—"Now, sir, bring forward your chair." And we all, including the **rustic** youth, drew round the table, an **austere** silence **prevailing** while we discussed our meal.

I thought, if I had caused the cloud, it was my duty to make an effort to **dispel** it. They could not every day sit so grim and **taciturn**; and it was impossible, however ill-tempered they might be, that the universal scowl they wore was their every-day **countenance**.

"It is strange," I began, in the interval of swallowing one cup of tea and receiving another—"it is strange how custom can mould our tastes and ideas: many could not imagine the existence of happiness in a life of such complete **exile** from the world as you spend, Mr. Heathcliff; yet I'll venture to say, that, surrounded by your family, and with your **amiable** lady as the presiding genius over your home and heart—"

"My **amiable** lady!" he interrupted, with an almost **diabolical** sneer on his face. "Where is she—my **amiable** lady?"

"Mrs. Heathcliff, your wife, I mean."

"Well, yes—Oh, you would **intimate** that her spirit has taken the post of ministering angel, and guards the fortunes of Wuthering Heights even when her body is gone. Is that it?"

Perceiving myself in a blunder, I attempted to correct it. I might have seen there was too great a **disparity** between the ages of the parties to make it likely that they were man and wife. One was about forty: a period of mental vigour at which men seldom cherish the delusion of being married for love by girls: that dream is reserved for the **solace** of our declining years. The other did not look seventeen.

Then it flashed upon me—the clown at my elbow, who is drinking his tea out of a basin and eating his bread with unwashed hands, may be her husband: Heathcliff, junior,

BOOR (bohr) *n.*
   crude person, one lacking manners or taste
      Synonyms: lout, clod, oaf, vulgarian, yahoo
REPULSIVE (rih <u>puhl</u> sihv) *adj.*
   repellant; sickening, disgusting
      Synonyms: offensive; nauseating
CORROBORATE (kuh <u>rahb</u> uhr ayt) *v.* **-ing,-ed.**
   to confirm, verify
      Synonyms: prove, substantiate, warrant
SURMISE (suhr <u>miez</u>) *n.*
   an educated guess
      Synonyms: conjecture, speculation,
      inference
PERVERSE (puhr <u>vuhrs</u>) *adj.*
   1. having the tendency to oppose or contradict
      Synonyms: contrary, improper, obstinate
   2. immoral, mean
      Synonyms: corrupted, disobedient, depraved
BENEFICENT (buh <u>neh</u> fih sihnt) *adj.*
   characterized by kindness and goodness
      Synonyms: benevolent, gracious, philanthropic, kind

CONJECTURE (kuhn <u>jehk</u> shuhr) *n.*
   speculation, prediction
      Synonyms: postulation, hypothesis, supposition, guess

PATERNITY (puh <u>tuhr</u> nih tee) *n.*
   fatherhood; descent from father's ancestors
      Synonyms: siring, begetting; origin

AUDIBLE (<u>aw</u> dih buhl) *adj.*
   capable of being heard
      Synonyms: detectable, perceptible

of course. Here is the consequence of being buried alive: she has thrown herself away upon that **boor** from sheer ignorance that better individuals existed! A sad pity—I must beware how I cause her to regret her choice. The last reflection may seem conceited; it was not. My neighbour struck me as bordering on **repulsive**; I knew, through experience, that I was tolerably attractive.

"Mrs. Heathcliff is my daughter-in-law," said Heathcliff, **corroborating** my **surmise**. He turned, as he spoke, a peculiar look in her direction: a look of hatred; unless he has a most **perverse** set of facial muscles that will not, like those of other people, interpret the language of his soul.

"Ah, certainly—I see now: you are the favoured possessor of the **beneficent** fairy," I remarked, turning to my neighbour.

This was worse than before: the youth grew crimson, and clenched his fist, with every appearance of a meditated assault. But he seemed to recollect himself presently, and smothered the storm in a brutal curse, muttered on my behalf: which, however, I took care not to notice.

"Unhappy in your **conjectures**, sir," observed my host. "We neither of us have the privilege of owning your good fairy; her mate is dead. I said she was my daughter-in-law, therefore, she must have married my son."

"And this young man is—"

"Not my son, assuredly."

Heathcliff smiled again, as if it were rather too bold a jest to attribute the **paternity** of that bear to him.

"My name is Hareton Earnshaw," growled the other, "and I'd counsel you to respect it!"

"I've shown no disrespect," was my reply, laughing internally at the dignity with which he announced himself.

He fixed his eye on me longer than I cared to return the stare, for fear I might be tempted either to box his ears or render my hilarity **audible**. I began to feel unmistakably

RESOLVE (rih <u>sahlv</u>) *v.* **-ing,-ed.**
. to determine or to make a firm decision about
Synonyms: solve, decide

DIVERT (die <u>vuhrt</u>) *v.* **-ing,-ed.**
to distract or amuse; to move in different directions
from a particular point
Synonyms: deter, occupy, entertain; deviate, separate

ELOQUENCE (<u>eh</u> luh kwuhns) *n.*
persuasive and effective speech
Synonyms: expressiveness, fluency

HYPOCRITE (<u>hih</u> puh kriht) *n.*
person claiming beliefs or virtues he or she doesn't
really possess
Synonyms: fraud, liar, sham, fake, phony

out of place in that pleasant family circle. The dismal spiritual atmosphere overcame, and more than neutralized, the glowing physical comforts round me; and I **resolved** to be cautious how I ventured under those rafters a third time.

The business of eating being concluded, and no one uttering a word of sociable conversation, I approached a window to examine the weather. A sorrowful sight I saw: dark night coming down prematurely, and sky and hills mingled in one bitter whirl of wind and suffocating snow.

"I don't think it possible for me to get home now without a guide," I could not help exclaiming. "The roads will be buried already; and, if they were bare, I could scarcely distinguish a foot in advance."

"Hareton, drive those dozen sheep into the barn porch. They'll be covered if left in the <u>fold</u> all night: and put a plank before them," said Heathcliff.

"How must I do?" I continued, with rising irritation.

There was no reply to my question; and on looking round I saw only Joseph bringing in a pail of porridge for the dogs, and Mrs. Heathcliff leaning over the fire, **diverting** herself with burning a bundle of matches which had fallen from the chimney-piece as she restored the tea canister to its place. The former, when he had deposited his burden, took a critical survey of the room, and in cracked tones, grated out:

"Aw wonder how yah can faishion to stand thear i' idleness un war, when all on 'em's goan out! Bud yah're a nowt, and it's no use talking—yah'll niver mend o' yer ill ways, but goa raight to t' devil, like yer mother afore ye!"

I imagined, for a moment, that this piece of **eloquence** was addressed to me; and, sufficiently enraged, stepped towards the aged rascal with an intention of kicking him out of the door. Mrs. Heathcliff, however, checked me by her answer.

"You scandalous old **hypocrite**!" she replied. "Are you not afraid of being carried away bodily, whenever you mention the devil's name? I warn you to refrain from

PROVOKE (proh <u>vohk</u>) *v.* **-ing,-ed.**
to cause a response, e.g., anger or disagreement
Synonyms: aggravate, stimulate, vex, incite

PROVIDENTIAL (prah vih <u>dehn</u> shuhl) *adj.*
resulting from divine intervention
Synonyms: heavenly, miraculous, fortunate, lucky

REPROBATE (<u>reh</u> pruh bayt) *n.*
morally unprincipled person
Synonyms: sinner, knave, scoundrel, rogue, rake

MALIGNITY (muh <u>lihg</u> nih tee) *n.*
evil or aggressive malice; something that produces death
Synonyms: bitterness, resentment; malevolence

EJACULATE (ih <u>jaak</u> yuh layt) *v.* **-ing,-ed.**
to exclaim suddenly
Synonyms: blurt, shout, declare

ENSCONCE (ehn <u>skahns</u>) *v.* **-ing,-ed.**
to settle into comfortably; to hide in a secure place
Synonyms: nestle, snuggle; conceal, enshroud

provoking me, or I'll ask your abduction as a special favour. Stop! Look here, Joseph," she continued, taking a long, dark book from a shelf. "I'll show you how far I've progressed in the Black Art: I shall soon be competent to make a clear house of it. The red cow didn't die by chance; and your <u>rheumatism</u> can hardly be reckoned among **providential** visitations!"

"Oh, wicked, wicked!" gasped the elder. "May the Lord deliver us from evil!"

"No, **reprobate**! You are a castaway—be off, or I'll hurt you seriously! I'll have you all modelled in wax and clay; and the first who passes the limits I fix, shall—I'll not say what he shall be done to—but, you'll see! Go, I'm looking at you!"

The little witch put a mock **malignity** into her beautiful eyes, and Joseph, trembling with sincere horror, hurried out praying and **ejaculating** "wicked" as he went. I thought her conduct must be prompted by a species of dreary fun; and, now that we were alone, I endeavoured to interest her in my distress.

"Mrs. Heathcliff," I said earnestly, "you must excuse me for troubling you. I presume, because, with that face, I'm sure you cannot help being good-hearted. Do point out some landmarks by which I may know my way home: I have no more idea how to get there than you would have how to get to London!"

"Take the road you came," she answered, **ensconcing** herself in a chair, with a candle, and the long book open before her. "It is brief advice, but as sound as I can give."

"Then, if you hear of me being discovered dead in a bog or a pit full of snow, your conscience won't whisper that it is partly your fault?"

"How so? I cannot escort you. They wouldn't let me go to the end of the garden-wall."

"*You*! I should be sorry to ask you to cross the threshold, for my convenience, on such a night," I cried. "I want you to *tell* me my way, not to *show* it; or else to persuade Mr. Heathcliff to give me a guide."

COMPEL (kuhm <u>pehl</u>) *v.* **-ling,-led.**
    to urge or force
        Synonyms: coerce, oblige, constrain
RASH (raash) *adj.*
    careless, hasty, reckless
        Synonyms: foolhardy, impulsive, precipitate

CIVIL (<u>sih</u> vuhl) *adj.*
    polite; involving the public
        Synonyms: courteous; communal

RETORT (rih <u>tohrt</u>) *v.* **-ing,-ed.**
    to make a cutting response
        Synonyms: retaliate, talk back, counter

"Who? There is himself, Earnshaw, Zillah, Joseph and I. Which would you have?"

"Are there no boys at the farm?"

"No; those are all."

"Then, it follows that I am **compelled** to stay."

"That you may settle with your host. I have nothing to do with it."

"I hope it will be a lesson to you to make no more **rash** journeys on these hills," cried Heathcliff's stern voice from the kitchen entrance. "As to staying here, I don't keep accommodations for visitors: you must share a bed with Hareton or Joseph, if you do."

"I can sleep on a chair in this room," I replied.

"No, no! A stranger is a stranger, be he rich or poor. It will not suit me to permit any one the range of the place while I am off guard!" said the unmannerly wretch.

With this insult, my patience was at an end. I uttered an expression of disgust, and pushed past him into the yard, running against Earnshaw in my haste. It was so dark that I could not see the means of exit; and, as I wandered round, I heard another specimen of their **civil** behaviour amongst each other. At first the young man appeared about to befriend me.

"I'll go with him as far as the park," he said.

"You'll go with him to hell!" exclaimed his master, or whatever relation he bore. "And who is to look after the horses, eh?"

"A man's life is of more consequence than one evening's neglect of the horses: somebody must go," murmured Mrs. Heathcliff, more kindly than I expected.

"Not at your command!" **retorted** Hareton. "If you set store on him, you'd better be quiet."

"Then I hope his ghost will haunt you; and I hope Mr. Heathcliff will never get another tenant till the Grange is a ruin!" she answered sharply.

"Hearken, hearken, shoo's cursing on 'em!" muttered Joseph, towards whom I had been steering.

31

MALIGNANT (muh <u>lihg</u> nehnt) *adj.*
   evil in influence or effect; aggressively malicious;
   tending to produce death
   Synonyms: vindictive, threatening; destructive,
   harmful; lethal, fatal
WRATH (raath) *n.*
   anger, rage
   Synonyms: fury, ire, resentment, indignation
PERIL (<u>pehr</u> ihl) *n.*
   danger
   Synonyms: trouble, hazard, vulnerability, risk
INCOHERENT (ihn koh <u>hihr</u> uhnt) *adj.*
   lacking cohesion or connection; unable to think or
   express one's thoughts in a clear or orderly manner
   Synonyms: disordered, incohesive; unintelligible
VIRULENCY (<u>veer</u> uh luhn see) *n.*
   extreme poisonousness, malignity; hatred
   Synonyms: infection, toxicity, pestilence; hostility
VEHEMENCE (<u>vee</u> huh muhnts) *n.*
   strength, urgency
   Synonyms: fervor, intensity, ferocity, passion, ardor
AGITATION (aa gih <u>tay</u> shuhn) *n.*
   commotion, excitement; uneasiness
   Synonyms: disturbance; restlessness, anxiety
COPIOUS (<u>koh</u> pee uhs) *adj.*
   abundant, plentiful
   Synonyms: ample, abounding
BENEVOLENT (buh <u>neh</u> vuh luhnt) *adj.*
   kind, compassionate
   Synonyms: charitable, altruistic, beneficent,
   generous, good
UPROAR (<u>uhp</u> rohr) *n.*
   a situation of loud and confusing excitement
   Synonyms: noise, hubbub, commotion, fracas

He sat within earshot, milking the cows by the light of a lantern, which I seized unceremoniously, and, calling out that I would send it back on the morrow, rushed to the nearest <u>postern</u>.

"Maister, maister, he's staling t' lanthern!" shouted the ancient, pursuing my retreat. "Hey, Gnasher! Hey, dog! Hey, Wolf, holld him, holld him!"

On opening the little door, two hairy monsters flew at my throat, bearing me down and extinguishing the light; while a mingled guffaw from Heathcliff and Hareton, put the copestone on my rage and humiliation. Fortunately, the beasts seemed more bent on stretching their paws and yawning and flourishing their tails, than devouring me alive; but they would suffer no <u>resurrection</u>, and I was forced to lie till their **malignant** masters pleased to deliver me: then, hatless and trembling with **wrath**, I ordered the <u>miscreants</u> to let me out—on their **peril** to keep me one minute longer—with several **incoherent** threats of retaliation that, in their indefinite depth of **virulency**, smacked of King Lear.

The **vehemence** of my **agitation** brought on a **copious** bleeding at the nose, and still Heathcliff laughed, and still I scolded. I don't know what would have concluded the scene, had there not been one person at hand rather more rational than myself, and more **benevolent** than my entertainer. This was Zillah, the stout housewife; who at length issued forth to inquire into the nature of the **uproar**. She thought that some of them had been laying violent hands on me; and, not daring to attack her master, she turned her vocal artillery against the younger scoundrel.

"Well, Mr. Earnshaw," she cried, "I wonder what you'll have agait next! Are we going to murder folk on our very doorstones? I see this house will never do for me—look at t' poor lad, he's fair choking! <u>Wisht</u>, <u>wisht</u>! You mun'n't go on so. Come in, and I'll cure that: there now, hold ye still."

With these words she suddenly splashed a pint of icy water down my neck, and pulled me into the kitchen. Mr.

EXPIRE (ehk <u>spier</u>) *v.* **-ing,-ed.**
   to come to an end; die; breathe out
      Synonyms: terminate; perish; exhale

MOROSENESS (muh <u>rohs</u> nehs) (maw <u>rohs</u> nehs) *n.*
   gloom, sadness, surliness
      Synonym: sullenness

COMPEL (kuhm <u>pehl</u>) *v.* **-ling,-led.**
   to urge or force
      Synonyms: coerce, oblige, constrain

CONDOLE (kuhn <u>dohl</u>) *v.* **-ing,-ed.**
   to grieve or express sympathy
      Synonyms: lament, pity, console

STUPEFIED (<u>stoo</u> puh fied) *adj.*
   having dulled senses; stunned, astonished
      Synonyms: benumbed; dazed, bemused, amazed

OBVIATE (<u>ahb</u> vee ayt) *v.* **-ing,-ed.**
   to make unnecessary; to anticipate and prevent
      Synonyms: preclude; avert, forestall, deter

VIGILANCE (<u>vih</u> juh lehnts) *n.*
   attentiveness, watchfulness
      Synonyms: alertness, awareness, care, diligence

Heathcliff followed, his accidental merriment **expiring** quickly in his habitual **moroseness**.

I was sick exceedingly, and dizzy and faint; and thus **compelled** perforce to accept lodgings under his roof. He told Zillah to give me a glass of brandy, and then passed on to the inner room; while she **condoled** with me on my sorry predicament, and having obeyed his orders, whereby I was somewhat revived, ushered me to bed.

Chapter 3

While leading the way upstairs, she recommended that I should hide the candle, and not make a noise; for her master had an odd notion about the chamber she would put me in, and never let anybody lodge there willingly. I asked the reason. She did not know, she answered: she had only lived there a year or two; and they had so many queer goings on, she could not begin to be curious.

Too **stupefied** to be curious myself, I fastened the door and glanced round for the bed. The whole furniture consisted of a chair, a clothes-press, and a large oak case, with squares cut out near the top resembling coach windows. Having approached this structure I looked inside, and perceived it to be a singular sort of old-fashioned couch, very conveniently designed to **obviate** the necessity for every member of the family having a room to himself. In fact, it formed a little closet, and the ledge of a window, which it enclosed, served as a table. I slid back the panelled sides, got in with my light, pulled them together again, and felt secure against the **vigilance** of Heathcliff, and every one else.

The ledge, where I placed my candle, had a few mildewed books piled up in one corner, and it was covered with writing scratched on the paint. This writing, however, was nothing but a name repeated in all kinds of characters, large and small—*Catherine Earnshaw*, here

VAPID (<u>vaa</u> pihd) (<u>vay</u> pihd) *adj.*
dull, tasteless
Synonyms: insipid, vacuous, inane
LISTLESSNESS (<u>lihst</u> lihs nehs) *n.*
lack of energy and enthusiasm
Synonyms: lethargy, sluggishness, languor, indolence
DISPEL (dihs <u>pehl</u>) *v.* **-ling,-led.**
to drive out or scatter
Synonyms: disband, disperse

TOME (tohm) *n.*
book, usually large and academic
Synonyms: volume, codex

DILAPIDATION (dih laap ih <u>day</u> shuhn) *n.*
disrepair
Synonyms: destruction, ruin, deterioration, decay

CARICATURE (<u>kaa</u> rih kah chuhr) *n.*
exaggerated portrait, cartoon
Synonyms: burlesque, travesty, lampoon
KINDLE (<u>kihn</u> duhl) *v.* **-ing,-ed.**
to excite or inspire; to set fire to or ignite
Synonyms: arouse, awaken; light, spark
DETESTABLE (dee <u>tehst</u> uh buhl) *adj.*
deserving of intense and violent hatred
Synonyms: disgusting, despicable, loathsome
ATROCIOUS (uh <u>troh</u> shuhs) *adj.*
revolting, shockingly bad, wicked
Synonyms: horrible, appalling, deplorable, direful
CONGREGATION (kahn grih <u>gay</u> shuhn) *n.*
a crowd of people, an assembly
Synonyms: group, gathering, fold, multitude

and there varied to *Catherine Heathcliff*, and then again to *Catherine Linton*.

In **vapid listlessness** I leant my head against the window, and continued spelling over Catherine Earnshaw—Heathcliff—Linton, till my eyes closed; but they had not rested five minutes when a glare of white letters started from the dark as vivid as <u>spectres</u>—the air swarmed with Catherines; and rousing myself to **dispel** the obtrusive name, I discovered my candle wick reclining on one of the antique volumes, and perfuming the place with an odour of roasted calf-skin. I <u>snuffed</u> it out, and, very ill at ease under the influence of cold and lingering nausea, sat up and spread open the injured **tome** on my knee. It was a Testament, in lean type, and smelling dreadfully musty: a fly-leaf bore the inscription—"Catherine Earnshaw, her book," and a date some quarter of a century back. I shut it, and took up another, and another, till I had examined all. Catherine's library was select, and its state of **dilapidation** proved it to have been well used; though not altogether for a legitimate purpose: scarcely one chapter had escaped a pen-and-ink commentary—at least, the appearance of one—covering every morsel of blank that the printer had left. Some were detached sentences; other parts took the form of a regular diary, scrawled in an unformed childish hand. At the top of an extra page (quite a treasure, probably, when first lighted on) I was greatly amused to behold an excellent **caricature** of my friend Joseph—rudely, yet powerfully sketched. An immediate interest **kindled** within me for the unknown Catherine, and I began forthwith to decipher her faded hieroglyphics.

"An awful Sunday!" commenced the paragraph beneath. "I wish my father were back again. Hindley is a **detestable** substitute—his conduct to Heathcliff is **atrocious**—H. and I are going to rebel—we took our initiatory step this evening.

"All day had been flooding with rain; we could not go to church, so Joseph must needs get up a **congregation** in

HOMILY (hah muh lee) *n.*
sermonlike speech
Synonyms: lecture, admonition, oration

DESCEND (dih sehnd) (dee sehnd) *v.* **-ing,-ed.**
to pass from a higher place to a lower place
Synonyms: fall, dismount, gravitate

SOBRIETY (suh brie eh tee) *n.*
state of being serious or sober
Synonyms: gravity, moderation, temperance

COMPEL (kuhm pehl) *v.* **-ling,-led.**
to urge or force
Synonyms: coerce, oblige, constrain

the <u>garret</u>; and, while Hindley and his wife basked down-stairs before a comfortable fire—doing anything but reading their Bibles, I'll answer for it—Heathcliff, myself, and the unhappy plough-boy, were commanded to take our Prayer-books, and mount: were ranged in a row, on a sack of corn, groaning and shivering, and hoping that Joseph would shiver too, so that he might give us a short **homily** for his own sake. A vain idea! The service lasted precisely three hours; and yet my brother had the face to exclaim, when he saw us **descending**, 'What, done already?' On Sunday evenings we used to be permitted to play, if we did not make much noise; now a mere titter is sufficient to send us into corners!

"'You forget you have a master here,' says the tyrant. 'I'll demolish the first who puts me out of temper! I insist on perfect **sobriety** and silence. Oh, boy! Was that you? Frances, darling, pull his hair as you go by. I heard him snap his fingers.' Frances pulled his hair heartily, and then went and seated herself on her husband's knee; and there they were, like two babies, kissing and talking nonsense by the hour—foolish <u>palaver</u> that we should be ashamed of. We made ourselves as snug as our means allowed in the arch of the dresser. I had just fastened our pinafores together, and hung them up for a curtain, when in comes Joseph on an errand from the stables. He tears down my handiwork, boxes my ears and croaks—

"'T' maister nobbut just buried, and Sabbath no o'ered, und t' sound o' t' gospel still i' yer lugs, and ye darr be laiking! Shame on ye! Sit ye down, ill childer! There's good books enough if ye'll read 'em! Sit ye down, and think o' yer sowls!'

"Saying this, he **compelled** us so to square our positions that we might receive from the far-off fire a dull ray to show us the text of the lumber he thrust upon us. I could not bear the employment. I took my dingy volume by the scroop, and hurled it into the dog-kennel, vowing I hated a good book. Heathcliff kicked his to the same place. Then there was a hubbub!

APPROPRIATE (uh <u>proh</u> pree ayt) *v*. **-ing,-ed.**
　　to take possession of; to set aside for a purpose
　　　　Synonyms: usurp, arrogate, commandeer; allocate,
　　　　designate
SURLY (<u>suhr</u> lee) *adj*.
　　rude and bad-tempered
　　　　Synonyms: gruff, testy, grumpy
PROPHECY (<u>prah</u> feh see) *n*.
　　the foretelling of events, a prediction of the future
　　　　Synonyms: dream, forecast, vision
WAX (waaks) *v*. **-ing,-ed.**
　　to begin to be; to increase gradually
　　　　Synonyms: become, grow; enlarge, expand, swell
LACHRYMOSE (<u>laak</u> ruh mohs) *adj*.
　　tearful
　　　　Synonyms: weepy, overemotional, sorrowful
VAGABOND (<u>vaa</u> guh bahnd) *n*.
　　one who moves from place to place with no fixed home
　　　　Synonyms: wanderer, floater, vagrant, nomad
LIBERALLY (<u>lihb</u> uh ruh lee) (<u>lihb</u> ruh lee) *adv*.
　　with tolerance and broad-mindedness; generously,
　　lavishly
　　　　Synonyms: progressively, permissively; bounteously,
　　　　munificently
PIOUS (<u>pie</u> uhs) *adj*.
　　dedicated, devout, extremely religious
　　　　Synonyms: observant, reverent, sanctimonious
DISCOURSE (<u>dihs</u> kohrs) *n*.
　　a formal, orderly, and extended expression of thought;
　　the verbal interchange of ideas
　　　　Synonyms: speech; dialogue, conversation

"'Maister Hindley!' shouted our chaplain. 'Maister, coom hither! Miss Cathy's <u>riven</u> th' back off *Th' Helmet o' Salvation*, un' Heathcliff's pawsed his fist into t' first part o' *T' Brooad Way to Destruction*! It's fair flaysome that ye let 'em go on this gait. Ech! Th' owd man wad ha' laced 'em properly—but he's goan!'

"Hindley hurried up from his paradise on the hearth, and seizing one of us by the collar, and the other by the arm, hurled both into the back kitchen; where, Joseph <u>asseverated</u>, 'owd Nick' would fetch us as sure as we were living: and, so comforted, we each sought a separate nook to await his <u>advent</u>. I reached this book, and a pot of ink from a shelf, and pushed the house-door ajar to give me light, and I have got the time on with writing for twenty minutes; but my companion is impatient, and proposes that we should **appropriate** the dairywoman's cloak, and have a scamper on the moors, under its shelter. A pleasant suggestion—and then, if the **surly** old man come in, he may believe his **prophecy** verified—we cannot be damper, or colder, in the rain than we are here."

I suppose Catherine fulfilled her project, for the next sentence took up another subject; she **waxed lachrymose**.

"How little did I dream that Hindley would ever make me cry so!" she wrote. "My head aches, till I cannot keep it on the pillow; and still I can't give over. Poor Heathcliff! Hindley calls him a **vagabond**, and won't let him sit with us, nor eat with us any more; and, he says, he and I must not play together, and threatens to turn him out of the house if we break his orders. He has been blaming our father (how dared he?) for treating H. too **liberally**; and he swears he will reduce him to his right place—"

I began to nod drowsily over the dim page: my eye wandered from manuscript to print. I saw a red ornamented title—*Seventy Times Seven, and the First of the Seventy-First. A **Pious Discourse** delivered by the Reverend Jabes Branderham, in the Chapel of*

FLOUNDER (<u>flown</u> duhr) *v.* **-ing,-ed.**
 to struggle, falter, waver
  Synonyms: blunder, stumble, bumble, lurch, lumber
REPROACH (rih <u>prohch</u>) *n.*
 expressed disappointment or displeasure; discredit
  Synonyms: rebuke, blame; disgrace

EXCOMMUNICATE (ehks kuh <u>myoo</u> nih kayt)
v. **-ing,-ed.**
 to bar from membership in the church
  Synonyms: exclude, ostracize, expel

STIPEND (<u>stie</u> pehnd) *n.*
 allowance, fixed amount of money paid regularly
  Synonyms: salary, reward, wage, emolument,
  endowment

CONGREGATION (kahn grih <u>gay</u> shuhn) *n.*
 a crowd of people, an assembly
  Synonyms: group, gathering, fold, multitude

Gimmerdon Sough. And while I was, half consciously, worrying my brain to guess what Jabes Branderham would make of his subject, I sank back in bed, and fell asleep. Alas, for the effects of bad tea and bad temper! What else could it be that made me pass such a terrible night? I don't remember another that I can at all compare with it since I was capable of suffering.

I began to dream, almost before I ceased to be sensible of my locality. I thought it was morning; and I had set out on my way home, with Joseph for a guide. The snow lay yards deep in our road; and, as we **floundered** on, my companion wearied me with constant **reproaches** that I had not brought a pilgrim's staff, telling me that I could never get into the house without one, and boastfully flourishing a heavy-headed <u>cudgel</u>, which I understood to be so <u>denominated</u>. For a moment I considered it absurd that I should need such a weapon to gain admittance into my own residence. Then a new idea flashed across me. I was not going there: we were journeying to hear the famous Jabes Branderham preach from the text—*Seventy Times Seven*; and either Joseph, the preacher, or I had committed the *First of the Seventy-First*, and were to be publicly exposed and **excommunicated**.

We came to the chapel. I have passed it really in my walks, twice or thrice; it lies in a hollow, between two hills: an elevated hollow, near a swamp, whose peaty moisture is said to answer all the purposes of <u>embalming</u> on the few corpses deposited there. The roof has been kept whole hitherto; but as the clergyman's **stipend** is only twenty pounds per <u>annum</u>, and a house with two rooms, threatening speedily to determine into one, no clergyman will undertake the duties of pastor especially as it is currently reported that his flock would rather let him starve than increase the living by one penny from their own pockets. However, in my dream, Jabes had a full and attentive **congregation**; and he preached. Good God! What a sermon: divided into *four hundred and ninety* parts, each fully equal to an ordinary address from the

TRANSGRESSION (traans <u>greh</u> shuhn) *n.*
  a trespass or violation of a law or command
    Synonyms: overstep, sin, offense
DESCEND (dih <u>sehnd</u>) (dee <u>sehnd</u>) *v.* **-ing,-ed.**
  1. to arrive in an overwhelming way
    Synonyms: overtake, cascade, surge
  2. to pass from a higher place to a lower place
    Synonyms: fall, dismount, gravitate
DENOUNCE (dih <u>nowns</u>) *v.* **-ing,-ed.**
  to accuse, blame
    Synonyms: censure, criticize, condemn, vilify, brand
DISCOURSE (<u>dihs</u> kohrs) *n. (See page 40.)*
PREPOSTEROUSLY (prih <u>pah</u> stehr uhs lee) *adv.*
  absurdly, illogically
    Synonyms: ridiculously, ludicrously, nonsensically
MARTYR (<u>mahr</u> tuhr) *n.*
  a person who dies for his or her beliefs
    Synonyms: saint, sufferer
SOLEMN (<u>sah</u> luhm) *adj.*
  quiet, deeply serious; somberly impressive
    Synonyms: earnest, brooding; dignified, ceremonial
VISAGE (<u>vih</u> sihj) *n.*
  the appearance of a person or place, face
    Synonyms: expression, look, style, manner
ABSOLVE (uhb <u>sahlv</u>) *v.* **-ing,-ed.**
  to forgive, free from blame
    Synonyms: acquit, exculpate, exonerate, pardon
EXECUTE (<u>ehk</u> sih kyoot) *v.* **-ing,-ed.**
  to carry out fully; to make or produce
    Synonyms: accomplish, achieve; perform, effectuate
EXALT (ihg <u>zahlt</u>) *v.* **-ing,-ed.**
  to elevate through praise; to enhance the activity of
    Synonyms: glorify; intensify
ASSAILANT (uh <u>sayl</u> ehnt) *n.*
  an attacker, one who assaults
    Synonyms: striker, aggressor, enemy, invader
CONFLUENCE (<u>kuhn</u> floo ehnts) *n.*
  a place where two or more things meet or flow together
    Synonyms: junction, merging, assemblage
MULTITUDE (<u>muhl</u> tuh tood) *n.*
  the state of being many, a great number
    Synonyms: mass, myriad, slew, crowd

44

pulpit, and each discussing a separate sin! Where he searched for them, I cannot tell. He had his private manner of interpreting the phrase, and it seemed necessary the brother should sin different sins on every occasion. They were of the most curious character: odd **transgressions** that I never imagined previously.

Oh, how weary I grew. How I writhed, and yawned, and nodded, and revived! How I pinched and pricked myself, and rubbed my eyes, and stood up, and sat down again, and nudged Joseph to inform me if he would *ever* have done. I was condemned to hear all out; finally, he reached the *First of the Seventy-First*. At that crisis, a sudden inspiration **descended** on me; I was moved to rise and **denounce** Jabes Branderham as the sinner of the sin that no Christian need pardon.

"Sir," I exclaimed, "sitting here within these four walls, at one stretch, I have endured and forgiven the four hundred and ninety heads of your **discourse**. Seventy times seven times have I plucked up my hat and been about to depart—Seventy times seven times have you **preposterously** forced me to resume my seat. The four hundred and ninety first is too much. Fellow-**martyrs**, have at him! Drag him down, and crush him to atoms, that the place which knows him may know him no more!"

"*Thou art the man!*" cried Jabes, after a **solemn** pause, leaning over his cushion. "Seventy times seven times didst thou gapingly contort thy **visage**. Seventy times seven did I take counsel with my soul. Lo, this is human weakness: this also may be **absolved**! The First of the Seventy-First is come. Brethren, **execute** upon him the judgment written. Such honour have all His saints!"

With that concluding word, the whole assembly, **exalting** their pilgrim's staves, rushed round me in a body; and I, having no weapon to raise in self-defence, commenced grappling with Joseph, my nearest and most ferocious **assailant**, for his. In the **confluence** of the **multitude**, several clubs crossed; blows, aimed at me, fell on other sconces. Presently the whole chapel resounded

ZEAL (zeel) *n.*
passion or devotion to a cause
Synonyms: fanaticism, enthusiasm

TUMULT (<u>tuh</u> muhlt) *n.*
state of confusion, agitation
Synonyms: disturbance, turmoil, din, commotion

ASCRIBE (uh <u>scrieb</u>) *v.* **-ing,-ed.**
to attribute to, assign
Synonyms: accredit, impute, refer

RESOLVE (rih <u>sahlv</u>) *v.* **-ing,-ed.**
to determine or to make a firm decision about
Synonyms: solve, decide

IMPORTUNATE (ihm <u>pohr</u> chuh niht) *adj.*
1. troublesome, difficult
Synonyms: annoying, disturbing
2. extremely urgent, pleading
Synonyms: craving, beseeching, earnest, imperative

DRAW *v.* **drawing, drew, drawn.**
to pull, drag; to attract or be attracted to; to lead, to
bring about on purpose
Synonyms: haul, tow, yank; lure, entice; provoke, elicit

MELANCHOLY (mehl uhn <u>kahl</u> ee) *adj.*
sad, depressing
Synonyms: dejected, despondent, woeful, sorrowful

DISCERN (dihs <u>uhrn</u>) *v.* **-ing,-ed.**
to perceive or recognize something
Synonyms: descry, observe, glimpse, distinguish

OBSCURELY (uhb <u>skyoor</u> lee) *adv.*
dimly, unclearly
Synonyms: faintly, remotely

with rappings and counter-tappings: every man's hand was against his neighbour, and Branderham, unwilling to remain idle, poured forth his **zeal** in a shower of loud taps on the boards of the pulpit, which responded so smartly that, at last, to my unspeakable relief, they woke me. And what was it that had suggested the tremendous **tumult**? What had played Jabes's part in the row? Merely, the branch of a fir-tree that touched my <u>lattice</u>, as the blast wailed by, and rattled its dry cones against the panes! I listened doubtingly an instant; detected the disturber, then turned and dozed, and dreamt again: if possible, still more disagreeably than before.

This time, I remembered I was lying in the oak closet, and I heard distinctly the gusty wind, and the driving of the snow; I heard, also, the fir-bough repeat its teasing sound, and **ascribed** it to the right cause: but it annoyed me so much, that I **resolved** to silence it, if possible; and, I thought, I rose and endeavoured to <u>unhasp</u> the <u>casement</u>. The hook was soldered into the staple: a circumstance observed by me when awake, but forgotten.

"I must stop it, nevertheless!" I muttered, knocking my knuckles through the glass, and stretching an arm out to seize the **importunate** branch; instead of which, my fingers closed on the fingers of a little, ice-cold hand!

The intense horror of nightmare came over me: I tried to **draw** back my arm, but the hand clung to it, and a most **melancholy** voice sobbed.

"Let me in—let me in!"

"Who are you?" I asked, struggling, meanwhile, to disengage myself.

"Catherine Linton," it replied, shiveringly (why did I think of *Linton*? I had read *Earnshaw* twenty times for *Linton*). "I'm come home: I'd lost my way on the moor!"

As it spoke, I **discerned**, **obscurely**, a child's face looking through the window. Terror made me cruel; and, finding it useless to attempt shaking the creature off, I pulled its wrist on to the broken pane, and rubbed it to and fro till the blood ran down and soaked the

TENACIOUS (tuh <u>nay</u> shuhs) *adj.*
  stubborn, holding firm
    Synonyms: persistent, strong, stout, sturdy, stalwart

LAMENTABLE (luh <u>mehn</u> tuh buhl) *adj.*
  deplorable, grievous
    Synonyms: mournful, sorrowful, tragic

DOLEFUL (<u>dohl</u> fuhl) *adj.*
  sad, mournful
    Synonyms: funereal, somber, lugubrious, dismal,
    woeful

WAIF (wayf) *n.*
  anything or anyone without a home or owner;
  a homeless child
    Synonyms: castaway, stray; orphan, foundling

AGITATION (aa gih <u>tay</u> shuhn) *n.*
  uneasiness; commotion, excitement
    Synonyms: restlessness, anxiety; disturbance

bedclothes: still it wailed, "Let me in!" and maintained its **tenacious** gripe, almost maddening me with fear.

"How can I?" I said at length. "Let *me* go, if you want me to let you in!"

The fingers relaxed, I snatched mine through the hole, hurriedly piled the books up in a pyramid against it, and stopped my ears to exclude the **lamentable** prayer. I seemed to keep them closed above a quarter of an hour, yet, the instant I listened again, there was the **doleful** cry moaning on!

"Begone!" I shouted, "I'll never let you in, not if you beg for twenty years."

"It is twenty years," mourned the voice. "Twenty years. I've been a **waif** for twenty years!"

Thereat began a feeble scratching outside, and the pile of books moved as if thrust forward. I tried to jump up; but could not stir a limb; and so yelled aloud, in a frenzy of fright. To my confusion, I discovered the yell was not ideal: hasty footsteps approached my chamber door, somebody pushed it open, with a vigorous hand, and a light glimmered through the squares at the top of the bed. I sat shuddering yet, and wiping the perspiration from my forehead. The intruder appeared to hesitate, and muttered to himself.

At last, he said in a half-whisper, plainly not expecting an answer, "Is anyone here?"

I considered it best to confess my presence; for I knew Heathcliff's accents, and feared he might search further, if I kept quiet. With this intention, I turned and opened the panels. I shall not soon forget the effect my action produced.

Heathcliff stood near the entrance, in his shirt and trousers: with a candle dripping over his fingers, and his face as white as the wall behind him. The first creak of the oak startled him like an electric shock! The light leaped from his hold to a distance of some feet, and his **agitation** was so extreme, that he could hardly pick it up.

CONFOUND (kuhn <u>fownd</u>) *v.* **-ing,-ed.**
1. to damn or condemn
   Synonyms: doom, jinx, revile, punish
2. to mistake something for another; to baffle, perplex
   Synonyms: confuse, misidentify; overwhelm,
   disconcert, entangle, muddle

TRANSGRESSION (traans <u>greh</u> shuhn) *n.*
a trespass or violation of a law or command
   Synonyms: overstep, sin, offense

"It is only your guest, sir," I called out, desirous to spare him the humiliation of exposing his cowardice further. "I had the misfortune to scream in my sleep, owing to a frightful nightmare. I'm sorry I disturbed you."

"Oh, God **confound** you, Mr. Lockwood! I wish you were at the—" commenced my host, setting the candle on a chair, because he found it impossible to hold it steady. "And who showed you up into this room?" he continued, crushing his nails into his palms, and grinding his teeth to subdue the <u>maxillary</u> convulsions. "Who was it? I've a good mind to turn them out of the house this moment!"

"It was your servant, Zillah," I replied, flinging myself on to the floor, and rapidly resuming my garments. "I should not care if you did, Mr. Heathcliff; she richly deserves it. I suppose that she wanted to get another proof that the place was haunted, at my expense. Well, it is—swarming with ghosts and goblins! You have reason in shutting it up, I assure you. No one will thank you for a doze in such a den!"

"What do you mean?" asked Heathcliff. "And what are you doing? Lie down and finish out the night, since you *are* here; but, for Heaven's sake! Don't repeat that horrid noise; nothing could excuse it, unless you were having your throat cut!"

"If the little fiend had got in at the window, she probably would have strangled me!" I returned. "I'm not going to endure the persecutions of your hospitable ancestors again. Was not the Reverend Jabes Branderham akin to you on the mother's side? And that minx, Catherine Linton, or Earnshaw, or however she was called—she must have been a <u>changeling</u>—wicked little soul! She told me she had been walking the earth those twenty years: a just punishment for her mortal **transgressions**, I've no doubt!"

Scarcely were these words uttered, when I recollected the association of Heathcliff's with Catherine's name in the book, which had completely slipped from my memory, till thus awakened. I blushed at my inconsideration;

PERUSE (puh <u>roos</u>) *v.* **-ing,-ed.**
to examine closely
Synonyms: scrutinize, inspect, study; browse

MONOTONOUS (muh <u>nah</u> tuh nihs) *adj.*
repetitive, unvaried
Synonyms: recurrent, tedious, boring, dull

VEHEMENCE (<u>vee</u> huh muhnts) *n.*
strength, urgency
Synonyms: fervor, intensity, ferocity, passion, ardor

AFFIRM (uh <u>fihrm</u>) *v.* **-ing,-ed.**
to state positively, to assert as valid or confirmed
Synonyms: declare, avow, maintain

APPELLATION (aa puhl <u>ay</u> shuhn) *n.*
a title or name
Synonyms: denomination, designation, moniker, tag

VANQUISH (<u>vaan</u> kwihsh) *v.* **-ing,-ed.**
to conquer, defeat
Synonyms: subjugate, overcome, subdue, suppress, trounce

SOLILOQUIZE (suh <u>lih</u> luh kwiez) *v.* **-ing,-ed.**
to make a literary or dramatic speech; to talk to oneself
Synonyms: dramatize; express, verbalize

STAGNATE (<u>staag</u> nayt) *v.* **-ing,-ed.**
to be immobile or motionless
Synonyms: stifle, decay, deteriorate, stall, vegetate

SUPPRESS (suh <u>prehs</u>) *v.* **-ing,-ed.**
to hold back, restrain
Synonyms: subdue, stifle, muffle, quell, curb

but, without showing further consciousness of the offence, I hastened to add—"The truth is, sir, I passed the first part of the night in"—Here I stopped afresh—I was about to say "**perusing** those old volumes," then it would have revealed my knowledge of their written, as well as their printed contents: so, correcting myself, I went on, "in spelling over the name scratched on that window-ledge. A **monotonous** occupation, calculated to set me asleep, like counting, or—"

"What *can* you mean by talking in this way to *me*?" thundered Heathcliff with savage **vehemence**. "How—how *dare* you, under my roof?—God! He's mad to speak so!" And he struck his forehead with rage.

I did not know whether to resent this language or pursue my explanation; but he seemed so powerfully affected that I took pity and proceeded with my dreams; **affirming** that I had never heard the **appellation** of "Catherine Linton" before, but reading it often over produced an impression which personified itself when I had no longer my imagination under control. Heathcliff gradually fell back into the shelter of the bed, as I spoke; finally sitting down almost concealed behind it I guessed. However, by his irregular and intercepted breathing, that he struggled to **vanquish** an excess of violent emotion. Not liking to show him that I had heard the conflict, I continued my <u>toilette</u> rather noisily, looked at my watch, and **soliloquized** on the length of the night: "Not three o'clock yet! I could have taken oath it had been six—time **stagnates** here: we must surely have retired to rest at eight!"

"Always at nine in winter, and rise at four," said my host, **suppressing** a groan: and, as I fancied by the motion of his arm's shadow, dashing a tear from his eyes. "Mr. Lockwood," he added, "you may go into my room: you'll only be in the way, coming downstairs so early; and your childish outcry has sent sleep to the devil for me."

"And for me, too," I replied. "I'll walk in the yard till daylight, and then I'll be off; and you need not dread a

SENTINEL (<u>sehn</u> tih nuhl) *n.*
surveillance, patrol, watch; a watch guard
Synonyms: lookout, vigilance; scout, protector

CAPRICE (kuh <u>prees</u>) *n.*
an impulsive change of mind, fickleness
Synonym: whim

VEX (vehks) *v.* **-ing,-ed.**
to irritate, annoy; confuse, puzzle
Synonyms: bother, plague, afflict, irk; perplex, perturb

DESCEND (dih <u>sehnd</u>) (dee <u>sehnd</u>) *v.* **-ing,-ed.**
to pass from a higher place to a lower place
Synonyms: fall, dismount, gravitate

REKINDLE (ree <u>kihn</u> duhl) *v.* **-ing,-ed.**
to set fire to again, or reignite; excite or inspire again
Synonyms: relight; reawaken

QUERULOUS (<u>kwehr</u> uh luhs) *adj.*
inclined to complain, irritable
Synonyms: peevish, whiny, sniveling, puling

repetition of my intrusion. I'm now quite cured of seeking pleasure in society, be it country or town. A sensible man ought to find sufficient company in himself."

"Delightful company!" muttered Heathcliff. "Take the candle, and go where you please. I shall join you directly. Keep out of the yard, though, the dogs are unchained; and the house—Juno mounts **sentinel** there, and—nay, you can only ramble about the steps and passages. But, away with you! I'll come in two minutes!"

I obeyed, so far as to quit the chamber; when, ignorant where the narrow lobbies led, I stood still, and was witness, involuntarily, to a piece of superstition on the part of my landlord, which belied, oddly, his apparent sense.

He got on to the bed, and wrenched open the <u>lattice</u>, bursting, as he pulled at it, into an uncontrollable passion of tears.

"Come in! Come in!" he sobbed. "Cathy, do come. Oh do—*once* more! Oh! My heart's darling; hear me *this* time, Catherine, at last!"

The <u>spectre</u> showed a <u>spectre</u>'s ordinary **caprice**: it gave no sign of being; but the snow and wind whirled wildly through, even reaching my station, and blowing out the light.

There was such an anguish in the gush of grief that accompanied this raving, that my compassion made me overlook its folly, and I drew off, half angry to have listened at all, and **vexed** at having related my ridiculous nightmare, since it produced that agony; though *why* was beyond my comprehension. I **descended** cautiously to the lower regions, and landed in the back kitchen, where a gleam of fire, raked compactly together, enabled me to **rekindle** my candle. Nothing was stirring except a <u>brindled</u>, grey cat, which crept from the ashes, and saluted me with a **querulous** mew.

Two benches, shaped in sections of a circle, nearly enclosed the hearth; on one of these I stretched myself, and Grimalkin mounted the other. We were both of us nodding, ere any one invaded our retreat, and then it was

SAT Vocabulary

ASCENT (uh <u>sehnt</u>) *n.*
    a climb or rising to another level; movement upward;
    an upward slope
        Synonyms: mounting; scaling, escalation; incline, upgrade

BESTOW (bih <u>stoh</u>) *v.* **-ing,-ed.**
    1. to stow or place
        Synonyms: position, set, arrange, plant
    2. to give as a gift; to apply or devote, as in time or effort
        Synonyms: endow, confer, present; allocate, dedicate

SANCTUM (<u>saank</u> tuhm) *n.*
    a private place; a sacred or holy place
        Synonyms: refuge, asylum, shelter, retreat; altar, temple

IMPUDENCE (<u>ihm</u> pyuh duhnts) *n.*
    arrogance, audacity
        Synonyms: insolence, impertinence, boldness

PROFOUND (pruh <u>fownd</u>) (proh <u>fownd</u>) *adj.*
    deep; having intellectual depth, difficult to understand
        Synonyms: bottomless; serious, thorough, weighty

SOLEMNLY (<u>sah</u> luhm lee) *adv.*
    seriously or somberly
        Synonyms: quietly, earnestly, ceremonially

SALUTATION (saal yoo <u>tay</u> shuhn) *n.*
    greeting
        Synonyms: regards, welcome, hello

DILATE (<u>die</u> layt) (die <u>layt</u>) *v.* **-ing,-ed.**
    to enlarge, swell, extend
        Synonyms: expand, spread, distend

CIVILITY (sih <u>vihl</u> ih tee) *n.*
    a courteous behavior or politeness
        Synonyms: compliment, pleasantry

EGRESS (<u>ee</u> grehs) *n.*
    the act of leaving or the ability to leave; an exit
        Synonyms: emergence, departure; escape, doorway

INTIMATE (<u>ihn</u> tuh mayt) *v.* **-ing,-ed.** *(See page 22.)*

INARTICULATE (ihn ahr <u>tihk</u> yuh liht) *adj.*
    tongue-tied, unable to speak clearly
        Synonyms: incomprehensible, unintelligible

DESIST (dih <u>sihst</u>) (dih <u>zihst</u>) *v.* **-ing,-ed.**
    to stop doing something
        Synonyms: cease, abort, discontinue, end, quit

CHIDE (chied) *v.* **-ing,-ed.**
    to scold, express disapproval
        Synonyms: chastise, admonish, reprimand, reprove

Joseph, shuffling down a wooden ladder that vanished in the roof, through a trap: the **ascent** to his <u>garret</u>, I suppose. He cast a sinister look at the little flame which I had enticed to play between the ribs, swept the cat from its elevation, and **bestowing** himself in the vacancy, commenced the operation of stuffing a three-inch pipe with tobacco. My presence in his **sanctum** was evidently esteemed a piece of **impudence** too shameful for remark: he silently applied the tube to his lips, folded his arms, and puffed away. I let him enjoy the luxury unannoyed; and after sucking out his last breath, and heaving a **profound** sigh, he got up, and departed as **solemnly** as he came.

A more elastic footstep entered next; and now I opened my mouth for a "good morning," but closed it again, the **salutation** unachieved; for Hareton Earnshaw was performing his <u>orisons</u> *sotto voce*, in a series of curses directed against every object he touched, while he rummaged a corner for a spade or shovel to dig through the drifts. He glanced over the back of the bench, **dilating** his nostrils, and thought as little of exchanging **civilities** with me as with my companion the cat. I guessed, by his preparations, that **egress** was allowed, and, leaving my hard couch, made a movement to follow him. He noticed this, and thrust at an inner door with the end of his spade, **intimating** by an **inarticulate** sound that there was the place where I must go, if I changed my locality.

It opened into the house, where the females were already astir. Zillah urging flakes of flame up the chimney with a colossal bellows; and Mrs. Heathcliff, kneeling on the hearth, reading a book by the aid of the blaze. She held her hand <u>interposed</u> between the furnace-heat and her eyes, and seemed absorbed in her occupation; **desisting** from it only to **chide** the servant for covering her with sparks, or to push away a dog, now and then, that snoozled its nose overforwardly into her face. I was surprised to see Heathcliff there also. He stood by the fire, his back towards me, just finishing a stormy scene to poor Zillah; who ever and anon interrupted her labour to

INDIGNANT (ihn <u>dihg</u> nuhnt) *adj.*
   angry, incensed, offended
      Synonyms: furious, irate, mad, wrathful, ireful
EPITHET (<u>eh</u> puh theht) *n.*
   an abusive word or phrase; a descriptive term or
   phrase substituted for a real name
      Synonyms: invective; nickname, motto, catchphrase

DECORUM (deh <u>kuhr</u> uhm) (deh <u>kohr</u> uhm) *n.*
   propriety, taste, social correctness
      Synonyms: politeness, courtesy, appropriateness
SUSPEND (suh <u>spehnd</u>) *v.* **-ing,-ed.**
   to delay, interrupt; to dangle, hang
      Synonyms: defer, cease, disrupt, halt, discontinue;
      swing

IMPALPABLE (ihm <u>paalp</u> uh buhl) *adj.*
   unreal, intangible
      Synonyms: imperceptible, tenuous, unsubstantial

BILLOWY (<u>bih</u> loh ee) *adj.*
   characterized by swelling or surging
      Synonyms: bouncy, heaving, undulating, rolling

pluck up the corner of her apron, and heave an **indignant** groan.

"And you, you worthless"—he broke out as I entered, turning to his daughter-in-law, and employing an **epithet** as harmless as duck, or sheep, but generally represented by a dash. "There you are, at your idle tricks again! The rest of them do earn their bread—you live on my charity! Put your trash away, and find something to do. You shall pay me for the plague of having you eternally in my sight—do you hear, damnable jade?"

"I'll put my trash away, because you can make me, if I refuse," answered the young lady, closing her book, and throwing it on a chair. "But I'll not do anything, though you should swear your tongue out, except what I please!"

Heathcliff lifted his hand, and the speaker sprang to a safer distance, obviously acquainted with its weight. Having no desire to be entertained by a cat-and-dog combat, I stepped forward briskly, as if eager to partake the warmth of the hearth, and innocent of any knowledge of the interrupted dispute. Each had enough **decorum** to **suspend** further hostilities: Heathcliff placed his fists, out of temptation, in his pockets; Mrs. Heathcliff curled her lip, and walked to a seat far off, where she kept her word by playing the part of a statue during the remainder of my stay. That was not long. I declined joining their breakfast, and, at the first gleam of dawn, took an opportunity of escaping into the free air, now clear, and still, and cold as **impalpable** ice.

My landlord hallooed for me to stop, ere I reached the bottom of the garden, and offered to accompany me across the moor. It was well he did, for the whole hillback was one **billowy**, white ocean; the swells and falls not indicating corresponding rises and depressions in the ground: many pits, at least, were filled to a level; and entire ranges of mounds, the refuse of the quarries, blotted from the chart which my yesterday's walk left pictured in my mind. I had remarked on one side of the road, at intervals of six or seven yards, a line of upright stones,

DAUB (dawb) *v.* **-ing,-ed.**
  to apply with short, quick strokes; to dab
    Synonyms: smudge, smear, blot, spot

CONFOUND (kuhn <u>fownd</u>) *v.* **-ing,-ed.**
  1. to mistake something for another; to baffle, perplex
    Synonyms: confuse, misidentify; overwhelm,
    disconcert, entangle, muddle
  2. to damn or condemn
    Synonyms: doom, jinx, revile, punish

TUMULTUOUSLY (tuh <u>muhl</u> choo uhs lee) *adv.*
  confusedly, noisily and disorderly
    Synonyms: turbulently, excitedly

CONJECTURE (kuhn <u>jehk</u> shuhr) *v.* **-ing,-ed.**
  to infer, predict, guess
    Synonyms: postulate, hypothesize, suppose, surmise

continued through the whole length of the barren: these were erected, and **daubed** with lime on the purpose to serve as guides in the dark; and also when a fall, like the present, **confounded** the deep swamps on either hand with the firmer path: but, excepting a dirty dot pointing up here and there, all traces of their existence had vanished: and my companion found it necessary to warn me frequently to steer to the right or left, when I imagined I was following, correctly, the windings of the road.

We exchanged little conversation, and he halted at the entrance of Thrushcross Park, saying, I could make no error there. Our <u>adieux</u> were limited to a hasty bow, and then I pushed forward, trusting to my own resources; for the porter's lodge is untenanted as yet. The distance from the gate to the Grange is two miles. I believe I managed to make it four; what with losing myself among the trees and sinking up to the neck in snow, a predicament which only those who have experienced it can appreciate. At any rate, whatever were my wanderings, the clock chimed twelve as I entered the house; and that gave me exactly an hour for every mile of the usual way from Wuthering Heights.

My human fixture and her satellites rushed to welcome me; exclaiming, **tumultuously**, they had completely given me up. Everybody **conjectured** that I had perished last night; and they were wondering how they must set about the search for my remains. I bid them be quiet, now that they saw me returned, and, benumbed to my very heart, I dragged upstairs; whence, after putting on dry clothes, and pacing to and fro thirty or forty minutes, to restore the animal heat, I am <u>adjourned</u> to my study, feeble as a kitten: almost too much so to enjoy the cheerful fire and smoking coffee which the servant has prepared for my refreshment.

IMPRACTICABLE (ihm <u>praak</u> tih kuh buhl) *adj.*
impassable; incapable of being performed by the
means employed
Synonyms: blocked; insane, imprudent, absurd,
impossible
COMPEL (kuhm <u>pehl</u>) *v.* **-ling,-led.**
to urge or force
Synonyms: coerce, oblige, constrain
PRETENSE (<u>pree</u> tehnts) (prih <u>tehnts</u>) *n.*
a fake reason or excuse; an act of pretending
Synonyms: falsehood, fabrication, guise; feigning
ANIMATION (aa nih <u>may</u> shuhn) *n.*
enthusiasm, excitement
Synonyms: elation, vivacity, brio, spirit, verve
RETAIN (rih <u>tayn</u>) *v.* **-ing,-ed.**
to hold, keep possession of
Synonyms: withhold, reserve, maintain, remember
RUDDY (<u>ruh</u> dee) *adj.*
healthily reddish or rosy
Synonyms: flushed, sanguine, fresh, pinkish
COUNTENANCE (<u>kown</u> tuh nuhns) *n.*
appearance, facial expression
Synonyms: face, features, visage
EJACULATE (ih <u>jaak</u> yuh layt) *v.* **-ing,-ed.**
to exclaim suddenly
Synonyms: blurt, shout, declare
EXOTIC (ihg <u>zah</u> tihk) *n.*
a foreigner
Synonyms: alien, gypsy
SURLY (<u>suhr</u> lee) *adj.*
rude and bad-tempered
Synonyms: gruff, testy, grumpy
INDIGENAE (ihn <u>dihj</u> uh nay) *n.pl.*
the native people of an area
Synonyms: residents, countrymen

Chapter 4

What vain weather-cocks we are! I, who had determined to hold myself independent of all social intercourse, and thanked my stars that, at length, I had lighted on a spot where it was next to **impracticable**—I, weak wretch, after maintaining till dusk a struggle with low spirits and solitude was finally **compelled** to strike my colours; and, under **pretense** of gaining information concerning the necessities of my establishment, I desired Mrs. Dean, when she brought in supper, to sit down while I ate it; hoping sincerely she would prove a regular gossip, and either rouse me to **animation** or lull me to sleep by her talk.

"You have lived here a considerable time," I commenced. "Did you not say sixteen years?"

"Eighteen, sir: I came, when the mistress was married, to wait on her; after she died, the master **retained** me for his housekeeper."

"Indeed."

There <u>ensued</u> a pause. She was not a gossip, I feared; unless about her own affairs, and those could hardly interest me. However, having studied for an interval, with a fist on either knee, and a cloud of meditation over her **ruddy countenance**, she **ejaculated**:

"Ah, times are greatly changed since then!"

"Yes," I remarked, "you've seen a good many alterations, I suppose?"

"I have, and troubles too," she said.

Oh, I'll turn the talk on my landlord's family! I thought to myself. A good subject to start! And that pretty girl-widow, I should like to know her history: whether she be a native of the country, or, as is more probable, an **exotic** that the **surly indigenae** will not recognize for kin. With this intention I asked Mrs. Dean why Heathcliff let

Thrushcross Grange, and preferred living in a situation and residence so much inferior. "Is he not rich enough to keep the estate in good order?" I inquired.

"Rich, sir!" she returned. "He has, nobody knows what money, and every year it increases. Yes, yes, he's rich enough to live in a finer house than this: but he's very near—close-handed; and, if he had meant to flit to Thrushcross Grange, as soon as he heard of a good tenant he could not have borne to miss the chance of getting a few hundreds more. It is strange people should be so greedy, when they are alone in the world!"

"He had a son, it seems?"

"Yes, he had one—he is dead."

"And that young lady, Mrs. Heathcliff, is his widow?"

"Yes."

"Where did she come from originally?"

"Why, sir, she is my late master's daughter: Catherine Linton was her maiden name. I nursed her, poor thing! I did wish Mr. Heathcliff would remove here, and then we might have been together again."

"What! Catherine Linton?" I exclaimed, astonished. But a minute's reflection convinced me it was not my ghostly Catherine. "Then," I continued, "my predecessor's name was Linton?"

"It was."

"And who is that Earnshaw: Hareton Earnshaw, who lives with Mr. Heathcliff? Are they relations?"

"No; he is the late Mrs. Linton's nephew."

"The young lady's cousin, then?"

"Yes; and her husband was her cousin also: one on the mother's, the other on the father's side. Heathcliff married Mr. Linton's sister."

"I see the house at Wuthering Heights has 'Earnshaw' carved over the front door. Are they an old family?"

"Very old, sir; and Hareton is the last of them, as our Miss Cathy is of us—I mean of the Lintons. Have you been to Wuthering Heights? I beg pardon for asking; but I should like to hear how she is!"

MEDDLE (<u>meh</u> duhl) *v.* **-ing,-ed.**
    to interfere in others' affairs, to impose
        Synonyms: interlope, tamper, snoop, encroach
CHURL (chuhrl) *n.*
    a rude, uncultured person
        Synonyms: boor, rustic, peasant, barbarian
UNFLEDGED (uhn <u>flehjd</u>) *adj.*
    immature, juvenile, inexperienced
        Synonyms: unprepared, untrained

BUSTLE (<u>buh</u> suhl) *v.* **-ing,-ed.**
    to move quickly and energetically
        Synonyms: scurry, scramble, dash, whirl, fuss

"Mrs. Heathcliff? She looked very well, and very handsome; yet, I think, not very happy."

"O dear, I don't wonder! And how did you like the master?"

"A rough fellow, rather, Mrs. Dean. Is not that his character?"

"Rough as a saw-edge, and hard as whinstone! The less you **meddle** with him the better."

"He must have had some ups and downs in life to make him such a **churl**. Do you know anything of his history?"

"It's a cuckoo's, sir—I know all about it: except where he was born, and who were his parents, and how he got his money, at first. And Hareton has been cast out like an **unfledged** dunnock! The unfortunate lad is the only one in all this parish that does not guess how he has been cheated."

"Well, Mrs. Dean, it will be a charitable deed to tell me something of my neighbours. I feel I shall not rest, if I go to bed; so be good enough to sit and chat an hour."

"Oh, certainly, sir! I'll just fetch a little sewing, and then I'll sit as long as you please. But you've caught cold: I saw you shivering, and you must have some gruel to drive it out."

The worthy woman **bustled** off, and I crouched nearer the fire. My head felt hot, and the rest of me chill. Moreover, I was excited, almost to a pitch of foolishness, through my nerves and brain. This caused me to feel, not uncomfortable, but rather fearful (as I am still) of serious effects from the incidents of to-day and yesterday. She returned presently, bringing a smoking basin and a basket of work; and, having placed the former on the hob, drew in her seat, evidently pleased to find me so companionable.

Before I came to live here, she commenced—waiting no farther invitation to her story—I was almost always at Wuthering Heights; because my mother had nursed Mr. Hindley Earnshaw, that was Hareton's father, and I got used to playing with the children: I ran errands too, and

helped to make hay, and hung about the farm ready for anything that anybody would set me to. One fine summer morning—it was the beginning of harvest, I remember—Mr. Earnshaw, the old master, came downstairs, dressed for a journey; and after he had told Joseph what was to be done during the day, he turned to Hindley, and Cathy, and me—for I sat eating my porridge with them—and he said, speaking to his son, "Now my <u>bonny</u> man, I'm going to Liverpool to-day, what shall I bring you? You may choose what you like: only let it be little, for I shall walk there and back: sixty miles each way, that is a long spell!" Hindley named a fiddle, and then he asked Miss Cathy; she was hardly six years old, but she could ride any horse in the stable, and she chose a whip. He did not forget me; for he had a kind heart, though he was rather severe sometimes. He promised to bring me a pocketful of apples and pears, and then he kissed his children, said good-bye, and set off.

It seemed a long while to us all—the three days of his absence—and often did little Cathy ask when he would be home. Mrs. Earnshaw expected him by supper-time on the third evening, and she put the meal off hour after hour. There were no signs of his coming, however, and at last the children got tired of running down to the gate to look. Then it grew dark; she would have had them to bed, but they begged sadly to be allowed to stay up; and, just about eleven o'clock, the door-latch was raised quietly and in stepped the master. He threw himself into a chair, laughing and groaning, and bid them all stand off, for he was nearly killed—he would not have such another walk for the three kingdoms.

"And at the end of it, to be <u>flighted</u> to death!" he said, opening his great-coat which he held bundled up in his arms. "See here, wife! I was never so beaten with anything in my life: but you must e'en take it as a gift of God; though it's as dark almost as if it came from the devil."

We crowded round, and over Miss Cathy's head, I had a peep at a dirty, ragged, black-haired child, big enough

both to walk and talk. Indeed, its face looked older than Catherine's; yet, when it was set on its feet, it only stared round, and repeated over and over again some gibberish, that nobody could understand. I was frightened, and Mrs. Earnshaw was ready to fling it out of doors: she did fly up, asking how he could fashion to bring that gypsy brat into the house, when they had their own <u>bairns</u> to feed and fend for? What he meant to do with it, and whether he were mad? The master tried to explain the matter; but he was really half dead with fatigue, and all that I could make out, amongst her scolding, was a tale of his seeing it starving, and houseless, and as good as dumb, in the streets of Liverpool, where he picked it up and inquired for its owner. Not a soul knew to whom it belonged, he said; and his money and time being both limited, he thought it better to take it home with him at once than run into vain expenses there, because he was determined he would not leave it as he found it. Well, the conclusion was that my mistress grumbled herself calm; and Mr. Earnshaw told me to wash it, and give it clean things, and let it sleep with the children.

Hindley and Cathy contented themselves with looking and listening till peace was restored: then, both began searching their father's pockets for the presents he had promised them. The former was a boy of fourteen, but when he drew out what had been a fiddle crushed to morsels in the great-coat, he blubbered aloud; and Cathy, when she learned the master had lost her whip in attending on the stranger, showed her humour by grinning and spitting at the stupid little thing; earning for her pains a sound blow from her father to teach her cleaner manners. They entirely refused to have it in bed with them, or even in their room; and I had no more sense, so I put it on the landing of the stairs, hoping it might be gone on the morrow. By chance, or else attracted by hearing his voice, it crept to Mr. Earnshaw's door, and there he found it on quitting his chamber. Inquiries were made as to how it

OBLIGE (uh <u>bliej</u>) *v.* **-ing,-ed.**
 to be obligated, to require or force someone to obey
  Synonyms: compel, constrain, bind, favor

RECOMPENSE (<u>reh</u> kuhm pehns) *n.*
 something given as a means of compensation;
 something returned in kind
  Synonyms: repayment, reimbursement; indemnity

BANISHMENT (<u>baan</u> ish mehnt) *n.*
 the act of forcing someone to leave, exile, ostracism
  Synonyms: deportment, expatriation, removal

PERPETUAL (puhr <u>peht</u> chyoo uhl) *adj.*
 endless, lasting
  Synonyms: continuous, constant, ceaseless, eternal

SULLEN (<u>suh</u> luhn) *adj.*
 brooding, gloomy
  Synonyms: morose, sulky, somber, glum

USURPER (yoo <u>suhrp</u> uhr) *n.*
 one who seizes by force or without right
  Synonyms: preemptor, hijacker, thief

BROODING (<u>brood</u> ihng) *v.*
 thinking persistent and morbid thoughts
  Synonyms: worrying, comtemplating

COMPEL (kuhm <u>pehl</u>) *v.* **-ling,-led.**
 to urge or force
  Synonyms: coerce, oblige, constrain

got there; I was **obliged** to confess, and in **recompense** for my <u>cowardice</u> and inhumanity was sent out of the house.

This was Heathcliff's first introduction to the family. On coming back a few days afterwards (for I did not consider my **banishment perpetual**) I found they had christened him "Heathcliff." It was the name of a son who died in childhood, and it has served him ever since, both for Christian and surname. Miss Cathy and he were now very thick, but Hindley hated him! And to say the truth I did the same; and we plagued and went on with him shamefully: for I wasn't reasonable enough to feel my injustice, and the mistress never put in a word on his behalf when she saw him wronged.

He seemed a **sullen**, patient child, hardened, perhaps, to ill-treatment. He would stand Hindley's blows without winking or shedding a tear, and my pinches moved him only to draw in a breath and open his eyes, as if he had hurt himself by accident and nobody was to blame. This endurance made old Earnshaw furious, when he discovered his son persecuting the poor, fatherless child, as he called him. He took to Heathcliff strangely, believing all he said (for that matter, he said precious little, and generally the truth), and petting him up far above Cathy, who was too mischievous and wayward for a favourite.

So, from the very beginning, he bred bad feeling in the house; and at Mrs. Earnshaw's death, which happened in less than two years after, the young master had learned to regard his father as an oppressor rather than a friend, and Heathcliff as a **usurper** of his parent's affections and his privileges; and he grew bitter with **brooding** over these injuries. I sympathised a while; but when the children fell ill of the measles, and I had to tend them and take on me the cares of a woman at once, I changed my ideas. Heathcliff was dangerously sick, and while he lay at the worst he would have me constantly by his pillow. I suppose he felt I did a good deal for him, and he hadn't wit to guess that I was **compelled** to do it. However, I will say this, he was the quietest child that ever a nurse watched

PARTIAL (<u>pahr</u> shuhl) *adj.*
  biased; showing favoritism or a fondness
    Synonyms: unfair, one-sided, prejudiced;
    affectionate, sympathetic

AFFIRM (uh <u>fihrm</u>) *v.* **-ing,-ed.**
  to state positively, to assert as valid or confirmed
    Synonyms: declare, avow, maintain

COMMENDATION (kah mehn <u>day</u> shuhn) *n.*
  an act of praise or a show of respect; an award; the
  act of entrusting into someone's care
    Synonyms: acclaim, approval, flattery; tribute,
    reward; relegation, assignment

DOTE (doht) *v.* **-ing,-ed.**
  to lavish attention, to love to excess
    Synonyms: adore, cherish, tender

SULLEN (<u>suh</u> luhn) *adj.*
  brooding, gloomy
    Synonyms: morose, sulky, somber, glum

INDULGENCE (ihn <u>duhl</u> jehns) *n.*
  lenience, the act of giving in to desires
    Synonyms: gratification, tolerance, pampering

INSOLENT (<u>ihn</u> suh luhnt) *adj.*
  insulting, arrogant
    Synonyms: audacious, rude, presumptuous,
    impertinent

BENEFACTOR (<u>behn</u> uh faak tohr) *n.*
  someone giving aid or money
    Synonyms: contributor, backer, donor, patron

OBLIGE (uh <u>bliej</u>) *v.* **-ing,-ed.**
  to be obligated, to require or force someone to obey
    Synonyms: compel, constrain, bind, favor

over. The difference between him and the others forced me to be less **partial**. Cathy and her brother harassed me terribly. *He* was as uncomplaining as a lamb; though hardness, not gentleness, made him give little trouble.

He got through, and the doctor **affirmed** it was in a great measure owing to me, and praised me for my care. I was vain of his **commendations**, and softened towards the being by whose means I earned them, and thus Hindley lost his last ally. Still I couldn't **dote** on Heathcliff, and I wondered often what my master saw to admire so much in the **sullen** boy, who never, to my recollection, repaid his **indulgence** by any sign of gratitude. He was not **insolent** to his **benefactor**, he was simply insensible; though knowing perfectly the hold he had on his heart, and conscious he had only to speak and all the house would be **obliged** to bend to his wishes. As an instance, I remember Mr. Earnshaw once bought a couple of colts at the parish fair, and gave the lads each one. Heathcliff took the handsomest, but it soon fell lame, and when he discovered it, he said to Hindley—

"You must exchange horses with me—I don't like mine; and if you won't I shall tell your father of the three thrashings you've given me this week, and show him my arm, which is black to the shoulder."

Hindley put out his tongue and cuffed him over the ears.

"You'd better do it at once," he persisted, escaping to the porch. (They were in the stable.). "You will have to; and if I speak of these blows, you'll get them again with interest."

"Off, dog!" cried Hindley, threatening him with an iron weight used for weighing potatoes and hay.

"Throw it," he replied, standing still, "and then I'll tell how you boasted that you would turn me out of doors as soon as he died, and see whether he will not turn you out directly."

Hindley threw it, hitting him on the breast, and down he fell, but staggered up immediately, breathless and white; and, had not I prevented it, he would have gone

INTIMATE (<u>ihn</u> tuh mayt) *v.* **-ing,-ed.**
  to hint or suggest obscurely
    Synonyms: implicate, allude, insinuate
INTERLOPER (<u>ihn</u> tuhr loh puhr) *n.*
  a meddler, a person who interferes in others' affairs
    Synonyms: intruder, trespasser
WHEEDLE (<u>weed</u> uhl) *v.* **-ing,-ed.**
  to use flattery and charm in order to persuade
    Synonyms: entice, coax, cajole, sweet-talk

VINDICTIVE (vihn <u>dihk</u> tihv) *adj.*
  disposed to seek revenge
    Synonyms: spiteful, vengeful, unforgiving
GRIEVOUSLY (<u>gree</u> vuhs lee) *adv.*
  seriously and distressingly; with grief or sorrow
    Synonyms: gravely; mournfully
VEX (vehks) *v.* **-ing,-ed.**
  to irritate, annoy; confuse, puzzle
    Synonyms: bother, plague, afflict, irk; perplex, perturb
SLIGHT (sliet) *n.*
  an act of discourteous treatment
    Synonyms: snub, insult
IMPOSE (ihm <u>pohz</u>) *v.* **-ing,-ed.**
  to inflict, force upon
    Synonyms: dictate, decree, demand, ordain, prescribe
DOMINEER (dahm uh <u>neer</u>) *v.* **-ing,-ed.**
  to rule over something in a tyrannical way
    Synonyms: govern, reign
AMISS (uh <u>mihs</u>) *adv.*
  mistakenly; in a defective way
    Synonyms: astray, awry, improperly; faultily

just so to the master, and got full revenge by letting his condition plead for him, **intimating** who had caused it.

"Take my colt, gypsy, then!" said young Earnshaw. "And I pray that he may break your neck. Take him, and be damned, you beggarly **interloper**! And **wheedle** my father out of all he has; only afterwards show him what you are, <u>imp</u> of Satan. And after that, I hope he'll kick out your brains!"

Heathcliff had gone to loose the beast and shift it to his own stall. He was passing behind it, when Hindley finished his speech by knocking him under its feet, and without stopping to examine whether his hopes were fulfilled, ran away as fast as he could. I was surprised to witness how coolly the child gathered himself up, and went on with his intention; exchanging saddles and all, and then sitting down on a bundle of hay to overcome the <u>qualm</u> which the violent blow occasioned, before he entered the house. I persuaded him easily to let me lay the blame for his bruises on the horse: he minded little what tale was told since he had what he wanted. He complained so seldom, indeed, of such stirs as these, that I really thought him not **vindictive**. I was deceived completely, as you will hear.

Chapter 5

In the course of time, Mr. Earnshaw began to fail. He had been active and healthy, yet his strength left him suddenly; and when he was confined to the chimney-corner he grew **grievously** irritable. A nothing **vexed** him; and suspected **slights** of his authority nearly threw him into fits. This was especially to be remarked if any one attempted to **impose** upon, or **domineer** over, his favourite. He was painfully jealous lest a word should be spoken **amiss** to him, seeming to have got into his head the notion that, because he liked Heathcliff, all hated, and longed to do

PARTIALITY (pahr shee <u>aal</u> ih tee) *n.*
favoritism or favorable bias; a special liking for
something
    Synonyms: preference, inclination; fondness, fancy
MANIFESTATION (maan uh fehs <u>tay</u> shuhn) *n.*
a clear appearance or certain display
    Synonyms: expression, exhibition, indication

PIOUS (<u>pie</u> uhs) *adj.*
dedicated, devout, extremely religious
    Synonyms: observant, reverent, sanctimonious
DISCOURSE (<u>dihs</u> kohrs) *v.* **-ing,-ed.**
to talk or converse
    Synonyms: speak, discuss, lecture
CONTRIVE (kuhn <u>triev</u>) *v.* **-ing,-ed.**
to devise, plan, or manage; to form in an artistic manner
    Synonyms: concoct, scheme; create, design
REPROBATE (<u>reh</u> pruh bayt) *n.*
morally unprincipled person
    Synonyms: sinner, knave, scoundrel, rogue, rake

him an ill turn. It was a disadvantage to the lad; for the kinder among us did not wish to fret the master, so we humoured his **partiality**; and that humouring was rich nourishment to the child's pride and black tempers. Still it became in a manner necessary; twice, or thrice, Hindley's **manifestation** of scorn, while his father was near, roused the old man to a fury: he seized his stick to strike him, and shook with rage that he could not do it.

At last, our <u>curate</u> (we had a <u>curate</u> then who made the living answer by teaching the little Lintons and Earnshaws, and farming his bit of land himself) advised that the young man should be sent to college; and Mr. Earnshaw agreed, though with a heavy spirit, for he said,"Hindley was <u>nought</u>, and would never thrive as where he wandered."

I hoped heartily we should have peace now. It hurt me to think the master should be made uncomfortable by his own good deed. I fancied the discontent of age and disease arose from his family disagreements, as he would have it that it did. Really, you know, sir, it was in his sinking frame. We might have got on tolerably, notwithstanding, but for two people, Miss Cathy and Joseph, the servant: you saw him I daresay, up yonder. He was, and is yet most likely, the wearisomest self-righteous Pharisee that ever ransacked a Bible to rake the promises to himself and fling the curses to his neighbours. By his knack of sermonising and **pious discoursing**, he **contrived** to make a great impression on Mr. Earnshaw; and the more feeble the master became, the more influence he gained. He was relentless in worrying him about his soul's concerns, and about ruling his children rigidly. He encouraged him to regard Hindley as a **reprobate**; and, night after night, he regularly grumbled out a long string of tales against Heathcliff and Catherine: always minding to flatter Earnshaw's weakness by heaping the heaviest blame on the latter.

Certainly, she had ways with her such as I never saw a child take up before; and she put all of us past our

OBLIGE (uh bliej) *v.* **-ing,-ed.**
  to be obligated, to require or force someone to obey
    Synonyms: compel, constrain, bind, favor
CHIDE (chied) *v.* **-ing,-ed.**
  to scold, express disapproval
    Synonyms: chastise, admonish, reprimand, reprove

REPROOF (rih proof) *n.*
  a criticism or correction
    Synonyms: admonition, reprimand, rebuke, censure
PROVOKE (proh vohk) *v.* **-ing,-ed.**
  to cause a response, e.g., anger or disagreement
    Synonyms: aggravate, stimulate, vex, incite
INSOLENCE (ihn suh luhnts) *n.*
  a tendency to be insulting; arrogance
    Synonyms: audacity, rudeness, presumption,
    impertinence; superiority, haughtiness
INCLINATION (ihn cluh nay shuhn) *n.*
  tendency toward
    Synonyms: leaning, trend, preference, disposition,
    propensity
RUE (roo) *v.* **ruing,-ed.**
  to regret
    Synonyms: deplore, repent
REPULSE (rih puhls) *v.* **-ing,-ed.**
  to repel; to sicken or disgust
    Synonyms: reject; nauseate

patience fifty times and oftener in a day. From the hour
she came downstairs till the hour she went to bed, we had
not a minute's security that she wouldn't be in mischief.
Her spirits were always at high-water mark, her tongue
always going—singing, laughing, and plaguing everybody
who would not do the same. A wild, wicked slip she
was—but she had the <u>bonniest</u> eye, the sweetest smile,
and lightest foot in the parish; and, after all, I believe she
meant no harm; for when once she made you cry in good
earnest, it seldom happened that she would not keep you
company, and **oblige** you to be quiet that you might comfort her. She was much too fond of Heathcliff. The
greatest punishment we could invent for her was to keep
her separate from him: yet she got **chided** more than any
of us on his account. In play, she liked exceedingly to act
the little mistress; using her hands freely, and commanding her companions. She did so to me, but I would not
bear shopping and ordering; and so I let her know.

Now, Mr. Earnshaw did not understand jokes from his
children. He had always been strict and grave with them;
and Catherine, on her part, had no idea why her father
should be crosser and less patient in his ailing condition,
than he was in his prime. His <u>peevish</u> **reproofs** wakened in
her a naughty delight to **provoke** him. She was never so
happy as when we were all scolding her at once, and she
defying us with her bold, saucy look, and her ready
words; turning Joseph's religious curses into ridicule,
baiting me, and doing just what her father hated most—
showing how her pretended **insolence**, which he thought
real, had more power over Heathcliff than his kindness:
how the boy would do *her* bidding in anything, and *his*
only when it suited his own **inclination**. After behaving as
badly as possible all day, she sometimes came <u>fondling</u> to
make it up at night. "Nay, Cathy," the old man would say,
"I cannot love thee; thou'rt worse than thy brother. Go
say thy prayers, child, and ask God's pardon. I doubt thy
mother and I must **rue** that we ever reared thee!" That
made her cry, at first: and then being **repulsed** continually

VEX (vehks) *v.* **-ing,-ed.**
to irritate, annoy; confuse, puzzle
Synonyms: bother, plague, afflict, irk; perplex, perturb

DIN (dihn) *n.*
blaring noise
Synonyms: loudness, clamor, cacophony, commotion
HINDER (<u>hihn</u> duhr) *v.* **-ing,-ed.**
to prevent action; to delay or impede
Synonyms: restrain; hamper, inhibit, obstruct

hardened her, and she laughed if I told her to say she was sorry for her faults, and beg to be forgiven.

But the hour came, at last, that ended Mr. Earnshaw's troubles on earth. He died quietly in his chair one October evening, seated by the fireside. A high wind blustered round the house, and roared in the chimney: it sounded wild and stormy, yet it was not cold, and we were all together—I, a little removed from the hearth, busy at my knitting, and Joseph reading his Bible near the table (for the servants generally sat in the house then, after their work was done). Miss Cathy had been sick, and that made her still; she leant against her father's knee, and Heathcliff was lying on the floor with his head in her lap. I remember the master, before he fell into a doze, stroking her <u>bonny</u> hair—It pleased him rarely to see her gentle— and saying, "Why canst thou not always be a good lass, Cathy?"

And she turned her face up to his, and laughed, and answered, "Why cannot you always be a good man, father?" But as soon as she saw him **vexed** again, she kissed his hand, and said she would sing him to sleep. She began singing very low, till his fingers dropped from hers, and his head sank on his breast. Then I told her to hush, and not stir, for fear she should wake him. We all kept as mute as mice a full half-hour, and should have done so longer, only Joseph, having finished his chapter, got up and said that he must rouse the master for prayers and bed. He stepped forward, and called him by name, and touched his shoulder; but he would not move, so he took the candle and looked at him. I thought there was something wrong as he set down the light; and seizing the children each by an arm, whispered them to "<u>frame</u> upstairs, and make little **din**—they might pray alone that evening—he had summut to do."

"I shall bid father good-night first," said Catherine, putting her arms round his neck, before we could **hinder** her. The poor thing discovered her loss directly. She

CONSOLE (kuhn <u>sohl</u>) *v.* **-ing,-ed.**
to alleviate grief and raise the spirits of, provide solace
Synonyms: relieve, comfort, soothe

screamed out, "Oh, he's dead, Heathcliff! He's dead!" And they both set up a heart-breaking cry.

I joined my wail to theirs, loud and bitter; but Joseph asked what we could be thinking of to roar in that way over a saint in heaven. He told me to put on my cloak and run to Gimmerton for the doctor and the parson. I could not guess the use that either would be of, then. However, I went, through wind and rain, and brought one, the doctor, back with me; the other said he would come in the morning. Leaving Joseph to explain matters, I ran to the children's room: their door was ajar, I saw they had never laid down, though it was past midnight; but they were calmer, and did not need me to **console** them. The little souls were comforting each other with better thoughts than I could have hit on. No parson in the world ever pictured heaven so beautifully as they did, in their innocent talk: and, while I sobbed and listened, I could not help wishing we were all there safe together.

Chapter 6

Mr. Hindley came home to the funeral and—a thing that amazed us and set the neighbours gossiping right and left—he brought a wife with him. What she was, and where she was born, he never informed us. Probably she had neither money nor name to recommend her, or he would scarcely have kept the union from his father.

She was not one that would have disturbed the house much on her own account. Every object she saw, the moment she crossed the threshold, appeared to delight her; and every circumstance that took place about her except the preparing for the burial, and the presence of the mourners. I thought she was half silly, from her behaviour while that went on. She ran into her chamber, and made me come with her, though I should have been dressing the children; and there she sat shivering and

PORTEND (pohr <u>tehnd</u>) *v.* **-ing,-ed.**
　to act as an omen, to foreshadow
　　Synonyms: foretell, herald, forecast, predict

IMPULSE (<u>ihm</u> puhls) *n.*
　sudden tendency, inclination
　　Synonyms: urge, whim

PRATTLE (<u>praa</u> tuhl) *v.* **-ing,-ed.**
　to talk foolishly and meaninglessly
　　Synonyms: chatter, babble, drivel, blather

EVINCE (ih <u>vihns</u>) *v.* **-ing,-ed.**
　to show clearly or display
　　Synonyms: express, exhibit, demonstrate, manifest

clasping her hands, and asking repeatedly, "Are they gone yet?" Then she began describing with hysterical emotion the effect it produced on her to see black; and started, and trembled, and, at last, fell a-weeping—and when I asked what was the matter? answered, she didn't know; but she felt so afraid of dying! I imagined her as little likely to die as myself. She was rather thin, but young, and fresh-complexioned, and her eyes sparkled as bright as diamonds. I did remark, to be sure, that mounting the stairs made her breathe very quick: that the least sudden noise set her all in a quiver, and that she coughed troublesomely sometimes: but I knew nothing of what these symptoms **portended**, and had no **impulse** to sympathize with her. We don't in general take to foreigners here, Mr. Lockwood, unless they take to us first.

Young Earnshaw was altered considerably in the three years of his absence. He had grown sparer, and lost his colour, and spoke and dressed quite differently; and, on the very day of his return, he told Joseph and me we must thenceforth quarter ourselves in the back-kitchen, and leave the house for him. Indeed, he would have carpeted and papered a small spare room for a parlour, but his wife expressed such pleasure at the white floor and huge glowing fire-place, at the pewter dishes and <u>delft</u>-case, and dog-kennel, and the wide space there was to move about in where they usually sat, that he thought it unnecessary to her comfort, and so dropped the intention.

She expressed pleasure, too, at finding a sister among her new acquaintances; and she **prattled** to Catherine, and kissed her, and ran about with her, and gave her quantities of presents, at the beginning. Her affection tired very soon, however, and when she grew <u>peevish</u>, Hindley became tyrannical. A few words from her, **evincing** a dislike to Heathcliff, were enough to rouse in him all his old hatred of the boy. He drove him from their company to the servants, deprived him of the instructions of the <u>curate</u>, and insisted that he should labour out of

COMPEL (kuhm <u>pehl</u>) *v.* **-ling,-led.**
to urge or force
Synonyms: coerce, oblige, constrain

DEGRADATION (day greh <u>day</u> shuhn) *n.*
the act of falling in rank or status; the act of losing
moral or intellectual character
Synonyms: demotion; abasement, disgrace, shame

NEGLIGENT (<u>nehg</u> lih jehnt) *adj.*
careless, inattentive
Synonyms: derelict, lax, remiss, slack, casual

CONTRIVE (kuhn <u>triev</u>) *v.* **-ing,-ed.**
to devise, plan, or manage; to form in an artistic manner
Synonyms: concoct, scheme; create, design

RETAIN (rih <u>tayn</u>) *v.* **-ing,-ed.**
to hold, keep possession of
Synonyms: withhold, reserve, maintain, remember

BANISH (<u>baan</u> ish) *v.* **-ing,-ed.**
to force to leave, exile
Synonyms: expel, deport

doors instead, **compelling** him to do so as hard as any other hand on the farm.

Heathcliff bore his **degradation** pretty well at first, because Cathy taught him what she learnt, and worked or played with him in the fields. They both promised fair to grow up as rude as savages; the young master being entirely **negligent** how they behaved, and what they did, so they kept clear of him. He would not even have seen after their going to church on Sundays, only Joseph and the <u>curate</u> reprimanded his carelessness when they absented themselves; and that reminded him to order Heathcliff a flogging, and Catherine a fast from dinner or supper. But it was one of their chief amusements to run away to the moors in the morning and remain there all day, and the after punishment grew a mere thing to laugh at. The <u>curate</u> might set as many chapters as he pleased for Catherine to get by heart, and Joseph might thrash Heathcliff till his arm ached. They forgot everything the minute they were together again, at least the minute they had **contrived** some naughty plan of revenge; and many a time I've cried to myself to watch them growing more reckless daily, and I not daring to speak a syllable, for fear of losing the small power I still **retained** over the unfriended creatures. One Sunday evening, it chanced that they were **banished** from the sitting-room, for making a noise, or a light offence of the kind; and when I went to call them to supper, I could discover them nowhere. We searched the house, above and below, and the yard and stables. They were invisible: and at last, Hindley in a passion told us to bolt the doors, and swore nobody should let them in that night. The household went to bed; and I, too anxious to lie down, opened my <u>lattice</u> and put my head out to hearken, though it rained, determined to admit them in spite of the prohibition, should they return. In a while, I distinguished steps coming up the road, and the light of a lantern glimmered through the gate. I threw a shawl over my head and ran to prevent

them from waking Mr. Earnshaw by knocking. There was Heathcliff by himself. It gave me a start to see him alone.

"Where is Miss Catherine?" I cried hurriedly. "No accident, I hope?"

"At Thrushcross Grange," he answered; "and I would have been there too, but they had not the manners to ask me to stay."

"Well, you will catch it!" I said. "You'll never be content till you're sent about your business. What in the world led you wandering to Thrushcross Grange?"

"Let me get off my wet clothes, and I'll tell you all about it, Nelly," he replied.

I bid him beware of rousing the master, and while he undressed and I waited to put out the candle, he continued, "Cathy and I escaped from the wash-house to have a ramble at liberty, and getting a glimpse of the Grange lights, we thought we would just go and see whether the Lintons passed their Sunday evenings standing shivering in corners, while their father and mother sat eating and drinking, and singing and laughing, and burning their eyes out before the fire. Do you think they do? Or reading sermons and being catechised by their man-servant, and set to learn a column of Scripture names if they don't answer properly?"

"Probably not," I responded. "They are good children, no doubt, and don't deserve the treatment you receive, for your bad conduct."

"Don't you cant, Nelly," he said. "Nonsense! We ran from the top of the Heights to the park, without stopping—Catherine completely beaten in the race because she was barefoot. You'll have to seek for her shoes in the bog to-morrow. We crept through a broken hedge, groped our way up the path, and planted ourselves on a flower-plot under the drawing-room window. The light came from thence; they had not put up the shutters, and the curtains were only half closed. Both of us were able to look in by standing on the basement, and clinging to the ledge, and we saw—ah! It was beautiful—a splendid place

carpeted with crimson, and crimson-covered chairs and tables, and a pure white ceiling bordered by gold, a shower of glass-drops hanging in silver chains from the centre, and shimmering with little soft <u>tapers</u>. Old Mr. and Mrs. Linton were not there; Edgar and his sister had it entirely to themselves. Shouldn't they have been happy? We should have thought ourselves in heaven! And now, guess what your good children were doing? Isabella—I believe she is eleven, a year younger than Cathy—lay screaming at the farther end of the room, shrieking as if witches were running red-hot needles into her. Edgar stood on the hearth weeping silently, and in the middle of the table sat a little dog, shaking its paw and yelping; which, from their mutual accusations, we understood they had nearly pulled in two between them. The idiots! That was their pleasure! To quarrel who should hold a heap of warm hair, and each begin to cry because both, after struggling to get it, refused to take it. We laughed outright at the petted things; we did despise them! When would you catch me wishing to have what Catherine wanted? Or find us by ourselves, seeking entertainment in yelling, and sobbing, and rolling on the ground, divided by the whole room? I'd not exchange, for a thousand lives, my condition here, for Edgar Linton's at Thrushcross Grange—not if I might have the privilege of flinging Joseph off the highest gable, and painting the house-front with Hindley's blood!"

"Hush, hush!" I interrupted. "Still you have not told me, Heathcliff, how Catherine is left behind?"

"I told you we laughed," he answered. "The Lintons heard us, and with one accord, they shot like arrows to the door. There was silence, and then a cry, 'Oh, Mamma, Mamma! Oh, Papa! Oh, Mamma, come here, Oh, Papa, oh!' They really did howl out something in that way. We made frightful noises to terrify them still more, and then we dropped off the ledge, because somebody was drawing the bars, and we felt we had better flee. I had Cathy by the hand, and was urging her on, when all at once she fell down.

ABOMINABLE (uh <u>bah</u> mihn uh buhl) *adj.*
loathsome, detestable
Synonyms: abhorrent, terrible, beastly, deplorable

VOCIFERATE (voh <u>sih</u> fuhr ayt) *v.* **-ing,-ed.**
to speak or yell loudly and noisily
Synonyms: clamor, holler, scream, bark

EXECRATION (ehk sih <u>kray</u> shun) *n.*
a curse or the act of cursing
Synonyms: hatred, denouncement, loathing, abhorrence

VENGEANCE (<u>vehn</u> juhns) *n.*
punishment inflicted in retaliation; vehemence
Synonyms: revenge, repayment; wrath

MAGISTRATE (<u>maa</u> juh strayt) *n.*
an official who can administrate laws
Synonyms: judge, arbiter, authority, marshal

INSOLENCE (<u>ihn</u> suh luhnts) *n.*
a tendency to be insulting; arrogance
Synonyms: audacity, rudeness, presumption, impertinence; superiority, haughtiness

"'Run, Heathcliff, run!' she whispered. 'They have let the bull-dog loose, and he holds me!'

"The devil had seized her ankle, Nelly, I heard his **abominable** snorting. She did not yell out—no! She would have scorned to do it, if she had been spitted on the horns of a mad cow. I did, though! I **vociferated** curses enough to annihilate any fiend in Christendom; and I got a stone and thrust it between his jaws, and tried with all my might to cram it down his throat. A beast of a servant came up with a lantern, at last, shouting—

"'Keep fast, Skulker, keep fast!' He changed his note, however, when he saw Skulker's game. The dog was throttled off, his huge, purple tongue hanging half a foot out of his mouth, and his pendant lips streaming with bloody <u>slaver</u>. The man took Cathy up: she was sick: not from fear, I'm certain, but from pain. He carried her in; I followed, grumbling **execrations** and **vengeance**.

"'What prey, Robert?' hallooed Linton from the entrance.

"'Skulker has caught a little girl, sir,' he replied, 'and there's a lad here,' he added, making a clutch at me, 'who looks an out-and-outer! Very like, the robbers were for putting them through the window to open the doors to the gang after all were asleep, that they might murder us at their ease. Hold your tongue, you foul-mouthed thief, you! You shall go to the gallows for this. Mr. Linton, sir, don't lay by your gun.'

"'No, no, Robert,' said the old fool. 'The rascals knew that yesterday was my rent day; they thought to have me cleverly. Come in; I'll furnish them a reception. There, John, fasten the chain. Give Skulker some water, Jenny. To beard a **magistrate** in his stronghold, and on the Sabbath, too! Where will their **insolence** stop? Oh, my dear Mary, look here! Don't be afraid, it is but a boy—yet the villain scowls so plainly in his face; would it not be a kindness to the country to hang him at once, before he shows his nature in acts as well as features?'

"He pulled me under the chandelier, and Mrs. Linton placed her spectacles on her nose and raised her hands in

CULPABLE (<u>kuhl</u> puh buhl) *adj.*
   guilty, responsible for wrong
      Synonyms: blameworthy, answerable

HEATHENISM (<u>hee</u> thuhn ihz uhm) *n.*
   uncivilized and irreligious manners and morals;
   paganism
      Synonyms: barbarism; irreligion, disbelief

horror. The cowardly children crept nearer also, Isabella lisping, 'Frightful thing! Put him in the cellar, Papa. He's exactly like the son of the fortune-teller that stole my tame pheasant. Isn't he, Edgar?'

"While they examined me, Cathy came round; she heard the last speech, and laughed. Edgar Linton, after an inquisitive stare, collected sufficient wit to recognise her. They see us at church, you know, though we seldom meet them elsewhere.

"'That's Miss Earnshaw!' he whispered to his mother, 'And look how Skulker has bitten her—how her foot bleeds!'

"'Miss Earnshaw? Nonsense!' cried the dame. 'Miss Earnshaw scouring the country with a gypsy! And yet, my dear, the child is in mourning—surely it is—and she may be maimed for life!'

"'What **culpable** carelessness in her brother!' exclaimed Mr. Linton, turning from me to Catherine. 'I've understood from Shielders' (that was the <u>curate</u>, sir) that he lets her grow up in absolute **heathenism**. But who is this? Where did she pick up this companion? Oho! I declare he is that strange acquisition my late neighbour made, in his journey to Liverpool—a little <u>Lascar</u>, or an American or Spanish castaway.'

"'A wicked boy, at all events,' remarked the old lady, 'and quite unfit for a decent house! Did you notice his language, Linton? I'm shocked that my children should have heard it.'

"I recommended cursing—don't be angry, Nelly—and so Robert was ordered to take me off. I refused to go without Cathy. He dragged me into the garden, pushed the lantern into my hand, assured me that Mr. Earnshaw should be informed of my behaviour, and, bidding me march directly, secured the door again. The curtains were still looped up at one corner, and I resumed my station as spy; because, if Catherine had wished to return, I intended shattering their great glass panes to a million of fragments, unless they let her out. She sat on a sofa

EXPOSTULATE (ihk <u>spahs</u> chuh layt) *v.* **-ing,-ed.**
to reason earnestly with another; to discuss or examine
Synonyms: argue, protest, dissuade; debate

KINDLE (<u>kihn</u> duhl) *v.* **-ing,-ed.**
to set fire to or ignite; excite or inspire
Synonyms: light, spark; arouse, awaken

RESTRAINT (rih <u>straynt</u>) *n.*
control, repression, restriction; a rule or limitation
Synonyms: confinement; barrier, order, rein

quietly. Mrs. Linton took off the grey cloak of the dairy-maid which we had borrowed for our excursion, shaking her head and **expostulating** with her, I suppose. She was a young lady, and they made a distinction between her treatment and mine. Then the woman-servant brought a basin of warm water, and washed her feet; and Mr. Linton mixed a tumbler of <u>negus</u>, and Isabella emptied a plateful of cakes into her lap, and Edgar stood gaping at a distance. Afterwards, they dried and combed her beautiful hair, and gave her a pair of enormous slippers, and wheeled her to the fire; and I left her, as merry as she could be, dividing her food between the little dog and Skulker, whose nose she pinched as he ate; and **kindling** a spark of spirit in the vacant blue eyes of the Lintons—a dim reflection from her own enchanting face. I saw they were full of stupid admiration; she is so immeasurably superior to them—to everybody on earth, is she not, Nelly?"

"There will more come of this business than you reckon on," I answered, covering him up and extinguishing the light. "You are incurable, Heathcliff; and Mr. Hindley will have to proceed to extremities, see if he won't!" My words came truer than I desired. The luckless adventure made Earnshaw furious. And then Mr. Linton, to mend matters, paid us a visit himself on the morrow, and read the young master such a lecture on the road he guided his family, that he was stirred to look about him, in earnest. Heathcliff received no flogging, but he was told that the first word he spoke to Miss Catherine should ensure a dismissal; and Mrs. Earnshaw undertook to keep her sister-in-law in due **restraint** when she returned home; employing art, not force: with force she would have found it impossible.

OBLIGE (uh <u>bliej</u>) *v.* **-ing,-ed.**
to be obligated, to require or force someone to obey
Synonyms: compel, constrain, bind, favor

BURNISH (<u>buhr</u> nihsh) *v.* **-ing,-ed.**
to polish, make smooth and bright
Synonyms: shine, buff

FAWN *v.* **-ing,-ed.**
to seek the favor of, to flatter excessively
Synonyms: kowtow, toady, grovel, truckle, apple-polish

Chapter 7

Cathy stayed at Thrushcross Grange five weeks: till Christmas. By that time her ankle was thoroughly cured, and her manners much improved. The mistress visited her often in the interval, and commenced her plan of reform by trying to raise her self-respect with fine clothes and flattery, which she took readily; so that, instead of a wild, hatless little savage jumping into the house, and rushing to squeeze us all breathless, there 'lighted from a handsome black pony a very dignified person, with brown ringlets falling from the cover of a feathered beaver, and a long cloth <u>habit</u>, which she was **obliged** to hold up with both hands that she might sail in.

Hindley lifted her from her horse, exclaiming delightedly, "Why, Cathy, you are quite a beauty! I should scarcely have known you: you look like a lady now. Isabella Linton is not to be compared with her, is she, Frances?"

"Isabella has not her natural advantages," replied his wife, "but she must mind and not grow wild again here. Ellen, help Miss Catherine off with her things—stay, dear, you will disarrange your curls—let me untie your hat."

I removed the <u>habit</u>, and there shone forth beneath, a grand plaid silk frock, white trousers, and **burnished** shoes; and, while her eyes sparkled joyfully when the dogs came bounding up to welcome her, she dare hardly touch them lest they should **fawn** upon her splendid garments. She kissed me gently. I was all flour, making the Christmas cake, and it would not have done to give me a hug and, then, she looked round for Heathcliff. Mr. and Mrs. Earnshaw watched anxiously their meeting; thinking it would enable them to judge, in some measure, what

SKULK (skuhlk) *v.* **-ing,-ed.**
to move in a stealthy or cautious manner, to sneak
Synonyms: lurk, shirk, hide, evade, prowl

DISCOMFITURE (dihs <u>kuhm</u> fih chuhr) *n.*
embarrassed frustration
Synonyms: discomfort, confusion, chagrin

COMPEL (kuhm <u>pehl</u>) *v.* **-ling,-led.**
to urge or force
Synonyms: coerce, oblige, constrain

BESTOW (bih <u>stoh</u>) *v.* **-ing,-ed.**
to give as a gift; to apply or devote, as in time or effort
Synonyms: endow, confer, present; allocate, dedicate

COUNTENANCE (<u>kown</u> tuh nuhns) *n.*
appearance, facial expression
Synonyms: face, features, visage

CONDESCENDINGLY (kahn dih <u>sehn</u> ding lee) *adv.*
with an attitude of superiority, in a superior manner
Synonyms: patronizingly, smuggly, superciliously

grounds they had for hoping to succeed in separating the two friends.

Heathcliff was hard to discover, at first. If he were careless, and uncared for before Catherine's absence, he had been ten times more so, since. Nobody but I even did him the kindness to call him a dirty boy, and bid him wash himself, once a week; and children of his age seldom have a natural pleasure in soap and water. Therefore, not to mention his clothes, which had seen three months' service in <u>mire</u> and dust, and his thick uncombed hair, the surface of his face and hands was dismally beclouded. He might well **skulk** behind the <u>settle</u>, on beholding such a bright, graceful damsel enter the house, instead of a rough-headed counterpart of himself, as he expected.

"Is Heathcliff not here?" she demanded, pulling off her gloves, and displaying fingers wonderfully whitened with doing nothing and staying indoors.

"Heathcliff, you may come forward," cried Mr. Hindley, enjoying his **discomfiture**, and gratified to see what a forbidding young blackguard he would be **compelled** to present himself. "You may come and wish Miss Catherine welcome, like the other servants."

Cathy, catching a glimpse of her friend in his conceal-ment, flew to embrace him; she **bestowed** seven or eight kisses on his cheek within the second, and then stopped, and drawing back, burst into a laugh, exclaiming, "Why, how very black and cross you look! And how—how funny and grim! But that's because I'm used to Edgar and Isabella Linton. Well, Heathcliff, have you forgotten me?"

She had some reason to put the question, for shame and pride threw double gloom over his **countenance**, and kept him immovable.

"Shake hands, Heathcliff," said Mr. Earnshaw **condescendingly**, "once in a way that is permitted."

"I shall not," replied the boy, finding his tongue at last. "I shall not stand to be laughed at. I shall not bear it!"

And he would have broken from the circle, but Miss Cathy seized him again.

HINDER (<u>hihn</u> duhr) *v.* **-ing,-ed.**
to prevent action; to delay or impede
Synonyms: restrain; hamper, inhibit, obstruct

EMBELLISHMENT (ehm <u>behl</u> ihsh mehnt) *n.*
something that adds beauty; an ornament or a
decorative detail
Synonyms: enhancement; adornment, embroidery,
garnish

AFFIRMATION (uh fuhr <u>may</u> shuhn) *n.*
a statement of agreement, a valid confirmation
Synonyms: assent, nod, yes

TRIFLE (<u>trie</u> fuhl) *n.*
something of slight worth or little importance
Synonyms: triviality, novelty, trinket

"I did not mean to laugh at you," she said. "I could not **hinder** myself. Heathcliff, shake hands at least! What are you sulky for? It was only that you looked odd. If you wash your face and brush your hair, it will be all right; but you are so dirty!"

She gazed concernedly at the dusky fingers she held in her own, and also at her dress; which she feared had gained no **embellishment** from its contact with his.

"You needn't have touched me!" he answered, following her eye and snatching away his hand. "I shall be as dirty as I please: and I like to be dirty, and I will be dirty."

With that he dashed head foremost out of the room, amid the merriment of the master and mistress, and to the serious disturbance of Catherine, who could not comprehend how her remarks should have produced such an exhibition of bad temper.

After playing lady's-maid to the new-comer, and putting my cakes in the oven, and making the house and kitchen cheerful with great fires, befitting Christmas Eve, I prepared to sit down and amuse myself by singing carols, all alone; regardless of Joseph's **affirmations** that he considered the merry tunes I chose as next door to songs. He had retired to private prayer in his chamber, and Mr. and Mrs. Earnshaw were engaging Missy's attention by <u>sundry</u> gay **trifles** bought for her to present to the little Lintons, as an acknowledgment of their kindness. They had invited them to spend the morrow at Wuthering Heights, and the invitation had been accepted, on one condition: Mrs. Linton begged that her darlings be kept carefully apart from that "naughty swearing boy."

Under these circumstances I remained solitary. I smelt the rich scent of the heating spices; and admired the shining kitchen utensils, the polished clock, decked in holly, the silver mugs ranged on a tray ready to be filled with mulled ale for supper, and above all, the speckless purity of my particular care—the scoured and well-swept floor. I gave due inward applause to every object, and then I remembered how old Earnshaw used to come in when all

REPROOF (rih <u>proof</u>) *n.*
   a criticism or correction
     Synonyms: admonition, reprimand, rebuke, censure

DOUR (<u>doo</u> uhr) (<u>dow</u> uhr) *adj.*
   sullen and gloomy; stern and severe
     Synonyms: grave, solemn, somber; austere, strict

was tidied, and call me a <u>cant</u> lass, and slip a shilling into my hand as a Christmas-<u>box</u>; and from that I went on to think of his fondness for Heathcliff, and his dread lest he should suffer neglect after death had removed him; and that naturally led me to consider the poor lad's situation now, and from singing I changed my mind to crying. It struck me soon, however, there would be more sense in endeavouring to repair some of his wrongs than shedding tears over them: I got up and walked into the court to seek him. He was not far, I found him smoothing the glossy coat of the new pony in the stable, and feeding the other beasts, according to custom.

"Make haste, Heathcliff!" I said. "The kitchen is so comfortable; and Joseph is upstairs. Make haste, and let me dress you smart before Miss Cathy comes out, and then you can sit together, with the whole hearth to yourselves, and have a long chatter till bedtime."

He proceeded with his task and never turned his head towards me.

"Come—are you coming?" I continued. "There's little cake for each of you, nearly enough; and you'll need half an hour's donning."

I waited five minutes, but getting no answer, left him. Catherine supped with her brother and sister-in-law: Joseph and I joined in an unsociable meal, seasoned with **reproofs** on one side and sauciness on the other. His cake and cheese remained on the table all night for the fairies. He managed to continue work till nine o'clock, and then marched dumb and **dour** to his chamber. Cathy sat up late, having a world of things to order for the reception of her new friends. She came into the kitchen once to speak to her old one; but he was gone, and she only stayed to ask what was the matter with him, and then went back. In the morning he rose early; and as it was a holiday carried his ill-humour on to the moors; not reappearing till the family were departed for church. Fasting and reflection seemed to have brought him to a better spirit. He hung

about me for a while, and having screwed up his courage, exclaimed abruptly:

"Nelly, make me decent, I'm going to be good."

"High time, Heathcliff," I said. "You *have* grieved Catherine: she's sorry she ever came home, I dare say! It looks as if you envied her, because she is more thought of than you."

The notion of *envying* Catherine was incomprehensible to him, but the notion of grieving her he understood clearly enough.

"Did she say she was grieved?" he inquired, looking very serious.

"She cried when I told her you were off again this morning."

"Well, *I* cried last night," he returned, "and I had more reason to cry than she."

"Yes: you had the reason of going to bed with a proud heart and an empty stomach," said I. "Proud people breed sad sorrows for themselves. But, if you be ashamed of your touchiness, you must ask pardon, mind, when she comes in. You must go up and offer to kiss her, and say— you know best what to say; only do it heartily, and not as if you thought her converted into a stranger by her grand dress. And now, though I have dinner to get ready, I'll steal time to arrange you so that Edgar Linton shall look quite a doll beside you: and that he does. You are younger, and yet, I'll be bound, you are taller and twice as broad across the shoulders: you could knock him down in a twinkling: don't you feel that you could?"

Heathcliff's face brightened for a moment; then it was overcast afresh, and he sighed.

"But, Nelly, if I knocked him down twenty times, that wouldn't make him less handsome or me more so. I wish I had light hair and a fair skin, and was dressed and behaved as well, and had a chance of being as rich as he will be!"

"And cried for Mamma at every turn," I added, "and trembled if a country lad heaved his fist against you, and

LURK (luhrk) *v.* **-ing,-ed.**
    to hide, to lie hidden or unsuspected; to prowl, sneak
        Synonyms: conceal; stalk, creep, skulk, slink

SURLY (<u>suhr</u> lee) *adj.*
    rude and bad-tempered
        Synonyms: gruff, testy, grumpy

DESCEND (dih <u>sehnd</u>) (dee <u>sehnd</u>) *v.* **-ing,-ed.**
    to pass from a higher place to a lower place
        Synonyms: fall, dismount, gravitate

sat at home all day for a shower of rain. Oh, Heathcliff, you are showing a poor spirit! Come to the glass, and I'll let you see what you should wish. Do you mark those two lines between your eyes; and those thick brows, that instead of rising arched, sink in the middle; and that couple of black fiends, so deeply buried, who never open their windows boldly, but **lurk** glinting under them, like devil's spies? Wish and learn to smooth away the **surly** wrinkles, to raise your lids frankly, and change the fiends to confident, innocent angels, suspecting and doubting nothing, and always seeing friends where they are not sure of foes. Don't get the expression of a vicious <u>cur</u> that appears to know the kicks it gets are its desert, and yet hates all the world as well as the kicker, for what it suffers."

"In other words, I must wish for Edgar Linton's great blue eyes and even forehead," he replied. "I do—and that won't help me to them."

"A good heart will help you to a <u>bonny</u> face, my lad," I continued, "if you were a regular black; and a bad one will turn the <u>bonniest</u> into something worse than ugly. And now that we've done washing, and combing, and sulking—tell me whether you don't think yourself rather handsome? I'll tell you, I do. You're fit for a prince in disguise. Who knows but your father was Emperor of China, and your mother an Indian queen, each of them able to buy up, with one week's income, Wuthering Heights and Thrushcross Grange together? And you were kidnapped by wicked sailors and brought to England. Were I in your place, I would <u>frame</u> high notions of my birth; and the thoughts of what I was should give me courage and dignity to support the oppressions of a little farmer!"

So I chattered on; and Heathcliff gradually lost his frown and began to look quite pleasant, when all at once our conversation was interrupted by a rumbling sound moving up the road and entering the court. He ran to the window and I to the door, just in time to behold the two Lintons **descend** from the family carriage, smothered in cloaks and furs, and the Earnshaws dismount from their

SAT Vocabulary

AMIABLE (<u>ay</u> mee uh buhl) *adj.*
friendly, pleasant, likable
Synonyms: affable, convivial, amicable, agreeable

VAGABOND (<u>vaa</u> guh bahnd) *n.*
one who moves from place to place with no fixed home
Synonyms: wanderer, floater, vagrant, nomad

IMPERTINENCE (ihm <u>puhr</u> tuh nuhnts) *n.*
rudeness, audacity
Synonyms: boldness, gall, impropriety

LAMENT (luh <u>mehnt</u>) *n.*
an expression of grief or sorrow, a loud cry; discontent
Synonyms: moaning, sobbing, tears; complaint

CULPRIT (<u>kuhl</u> priht) *n.*
one who is guilty or responsible for wrongdoing
Synonyms: criminal, offender, malefactor

horses: they often rode to church in winter. Catherine took a hand of each of the children, and brought them into the house and set them before the fire, which quickly put colour into their white faces.

I urged my companion to hasten now and show his **amiable** humour, and he willingly obeyed; but ill luck would have it that, as he opened the door leading from the kitchen on one side, Hindley opened it on the other. They met, and the master, irritated at seeing him clean and cheerful; or, perhaps, eager to keep his promise to Mrs. Linton, shoved him back with a sudden thrust, and angrily bade Joseph, "Keep the fellow out of the room—send him into the <u>garret</u> till dinner is over. He'll be cramming his fingers in the tarts and stealing the fruit, if left alone with them a minute."

"Nay, sir," I could not avoid answering, "he'll touch nothing, not he: and I suppose he must have his share of the dainties as well as we."

"He shall have his share of my hand, if I catch him downstairs till dark," cried Hindley. "Begone, you **vagabond**! What! You are <u>attempting the coxcomb</u>, are you? Wait till I get hold of those elegant locks—see if I won't pull them a bit longer."

"They are long enough, already," observed Master Linton, peeping from the doorway. "I wonder they don't make his head ache. It's like a colt's mane over his eyes!"

He ventured this remark without any intention to insult; but Heathcliff's violent nature was not prepared to endure the appearance of **impertinence** from one whom he seemed to hate, even then, as a rival. He seized a tureen of hot apple sauce (the first thing that came under his <u>gripe</u>) and dashed it full against the speaker's face and neck; who instantly commenced a **lament** that brought Isabella and Catherine hurrying to the place. Mr. Earnshaw snatched up the **culprit** directly and conveyed him to his chamber, where, doubtless, he administered a rough remedy to cool the fit of passion, for he appeared red and breathless. I got the dish-cloth, and rather spite-

AFFIRM (uh <u>fihrm</u>) *v.* **-ing,-ed.**
to state positively, to assert as valid or confirmed
Synonyms: declare, avow, maintain

MEDDLE (<u>meh</u> duhl) *v.* **-ing,-ed.**
to interfere in others' affairs, to impose
Synonyms: interlope, tamper, snoop, encroach

CONFOUND (kuhn <u>fownd</u>) *v.* **-ing,-ed.**
1. to baffle, perplex; to mistake something for another
Synonyms: overwhelm, disconcert, entangle,
muddle; confuse, misidentify
2. to damn or condemn
Synonyms: doom, jinx, revile, punish

EXPOSTULATE (ihk <u>spahs</u> chuh layt) *v.* **-ing,-ed.**
to reason earnestly with another; to discuss or examine
Synonyms: argue, protest, dissuade; debate

CONTEMPTUOUSLY (kuhn <u>tehmp</u> choo uhs lee) *adv.*
scornfully
Synonyms: derisively, disdainfully, superciliously

BUSTLE (<u>buh</u> suhl) *v.* **-ing,-ed.**
to move quickly and energetically
Synonyms: scurry, scramble, dash, whirl, fuss

EQUANIMITY (ee kwuh <u>nihm</u> ih tee)
(ehk wuh <u>nihm</u> ih tee) *n.*
calmness, composure
Synonyms: coolness, poise, sang-froid, serenity

CONSOLE (kuhn <u>sohl</u>) *v.* **-ing,-ed.**
to alleviate grief and raise the spirits of, provide solace
Synonyms: relieve, comfort, soothe

BOUNTIFUL (<u>bown</u> tih fuhl) *adj.*
abundant and plentiful; generous
Synonyms: ample, luxuriant; liberal, benevolent

INDIFFERENT (ihn <u>dihf</u> ruhnt) (ihn <u>dihf</u> uhr uhnt) *adj.*
uncaring, unbiased
Synonyms: unconcerned, uncurious, detached,
uninterested, apathetic

fully scrubbed Edgar's nose and mouth, **affirming** it served him right for **meddling**. His sister began weeping to go home, and Cathy stood by **confounded**, blushing for all.

"You should not have spoken to him!" she **expostulated** with Master Linton. "He was in a bad temper, and now you've spoilt your visit; and he'll be flogged: I hate him to be flogged! I can't eat my dinner. Why did you speak to him, Edgar?"

"I didn't," sobbed the youth, escaping from my hands, and finishing the remainder of the purification with his cambric pocket-handkerchief. "I promised Mamma that I wouldn't say one word to him, and I didn't."

"Well, don't cry," replied Catherine **contemptuously**. "You're not killed. Don't make more mischief; my brother is coming: be quiet! Hush! Isabella! Has anybody hurt *you?*"

"There, there, children—to your seats!" cried Hindley, **bustling** in. "That <u>brute</u> of a lad has warmed me nicely. Next time, Master Edgar, take the law into your own fists—it will give you an appetite!"

The little party recovered its **equanimity** at sight of the fragrant feast. They were hungry after their ride, and easily **consoled**, since no real harm had befallen them. Mr. Earnshaw carved **bountiful** platefuls, and the mistress made them merry with lively talk. I waited behind her chair, and was pained to behold Catherine, with dry eyes and an **indifferent** air, commence cutting up the wing of a goose before her. An unfeeling child, I thought to myself; how lightly she dismisses her old playmate's troubles. I could not have imagined her to be so selfish. She lifted a mouthful to her lips; then she set it down again: her cheeks flushed, and the tears gushed over them. She slipped her fork to the floor, and hastily dived under the cloth to conceal her emotion. I did not call her unfeeling long; for I perceived she was in <u>purgatory</u> throughout the day, and wearying to find an opportunity of getting by herself, or paying a visit to Heathcliff, who had been locked up by the master as I discovered, on endeavouring to introduce to him a private mess of <u>victuals</u>.

ENTREATY (ehn <u>tree</u> tee) *n.*
 a plea or request
  Synonyms: imploration, prayer, petition

PERSEVERE (pehr suh <u>veer</u>) *v.* **-ing,-ed.**
 to continue with determination, remain steadfast
  Synonyms: persist, endure, plod

In the evening we had a dance. Cathy begged that he might be liberated then, as Isabella Linton had no partner; her **entreaties** were vain, and I was appointed to supply the deficiency. We got rid of all gloom in the excitement of the exercise, and our pleasure was increased by the arrival of the Gimmerton band, mustering fifteen strong: a trumpet, a trombone, clarionets, bassoons, French horns, and a bass viol, besides singers. They go the rounds of all the respectable houses, and receive contributions every Christmas, and we esteemed it a first-rate treat to hear them. After the usual carols had been sung, we set them to songs and glees. Mrs. Earnshaw loved music, and so they gave us plenty.

Catherine loved it too; but she said it sounded sweetest at the top of the steps, and she went up in the dark; I followed. They shut the house door below, never noting our absence, it was so full of people. She made no stay at the stair's head, but mounted farther, to the garret where Heathcliff was confined, and called him. He stubbornly declined answering for a while; she **persevered**, and finally persuaded him to hold communion with her through the boards. I let the poor things converse unmolested, till I supposed the songs were going to cease, and the singers to get some refreshment; then, I clambered up the ladder to warn her. Instead of finding her outside, I heard her voice within. The little monkey had crept by the skylight of one garret, along the roof, into the skylight of the other, and it was with the utmost difficulty I could coax her out again. When she did come Heathcliff came with her, and she insisted that I should take him into the kitchen, as my fellow-servant had gone to a neighbour's to be removed from the sound of our "devil's psalmody," as it pleased him to call it. I told them I intended by no means to encourage their tricks; but as the prisoner had never broken his fast since yesterday's dinner, I would wink at his cheating Mr. Hindley that once. He went down; I set him a stool by the fire, and offered him a quantity of good things; but he was sick and could eat little, and my

DIVERT (die <u>vuhrt</u>) *v.* **-ing,-ed.**
to distract or amuse; to move in different directions
from a particular point
Synonyms: deter, occupy, entertain; deviate, separate

PROGNOSTICATE (prahg <u>nahs</u> tih kayt) *v.* **-ing,-ed.**
to indicate in advance, to forecast
Synonyms: predict, foreshadow, portend
OBSTINATE (<u>ahb</u> stih nuht) *adj.*
stubborn
Synonyms: headstrong, stiff-necked, bullheaded,
pigheaded, mulish

attempts to entertain him were thrown away. He leant his two elbows on his knees, and his chin on his hands, and remained wrapt in dumb meditation. On my inquiring the subject of his thoughts, he answered gravely:

"I'm trying to settle how I shall pay Hindley back. I don't care how long I wait, if I can only do it at last. I hope he will not die before I do!"

"For shame, Heathcliff!" said I. "It is for God to punish wicked people; we should learn to forgive."

"No, God won't have the satisfaction that I shall," he returned. "I only wish I knew the best way! Let me alone, and I'll plan it out: while I'm thinking of that I don't feel pain."

But, Mr. Lockwood, I forget these tales cannot **divert** you. I'm annoyed how I should dream of chattering on at such a rate; and your gruel cold, and you nodding for bed! I could have told Heathcliff's history, all that you need hear, in a half-a-dozen words. Thus interrupting herself, the housekeeper rose, and proceeded to lay aside her sewing; but I felt incapable of moving from the hearth, and I was very far from nodding.

"Sit still, Mrs. Dean," I cried, "do sit still, another half-hour. You've done just right to tell the story leisurely. That is the method I like; and you must finish it in the same style. I am interested in every character you have mentioned, more or less."

"The clock is on the stroke of eleven, sir."

"No matter—I'm not accustomed to go to bed in the long hours. One or two is early enough for a person who lies till ten."

"You shouldn't lie till ten. There's the very prime of the morning gone long before that time. A person who has not done one half his day's work by ten o'clock, runs a chance of leaving the other half undone."

"Nevertheless, Mrs. Dean, resume your chair; because to-morrow I intend lengthening the night till afternoon. I **prognosticate** for myself an **obstinate** cold, at least."

FRIVOLOUS (<u>frihv</u> uh luhs) *adj.*
   petty, trivial; flippant, silly
      Synonyms: inconsequential, worthless; frothy, light,
      vapid

PROVINCIALISM (pruh <u>vihn</u> shuhl ihz uhm) *n.*
   lack of sophistication; a trait or quality specific to a
   country or region
      Synonyms: barbarity, unrefinement; localism
COMPEL (kuhm <u>pehl</u>) *v.* **-ling,-led.**
   to urge or force
      Synonyms: coerce, oblige, constrain
FACULTY (<u>faa</u> kuhl tee) *n.*
   the ability to act or do
      Synonyms: aptitude, capability, sense, skill
TRIFLE (<u>trie</u> fuhl) *n.*
   something of slight worth or little importance
      Synonyms: triviality, novelty, trinket

"I hope not, sir. Well, you must allow me to leap over some three years; during that space Mrs. Earnshaw—"

"No, no, I'll allow nothing of the sort! Are you acquainted with the mood of mind in which, if you were seated alone, and the cat licking its kitten on the rug before you, you would watch the operation so intently that puss's neglect of one ear would put you seriously out of temper?"

"A terribly lazy mood, I should say."

"On the contrary, a tiresomely active one. It is mine, at present; and, therefore, continue minutely. I perceive that people in these regions acquire over people in towns the value that the spider in a dungeon does over a spider in a cottage, to their various occupants; and yet the deepened attraction is not entirely owing to the situation of the looker-on. They *do* live more in earnest, more in themselves, and less in surface, change, and **frivolous** external things. I could fancy a love for life here almost possible; and I was a fixed unbeliever in any love of a year's standing. One state resembles setting a hungry man down to a single dish, on which he may concentrate his entire appetite and do it justice; the other, introducing him to a table laid out by French cooks: he can perhaps extract as much enjoyment from the whole; but each part is a mere atom in his regard and remembrance."

"Oh! Here we are the same as anywhere else, when you get to know us," observed Mrs. Dean, somewhat puzzled at my speech.

"Excuse me," I responded. "You, my good friend, are a striking evidence against that assertion. Excepting a few **provincialisms** of slight consequence, you have no marks of the manners which I am habituated to consider as peculiar to your class. I am sure you have thought a great deal more than the generality of servants think. You have been **compelled** to cultivate your reflective **faculties** for want of occasions for frittering your life away in silly **trifles**."

Mrs. Dean laughed.

"I certainly esteem myself a steady, reasonable kind of body," she said, "not exactly from living among the hills and seeing one set of faces, and one series of actions, from year's end to year's end. But I have undergone sharp discipline, which has taught me wisdom; and then, I have read more than you would fancy, Mr. Lockwood. You could not open a book in this library that I have not looked into, and got something out of also: unless it be that range of Greek and Latin, and that of French; and those I know one from another, it is as much as you can expect of a poor man's daughter. However, if I am to follow my story in true gossip's fashion, I had better go on; and instead of leaping three years, I will be content to pass to the next summer—the summer of 1778, that is, nearly twenty-three years ago."

Chapter 8

On the morning of a fine June day, my first <u>bonny</u> little nursling, and the last of the ancient Earnshaw stock, was born. We were busy with the hay in a far away field, when the girl that usually brought our breakfasts, came running an hour too soon, across the meadow and up the lane, calling me as she ran.

"Oh, such a grand <u>bairn</u>!" she panted out. "The finest lad that ever breathed! But the doctor says Missis must go. He says she's been in a <u>consumption</u> these many months. I heard him tell Mr. Hindley—and now she has nothing to keep her, and she'll be dead before winter. You must come home directly. You're to nurse it, Nelly: to feed it with sugar and milk, and take care of it day and night. I wish I were you, because it will be all yours when there is no Missis!"

"But is she very ill?" I asked, flinging down my rake, and tying my bonnet.

CHERUB (<u>cheh</u> ruhb) *n.*
an adorable child; a winged angel
Synonyms: baby, doll; guardian, heavenly being

RAPTUROUSLY (<u>raap</u> chuhr uhs lee) *adv.*
with extreme joy or ecstasy
Synonyms: blissfully, delightfully

ZEALOUS (<u>zeh</u> luhs) *adj.*
passionate, devoted
Synonyms: fanatical, enthusiastic, militant, radical

DOTE (doht) *v.* **-ing,-ed.**
to lavish attention, to love to excess
Synonyms: adore, cherish, tender

"I guess she is; yet she looks bravely," replied the girl, "and she talks as if she thought of living to see it grow a man. She's out of her head for joy, it's such a beauty! If I were her, I'm certain I should not die: I should get better at the bare sight of it, in spite of Kenneth. I was fairly mad at him. Dame Archer brought the **cherub** down to master, in the house, and his face just began to light up, when the old croaker steps forward, and says he: 'Earnshaw, it's a blessing your wife has been spared to leave you this son. When she came, I felt convinced we shouldn't keep her long; and now, I must tell you, the winter will probably finish her. Don't take on, and fret about it too much! It can't be helped. And besides, you should have known better than to choose such a rush of a lass!'"

"And what did the master answer?" I enquired.

"I think he swore; but I didn't mind him, I was straining to see the <u>bairn</u>," and she began again to describe it **rapturously**. I, as **zealous** as herself, hurried eagerly home to admire, on my part; though I was very sad for Hindley's sake. He had room in his heart for only two idols—his wife and himself: he **doted** on both, and adored one, and I couldn't conceive how he would bear the loss.

When we got to Wuthering Heights, there he stood at the front door, and, as I passed in, I asked, "How was the baby?"

"Nearly ready to run about, Nell," he replied, putting on a cheerful smile.

"And the mistress?" I ventured to inquire. "The doctor says she's—"

"Damn the doctor!" he interrupted, reddening. "Frances is quite right; she'll be perfectly well by this time next week. Are you going upstairs? Will you tell her that I'll come, if she'll promise not to talk. I left her because she would not hold her tongue; and she must—tell her Mr. Kenneth says she must be quiet."

I delivered this message to Mrs. Earnshaw; she seemed in flighty spirits, and replied merrily:

DOGGEDLY (<u>daw</u> guhd lee) *adv.*
   stubbornly or persistently
     Synonyms: tenaciously, obstinately, pertinaciously
AFFIRM (uh <u>fihrm</u>) *v.* **-ing,-ed.**
   to state positively, to assert as valid or confirmed
     Synonyms: declare, avow, maintain
MALADY (<u>maal</u> uh dee) *n.*
   illness
     Synonyms: disease, disorder, ailment, affliction,
     infirmity
RETORT (rih <u>tohrt</u>) *v.* **-ing,-ed.**
   to make a cutting response
     Synonyms: retaliate, talk back, counter

LAMENT (luh <u>mehnt</u>) *v.* **-ing,-ed.**
   to deplore, grieve
     Synonyms: mourn, sorrow, regret, bewail
EXECRATE (<u>ehk</u> sih krayt) *v.* **-ing,-ed.**
   to curse; to imprecate
     Synonyms: hate, denounce, loathe, abhor
DISSIPATION (dihs uh <u>pay</u> shuhn) *n.*
   the pursuance of pleasure to excess; a scattering
     Synonyms: self-indulgence, squandering,
     consumption; dispersal, diffusion
REPROVE (rih <u>proov</u>) *v.* **-ing,-ed.**
   to criticize or correct
     Synonyms: rebuke, admonish, reprimand, chide,
     reproach
DIABOLICAL (die uh <u>bah</u> lih kuhl) *adj.*
   characteristic of the devil
     Synonyms: fiendish, wicked, evil

"I hardly spoke a word, Ellen, and there he has gone out twice, crying. Well, say I promise I won't speak: but that does not bind me not to laugh at him!"

Poor soul! Till within a week of her death that gay heart never failed her, and her husband persisted **doggedly**, nay, furiously, in **affirming** her health improved every day. When Kenneth warned him that his medicines were useless at that stage of the **malady**, and he needn't put him to further expense by attending her, he **retorted**:

"I know you need not—she's well—she does not want any more attendance from you! She never was in a <u>consumption</u>. It was a fever, and it is gone: her pulse is as slow as mine now, and her cheek as cool."

He told his wife the same story, and she seemed to believe him; but one night, while leaning on his shoulder, in the act of saying she thought she should be able to get up tomorrow, a fit of coughing took her—a very slight one—he raised her in his arms; she put her two hands about his neck, her face changed, and she was dead.

As the girl had anticipated, the child Hareton fell wholly into my hands. Mr. Earnshaw, provided he saw him healthy and never heard him cry, was contented, as far as regarded him. For himself, he grew desperate: his sorrow was of that kind that will not **lament**. He neither wept nor prayed: he cursed and defied; **execrated** God and man, and gave himself up to reckless **dissipation**. The servants could not bear his tyrannical and evil conduct long: Joseph and I were the only two that would stay. I had not the heart to leave my charge; and besides, you know I had been his foster-sister, and excused his behaviour more readily than a stranger would. Joseph remained to <u>hector</u> over tenants and labourers; and because it was his <u>vocation</u> to be where he had plenty of wickedness to **reprove**.

The master's bad ways and bad companions formed a pretty example for Catherine and Heathcliff. His treatment of the latter was enough to make a fiend of a saint. And, truly, it appeared as if the lad *were* possessed of something **diabolical** at that period. He delighted to

DEGRADE (dih <u>grayd</u>) (dee <u>grayd</u>) *v.* **-ing,-ed.**
  to drag down in moral or intellectual character; to
  lower in rank or status
    Synonyms: shame, demean, dishonor, weaken; demote
SULLENNESS (<u>suh</u> luhn nehs) *n.*
  gloom, dreariness
    Synonyms: moroseness, sulkiness, glumness
INFERNAL (ihn <u>fuhr</u> nuhl) *adj.*
  relating to the dead or hell; devilish
    Synonyms: damned, accursed; fiendish, awful, malicious
PEER *n.*
  contemporary, a person or thing of equal standing
    Synonyms: fellow, coeval, colleague
HAUGHTY (<u>haw</u> tee) (<u>hah</u> tee) *adj.*
  arrogant and condescending
    Synonyms: proud, disdainful, supercilious, scornful,
    vainglorious
VEX (vehks) *v.* **-ing,-ed.**
  to irritate, annoy; confuse, puzzle
    Synonyms: bother, plague, afflict, irk; perplex, perturb
AVERSION (uh <u>vuhr</u> zhuhn) *n.*
  intense dislike
    Synonyms: antagonism, antipathy, abhorrence,
    repulsion, repugnance
DISCERN (dihs <u>uhrn</u>) *v.* **-ing,-ed.**
  to perceive or recognize something obscure
    Synonyms: descry, observe, glimpse, distinguish
PENSIVE (<u>pehn</u> sihv) *adj.*
  thoughtful
    Synonyms: contemplative, reflective, meditative
AMIABLE (<u>ay</u> mee uh buhl) *adj.*
  friendly, pleasant, likable
    Synonyms: affable, convivial, amicable, agreeable
ANIMATE (<u>aa</u> nih mayt) *v.* **-ing,-ed.**
  to make lively and excited, to fill with spirit
    Synonyms: elate, inspire, stimulate
COUNTENANCE (<u>kown</u> tuh nuhns) *n. (See page 102.)*

witness Hindley **degrading** himself past redemption; and became daily more notable for savage **sullenness** and <u>ferocity</u>. I could not half tell what an **infernal** house we had. The <u>curate</u> dropped calling, and nobody decent came near us, at last; unless Edgar Linton's visits to Miss Cathy might be an exception. At fifteen she was the queen of the country side; she had no **peer**, and she did turn out a **haughty**, headstrong creature! I own I did not like her, after her infancy was past; and I **vexed** her frequently by trying to bring down her arrogance: she never took an **aversion** to me, though. She had a wondrous constancy to old attachments: even Heathcliff kept his hold on her affections unalterably; and young Linton, with all his superiority, found it difficult to make an equally deep impression. He was my late master. That is his portrait over the fireplace. It used to hang on one side, and his wife's on the other, but hers has been removed, or else you might see something of what she was. Can you make that out?

Mrs. Dean raised the candle, and I **discerned** a soft-featured face, exceedingly resembling the young lady at the Heights, but more **pensive** and **amiable** in expression. It formed a sweet picture. The long light hair curled slightly on the temples; the eyes were large and serious; the figure almost too graceful. I did not marvel how Catherine Earnshaw could forget her first friend for such an individual. I marvelled much how he, with a mind to correspond with his person, could fancy my idea of Catherine Earnshaw.

"A very agreeable portrait," I observed to the housekeeper. "Is it like?"

"Yes," she answered, "but he looked better when he was **animated**. That is his everyday **countenance**; he wanted spirit in general."

Catherine had kept up her acquaintance with the Lintons since her five weeks' residence among them; and as she had no temptation to show her rough side in their company, and had the sense to be ashamed of being rude where she experienced such invariable courtesy, she

IMPOSE (ihm <u>pohz</u>) *v.* **-ing,-ed.**
to inflict, force oneself upon
Synonyms: dictate, demand, ordain, intrude
UNWITTINGLY (uhn <u>wih</u> ting lee) *adv.*
unconsciously, unintentionally
Synonyms: obliviously, inadvertently
INGENUOUS (ihn <u>jehn</u> yoo uhs) *adj.*
naive and unsophisticated; straightforward, open
Synonyms: simple, childlike; honest, candid
INCLINATION (ihn cluh <u>nay</u> shuhn) *n.* *(See page 80.)*
RESTRAIN (rih <u>strayn</u>) *v.* **-ing,-ed.**
to control, repress, restrict, hold back
Synonyms: hamper, bridle, curb, check
CIVILITY (sih <u>vihl</u> ih tee) *n.*
a courteous behavior or politeness
Synonyms: compliment, pleasantry
COQUETTE (koh <u>keht</u>) *n.*
a flirty woman who uses sex appeal to exploit men
Synonyms: seductress, vamp, tease
CONTEMPT (kuhn <u>tehmpt</u>) *n.*
disrespect, scorn
Synonyms: derision, disdain
EVINCE (ih <u>vihns</u>) *v.* **-ing,-ed.** *(See page 86.)*
ANTIPATHY (aan <u>tih</u> puh thee) *n.*
dislike, hostility; extreme opposition or aversion
Synonyms: antagonism; enmity, malice
SENTIMENT (<u>sehn</u> tuh muhnt) *n.*
an attitude, thought, or judgment prompted by
feeling; a romantic or nostalgic feeling
Synonyms: idea; emotion
INDIFFERENCE (ihn <u>dihf</u> ruhnts) *n.*
lack of caring
Synonyms: detachment, disinterest, apathy
DEPRECIATION (dih pree shee <u>ay</u> shuhn) *n.*
belittlement of character; a decrease in value or worth
Synonyms: disparagement; reduction
CHASTEN (<u>chay</u> sehn) *v.* **-ing,-ed.**
to correct with punishment or restraint
Synonyms: discipline, castigate, moderate

130

imposed unwittingly on the old lady and gentleman, by her **ingenuous** cordiality; gained the admiration of Isabella, and the heart and soul of her brother: acquisitions that flattered her from the first, for she was full of ambition, and led her to adopt a double character without exactly intending to deceive any one. In the place where she heard Heathcliff termed a "vulgar young <u>ruffian</u>," and "worse than a <u>brute</u>," she took care not to act like him; but at home she had small **inclination** to practise politeness that would only be laughed at, and **restrain** an unruly nature when it would bring her neither credit nor praise.

Mr. Edgar seldom mustered courage to visit Wuthering Heights openly. He had a terror of Earnshaw's reputation, and·shrunk from encountering him; and yet he was always received with our best attempts at **civility**: the master himself avoided offending him, knowing why he came; and if he could not be gracious, kept out of the way. I rather think his appearance there was distasteful to Catherine: she was not artful, never played the **coquette**, and had evidently an objection to her two friends meeting at all; for when Heathcliff expressed **contempt** of Linton in his presence, she could not half coincide, as she did in his absence; and when Linton **evinced** disgust and **antipathy** to Heathcliff, she dared not treat his **sentiments** with **indifference**, as if **depreciation** of her playmate were of scarcely any consequence to her. I've had many a laugh at her <u>perplexities</u> and untold troubles, which she vainly strove to hide from my mockery. That sounds ill-natured: but she was so proud, it became really impossible to pity her distresses, till she should be **chastened** into more humility. She did bring herself, finally, to confess, and to confide in me: there was not a soul else that she might fashion into an adviser.

Mr. Hindley had gone from home one afternoon, and Heathcliff presumed to give himself a holiday on the strength of it. He had reached the age of sixteen then, I think, and without having bad features, or being deficient

CONTRIVE (kuhn <u>triev</u>) *v.* **-ing,-ed.**
  to devise, plan, or manage; to form in an artistic manner
    Synonyms: concoct, scheme; create, design
REPULSIVENESS (rih <u>puhl</u> sihv nehs) *n.*
  the quality of being repellant or disgusting
    Synonyms: ugliness, corruption, grossness
RETAIN (rih <u>tayn</u>) *v.* **-ing,-ed.**
  to hold, keep possession of
    Synonyms: withhold, reserve, maintain, remember
POIGNANT (<u>poy</u> nyaant) *adj.*
  emotionally moving
    Synonyms: stirring, touching, pathetic, piquant
PREVAIL (prih <u>vayl</u>) *v.* **-ing,-ed.**
  1. to persuade or convince
    Synonyms: influence, induce, affect
  2. to overcome; to succeed lastingly
    Synonyms: dominate, triumph; persist, endure
GAIT (gayt) *n.*
  the way one moves on foot, a manner of walking
    Synonyms: tread, march, pace
IGNOBLE (ihg <u>noh</u> buhl) *adj.*
  dishonorable, not noble in character
    Synonyms: mean, low, base, disreputable, sordid
DISPOSITION (dihs puh <u>zih</u> shuhn) *n.*
  mood or temperament
    Synonyms: behavior, tendency, inclination, nature
MOROSENESS (muh <u>rohs</u> nehs) (maw <u>rohs</u> nehs) *n.*
  gloom, sadness, surliness
    Synonym: sullenness
AVERSION (uh <u>vuhr</u> zhuhn) *n.* *(See page 128.)*
RESPITE (<u>reh</u> spiht) *n.*
  interval of relief
    Synonyms: rest, pause, intermission, recess
LAVISH (<u>laa</u> vihsh) *v.* **-ing,-ed.**
  to shower with abundance or extravagance; to waste
  or spend excessively
    Synonyms: cram, overflow, saturate, teem; squander

in intellect, he **contrived** to convey an impression of inward and outward **repulsiveness** that his present aspect **retains** no traces of. In the first place, he had by that time lost the benefit of his early education: continual hard work, begun soon and concluded late, had extinguished any curiosity he once possessed in pursuit of knowledge, and any love for books or learning. His childhood's sense of superiority, instilled into him by the favours of old Mr. Earnshaw, was faded away. He struggled long to keep up an equality with Catherine in her studies, and yielded with **poignant** though silent regret: but he yielded completely; and there was no **prevailing** on him to take a step in the way of moving upward, when he found he must, necessarily, sink beneath his former level. Then personal appearance sympathized with mental deterioration: he acquired a slouching **gait**, and **ignoble** look; his naturally reserved **disposition** was exaggerated into an almost idiotic excess of unsociable **moroseness**; and he took a grim pleasure, apparently, in exciting the **aversion** rather than the esteem of his few acquaintances.

Catherine and he were constant companions still at his seasons of **respite** and labour; but he had ceased to express his fondness for her in words, and recoiled with angry suspicion from her girlish caresses, as if conscious there could be no gratification in **lavishing** such marks of affection on him. On the before-named occasion he came into the house to announce his intention of doing nothing, while I was assisting Miss Cathy to arrange her dress: she had not reckoned on his taking it into his head to be idle; and imagining she would have the whole place to herself, she managed, by some means, to inform Mr. Edgar of her brother's absence, and was then preparing to receive him.

"Cathy, are you busy, this afternoon?" asked Heathcliff. "Are you going anywhere?"

"No, it is raining," she answered.

"Why have you that silk frock on, then?" he said. "Nobody coming here, I hope?"

COUNTENANCE (<u>kown</u> tuh nuhns) *n.*
  appearance, facial expression
    Synonyms: face, features, visage
PETULANTLY (<u>peh</u> chuh luhnt lee) *adv.*
  rudely, peevishly
    Synonyms: irritably, testily, fretfully

"Not that I know of," stammered Miss, "but you should be in the field now, Heathcliff. It is an hour past dinner time. I thought you were gone."

"Hindley does not often free us from his <u>accursed</u> presence," observed the boy. "I'll not work any more to-day. I'll stay with you."

"Oh, but Joseph will tell," she suggested; "you'd better go!"

"Joseph is loading lime on the further side of Pennistow Crag. It will take him till dark, and he'll never know."

So saying, he lounged to the fire, and sat down. Catherine reflected an instant, with knitted brows—she found it needful to smooth the way for an intrusion. "Isabella and Edgar Linton talked of calling this afternoon," she said, at the conclusion of a minute's silence. "As it rains, I hardly expect them; but they may come, and if they do, you run the risk of being scolded for no good."

"Order Ellen to say you are engaged, Cathy," he persisted. "Don't turn me out for those pitiful, silly friends of yours! I'm on the point, sometimes, of complaining that they—but I'll not—"

"That they what?" cried Catherine, gazing at him with a troubled **countenance**. "Oh, Nelly!" she added **petulantly**, jerking her head away from my hands, "you've combed my hair quite out of curl! That's enough; let me alone. What are you on the point of complaining about, Heathcliff?"

"Nothing—only look at the almanac on that wall." He pointed to a framed sheet hanging near the window, and continued. "The crosses are for the evenings you have spent with the Lintons, the dots for those spent with me. Do you see? I've marked every day."

"Yes—very foolish: as if I took notice!" replied Catherine in a <u>peevish</u> tone. "And where is the sense of that?"

"To show that I *do* take notice," said Heathcliff.

"And should I always be sitting with you?" she demanded, growing more irritated. "What good do I get?

AGITATION (aa gih <u>tay</u> shuhn) *n.*
    commotion, excitement; uneasiness
        Synonyms: disturbance; restlessness, anxiety

IMPERIOUSLY (ihm <u>pihr</u> ee uhs lee) *adv.*
    in a majestic or domineering manner; urgently
        Synonyms: arrogantly, overbearingly; imperatively

What do you talk about? You might be dumb, or a baby, for anything you say to amuse me, or for anything you do, either!"

"You never told me before that I talked too little, or that you disliked my company, Cathy!" exclaimed Heathcliff, in much **agitation**.

"It's no company at all, when people know nothing and say nothing," she muttered.

Her companion rose up, but he hadn't time to express his feelings further, for a horse's feet were heard on the flags, and having knocked gently, young Linton entered, his face brilliant with delight at the unexpected summons he had received. Doubtless Catherine marked the difference between her friends, as one came in and the other went out. The contrast resembled what you see in exchanging a bleak, hilly, coal country for a beautiful fertile valley; and his voice and greeting were as opposite as his aspect. He had a sweet, low manner of speaking, and pronounced his words as you do: that's less gruff than we talk here, and softer.

"I'm not come too soon, am I?" he said, casting a look at me: I had begun to wipe the plate, and tidy some drawers at the far end in the dresser.

"No," answered Catherine. "What are you doing there, Nelly?"

"My work, Miss," I replied. (Mr. Hindley had given me directions to make a third party in any private visits Linton chose to pay.)

She stepped behind me and whispered crossly, "Take yourself and your dusters off. When company are in the house, servants don't commence scouring and cleaning in the room where they are!"

"It's a good opportunity, now that the master is away," I answered aloud. "He hates me to be fidgeting over these things in his presence. I'm sure Mr. Edgar will excuse me."

"I hate you to be fidgeting in *my* presence," exclaimed the young lady **imperiously**, not allowing her guest time to

EQUANIMITY (ee kwuh <u>nihm</u> ih tee)
(ehk wuh <u>nihm</u> ih tee) *n.*
   calmness, composure
      Synonyms: coolness, poise, sang-froid, serenity
ASSIDUOUSLY (uh <u>sih</u> joo uhs lee) *adv.*
   diligently, attentively
      Synonyms: industriously, steadfastly, thoroughly
RELISH (<u>reh</u> lihsh) *v.* **-ing,-ed.**
   to enjoy greatly
      Synonyms: savor, love, fancy

RETORT (rih <u>tohrt</u>) *v.* **-ing,-ed.**
   to make a cutting response
      Synonyms: retaliate, talk back, counter
REFUTE (rih <u>fyoot</u>) *v.* **-ing,-ed.**
   to contradict, discredit
      Synonyms: deny, controvert, confute, debunk,
      disprove
IMPEL (ihm <u>pehl</u>) *v.* **-ling,-led.**
   to urge forward as if driven by a strong moral pressure
      Synonyms: push, prompt, drive, incite, instigate

WAX (waaks) *v.* **-ing,-ed.**
   to begin to be; to increase gradually
      Synonyms: become, grow; enlarge, expand, swell
LIVID (<u>lih</u> vihd) *adj.*
   reddened with anger; discolored from a bruise; pale
      Synonyms: furious; black-and-blue; ashen, pallid
CONSTERNATION (kahn stuhr <u>nay</u> shuhn) *n.*
   amazement or distress that leads to confusion
      Synonyms: alarm, bewilderment, perplexity

138

speak—she had failed to recover her **equanimity** since the little dispute with Heathcliff.

"I'm sorry for it, Miss Catherine," was my response; and I proceeded **assiduously** with my occupation.

She, supposing Edgar could not see her, snatched the cloth from my hand, and pinched me, with a prolonged wrench, very spitefully on the arm. I've said I did not love her, and rather **relished** mortifying her vanity now and then: besides, she hurt me extremely; so I started up from my knees, and screamed out, "Oh, Miss, that's a nasty trick! You have no right to nip me, and I'm not going to bear it."

"I didn't touch you, you lying creature!" cried she, her fingers tingling to repeat the act, and her ears red with rage. She never had power to conceal her passion, it always set her whole complexion in a blaze.

"What's that, then?" I **retorted**, showing a decided purple witness to **refute** her.

She stamped her foot, wavered a moment, and then irresistibly **impelled** by the naughty spirit within her, slapped me on the cheek: a stinging blow that filled both eyes with water.

"Catherine, love! Catherine!" interposed Linton, greatly shocked at the double fault of falsehood and violence which his idol had committed.

"Leave the room, Ellen!" she repeated, trembling all over.

Little Hareton, who followed me everywhere, and was sitting near me on the floor, at seeing my tears commenced crying himself, and sobbed out complaints against "wicked Aunt Cathy," which drew her fury on to his unlucky head: she seized his shoulders, and shook him till the poor child **waxed livid**, and Edgar thoughtlessly laid hold of her hands to deliver him. In an instant one was wrung free, and the astonished young man felt it applied over his own ear in a way that could not be mistaken for jest. He drew back in **consternation**. I lifted Hareton in my arms, and walked off to the kitchen with

DISPOSITION (dihs puh <u>zih</u> shuhn) *n.*
mood or temperament
Synonyms: behavior, tendency, inclination, nature

PERSEVERE (pehr suh <u>veer</u>) *v.* **-ing,-ed.**
to continue with determination, remain steadfast
Synonyms: persist, endure, plod
RESOLUTION (reh suh <u>loo</u> shuhn) *n.*
a firm decision
Synonyms: determination, will, explanation
RESOLVE (rih <u>sahlv</u>) *v.* **-ing,-ed.**
to determine or to make a firm decision about
Synonyms: solve, decide
MARRED (mahrd) *adj.*
damaged, defaced; spoiled
Synonyms: injured, disfigured, blemished
scarred; impaired

him, leaving the door of communication open, for I was curious to watch how they would settle their disagreement. The insulted visitor moved to the spot where he had laid his hat, pale and with a quivering lip.

"That's right!" I said to myself. "Take warning and begone! It's a kindness to let you have a glimpse of her genuine **disposition**."

"Where are you going?" demanded Catherine, advancing to the door.

He swerved aside, and attempted to pass.

"You must not go!" she exclaimed energetically.

"I must and shall!" he replied in a subdued voice.

"No," she persisted, grasping the handle, "not yet, Edgar Linton. Sit down; you shall not leave me in that temper. I should be miserable all night, and I won't be miserable for you!"

"Can I stay after you have struck me?" asked Linton.

Catherine was mute.

"You've made me afraid and ashamed of you," he continued. "I'll not come here again!"

Her eyes began to glisten, and her lids to twinkle.

"And you told a deliberate untruth!" he said.

"I didn't!" she cried, recovering her speech. "I did nothing deliberately. Well, go, if you please—get away! And now I'll cry—I'll cry myself sick!"

She dropped down on her knees by a chair, and set to weeping in serious earnest. Edgar **persevered** in his **resolution** as far as the court; there he lingered. I **resolved** to encourage him.

"Miss is dreadfully wayward, sir," I called out. "As bad as any **marred** child. You'd better be riding home, or else she will be sick only to grieve us."

The soft thing looked askance through the window: he possessed the power to depart, as much as a cat possesses the power to leave a mouse half killed, or a bird half eaten. Ah, I thought, there will be no saving him: he's doomed, and flies to his fate! And so it was: he turned abruptly, hastened into the house again, shut the

FORSAKE (fohr <u>sayk</u>) *v.* **-saking,-sook,-saken.**
  to abandon, withdraw from
    Synonyms: desert, renounce, leave, quit

PROVOKE (proh <u>vohk</u>) *v.* **-ing,-ed.**
  to cause a response, e.g., anger or disagreement
    Synonyms: aggravate, stimulate, vex, incite

VOCIFERATE (voh <u>sih</u> fuhr ayt) *v.* **-ing,-ed.**
  to speak or yell loudly and noisily
    Synonyms: clamor, holler, scream, bark

door behind him; and when I went in a while after to inform them that Earnshaw had come home rabid drunk, ready to pull the whole place about our ears (his ordinary frame of mind in that condition), I saw the quarrel had merely effected a closer intimacy—had broken the outworks of youthful timidity, and enabled them to **forsake** the disguise of friendship, and confess themselves lovers.

Intelligence of Mr. Hindley's arrival drove Linton speedily to his horse, and Catherine to her chamber. I went to hide little Hareton, and to take the shot out of the master's fowling-piece, which he was fond of playing with in his insane excitement, to the hazard of the lives of any who **provoked**, or even attracted his notice too much; and I had hit upon the plan of removing it, that he might do less mischief if he did go the length of firing the gun.

Chapter 9

He entered, **vociferating** oaths dreadful to hear, and caught me in the act of stowing his son away in the kitchen cupboard. Hareton was impressed with a wholesome terror of encountering either his wild beast's fondness or his madman's rage; for in one he ran a chance of being squeezed and kissed to death, and in the other of being flung into the fire, or dashed against the wall; and the poor thing remained perfectly quiet wherever I chose to put him.

"There, I've found it out at last!" cried Hindley, pulling me back by the skin of my neck, like a dog. "By heaven and hell, you've sworn between you to murder that child! I know how it is, now, that he is always out of my way. But, with the help of Satan, I shall make you swallow the carving-knife, Nelly! You needn't laugh; for I've just crammed Kenneth, head-downmost, in the Blackhorse

HINDER (<u>hihn</u> duhr) *v.* **-ing,-ed.**
   to prevent action; to delay or impede
     Synonyms: restrain; hamper, inhibit, obstruct
ABOMINABLE (uh <u>bah</u> mihn uh buhl) *adj.*
   loathsome, detestable
     Synonyms: abhorrent, terrible, beastly, deplorable
AFFIRM (uh <u>fihrm</u>) *v.* **-ing,-ed.**
   to state positively, to assert as valid or confirmed
     Synonyms: declare, avow, maintain
DETESTABLY (dee <u>tehst</u> uh blee) *adv.*
   in a manner deserving of intense and violent hatred
     Synonyms: disgustingly, despicably, grossly
IMPOSE (ihm <u>pohz</u>) *v.* **-ing,-ed.**
   to inflict, force upon
     Synonyms: dictate, decree, demand, ordain
INFERNAL (ihn <u>fuhr</u> nuhl) *adj.*
   devilish; relating to the dead or hell
     Synonyms: fiendish, awful, malicious; damned, accursed
AFFECTATION (aaf ehk <u>tay</u> shun) *n.*
   fakeness, phoniness, artificiality, false display
     Synonyms: insincerity, pose, pretension

marsh; and two is the same as one—and I want to kill some of you: I shall have no rest till I do!"

"But I don't like the carving-knife, Mr. Hindley," I answered. "It has been cutting red herrings. I'd rather be shot, if you please."

"You'd rather be damned!" he said. "And so you shall. No law in England can **hinder** a man from keeping his house decent, and mine's **abominable**! Open your mouth."

He held the knife in his hand, and pushed its point between my teeth: but, for my part, I was never much afraid of his <u>vagaries</u>. I spat out, and **affirmed** it tasted **detestably**—I would not take it on any account.

"Oh!" said he, releasing me, "I see that hideous little villain is not Hareton: I beg your pardon, Nell. If it be, he deserves flaying alive for not running to welcome me, and for screaming as if I were a goblin. Unnatural cub, come hither! I'll teach thee to **impose** on a good-hearted deluded father. Now, don't you think the lad would be handsomer cropped? It makes a dog fiercer, and I love something fierce—get me a scissors—something fierce and trim! Besides, it's **infernal affectation**—devilish conceit it is, to cherish our ears—we're asses enough without them. Hush, child, hush! Well, then, it is my darling! Whisht, dry thy eyes—there's a joy; kiss me. What! It won't? Kiss me, Hareton! Damn thee, kiss me! By God, I'll break the brat's neck."

Poor Hareton was squalling and kicking in his father's arms with all his might, and redoubled his yells when he carried him upstairs and lifted him over the banister. I cried out that he would frighten the child into fits, and ran to rescue him. As I reached them, Hindley leant forward on the rails to listen to a noise below; almost forgetting what he had in his hands. "Who is that?" he asked, hearing some one approaching the stair's foot. I leant forward also, for the purpose of signing to Heathcliff, whose step I recognised, not to come further, and, at the instant when my eye quitted Hareton, he gave a sudden spring,

IMPULSE (<u>ihm</u> puhls) *n.*
  sudden tendency, inclination
    Synonyms: urge, whim
DESCENT (dih <u>sehnt</u>) (dee <u>sehnt</u>) *n.*
  the passing from a higher place to a lower place
    Synonyms: lowering, dismount, gravitation
MISER (<u>mie</u> zuhr) *n.*
  an extremely stingy and greedy person
    Synonyms: cheapskate, scrooge, misanthrope
COUNTENANCE (<u>kown</u> tuh nuhns) *n.*
  appearance, facial expression
    Synonyms: face, features, visage
THWART (thwahrt) *v.* **-ing,-ed.**
  to block or prevent from happening; to frustrate
    Synonyms: oppose, defeat, foil, balk; hinder, baffle
DESCEND (dih <u>sehnd</u>) (dee <u>sehnd</u>) *v.* **-ing,-ed.**
  to pass from a higher place to a lower place
    Synonyms: fall, dismount, gravitate
SOBERED (<u>soh</u> buhrd) *adj.*
  not intoxicated; self-controlled; serious
    Synonyms: dry, not drunk; subdued, sedate; grave
ABASHED (uh <u>baasht</u>) *adj.*
  embarrassed
    Synonyms: disconcerted, discomfited, fazed,
    mortified
HEATHEN (<u>hee</u> thuhn) *n.*
  pagan, uncivilized and irreligious person
    Synonyms: idolater, polytheist, unbeliever

MEDDLE (<u>meh</u> duhl) *v.* **-ing,-ed.**
  to interfere in others' affairs, to impose
    Synonyms: interlope, tamper, snoop, encroach

delivered himself from the careless grasp that held him, and fell.

There was scarcely time to experience a thrill of horror before we saw that the little wretch was safe. Heathcliff arrived underneath just at the critical moment; by a natural **impulse**, he arrested his **descent**, and setting him on his feet, looked up to discover the author of the accident. A **miser** who has parted with a lucky lottery ticket for five shillings, and finds next day he has lost in the bargain five thousand pounds, could not show a blanker **countenance** than he did on beholding the figure of Mr. Earnshaw above. It expressed, plainer than words could do, the intense anguish at having made himself the instrument of **thwarting** his own revenge. Had it been dark, I dare say, he would have tried to remedy the mistake by smashing Hareton's skull on the steps; but we witnessed his salvation; and I was presently below with my precious charge pressed to my heart. Hindley **descended** more leisurely, **sobered** and **abashed**.

"It is your fault, Ellen," he said. "You should have kept him out of sight: you should have taken him from me! Is he injured anywhere?"

"Injured!" I cried angrily. "If he's not killed, he'll be an idiot! Oh! I wonder his mother does not rise from her grave to see how you use him. You're worse than a **heathen**—treating your own flesh and blood in that manner!"

He attempted to touch the child, who, on finding himself with me, sobbed off his terror directly. At the first finger his father laid on him, however, he shrieked again louder than before, and struggled as if he would go into convulsions.

"You shall not **meddle** with him!" I continued. "He hates you—they all hate you—that's the truth! A happy family you have: and a pretty state you've come to!"

"I shall come to a prettier, yet, Nelly," laughed the misguided man, recovering his hardness. "At present, convey yourself and him away. And, hark you, Heathcliff! Clear

ENTREAT (ehn <u>treet</u>) *v.* **-ing,-ed.**
to plead, beg
Synonyms: beseech, implore, importune, request

PERDITION (puhr <u>dih</u> shuhn) *n.*
eternal misery or damnation; a huge loss or total destruction
Synonyms: nightmare, inferno; catastrophe, ruin

BLASPHEMER (<u>blaas</u> fuh muhr) *n.*
one who curses, one who reviles sacred things
Synonyms: imp, liar, curser

IMPRECATION (ihm prih <u>kay</u> shuhn) *n.*
curse
Synonyms: execration, anathema, malediction

CONSTITUTION (kahn stih <u>too</u> shuhn) *n.*
the physical structure or health of something or someone; the sum of components, composition
Synonyms: disposition, nature, stature; formation, design, architecture, make-up

HOARY (<u>hohr</u> ee) (<u>haw</u> ree) *adj.*
very old; whitish or gray from age
Synonyms: antique, vintage, ancient, venerable; silvery

you too, quite from my reach and hearing. I wouldn't murder you to-night; unless, perhaps, I set the house on fire: but that's as my fancy goes."

While saying this he took a pint bottle of brandy from the dresser, and poured some into a tumbler.

"Nay, don't!" I **entreated**. "Mr. Hindley, do take warning. Have mercy on this unfortunate boy, if you care nothing for yourself!"

"Any one will do better for him than I shall," he answered.

"Have mercy on your own soul!" I said, endeavouring to snatch the glass from his hand.

"Not I! On the contrary, I shall have great pleasure in sending it to **perdition** to punish its Maker," exclaimed the **blasphemer**. "Here's to its hearty damnation!"

He drank the spirits and impatiently bade us go; terminating his command with a sequel of horrid **imprecations**, too bad to repeat or remember.

"It's a pity he cannot kill himself with drink," observed Heathcliff, muttering an echo of curses back when the door was shut. "He's doing his very utmost; but his **constitution** defies him. Mr. Kenneth says he would wager his mare, that he'll outlive any man on this side Gimmerton, and go to the grave a **hoary** sinner, unless some happy chance out of the common course befall him."

I went into the kitchen, and sat down to lull my little lamb to sleep. Heathcliff, as I thought, walked through to the barn. It turned out afterwards that he only got as far as the other side the <u>settle</u>, when he flung himself on a bench by the wall, removed from the fire, and remained silent.

I was rocking Hareton on my knee, and humming a song that began:

It was far in the night, and the <u>bairnies</u> grat,
The mither beneath the mools heard that—

NOVELTY (<u>nah</u> vuhl tee) *n.*
  something new and original
    Synonyms: surprise, change, innovation

WINSOME (<u>wihn</u> suhm) *adj.*
  charming, happily engaging
    Synonyms: attractive, delightful

INDULGE (ihn <u>duhlj</u>) *v.* **-ing,-ed.**
  to give in to a craving or desire
    Synonyms: humor, gratify, allow, pamper

when Miss Cathy, who had listened to the hubbub from her room, put her head in, and whispered:

"Are you alone, Nelly?"

"Yes, Miss," I replied.

She entered and approached the hearth. I, supposing she was going to say something, looked up. The expression of her face seemed disturbed and anxious. Her lips were half asunder, as if she meant to speak, and she drew a breath; but it escaped in a sigh instead of a sentence. I resumed my song; not having forgotten her recent behaviour.

"Where's Heathcliff?" she said, interrupting me.

"About his work in the stable," was my answer.

He did not contradict me; perhaps he had fallen into a doze. There followed another long pause, during which I perceived a drop or two trickle from Catherine's cheek to the flags. Is she sorry for her shameful conduct? I asked myself. That will be a **novelty**: but she may come to the point as she will—I shan't help her! No, she felt small trouble regarding any subject, save her own concerns.

"Oh, dear!" she cried at last. "I'm very unhappy!"

"A pity," observed I. "You're hard to please: so many friends and so few cares, and can't make yourself content!"

"Nelly, will you keep a secret for me?" she pursued, kneeling down by me, and lifting her **winsome** eyes to my face with that sort of look which turns off bad temper, even when one has all the right in the world to **indulge** it.

"Is it worth keeping?" I inquired, less sulkily.

"Yes, and it worries me, and I must let it out! I want to know what I should do. To-day, Edgar Linton has asked me to marry him, and I've given him an answer. Now, before I tell you whether it was a consent or denial, you tell me which it ought to have been."

"Really, Miss Catherine, how can I know?" I replied. "To be sure, considering the exhibition you performed in his presence this afternoon, I might say it would be wise to refuse him. Since he asked you after that, he must either be hopelessly stupid or a venturesome fool."

RETRACT (rih <u>traakt</u>) *v.* **-ing,-ed.**
to draw in or take back
Synonyms: disavow, recede, retreat, retrogress

SENTENTIOUSLY (sehn <u>tehn</u> shuhs lee) *adv.*
in a terse and moralizing manner
Synonyms: pompously, moralistically, ardently

INJUDICIOUS (ihn joo <u>dih</u> shuhs) *adj.*
insensible, showing bad judgment, foolish
Synonyms: imprudent, unwise, irresponsible

INDIFFERENT (ihn <u>dihf</u> ruhnt) (ihn <u>dihf</u> uhr uhnt) *adj.*
uncaring, unbiased
Synonyms: unconcerned, uncurious, detached,
uninterested, apathetic

"If you talk so, I won't tell you any more," she returned <u>peevishly</u>, rising to her feet. "I accepted him, Nelly. Be quick, and say whether I was wrong!"

"You accepted him! Then what good is it discussing the matter? You have pledged your word, and cannot **retract**."

"But, say whether I should have done so—do!" she exclaimed in an irritated tone; chafing her hands together, and frowning.

"There are many things to be considered before that question can be answered properly," I said **sententiously**. "First and foremost, do you love Mr. Edgar?"

"Who can help it? Of course I do," she answered.

Then I put her through the following <u>catechism</u>: for a girl of twenty-two it was not **injudicious**.

"Why do you love him, Miss Cathy?"

"Nonsense, I do—that's sufficient."

"By no means; you must say why?"

"Well, because he is handsome, and pleasant to be with."

"Bad!" was my commentary.

"And because he is young and cheerful."

"Bad still."

"And because he loves me."

"**Indifferent**, coming there."

"And he will be rich, and I shall like to be the greatest woman of the neighbourhood, and I shall be proud of having such a husband."

"Worst of all. And now, say how you love him?"

"As anybody loves— You're silly, Nelly."

"Not at all—Answer."

"I love the ground under his feet, and the air over his head, and everything he touches, and every word he says. I love all his looks, and all his actions, and him entirely and altogether. There now!"

"And why?"

"Nay; you are making a jest of it; it is exceedingly ill-natured! It's no jest to me!" said the young lady, scowling, and turning her face to the fire.

HINDER (<u>hihn</u> duhr) *v.* **-ing,-ed.**
to prevent action; to delay or impede
Synonyms: restrain; hamper, inhibit, obstruct

COUNTENANCE (<u>kown</u> tuh nuhns) *n.*
appearance, facial expression
Synonyms: face, features, visage

"I'm very far from jesting, Miss Catherine," I replied. "You love Mr. Edgar because he is handsome, and young, and cheerful, and rich, and loves you. The last, however, goes for nothing: you would love him without that, probably; and with it you wouldn't, unless he possessed the four former attractions."

"No, to be sure not: I should only pity him—hate him, perhaps, if he were ugly, and a clown."

"But there are several other handsome, rich young men in the world: handsomer, possibly, and richer than he is. What should **hinder** you from loving them?"

"If there be any, they are out of my way! I've seen none like Edgar."

"You may see some; and he won't always be handsome, and young, and may not always be rich."

"He is now, and I have only to do with the present. I wish you would speak rationally."

"Well, that settles it if you have only to do with the present, marry Mr. Linton."

"I don't want your permission for that—I *shall* marry him: and yet you have not told me whether I'm right."

"Perfectly right; if people be right to marry only for the present. And now, let us hear what you are unhappy about. Your brother will be pleased; the old lady and gentleman will not object, I think; you will escape from a disorderly, comfortless home into a wealthy, respectable one; and you love Edgar, and Edgar loves you. All seems smooth and easy; where is the obstacle?"

"*Here!* And *here!*" replied Catherine, striking one hand on her forehead, and the other on her breast. "In whichever place the soul lives. In my soul and in my heart, I'm convinced I'm wrong!"

"That's very strange! I cannot make it out."

"It's my secret. But if you will not mock at me, I'll explain it: I can't do it distinctly: but I'll give you a feeling of how I feel."

She seated herself by me again. Her **countenance** grew sadder and graver, and her clasped hands trembled.

CONJURE (<u>kahn</u> juhr) *v.* **-ing,-ed.**
to summon a devil or spirit by invocation; to affect or effect as if by magic; to bring to mind
Synonyms: materialize; invoke, arouse; recollect

OBLIGE (uh <u>bliej</u>) *v.* **-ing,-ed.**
to be obligated, to require or force someone to obey
Synonyms: compel, constrain, bind, favor
PROPHECY (<u>prah</u> feh see) *n.*
the foretelling of events, a prediction of the future
Synonyms: dream, forecast, vision
VEX (vehks) *v.* **-ing,-ed.**
to irritate, annoy; confuse, puzzle
Synonyms: bother, plague, afflict, irk; perplex, perturb

"Nelly, do you never dream queer dreams?" she said suddenly, after some minutes' reflection.

"Yes, now and then," I answered.

"And so do I. I've dreamt in my life dreams that have stayed with me ever after, and changed my ideas: they've gone through and through me, like wine through water, and altered the colour of my mind. And this is one; I'm going to tell it—but take care not to smile at any part of it."

"Oh! Don't, Miss Catherine!" I cried. "We're dismal enough without **conjuring** up ghosts and visions to perplex us. Come, come, be merry and like yourself! Look at little Hareton! *He's* dreaming nothing dreary. How sweetly he smiles in his sleep!"

"Yes; and how sweetly his father curses in his solitude! You remember him, I daresay, when he was just such another as that chubby thing: nearly as young and innocent. However, Nelly, I shall **oblige** you to listen: it's not long, and I've no power to be merry to-night."

"I won't hear it, I won't hear it!" I repeated hastily.

I was superstitious about dreams then, and am still; and Catherine had an unusual gloom in her aspect, that made me dread something from which I might shape a **prophecy**, and foresee a fearful catastrophe. She was **vexed**, but she did not proceed. Apparently taking up another subject, she recommenced in a short time.

"If I were in heaven, Nelly, I should be extremely miserable."

"Because you are not fit to go there," I answered. "All sinners would be miserable in heaven."

"But it is not for that. I dreamt once that I was there."

"I tell you I won't hearken to your dreams, Miss Catherine! I'll go to bed," I interrupted again.

She laughed, and held me down; for I made a motion to leave my chair.

"This is nothing," cried she. "I was only going to say that heaven did not seem to be my home; and I broke my heart with weeping to come back to earth; and the angels were so angry that they flung me out into the middle of

DEGRADE (dih <u>grayd</u>) (dee <u>grayd</u>) *v.* **-ing,-ed.**
to lower in rank or status; to drag down in moral or
intellectual character
   Synonyms: demote; shame, demean, dishonor, weaken

OPPORTUNELY (ah pohr <u>toon</u> lee) *adv.*
appropriately, favorably
   Synonyms: seasonably, timely, advantageously

the <u>heath</u> on the top of Wuthering Heights; where I woke sobbing for joy. That will do to explain my secret, as well as the other. I've no more business to marry Edgar Linton than I have to be in heaven; and if the wicked man in there had not brought Heathcliff so low, I shouldn't have thought of it. It would **degrade** me to marry Heathcliff now; so he shall never know how I love him: and that, not because he's handsome, Nelly, but because he's more myself than I am. Whatever our souls are made of, his and mine are the same; and Linton's is as different as a moonbeam from lightning, or frost from fire."

Ere this speech ended, I became sensible of Heathcliff's presence. Having noticed a slight movement, I turned my head, and saw him rise from the bench, and steal out noiselessly. He had listened till he heard Catherine say it would **degrade** her to marry him, and then he stayed to hear no further. My companion, sitting on the ground, was prevented by the back of the <u>settle</u> from remarking his presence or departure; but I started, and bade her hush!

"Why?" she asked, gazing nervously round.

"Joseph is here," I answered, catching **opportunely** the roll of his cart-wheels up the road, "and Heathcliff will come in with him. I'm not sure whether he were not at the door this moment."

"Oh, he couldn't overhear me at the door!" said she. "Give me Hareton, while you get the supper, and when it is ready ask me to sup with you. I want to cheat my uncomfortable conscience, and be convinced that Heathcliff has no notion of these things. He has not, has he? He does not know what being in love is?"

"I see no reason that he should not know, as well as you," I returned, "and if you are his choice, he will be the most unfortunate creature that ever was born! As soon as you become Mrs. Linton, he loses friend, and love, and all! Have you considered how you'll bear the separation, and how he'll bear to be quite deserted in the world? Because, Miss Catherine—"

INDIGNATION (ihn dihg <u>nay</u> shun) *n.*
anger caused by something mean or unjust
Synonyms: fury, ire, wrath

FORSAKE (fohr <u>sayk</u>) *v.* **-saking,-sook,-saken.**
to abandon, withdraw from
Synonyms: desert, renounce, leave, quit

ANTIPATHY (aan <u>tih</u> puh thee) *n.*
dislike, hostility; extreme opposition or aversion
Synonyms: antagonism; enmity, malice

PLIABLE (<u>plie</u> uh buhl) *adj.*
yielding, submissive; easily bent or changed
Synonyms: complacent; malleable, adaptable
RETORT (rih <u>tohrt</u>) *v.* **-ing,-ed.**
to make a cutting response
Synonyms: retaliate, talk back, counter

"He quite deserted! We separated!" she exclaimed, with an accent of **indignation**. "Who is to separate us, pray? They'll meet the fate of Milo! Not as long as I live, Ellen: for no mortal creature. Every Linton on the face of the earth might melt into nothing, before I could consent to **forsake** Heathcliff. Oh, that's not what I intend—that's not what I mean! I shouldn't be Mrs. Linton were such a price demanded! He'll be as much to me as he has been all his lifetime. Edgar must shake off his **antipathy**, and tolerate him, at least. He will, when he learns my true feelings towards him. Nelly, I see now, you think me a selfish wretch; but did it never strike you that if Heathcliff and I married, we should be beggars? Whereas, if I marry Linton, I can aid Heathcliff to rise, and place him out of my brother's power."

"With your husband's money, Miss Catherine?" I asked. "You'll find him not so **pliable** as you calculate upon: and, though I'm hardly a judge, I think that's the worst motive you've given yet for being the wife of young Linton."

"It is not," **retorted** she. "It is the best! The others were the satisfaction of my whims: and for Edgar's sake, too, to satisfy him. This is for the sake of one who comprehends in his person my feelings to Edgar and myself. I cannot express it; but surely you and everybody have a notion that there is or should be an existence of yours beyond you. What were the use of my creation, if I were entirely contained here? My great miseries in this world have been Heathcliff's miseries, and I watched and felt each from the beginning: my great thought in living is himself. If all else perished, and *he* remained, *I* should still continue to be; and if all else remained, and he were annihilated, the universe would turn to a mighty stranger I should not seem a part of it. My love for Linton is like the foliage in the woods: time will change it, I'm well aware, as winter changes the trees. My love for Heathcliff resembles the eternal rocks beneath: a source of little visible delight, but necessary. Nelly, I *am* Heathcliff! He's always, always in my mind: not as a pleasure, any more than I am always a

IMPRACTICABLE (ihm <u>praak</u> tih kuh buhl) *adj.*
  incapable of being performed by the means employed;
  impassable
    Synonyms: insane, imprudent, absurd, impossible;
    blocked

CONJECTURE (kuhn <u>jehk</u> shuhr) *v.* **-ing,-ed.**
  to infer, predict, guess
    Synonyms: postulate, hypothesize, suppose, surmise
PROTRACTED (proh <u>traak</u> tihd) *adj.*
  prolonged, drawn out, extended
    Synonyms: lengthy, elongated, stretched

pleasure to myself, but as my own being. So don't talk of our separation again: it is **impracticable**; and—"

She paused, and hid her face in the folds of my gown; but I jerked it forcibly away. I was out of patience with her folly!

"If I can make any sense of your nonsense, Miss," I said, "it only goes to convince me that you are ignorant of the duties you undertake in marrying; or else that you are a wicked, unprincipled girl. But trouble me with no more secrets: I'll not promise to keep them."

"You'll keep that?" she asked eagerly.

"No, I'll not promise," I repeated.

She was about to insist, when the entrance of Joseph finished our conversation; and Catherine removed her seat to a corner, and nursed Hareton, while I made the supper. After it was cooked, my fellow-servant and I began to quarrel who should carry some to Mr. Hindley; and we didn't settle it till all was nearly cold. Then we came to the agreement that we would let him ask, if he wanted any, for we feared particularly to go into his presence when he had been some time alone.

"And how isn't that nowt comed in fro' th' field, be this time? What is he about? Girt idle seegh!" demanded the old man, looking round for Heathcliff.

"I'll call him," I replied. "He's in the barn, I've no doubt."

I went and called, but got no answer. On returning, I whispered to Catherine that he had heard a good part of what she said, I was sure; and told how I saw him quit the kitchen just as she complained of her brother's conduct regarding him. She jumped up in a fine fright, flung Hareton on to the settle, and ran to seek for her friend herself; not taking leisure to consider why she was so flurried, or how her talk would have affected him. She was absent such a while that Joseph proposed we should wait no longer. He cunningly **conjectured** they were staying away in order to avoid hearing his **protracted** blessing. They were "ill enough for only fahl manners," he

AFFIRM (uh <u>fihrm</u>) *v.* **-ing,-ed.**
 to state positively, to assert as valid or confirmed
  Synonyms: declare, avow, maintain
SUPPLICATION (suh plih <u>kay</u> shun) *n.*
 a humble and earnest request
  Synonyms: petition, appellation, application

VEX (vehks) *v.* **-ing,-ed.**
 to irritate, annoy; confuse, puzzle
  Synonyms: bother, plague, afflict, irk; perplex, perturb
TRIFLE (<u>trie</u> fuhl) *n.*
 something of slight worth or little importance
  Synonyms: triviality, novelty, trinket
SAUNTER (<u>sawn</u> tuhr) *n.*
 a leisurely walk or amble
  Synonyms: stroll, ramble, perambulation
LURK (luhrk) *v.* **-ing,-ed.**
 to hide, to lie hidden or unsuspected; to prowl, sneak
  Synonyms: conceal; stalk, creep, skulk, slink
FERRET (<u>fehr</u> iht) *v.* **-ing,-ed.**
 to hunt or look intensively for something
  Synonyms: search, track, pursue, chase, root out

affirmed. And on their behalf he added that night a special prayer to the usual quarter of an hour's **supplication** before meat, and would have tacked another to the end of the grace, had not his young mistress broken in upon him with a hurried command that he must run down the road, and wherever Heathcliff had rambled, find and make him re-enter directly!

"I want to speak to him, and I *must*, before I go upstairs," she said. "And the gate is open: he is somewhere out of hearing; for he would not reply, though I shouted at the top of the <u>fold</u> as loud as I could."

Joseph objected at first; she was too much in earnest, however, to suffer contradiction; and at last he placed his hat on his head, and walked grumbling forth. Meantime, Catherine paced up and down the floor, exclaiming:

"I wonder where he is—I wonder where he *can* be? What did I say, Nelly? I've forgotten. Was he **vexed** at my bad humour this afternoon? Dear! Tell me what I've said to grieve him? I do wish he'd come. I do wish he would!"

"What a noise for nothing!" I cried, though rather uneasy myself. "What a **trifle** scares you! It's surely no great cause of alarm that Heathcliff should take a moonlight **saunter** on the moors, or even lie too sulky to speak to us in the hay-loft. I'll engage he's **lurking** there. See if I don't **ferret** him out!"

I departed to renew my search; its result was disappointment, and Joseph's quest ended in the same.

"Yon lad gets war un war!" observed he on re-entering. "He's left th' yate at t' full swing, and Miss's pony has trodden dahn two rigs o' corn, and plottered through, raight o'er into t' meadow! Hahsomdiver, t' maister 'ull play t' devil to-morn, and he'll do weel. He's patience itsseln wi' sich careless, offald craters—patience itsseln he is! Bud he'll not be soa allus—yah's see, all on ye! Yah mumn't drive him out of his heead for nowt!"

"Have you found Heathcliff, you ass?" interrupted Catherine. "Have you been looking for him, as I ordered?"

INCLINED (ihn <u>kliend</u>) *adj.*
   predisposed, having a certain tendency
      Synonyms: likely, prone

AGITATION (aa gih <u>tay</u> shuhn) *n.*
   uneasiness; commotion, excitement
      Synonyms: restlessness, anxiety; disturbance

REPOSE (rih <u>pohz</u>) *n.*
   relaxation, leisure; a state of peace or tranquility
      Synonyms: rest, ease, idleness; calmness, serenity

EXPOSTULATION (ihk spahs chuh <u>lay</u> shuhn) *n.*
   reasoning; an expression of opposition
      Synonyms: assertion; argument, dissuasion,
      remonstration

BESEECH (bih <u>seech</u>) *v.* **-ing,-ed.**
   to beg, plead, implore
      Synonyms: petition, supplicate, entreat

SENTIMENT (<u>sehn</u> tuh muhnt) *n.*
   an attitude, thought, or judgment prompted by
   feeling; a romantic or nostalgic feeling
      Synonyms: idea; emotion

ASCERTAIN (aa suhr <u>tayn</u>) *v.* **-ing,-ed.**
   to determine, discover, make certain of
      Synonyms: verify, calculate, detect

AUDIBLY (<u>aw</u> dih blee) *adv.*
   in a manner capable of being heard; aloud
      Synonyms: detectably, perceptibly, loudly, plainly

VOCIFERATE (voh <u>sih</u> fuhr ayt) *v.* **-ing,-ed.**
   to speak or yell loudly and noisily
      Synonyms: clamor, holler, scream, bark

CLAMOROUSLY (<u>klaa</u> muhr uhs lee) *adv.*
   in a manner that demands attention; loudly
      Synonyms: insistently; uproariously, noisily,
      obstreperously

UPROAR (<u>uhp</u> rohr) *n.*
   a situation of loud and confusing excitement
      Synonyms: noise, hubbub, commotion, fracas

OBSTINACY (<u>ahb</u> stih nuh see) *n.*
   stubbornness and determination
      Synonyms: bullheadedness, persistence, perseverance

"I sud more likker look for th' horse," he replied. "It 'ud be to more sense. Bud, I can look for norther horse nur man of a neeght loike this—as black as t' chimbley! und Heathcliff's noan t' chap to coom at *my* whistle— happen he'll be less hard o' hearing wi' *ye!*"

It *was* a very dark evening for summer. The clouds appeared **inclined** to thunder, and I said we had better all sit down; the approaching rain would be certain to bring him home without further trouble. However, Catherine would not be persuaded into tranquillity. She kept wandering to and fro, from the gate to the door, in a state of **agitation** which permitted no **repose**; and at length took up a permanent situation on one side of the wall, near the road: where, heedless of my **expostulations** and the growling thunder, and the great drops that began to splash around her, she remained, calling at intervals, and then listening, and then crying outright. She beat Hareton, or any child, at a good passionate fit of crying.

About midnight, while we still sat up, the storm came rattling over the Heights in full fury. There was a violent wind, as well as thunder, and either one or the other split a tree off at the corner of the building. A huge bough fell across the roof, and knocked down a portion of the east chimney-stack, sending a clatter of stones and soot into the kitchen fire. We thought a bolt had fallen in the middle of us; and Joseph swung on to his knees **beseeching** the Lord to remember the patriarchs Noah and Lot, and, as in former times, spare the righteous, though He smote the ungodly. I felt some **sentiment** that it must be a judgment on us also. The Jonah, in my mind, was Mr. Earnshaw; and I shook the handle of his den that I might **ascertain** if he were yet living. He replied **audibly** enough, in a fashion which made my companion **vociferate**, more **clamorously** than before, that a wide distinction might be drawn between saints like himself and sinners like his master. But the **uproar** passed away in twenty minutes, leaving us all unharmed; except Cathy, who got thoroughly drenched for her **obstinacy** in refusing to take

167

shelter, and standing bonnetless and shawlless to catch as much water as she could with her hair and clothes. She came in and lay down on the <u>settle</u>, all soaked as she was, turning her face to the back, and putting her hands before it.

"Well, Miss!" I exclaimed, touching her shoulder; "You are not bent on getting your death, are you? Do you know what o'clock it is? Half-past twelve. Come, come to bed! There's no use waiting longer on that foolish boy: he'll be gone to Gimmerton, and he'll stay there now. He guesses we shouldn't wait for him till this late hour at least, he guesses that only Mr. Hindley would be up; and he'd rather avoid having the door opened by the master."

"Nay, nay, he's noan at Gimmerton," said Joseph. "I's niver wonder but he's at t' bottom of a bog-hoile. This visitation worn't for nowt, and I wod hev ye to look out, Miss—yah muh be t' next. Thank Hivin for all! All warks togither for gooid to them as is chozzen, and picked out fro' th' rubbidge! Yah knaw whet t' Scripture ses." And he began quoting several texts, referring us to chapters and verses where we might find them.

I, having vainly begged the wilful girl to rise and remove her wet things, left him preaching and her shivering, and betook myself to bed with little Hareton, who slept as fast as if every one had been sleeping round him. I heard Joseph read on a while afterwards; then I distinguished his slow step on the ladder, and then I dropped asleep.

Coming down somewhat later than usual, I saw, by the sunbeams piercing the chinks of the shutters, Miss Catherine still seated near the fire-place. The house door was ajar, too; light entered from its unclosed windows; Hindley had come out, and stood on kitchen hearth, haggard and drowsy.

"What ails you, Cathy?" he was saying when I entered. "You look as dismal as a drowned <u>whelp</u>. Why are you so damp and pale, child?"

SOBER (<u>soh</u> buhr) *adj.*
   not intoxicated; self-controlled; serious
     Synonyms: dry, not drunk; subdued, sedate; grave

PREVAIL (prih <u>vayl</u>) *v.* **-ing,-ed.**
   1. to persuade or convince
     Synonyms: influence, induce, affect
   2. to overcome; to succeed lastingly
     Synonyms: dominate, triumph; persist, endure

LURK (luhrk) *v.* **-ing,-ed.**
   to prowl, sneak; to hide, to lie hidden or unsuspected
     Synonyms: stalk, creep, skulk, slink; conceal

DISCOURSE (<u>dihs</u> kohrs) *n.*
   the verbal interchange of ideas; a formal, orderly, and
   extended expression of thought
     Synonyms: speech; dialogue, conversation

"I've been wet," she answered reluctantly, "and I'm cold, that's all."

"Oh, she is naughty!" I cried, perceiving the master to be tolerably **sober**. "She got steeped in the shower of yesterday evening, and there she has sat the night through, and I couldn't **prevail** on her to stir."

Mr. Earnshaw stared at us in surprise. "The night through," he repeated. "What kept her up? Not fear of the thunder, surely? That was over hours since."

Neither of us wished to mention Heathcliff's absence, as long as we could conceal it; so I replied, I didn't know how she took it into her head to sit up; and she said nothing. The morning was fresh and cool; I threw back the <u>lattice</u>, and presently the room filled with sweet scents from the garden; but Catherine called <u>peevishly</u> to me, "Ellen, shut the window; I'm starving!" And her teeth chattered as she shrunk closer to the almost extinguished embers.

"She's ill," said Hindley, taking her wrist. "I suppose that's the reason she would not go to bed. Damn it! I don't want to be troubled with more sickness here. What took you into the rain!"

"Running after t' lads, as usuald!" croaked Joseph, catching an opportunity, from our hesitation, to thrust in his evil tongue. "If I war yah, maister, I'd just slam t' boards i' their faces all on 'em, gentle and simple! Never a day ut yah're off, but yon cat a Linton comes sneaking hither; and Miss Nelly, shoo's a fine lass! Shoo sits watching for ye i't' kitchen; and as yah're in at one door, he's out at t'other, and, then, wer grand lady goes a coorting of her side! It's <u>bonny</u> behaviour, **lurking** amang t' fields, after twelve o' t' night, wi' that fahl, flaysome divil of a gypsy, Heathcliff! They think *I'm* blind; but I'm noan: nowt ut t' soart!—I seed young Linton boath coming and going, and I seed *yah*" (directing his **discourse** to me), "yah gooid fur nowt, slattenly witch! Nip up and bolt into th' house, t' minute yah heard t' maister's horse fit clatter up t' road."

171

SAT Vocabulary

INSOLENCE (<u>ihn</u> suh luhnts) *n.*
  a tendency to be insulting; arrogance
    Synonyms: audacity, rudeness, presumption,
    impertinence; superiority, haughtiness

CONFOUND (kuhn <u>fownd</u>) *v.* **-ing,-ed.**
  1. to damn or condemn
    Synonyms: doom, jinx, revile, punish
  2. to baffle, perplex; to mistake something for another
    Synonyms: overwhelm, disconcert, entangle,
    muddle; confuse, misidentify

INARTICULATE (ihn ahr <u>tihk</u> yuh liht) *adj.*
  tongue-tied, unable to speak clearly
    Synonyms: incomprehensible, unintelligible
LAVISH (<u>laa</u> vihsh) *v.* **-ing,-ed.**
  to shower with abundance or extravagance
    Synonyms: pamper, spend, squander
OBLIGE (uh <u>bliej</u>) *v.* **-ing,-ed.**
  to be obligated, to require or force someone to obey
    Synonyms: compel, constrain, bind, favor

"Silence, eavesdropper!" cried Catherine. "None of your **insolence** before me! Edgar Linton came yesterday by chance, Hindley, and it was *I* who told him to be off: because I knew you would not like to have met him as you were."

"You lie, Cathy, no doubt," answered her brother, "and you are a **confounded** simpleton! But never mind Linton at present. Tell me, were you not with Heathcliff last night? Speak the truth, now. You need not be afraid of harming him. Though I hate him as much as ever, he did me a good turn a short time since, that will make my conscience tender of breaking his neck. To prevent it, I shall send him about his business, this very morning; and after he's gone, I'd advise you all to look sharp: I shall only have the more humour for you."

"I never saw Heathcliff last night," answered Catherine, beginning to sob bitterly, "and if you do turn him out of doors, I'll go with him. But, perhaps you'll never have an opportunity; perhaps he's gone." Here she burst into uncontrollable grief, and the remainder of her words were **inarticulate**.

Hindley **lavished** on her a torrent of scornful abuse, and bade her get to her room immediately, or she shouldn't cry for nothing! I **obliged** her to obey; and I shall never forget what a scene she acted when we reached her chamber. It terrified me—I thought she was going mad, and I begged Joseph to run for the doctor. It proved the commencement of delirium. Mr. Kenneth, as soon as he saw her, pronounced her dangerously ill; she had a fever. He bled her, and he told me to let her live on whey and water-gruel, and take care she did not throw herself downstairs or out of the window; and then he left: for he had enough to do in the parish, where two or three miles was the ordinary distance between cottage and cottage.

Though I cannot say I made a gentle nurse, and Joseph and the master were no better, and though our patient was as wearisome and headstrong as a patient could be, she weathered it through. Old Mrs. Linton paid us several

CONVALESCENT (kahn vuhl <u>ehs</u> uhnt) *adj.*
  partially recovered from an illness
    Synonyms: healed, recuperated, healthy

REPENT (rih <u>pehnt</u>) *v.* **-ing,-ed.**
  to regret a past action
    Synonyms: rue, atone, apologize

HAUGHTY (<u>haw</u> tee) (<u>hah</u> tee) *adj.*
  arrogant and condescending
    Synonyms: proud, disdainful, supercilious, scornful,
    vainglorious

PROVOKE (proh <u>vohk</u>) *v.* **-ing,-ed.**
  to cause a response, e.g., anger or disagreement
    Synonyms: aggravate, stimulate, vex, incite

BAN (baan) *n.*
  an order that prohibits something
    Synonyms: forbiddance, boycott, restriction

ALOOF (uh <u>loof</u>) *adj.*
  removed or distant
    Synonyms: remote, indifferent, withdrawn, unsociable

INDULGENT (ihn <u>duhl</u> jehnt) *adj.*
  lenient, tolerant
    Synonyms: gratifying, pleasing

CAPRICE (kuh <u>prees</u>) *n.*
  an impulsive change of mind, fickleness
    Synonym: whim

MULTITUDE (<u>muhl</u> tuh tood) *n.*
  the state of being many, a great number
    Synonyms: mass, myriad, slew, crowd

INFATUATE (ihn <u>faach</u> oo ayt) *v.* **-ing,-ed.**
  to become strongly or foolishly attached to, inspired
  with foolish passion, or overly in love
    Synonyms: besotted, enthralled, smitten, enamored

SUBSEQUENT (<u>suhb</u> suh kwehnt) *adj.*
  following in time or order
    Synonyms: succeeding, next, afterward

INCLINATION (ihn cluh <u>nay</u> shuhn) *n.*
  tendency toward
    Synonyms: leaning, trend, preference, disposition,
    propensity

visits, to be sure, and set things to rights, and scolded and ordered us all; and when Catherine was **convalescent**, she insisted on conveying her to Thrushcross Grange: for which deliverance we were very grateful. But the poor dame had reason to **repent** of her kindness: she and her husband both took the fever, and died within a few days of each other.

Our young lady returned to us, saucier and more passionate, and **haughtier** than ever. Heathcliff had never been heard of since the evening of the thunder-storm; and one day I had the misfortune, when she had **provoked** me exceedingly, to lay the blame of his disappearance on her: where indeed it belonged, as she well knew. From that period, for several months, she ceased to hold any communication with me, save in the relation of a mere servant. Joseph fell under a **ban** also: he *would* speak his mind, and lecture her all the same as if she were a little girl; and she esteemed herself a woman, and our mistress, and thought that her recent illness gave her a claim to be treated with consideration. Then the doctor had said that she would not bear crossing much; she ought to have her own way; and it was nothing less than murder in her eyes for any one to presume to stand up and contradict her. From Mr. Earnshaw and his companions she kept **aloof**; and tutored by Kenneth, and serious threats of a fit that often attended her rages, her brother allowed her whatever she pleased to demand, and generally avoided aggravating her fiery temper. He was rather too **indulgent** in humouring her **caprices**; not from affection, but from pride: he wished earnestly to see her bring honour to the family by an alliance with the Lintons, and as long as she let him alone she might trample on us like slaves, for aught he cared! Edgar Linton, as **multitudes** have been before and will be after him, was **infatuated**; and believed himself the happiest man alive on the day he led her to Gimmerton three years **subsequent** to his father's death.

Much against my **inclination**, I was persuaded to leave Wuthering Heights and accompany her here. Little

175

ENTREATY (ehn <u>tree</u> tee) *n.*
  a plea or request
    Synonyms: imploration, prayer, petition
LAMENT (luh <u>mehnt</u>) *v.* **-ing,-ed.**
  to deplore, grieve
    Synonyms: mourn, sorrow, regret, bewail
MUNIFICENT (myoo <u>nihf</u> ih suhnt) *adj.*
  generous, lavish
    Synonyms: liberal, bountiful

DISPOSE (dih <u>spohz</u>) *v.* **-ing,-ed.**
  to incline or give a tendency to; to put in place, to settle
    Synonyms: determine, motivate; organize, position
DEFER (dih <u>fuhr</u>) *v.* **-ring,-red.**
  to delay; to delegate to another
    Synonyms: extend, impede, postpone, stall; submit, yield

IMPASSABLE (ihm <u>paas</u> uh buhl) *adj.*
  blocked, impossible to cross or travel
    Synonyms: impenetrable, closed
DILATORY (<u>dihl</u> uh tohr ee) *adj.*
  slow, tending to delay
    Synonyms: sluggish, tardy, unhurried
DEARTH (duhrth) *n.*
  lack, scarcity, insufficiency
    Synonyms: absence, shortage, paucity
INTIMATION (ihn tuh <u>may</u> shuhn) *n.*
  clue, suggestion
    Synonyms: implication, allusion, insinuation

Hareton was nearly five years old, and I had just begun to teach him his letters. We made a sad parting; but Catherine's tears were more powerful than ours. When I refused to go, and when she found her **entreaties** did not move me, she went **lamenting** to her husband and brother. The former offered me **munificent** wages; the latter ordered me to pack up. He wanted no women in the house, he said, now that there was no mistress; and as to Hareton, the <u>curate</u> should take him in hand, by-and-by. And so I had but one choice left: to do as I was ordered. I told the master he got rid of all decent people only to run to ruin a little faster. I kissed Hareton, said good-bye; and since then he has been a stranger and it's very queer to think it, but I've no doubt he has completely forgotten all about Ellen Dean, and that he was ever more than all the world to her, and she to him!

At this point of the housekeeper's story, she chanced to glance towards the timepiece over the chimney; and was in amazement on seeing the minute-hand measure half-past one. She would not hear of staying a second longer. In truth, I felt rather **disposed** to **defer** the sequel of her narrative, myself. And now that she is vanished to her rest, and I have meditated for another hour or two, I shall summon courage to go, also, in spite of aching laziness of head and limbs.

Chapter 10

A charming introduction to a hermit's life! Four weeks' torture, tossing, and sickness! Oh! These bleak winds and bitter northern skies, and **impassable** roads, and **dilatory** country surgeons! And, oh, this **dearth** of the human <u>physiognomy</u>! and, worse than all, the terrible **intimation** of Kenneth that I need not expect to be out of doors till spring.

PHALANX (<u>fay</u> laanks) *n.*
massed group of soldiers, people, or things
Synonyms: body, infantry
DRAW *v.* **drawing, drew, drawn**
to pull, drag; to attract or be attracted to; to lead, to
bring about on purpose
Synonyms: haul, tow, yank; lure, entice; provoke, elicit

Mr. Heathcliff has just honoured me with a call. About seven days ago he sent me a brace of grouse—the last of the season. Scoundrel! He is not altogether guiltless in this illness of mine; and that I had a great mind to tell him. But, alas! How could I offend a man who was charitable enough to sit at my bedside a good hour, and talk on some other subject than pills and draughts, blisters and leeches? This is quite an easy interval. I am too weak to read; yet I feel as if I could enjoy something interesting. Why not have up Mrs. Dean to finish her tale? I can recollect its chief incidents as far as she had gone. Yes: I remember her hero had run off, and never been heard of for three years; and the heroine was married. I'll ring: she'll be delighted to find me capable of talking cheerfully.

Mrs. Dean came. "It wants twenty minutes, sir, to taking the medicine," she commenced.

"Away, away with it!" I replied. "I desire to have—"

"The doctor says you must drop the powders."

"With all my heart! Don't interrupt me. Come and take your seat here. Keep your fingers from that bitter **phalanx** of vials. **Draw** your knitting out of your pocket—that will do—now continue the history of Mr. Heathcliff, from where you left off, to the present day. Did he finish his education on the Continent, and come back a gentleman? Or did he get a <u>sizar</u>'s place at college, or escape to America, and earn honours by drawing blood from his foster-country? Or make a fortune more promptly on the English highways?"

"He may have done a little in all these <u>vocations</u>, Mr. Lockwood, but I couldn't give my word for any. I stated before that I didn't know how he gained his money; neither am I aware of the means he took to raise his mind from the savage ignorance into which it was sunk: but, with your leave, I'll proceed in my own fashion, if you think it will amuse and not weary you. Are you feeling better this morning?"

"Much."

INDIFFERENCE (ihn <u>dihf</u> ruhnts) *n.*
lack of caring
Synonyms: detachment, disinterest, apathy
IMPERIOUS (ihm <u>pihr</u> ee uhs) *adj.*
arrogantly self-assured, domineering, overbearing
Synonyms: authoritarian, despotic
AVER (uh <u>vuhr</u>) *v.* **-ring,-red.**
to declare to be true, affirm
Synonyms: assert, attest
VEX (vehks) *v.* **-ing,-ed.**
to irritate, annoy; confuse, puzzle
Synonyms: bother, plague, afflict, irk; perplex, perturb
ASCRIBE (uh <u>skrieb</u>) *v.* **-ing,-ed.**
to attribute to, assign
Synonyms: accredit, impute, refer
CONSTITUTION (kahn stih <u>too</u> shuhn) *n.*
the physical structure or health of something or
someone; the sum of components, composition
Synonyms: disposition, nature, stature; formation,
design, architecture, make-up
PERILOUS (<u>pehr</u> uh luhs) *adj.*
full of danger
Synonyms: risky, hazardous, unsafe

DOMINEERING (dahm uh <u>neer</u> ihng) *adj.*
tyrannical, dictatorial
Synonyms: bossy, despotic, totalitarian, harsh

"That's good news. I got Miss Catherine and myself to Thrushcross Grange; and, to my agreeable disappointment, she behaved infinitely better than I dared to expect. She seemed almost over-fond of Mr. Linton; and even to his sister she showed plenty of affection. They were both very attentive to her comfort, certainly. It was not the thorn bending to the honeysuckles, but the honeysuckles embracing the thorn. There were no mutual concessions; one stood erect, and the others yielded: and who *can* be ill-natured and bad-tempered when they encounter neither opposition nor **indifference**? I observed that Mr. Edgar had a deep-rooted fear of ruffling her humour. He concealed it from her, but if ever he heard me answer sharply, or saw any other servant grow cloudy at some **imperious** order of hers, he would show his trouble by a frown of displeasure that never darkened on his own account. He many a time spoke sternly to me about my pertness; and **averred** that the stab of a knife could not inflict a worse pang than he suffered at seeing his lady **vexed**. Not to grieve a kind master, I learned to be less touchy, and, for the space of half a year, the gun-powder lay as harmless as sand, because no fire came near to explode it. Catherine had seasons of gloom and silence now and then. They were respected with sympathizing silence by her husband, who **ascribed** them to an alteration in her **constitution**, produced by her **perilous** illness; as she was never subject to depression of spirits before. The return of sunshine was welcomed by answering sunshine from him. I believe I may assert that they were really in possession of deep and growing happiness.

It ended. Well, we *must* be for ourselves in the long run; the mild and generous are only more justly selfish than the **domineering**; and it ended when circumstances caused each to feel that the one's interest was not the chief consideration in the other's thoughts. On a mellow evening in September, I was coming from the garden with a heavy basket of apples which I had been gathering. It had got dusk, and the moon looked over the high wall of the

LURK (luhrk) *v.* **-ing,-ed.**
    to hide, to lie hidden or unsuspected; to prowl, sneak
        Synonyms: conceal; stalk, creep, skulk, slink

SALLOW (<u>saa</u> loh) *adj.*
    sickly yellow in color
        Synonyms: ashen, pasty, peaked, wan

court, causing undefined shadows to **lurk** in the corners of the numerous projecting portions of the building. I set my burden on the house steps by the kitchen door, and lingered to rest, and drew in a few more breaths of the soft, sweet air. My eyes were on the moon, and my back to the entrance, when I heard a voice behind me say—

"Nelly, is that you?"

It was a deep voice, and foreign in tone; yet there was something in the manner of pronouncing my name which made it sound familiar. I turned about to discover who spoke, fearfully; for the doors were shut, and I had seen nobody on approaching the steps. Something stirred in the porch; and, moving nearer, I distinguished a tall man dressed in dark clothes, with dark face and hair. He leant against the side, and held his fingers on the latch as if intending to open for himself. Who can it be? I thought. Mr. Earnshaw? Oh, no! The voice has no resemblance to his.

"I have waited here an hour," he resumed, while I continued staring, "and the whole of that time all round has been as still as death. I dared not enter. You do not know me? Look, I'm not a stranger!"

A ray fell on his features; the cheeks were **sallow**, and half covered with black whiskers; the brows lowering, the eyes deep set and singular. I remembered the eyes.

"What!" I cried, uncertain whether to regard him as a worldly visitor, and I raised my hands in amazement "What! You come back? Is it really you? Is it?"

"Yes, Heathcliff," he replied, glancing from me up to the windows, which reflected a score of glittering moons, but showed no lights from within. "Are they at home? Where is she? Nelly, you are not glad! You needn't be so disturbed. Is she here? Speak! I want to have one word with her—your mistress. Go, and say some person from Gimmerton desires to see her."

"How will she take it?" I exclaimed. "What will she do? The surprise bewilders me—it will put her out of her head! And you are Heathcliff! But altered! Nay, there's no comprehending it. Have you been for a soldier?"

RESOLVE (rih <u>sahlv</u>) *v.* **-ing,-ed.**
    to determine or to make a firm decision about
        Synonyms: solve, decide

COMPEL (kuhm <u>pehl</u>) *v.* **-ling,-led.**
    to urge or force
        Synonyms: coerce, oblige, constrain

JUBILEE (joo bih <u>lee</u>) *n.*
    a joyous celebration
        Synonyms: party, hoopla, festivity, jamboree

"Go and carry my message," he interrupted impatiently. "I'm in hell till you do!"

He lifted the latch, and I entered; but when I got to the parlour where Mr. and Mrs. Linton were, I could not persuade myself to proceed. At length, I **resolved** on making an excuse to ask if they would have the candles lighted, and I opened the door.

They sat together in a window whose <u>lattice</u> lay back against the wall, and displayed, beyond the garden trees and the wild green park, the valley of Gimmerton, with a long line of mist winding nearly to its top (for very soon after you pass the chapel, as you may have noticed, the <u>sough</u> that runs from the marshes joins a <u>beck</u> which follows the bend of the glen). Wuthering Heights rose above this silvery vapour; but our old house was invisible; it rather dips down on the other side. Both the room and its occupants, and the scene they gazed on, looked wondrously peaceful. I shrank reluctantly from performing my errand; and was actually going away leaving it unsaid, after having put my question about the candles, when a sense of my folly **compelled** me to return, and mutter—"A person from Gimmerton wishes to see you, ma'am."

"What does he want?" asked Mrs. Linton.

"I did not question him," I answered.

"Well, close the curtains, Nelly," she said, "and bring up tea. I'll be back again directly."

She quitted the apartment; Mr. Edgar inquired, carelessly, who it was.

"Some one mistress does not expect," I replied. "That Heathcliff—you recollect him, sir,—who used to live at Mr. Earnshaw's."

"What! The gypsy—the ploughboy?" he cried. "Why did you not say so to Catherine?"

"Hush! You must not call him by those names, master," I said. "She'd be sadly grieved to hear you. She was nearly heartbroken when he ran off. I guess his return will make a **jubilee** to her."

SURMISE (suhr <u>miez</u>) *v.* **-ing,-ed.**
  to make an educated guess.
    Synonyms: conjecture, speculate, infer
CALAMITY (kuh <u>laam</u> ih tee) *n.*
  misfortune; state of despair
    Synonyms: disaster, cataclysm; misery

VEX (vehks) *v.* **-ing,-ed.**
  to irritate, annoy; confuse, puzzle
    Synonyms: bother, plague, afflict, irk; perplex, perturb
DROLL (drohl) *adj.*
  amusing in a wry, subtle way
    Synonyms: witty, comic, funny, entertaining, risible
FASTIDIOUSNESS (faa <u>stihd</u> ee uhs nehs) *n.*
  careful attention or overattention to details
    Synonyms: meticulousness, precision, effort
GENTRY (<u>jehn</u> tree) *n.*
  people of a high social class
    Synonyms: nobility, aristocracy, landowners

DESCEND (dih <u>sehnd</u>) (dee <u>sehnd</u>) *v.* **-ing,-ed.**
  to pass from a higher place to a lower place
    Synonyms: fall, dismount, gravitate

Mr. Linton walked to a window on the other side of the room that overlooked the court. He unfastened it and leant out. I suppose they were below, for he exclaimed quickly—"Don't stand there, love! Bring the person in, if it be any one particular." Ere long I heard the click of the latch, and Catherine flew upstairs, breathless and wild; too excited to show gladness. Indeed, by her face, you would rather have **surmised** an awful **calamity**.

"Oh, Edgar, Edgar!" she panted, flinging her arms round his neck. "Oh, Edgar, darling! Heathcliff's come back—he is!" And she tightened her embrace to a squeeze.

"Well, well," cried her husband crossly, "don't strangle me for that! He never struck me as such a marvellous treasure. There is no need to be frantic!"

"I know you didn't like him," she answered, repressing a little the intensity of her delight. "Yet, for my sake, you must be friends now. Shall I tell him to come up?"

"Here?" he said. "Into the parlour?"

"Where else?" she asked.

He looked **vexed**, and suggested the kitchen as a more suitable place for him. Mrs. Linton eyed him with a **droll** expression—half angry, half laughing at his **fastidiousness**.

"No," she added after a while, "I cannot sit in the kitchen. Set two tables here, Ellen: one for your master and Miss Isabella, being **gentry**, the other for Heathcliff and myself, being of the lower orders. Will that please you, dear? Or must I have a fire lighted elsewhere? If so, give directions. I'll run down and secure my guest. I'm afraid the joy is too great to be real!"

She was about to dart off again, but Edgar arrested her.

"*You* bid him step up," he said, addressing me, "and, Catherine, try to be glad without being absurd! The whole household need not witness the sight of your welcoming a runaway servant as a brother."

I **descended** and found Heathcliff waiting under the porch, evidently anticipating an invitation to enter. He

COUNTENANCE (<u>kown</u> tuh nuhns) *n.*
appearance, facial expression
Synonyms: face, features, visage
RETAIN (rih <u>tayn</u>) *v.* **-ing,-ed.**
to hold, keep possession of
Synonyms: withhold, reserve, maintain, remember
DEGRADATION (day greh <u>day</u> shuhn) *n.*
the act of falling in rank or status; the act of losing
moral or intellectual character
Synonyms: demotion; abasement, disgrace, shame
CIVILISED or CIVILIZED (<u>sih</u> vuhl iezd) *adj.*
humane, ethical; politely sophisticated
Synonyms: refined, cultivated; courteous, pleasant,
affable
LURK (luhrk) *v.* **-ing,-ed.**
to hide, to lie hidden or unsuspected; to prowl, sneak
Synonyms: conceal; stalk, creep, skulk, slink
DIVEST (dih <u>vehst</u>) (die <u>vehst</u>) *v.* **-ing,-ed.**
to take away one's possessions or character
Synonyms: deprive, strip, dispossess, remove

followed my guidance without waste of words, and I
ushered him into the presence of the master and mistress, whose flushed cheeks betrayed signs of warm
talking. But the lady's glowed with another feeling when
her friend appeared at the door: she sprang forward,
took both his hands, and led him to Linton; and then
she seized Linton's reluctant fingers and crushed them
into his. Now fully revealed by the fire and candlelight, I
was amazed, more than ever, to behold the transformation of Heathcliff. He had grown a tall, athletic,
well-formed man; beside whom, my master seemed quite
slender and youth-like. His upright <u>carriage</u> suggested
the idea of his having been in the army. His **countenance**
was much older in expression and decision of feature
than Mr. Linton's; it looked intelligent, and **retained** no
marks of former **degradation**. A half-**civilised** <u>ferocity</u>
lurked yet in the depressed brows and eyes full of black
fire, but it was subdued; and his manner was even dignified: quite **divested** of roughness, though too stern for
grace. My master's surprise equalled or exceeded mine:
he remained for a minute at a loss how to address the
ploughboy, as he had called him. Heathcliff dropped his
slight hand, and stood looking at him coolly till he chose
to speak.

"Sit down, sir," he said, at length. "Mrs. Linton, recalling old times, would have me give you a cordial reception;
and, of course, I am gratified when anything occurs to
please her."

"And I also," answered Heathcliff, "especially if it be
anything in which I have a part. I shall stay an hour or
two willingly."

He took a seat opposite Catherine, who kept her gaze
fixed on him as if she feared he would vanish were she to
remove it. He did not raise his to her often: a quick
glance now and then sufficed; but it flashed back, each
time more confidently, the undisguised delight he drank
from hers. They were too much absorbed in their mutual
joy to suffer embarrassment. Not so Mr. Edgar. He grew

EXECUTION (ehk sih <u>kyoo</u> shuhn) *n.*
1. the act of putting to death
   Synonyms: killing, suicide, murder
2. the act of performing or carrying out a task
   Synonyms: accomplishment, achievement

PROTRACT (proh <u>traakt</u>) *v.* **-ing,-ed.**
to prolong, draw out, extend
   Synonyms: lengthen, elongate, stretch

pale with pure annoyance, a feeling that reached its climax when his lady rose, and stepping across the rug, seized Heathcliff's hands again, and laughed like one beside herself.

"I shall think it a dream to-morrow!" she cried. "I shall not be able to believe that I have seen, and touched, and spoken to you once more. And yet, cruel Heathcliff! You don't deserve this welcome. To be absent and silent for three years, and never to think of me!"

"A little more than you have thought of me," he murmured. "I heard of your marriage, Cathy, not long since; and, while waiting in the yard below, I meditated this plan—just to have one glimpse of your face, a stare of surprise, perhaps, and pretended pleasure; afterwards settle my score with Hindley; and then prevent the law by doing **execution** on myself. Your welcome has put these ideas out of my mind, but beware of meeting me with another aspect next time! Nay, you'll not drive me off again. You were really sorry for me, were you? Well, there was cause. I've fought through a bitter life since I last heard your voice; and you must forgive me, for I struggled only for you!"

"Catherine, unless we are to have cold tea, please to come to the table," interrupted Linton, striving to preserve his ordinary tone, and a due measure of politeness. "Mr. Heathcliff will have a long walk, wherever he may lodge to-night; and I'm thirsty."

She took her post before the urn; and Miss Isabella came, summoned by the bell; then, having handed their chairs forward, I left the room. The meal hardly endured ten minutes. Catherine's cup was never filled: she could neither eat nor drink. Edgar had made a slop in his saucer, and scarcely swallowed a mouthful. Their guest did not **protract** his stay that evening above an hour longer. I asked, as he departed, if he went to Gimmerton?

"No, to Wuthering Heights," he answered. "Mr. Earnshaw invited me, when I called this morning."

PONDER (<u>pahn</u> duhr) *v.* **-ing,-ed.**
to consider or think about something in depth
Synonyms: contemplate, reflect, ruminate

HYPOCRITE (<u>hih</u> puh kriht) *n.*
person claiming beliefs or virtues he or she doesn't
really possess
Synonyms: fraud, liar, sham, fake, phony

PRESENTIMENT (prih <u>sehn</u> tih mehnt) *n.*
the anticipation or sense that something may happen
Synonyms: expectation, premonition

AFFIRM (uh <u>fihrm</u>) *v.* **-ing,-ed.**
to state positively, to assert as valid or confirmed
Synonyms: declare, avow, maintain

CONTRIVE (kuhn <u>triev</u>) *v.* **-ing,-ed.**
to devise, plan, or manage; to form in an artistic manner
Synonyms: concoct, scheme; create, design

COMMENDATION (kah mehn <u>day</u> shuhn) *n.*
an act of praise or a show of respect; an award; the
act of entrusting into someone's care
Synonyms: acclaim, approval, flattery; tribute,
reward; relegation, assignment

AVERSION (uh <u>vuhr</u> zhuhn) *n.*
intense dislike
Synonyms: antagonism, antipathy, abhorrence,
repulsion, repugnance

DAINTY (<u>dayn</u> tee) *adj.*
delicate, sweet
Synonyms: fine, graceful

CHASTISEMENT (<u>chaa</u> stiez mehnt) (chaa <u>stiez</u> mehnt) *n.*
punishment, discipline, scolding
Synonyms: castigation, penalty

Mr. Earnshaw invited *him!* And *he* called on Mr. Earnshaw! I **pondered** this sentence painfully, after he was gone. Is he turning out a bit of a **hypocrite**, and coming into the country to work mischief under a cloak? I mused: I had a **presentiment** in the bottom of my heart that he had better have remained away.

About the middle of the night, I was wakened from my first nap by Mrs. Linton gliding into my chamber, taking a seat on my bedside, and pulling me by the hair to rouse me.

"I cannot rest, Ellen," she said, by way of apology. "And I want some living creature to keep me company in my happiness! Edgar is sulky, because I'm glad of a thing that does not interest him. He refuses to open his mouth, except to utter <u>pettish</u>, silly speeches; and he **affirmed** I was cruel and selfish for wishing to talk when he was so sick and sleepy. He always **contrives** to be sick at the least cross! I gave a few sentences of **commendation** to Heathcliff, and he, either for a headache or a pang of envy, began to cry: so I got up and left him."

"What use is it praising Heathcliff to him?" I answered. "As lads they had an **aversion** to each other, and Heathcliff would hate just as much to hear him praised: it's human nature. Let Mr. Linton alone about him, unless you would like an open quarrel between them."

"But does it not show great weakness?" pursued she. "I'm not envious. I never feel hurt at the brightness of Isabella's yellow hair and the whiteness of her skin, at her **dainty** elegance, and the fondness all the family exhibit for her. Even you, Nelly, if we have a dispute sometimes, you back Isabella at once; and I yield like a foolish mother. I call her a darling, and flatter her into a good temper. It pleases her brother to see us cordial, and that pleases me. But they are very much alike: they are spoiled children, and fancy the world was made for their accommodation; and though I humour both, I think a smart **chastisement** might improve them, all the same."

INDULGE (ihn <u>duhlj</u>) *v.* **-ing,-ed.**
  to give in to a craving or desire
    Synonyms: humor, gratify, allow, pamper

OBSTINATE (<u>ahb</u> stih nuht) *adj.*
  stubborn
    Synonyms: headstrong, stiff-necked, bullheaded,
    pigheaded, mulish

TRIFLE (<u>trie</u> fuhl) *n.*
  something of slight worth or little importance
    Synonyms: triviality, novelty, trinket

PRUDENTLY (<u>proo</u> dehnt lee) *adv.*
  carefully, cautiously
    Synonyms: pragmatically, judiciously, sensibly

"You're mistaken, Mrs. Linton," said I. "They humour you. I know what there would be to do if they did not. You can well afford to **indulge** their passing whims as long as their business is to anticipate all your desires. You may, however, fall out, at last, over something of equal consequence to both sides; and then those you term weak are very capable of being as **obstinate** as you."

"And then we shall fight to the death, shan't we, Nelly?" she returned, laughing. "No! I tell you, I have such faith in Linton's love, that I believe I might kill him, and he wouldn't wish to retaliate."

I advised her to value him the more for his affection.

"I do," she answered, "but he needn't resort to whining for **trifles**. It is childish; and, instead of melting into tears because I said that Heathcliff was now worthy of any one's regard, and it would honour the first gentleman in the country to be his friend, he ought to have said it for me, and been delighted from sympathy. He must get accustomed to him, and he may as well like him: considering how Heathcliff has reason to object to him, I'm sure he behaved excellently!"

"What do you think of his going to Wuthering Heights?" I inquired. "He is reformed in every respect, apparently—quite a Christian—offering the right hand of fellowship to his enemies all around!"

"He explained it," she replied. "I wondered as much as you. He said he called to gather information concerning me from you, supposing you resided there still; and Joseph told Hindley, who came out and fell to questioning him of what he had been doing, and how he had been living; and finally, desired him to walk in. There were some persons sitting at cards; Heathcliff joined them; my brother lost some money to him, and, finding him plentifully supplied, he requested that he would come again in the evening: to which he consented. Hindley is too reckless to select his acquaintance **prudently**: he doesn't trouble himself to reflect on the causes he might have for mistrusting one

BASELY (<u>bays</u> lee) *adv.*
without qualities of higher mind or spirit
Synonyms: vulgarly, corruptly, immorally, menially

AFFIRM (uh <u>fihrm</u>) *v.* **-ing,-ed.** *(See page 192.)*

LIBERAL (<u>lihb</u> uh ruhl) (<u>lihb</u> ruhl) *adj.*
generous, lavish; tolerant, broad-minded
Synonyms: bounteous, munificent; progressive, permissive

COVETOUSNESS (<u>kuh</u> vih tuhs nehs) *n.*
the strong desire to possess something had by another
Synonyms: envy, craving

RECONCILE (<u>reh</u> kuhn siel) *v.* **-ing,-ed.**
1. to bring to accept
Synonyms: resign, submit, placate, pacify, appease
2. to resolve a dispute
Synonyms: agree, accommodate, rectify, reunite

PETULANCE (<u>peh</u> chuh luhnts) *n.*
rudeness, peevishness
Synonyms: irritability, querulousness, testiness, fretfulness

INDUCE (ih <u>doos</u>) (ihn <u>dyoos</u>) *v.* **-ing,-ed.**
to persuade; bring about
Synonyms: convince, prevail; effect, lead, occasion

ALLEVIATION (uh lee vee <u>ay</u> shuhn) *n.*
relief, a partial improvement
Synonyms: assuagement, mitigation, quelling

ARDENTLY (<u>ahr</u> dihnt lee) *adv.*
passionately, enthusiastically, fervently
Synonyms: intensely, vehemently

PROVOKE (proh <u>vohk</u>) *v.* **-ing,-ed.** *(See page 174.)*

COMPLACENT (kuhm <u>play</u> sihnt) *adj.*
self-satisfied
Synonyms: contented, unconcerned

RESOLUTION (reh suh <u>loo</u> shuhn) *n.* *(See page 140.)*

ABJURE (aab <u>joor</u>) *v.* **-ing,-ed.**
to abandon or give up; to renounce solemnly
Synonyms: quit, surrender; reject, recant, forswear

EXUBERANCE (ihg <u>zoo</u> buhr uhnts) *n.*
an excessive quantity or supply
Synonyms: abundance, plenty, overflow

VIVACITY (vih <u>vahs</u> ih tee) *n.*
liveliness, spiritedness
Synonyms: vibrance, zest

whom he has **basely** injured. But Heathcliff **affirms** his principal reason for resuming a connection with his ancient persecutor is a wish to install himself in quarters at walking distance from the Grange, and an attachment to the house where we lived together, and likewise a hope that I shall have more opportunities of seeing him there than I could have if he settled in Gimmerton. He means to offer **liberal** payment for permission to lodge at the Heights; and doubtless my brother's **covetousness** will prompt him to accept the terms. He was always greedy, though what he grasps with one hand he flings away with the other."

"It's a nice place for a young man to fix his dwelling in!" said I. "Have you no fear of the consequences, Mrs. Linton?"

"None for my friend," she replied. "His strong head will keep him from danger; a little for Hindley: but he can't be made morally worse than he is; and I stand between him and bodily harm. The event of this evening has **reconciled** me to God and humanity! I had risen in angry rebellion against Providence. Oh, I've endured very, very bitter misery, Nelly! If that creature knew how bitter, he'd be ashamed to cloud its removal with idle **petulance**. It was kindness for him which **induced** me to it alone. Had I expressed the agony I frequently felt, he would have been taught to long for its **alleviation** as **ardently** as I. However, it's over, and I'll take no revenge on his folly; I can afford to suffer anything hereafter! Should the meanest thing alive slap me on the cheek, I'd not only turn the other, but I'd ask pardon for **provoking** it; and, as a proof, I'll go make my peace with Edgar instantly. Good-night! I'm an angel!"

In this self-**complacent** conviction she departed; and the success of her fulfilled **resolution** was obvious on the morrow: Mr. Linton had not only **abjured** his <u>peevishness</u> (though his spirits seemed still subdued by Catherine's **exuberance** of **vivacity**), but he ventured no objection to her taking Isabella with her to Wuthering Heights in the

PERPETUAL (puhr <u>peht</u> chyoo uhl) *adj. (See page 72.)*

JUDICIOUS (joo <u>dih</u> shuhs) *adj.*
   sensible, showing good judgment
      Synonyms: prudent, sagacious, sapient, circumspect

MODERATE (<u>mahd</u> uhr ayt) *v.* **-ing,-ed.**
   to make less excessive, restrain
      Synonyms: lessen, abate, qualify, temper, mitigate

RETAIN (rih <u>tayn</u>) *v.* **-ing,-ed.** *(See page 188.)*

DIVERT (die <u>vuhrt</u>) *v.* **-ing,-ed.** *(See page 118.)*

EVINCE (ih <u>vihns</u>) *v.* **-ing,-ed.**
   to show clearly or display
      Synonyms: express, exhibit, demonstrate, manifest

KEEN *adj.*
   intellectually sharp, perceptive; having a sharp edge
      Synonyms: acute, quick, canny; pointed, razorlike

APPALL (uh <u>pahl</u>) *v.* **-ing,-ed.**
   to overcome with shock or dismay
      Synonyms: horrify, astound, petrify

DEGRADATION (day greh <u>day</u> shuhn) *n. (See page 188.)*

DISPOSITION (dihs puh <u>zih</u> shuhn) *n.*
   mood or temperament
      Synonyms: behavior, tendency, inclination, nature

REVOLT (rih <u>vohlt</u>) *v.* **-ing,-ed.**
   to fill with repugnance, disgust, or dislike
      Synonyms: offend, shock, sicken, repel

FOREBODINGLY (fohr <u>boh</u> dihng lee) *adv.*
   in an ominous manner
      Synonyms: apprehensively, suspiciously

UNSOLICITED (uhn suh <u>lih</u> sih tihd) *adj.*
   not requested
      Synonyms: unwelcome, voluntary, unsought

BESTOW (bih <u>stoh</u>) *v.* **-ing,-ed.** *(See page 56.)*

RECIPROCATION (rih sihp ruh <u>kay</u> shuhn) *n.*
   mutual back-and-forth interaction
      Synonyms: interchange, exchange, give-and-take

SENTIMENT (<u>sehn</u> tuh muhnt) *n.*
   an attitude, thought, or judgment prompted by
   feeling; a romantic or nostalgic feeling
      Synonyms: idea; emotion

afternoon; and she rewarded him with such a summer of sweetness and affection in return, as made the house a paradise for several days; both master and servants profiting from the **perpetual** sunshine.

Heathcliff—Mr. Heathcliff I should say in future— used the liberty of visiting at Thrushcross Grange cautiously, at first: he seemed estimating how far its owner would bear his intrusion. Catherine, also, deemed it **judicious** to **moderate** her expressions of pleasure in receiving him; and he gradually established his right to be expected. He **retained** a great deal of the reserve for which his boyhood was remarkable; and that served to repress all startling demonstrations of feeling. My master's uneasiness experienced a lull, and further circumstances **diverted** it into another channel for a space.

His new source of trouble sprang from the not-anticipated misfortune of Isabella Linton **evincing** a sudden and irresistible attraction towards the tolerated guest. She was at that time a charming young lady of eighteen; infantile in manners, though possessed of **keen** wit, **keen** feelings, and a **keen** temper, too, if irritated. Her brother, who loved her tenderly, was **appalled** at this fantastic preference. Leaving aside the **degradation** of an alliance with a nameless man, and the possible fact that his property, in default of heirs male, might pass into such a one's power, he had sense to comprehend Heathcliff's **disposition**: to know that, though his exterior was altered, his mind was unchangeable and unchanged. And he dreaded that mind: it **revolted** him. He shrank **forebodingly** from the idea of committing Isabella to his keeping. He would have recoiled still more had he been aware that her attachment rose **unsolicited**, and was **bestowed** where it awakened no **reciprocation** of **sentiment**; for the minute he discovered its existence, he laid the blame on Heathcliff's deliberate designing.

We had all remarked, during some time, that Miss Linton fretted and pined over something. She grew cross

VEX (vehks) *v.* **-ing,-ed.**
   to irritate, annoy; confuse, puzzle
   Synonyms: bother, plague, afflict, irk; perplex, perturb
FRIVOLOUS (<u>frihv</u> uh luhs) *adj.*
   petty, trivial; flippant, silly
   Synonyms: inconsequential, worthless; frothy, light,
   vapid
PEREMPTORILY (puhr <u>ehm</u> tohr uh lee) *adv.*
   absolutely, in a commanding manner
   Synonyms: urgently, imperatively, decisively

SAUNTER (<u>sawn</u> tuhr) *v.* **-ing,-ed.**
   to walk leisurely or amble
   Synonyms: stroll, ramble, perambulate

SUPERFLUOUS (soo <u>puhr</u> floo uhs) *adj.*
   extra, more than necessary
   Synonyms: excess, spare, supernumerary, surplus

and wearisome; snapping at and teasing Catherine continually, at the imminent risk of exhausting her limited patience. We excused her, to a certain extent, on the plea of ill-health. She was dwindling and fading before our eyes. But one day, when she had been peculiarly wayward, rejecting her breakfast, complaining that the servants did not do what she told them; that the mistress would allow her to be nothing in the house, and Edgar neglected her that she had caught a cold with the doors being left open, and we let the parlour fire go out on purpose to **vex** her, with a hundred yet more **frivolous** accusations, Mrs. Linton **peremptorily** insisted that she should get to bed; and, having scolded her heartily, threatened to send for the doctor. Mention of Kenneth caused her to exclaim, instantly, that her health was perfect, and it was only Catherine's harshness which made her unhappy.

"How can you say I am harsh, you naughty <u>fondling</u>?" cried the mistress, amazed at the unreasonable assertion. "You are surely losing your reason. When have I been harsh, tell me?"

"Yesterday," sobbed Isabella, "and now!"

"Yesterday!" said her sister-in-law. "On what occasion?"

"In our walk along the moor, you told me to ramble where I pleased, while you **sauntered** on with Mr. Heathcliff!"

"And that's your notion of harshness?" said Catherine, laughing. "It was no hint that your company was **superfluous**. We didn't care whether you kept with us or not. I merely thought Heathcliff's talk would have nothing entertaining for your ears."

"Oh, no," wept the young lady, "you wished me away, because you knew I liked to be there!"

"Is she sane?" asked Mrs. Linton, appealing to me. "I'll repeat our conversation, word for word, Isabella, and you point out any charm it could have had for you."

"I don't mind the conversation," she answered. "I wanted to be with—"

KINDLE (<u>kihn</u> duhl) *v.* **-ing,-ed.**
  to excite or inspire; to set fire to or ignite
    Synonyms: arouse, awaken; light, spark
IMPERTINENT (ihm <u>puhr</u> tuh nuhnt) *adj.*
  rude, audacious; improper
    Synonyms: forward, bold; impolite, discourteous
COVET (<u>kuh</u> viht) *v.* **-ing,-ed.**
  to desire strongly (something possessed by another)
    Synonyms: envy, crave
INFATUATED (ihn <u>faach</u> oo ay tihd) *adj.*
  strongly or foolishly attached to, inspired with foolish
  passion, or overly in love
    Synonyms: besotted, enthralled, smitten, enamored
ARID (<u>aa</u> rihd) *adj.*
  extremely dry; lacking in interest
    Synonyms: thirsty, desiccated, parched; dull,
    lackluster
BESTOW (bih <u>stoh</u>) *v.* **-ing,-ed.**
  to give as a gift; to apply or devote, as in time or effort
    Synonyms: endow, confer, present; allocate, dedicate
DEPLORABLE (dih <u>plohr</u> uh buhl) *adj.*
  woeful; strongly regrettable or condemnable
    Synonyms: unfortunate, lamentable, pitiful; wretched
BENEVOLENCE (buh <u>neh</u> vuh luhnts) *n.*
  kindness, compassion
    Synonyms: charity, altruism, generosity
RUSTIC (<u>ruh</u> stihk) 1. *n.* 2. *adj.*
  1. a rural person with a simplistic character
    Synonyms: bumpkin, hick, clod, countryman
  2. simple and unsophisticated; typical of country life
    Synonyms: unrefined, crude; bucolic, pastoral
AVARICE (<u>aa</u> vuhr ihs) *n.*
  greed
    Synonyms: cupidity, rapacity
INDIGNATION (ihn dihg <u>nay</u> shun) *n.*
  anger caused by something mean or unjust
    Synonyms: fury, ire, wrath

"Well!" said Catherine, perceiving her hesitate to complete the sentence.

"With him, and I won't be always sent off!" she continued, **kindling** up. "You are a dog in the manger, Cathy, and desire no one to be loved but yourself!"

"You are an **impertinent** little monkey!" exclaimed Mrs. Linton, in surprise. "But I'll not believe this idiocy! It is impossible that you can **covet** the admiration of Heathcliff—that you consider him an agreeable person! I hope I have misunderstood you, Isabella?"

"No, you have not," said the **infatuated** girl. "I love him more than ever you loved Edgar; and he might love me, if you would let him!"

"I wouldn't be you for a kingdom, then!" Catherine declared emphatically, and she seemed to speak sincerely. "Nelly, help me to convince her of her madness. Tell her what Heathcliff is—an unreclaimed creature, without refinement, without cultivation—an **arid** wilderness of <u>furze</u> and whinstone. I'd as soon put that little canary into the park on a winter's day, as recommend you to **bestow** your heart on him! It is **deplorable** ignorance of his character, child, and nothing else, which makes that dream enter your head. Pray, don't imagine that he conceals depths of **benevolence** and affection beneath a stern exterior! He's not a rough diamond—a pearl-containing oyster of a **rustic**: he's a fierce, pitiless, wolfish man. I never say to him, 'Let this or that enemy alone, because it would be ungenerous or cruel to harm them.' I say, 'Let them alone, because *I* should hate them to be wronged.' And he'd crush you like a sparrow's egg, Isabella, if he found you a troublesome charge. I know he couldn't love a Linton; and yet he'd be quite capable of marrying your fortune and expectations! **Avarice** is growing with him a <u>besetting</u> sin. There's my picture: and I'm his friend—so much so, that had he thought seriously to catch you, I should, perhaps, have held my tongue, and let you fall into his trap."

Miss Linton regarded her sister-in-law with **indignation**.

RETORT (rih <u>tohrt</u>) *v.* **-ing,-ed.**
    to make a cutting response
        Synonyms: retaliate, talk back, counter
INSOLENCE (<u>ihn</u> suh luhnts) *n.*
    a tendency to be insulting; arrogance
        Synonyms: audacity, rudeness, presumption,
        impertinence; superiority, haughtiness
EGOTISM (<u>ee</u> goh tihz uhm) *n.*
    the belief that things are centered around oneself
        Synonyms: conceit, narcissism, selfishness
BLIGHT (bliet) *v.* **-ing,-ed.**
    to afflict, destroy
        Synonyms: damage, plague
CONSOLATION (kahn suh <u>lay</u> shuhn) *n.*
    something providing comfort or solace for a loss or
    hardship
        Synonym: condolence
BANISH (<u>baan</u> ish) *v.* **-ing,-ed.**
    to force to leave, exile
        Synonyms: expel, deport
ABHOR (uhb <u>hohr</u>) *v.* **-ring,-red.**
    to loathe, detest, despise
        Synonyms: hate, condemn, abominate, execrate

BRAZENED (<u>bray</u> zihnd) *adj.*
    shameless, defiant
        Synonyms: brash, audacious, forward

"For shame! For shame!" she repeated angrily. "You are worse than twenty foes, you poisonous friend!"

"Ah! You won't believe me, then?" said Catherine. "You think I speak from wicked selfishness?"

"I'm certain you do," **retorted** Isabella, "and I shudder at you!"

"Good!" cried the other. "Try for yourself if that be your spirit. I have done, and yield the argument to your saucy **insolence**."

"And I must suffer for her **egotism**!" she sobbed, as Mrs. Linton left the room. "All, all is against me; she has **blighted** my single **consolation**. But she uttered falsehoods, didn't she? Mr. Heathcliff is not a fiend. He has an honourable soul, and a true one, or how could he remember her?"

"**Banish** him from your thoughts, Miss," I said. "He's a bird of bad omen: no mate for you. Mrs. Linton spoke strongly, and yet I can't contradict her. She is better acquainted with his heart than I, or any one besides; and she would never represent him as worse than he is. Honest people don't hide their deeds. How has he been living? How has he got rich? Why is he staying at Wuthering Heights, the house of a man whom he **abhors**? They say Mr. Earnshaw is worse and worse since he came. They sit up all night together continually, and Hindley has been borrowing money on his land, and does nothing but play and drink. I heard only a week ago—it was Joseph who told me—I met him at Gimmerton.

"'Nelly,' he said, 'we's hae a crowner's 'quest enow, at ahr folks. One on 'em's a'most gotten his fingers cut off wi' hauding t'others fro' stickin hisseln loike a cawlf. That's maister, yah knaw, 'at's soa up o' going tub t' grand 'sizes. He's noan feared o't' bench o' judges, norther Paul, nur Peter, nur John, nur Matthew, nor noan on 'em, not he! He fair likes—he langs to set his **brazened** face agean 'em! And yon <u>bonny</u> lad Heathcliff, yah mind, he's a rare 'un! He can girn a laugh as well's onybody at a raight divil's jest. Does he niver say nowt of his fine living

205

MALEVOLENCE (muh <u>lehv</u> uh luhnts) *n.*
  ill-will; evil or harm done to hurt others
    Synonyms: spite; malice, malignance
PERSEVERE (pehr suh <u>veer</u>) *v.* **-ing,-ed.**
  to continue with determination, remain steadfast
    Synonyms: persist, endure, plod
PERPETUALLY (puhr <u>peht</u> chyoo uh lee) *adv.*
  endlessly, always
    Synonyms: continuously, constantly, eternally,
    perennially
OBLIGE (uh <u>bliej</u>) *v.* **-ing,-ed.**
  to be obligated, to require or force someone to obey
    Synonyms: compel, constrain, bind, favor
INDISCRETION (ihn dih <u>skrehsh</u> uhn) *n.*
  lack of good judgment, injudiciousness
    Synonyms: thoughtlessness, misjudgment
DISCLOSURE (dihs <u>kloh</u> shuhr) *n.*
  exposure, divulgence
    Synonyms: confession, revelation, impartance
TRANSIENT (<u>traan</u> see uhnt) *adj.*
  temporary, short-lived, fleeting
    Synonyms: transitory, ephemeral, fugitive,
    momentary, evanescent
INCLINE (ihn <u>klien</u>) *v.* **-ing,-ed.**
  to have a specific tendency, to be predisposed
    Synonyms: lean to, influence, impel, prefer
PRACTICABLE (<u>praak</u> tih kuh buhl) *adj.*
  possible, capable of being performed by the
  means employed
    Synonyms: sane, prudent, doable, viable

amang us, when he goes t' Grange? This is t' way on't: up at sundown: dice, brandy, cloised shutters, und can'le-light till next day at noon: then, t' fooil gangs banning un raving to his cham'er, makking dacent fowks dig thur fingers i' thur lugs fur varry shame; un' the knave, why he can caint his brass, un ate, un sleep, un off to his neighbour's to gossip wi' t' wife. I' course, he tells Dame Catherine how her fathur's goold runs into his pocket, and her father's son gallops down t' broad road, while he flees afore to oppen t' pikes?' Now, Miss Linton, Joseph is an old rascal, but no liar, and, if his account of Heathcliff's conduct be true, you would never think of desiring such a husband, would you?"

"You are leagued with the rest, Ellen!" she replied. "I'll not listen to your slanders. What **malevolence** you must have to wish to convince me that there is no happiness in the world!"

Whether she would have got over this fancy if left to herself, or **persevered** in nursing it **perpetually**, I cannot say. She had little time to reflect. The day after, there was a justice-meeting at the next town; my master was **obliged** to attend; and Mr. Heathcliff, aware of his absence, called rather earlier than usual. Catherine and Isabella were sitting in the library, on hostile terms, but silent. The latter alarmed at her recent **indiscretion**, and the **disclosure** she had made of her secret feelings in a **transient** fit of passion; the former, on mature consideration, really offended with her companion; and, if she laughed again at her pertness, **inclined** to make it no laughing matter to *her*. She did laugh as she saw Heathcliff pass the window. I was sweeping the hearth, and I noticed a mischievous smile on her lips. Isabella, absorbed in her meditations, or a book, remained till the door opened; and it was too late to attempt an escape, which she would gladly have done had it been **practicable**.

"Come in, that's right!" exclaimed the mistress gaily, pulling a chair to the fire. "Here are two people sadly in need of a third to thaw the ice between them; and you are

DOTE (doht) *v.* **-ing,-ed.**
to lavish attention, to love to excess
Synonyms: adore, cherish, tender
FEIGNED (faynd) *adj.*
not real, fictional
Synonyms: fake, counterfeit, insincere
CONFOUNDED (kuhn <u>fown</u> dihd) *adj.*
baffled, perplexed
Synonyms: overwhelmed, confused, disconcerted,
entangled, muddled
INDIGNANTLY (ihn <u>dihg</u> nuhnt lee) *adv.*
angrily
Synonyms: furiously, irately, madly, irefully
OBLIVION (oh <u>blih</u> vee uhn) *n.*
the state of being forgotten; lack of awareness
Synonyms: nothingness, nowhere, nonexistence;
mindlessness, forgetfulness, indifference
DISDAIN (dihs <u>dayn</u>) *v.* **-ing,-ed.**
to scorn; to reject as inferior
Synonyms: disrespect, disparage, despise, condemn;
dismiss, renounce
ADHERE (aad <u>heer</u>) *v.* **-ing,-ed.**
to cling or follow without deviation
Synonyms: cleave, stick
INDIFFERENT (ihn <u>dihf</u> ruhnt) (ihn <u>dihf</u> uhr uhnt) *adj.*
uncaring, unbiased
Synonyms: unconcerned, uncurious, detached,
uninterested, apathetic
SENTIMENT (<u>sehn</u> tuh muhnt) *n. (See page 198.)*
EVINCE (ih <u>vihns</u>) *v.* **-ing,-ed.**
to show clearly or display
Synonyms: express, exhibit, demonstrate, manifest
BELIE (bih <u>lie</u>) *v.* **belying,-ied.**
to misrepresent, expose as false
Synonyms: distort, refute

the very one we should both of us choose. Heathcliff, I'm proud to show you, at last, somebody that **dotes** on you more than myself. I expect you to feel flattered. Nay, it's not Nelly, don't look at her! My poor little sister-in-law is breaking her heart by mere contemplation of your physical and moral beauty. It lies in your own power to be Edgar's brother! No, no, Isabella, you shan't run off," she continued, arresting, with **feigned** playfulness, the **confounded** girl, who had risen **indignantly**. "We were quarrelling like cats about you, Heathcliff; and I was fairly beaten in protestations of devotion and admiration: and, moreover, I was informed that if I would but have the manners to stand aside, my rival, as she will have herself to be, would shoot a shaft into your soul that would fix you for ever, and send my image into eternal **oblivion**!"

"Catherine!" said Isabella, calling up her dignity, and **disdaining** to struggle from the tight grasp that held her. "I'd thank you to **adhere** to the truth and not slander me, even in joke! Mr. Heathcliff, be kind enough to bid this friend of yours release me—she forgets that you and I are not intimate acquaintances, and what amuses her is painful to me beyond expression."

As the guest answered nothing, but took his seat, and looked thoroughly **indifferent** what **sentiments** she cherished concerning him, she turned and whispered an earnest appeal for liberty to her tormentor.

"By no means!" cried Mrs. Linton in answer. "I won't be named a dog in the manger again. You *shall* stay. Now then! Heathcliff, why don't you **evince** satisfaction at my pleasant news? Isabella swears that the love Edgar has for me is nothing to that she entertains for you. I'm sure she made some speech of the kind. Did she not, Ellen? And she has fasted ever since the day before yesterday's walk, from sorrow and rage that I <u>despatched</u> her out of your society under the idea of its being unacceptable."

"I think you **belie** her," said Heathcliff, twisting his chair to face them. "She wishes to be out of my society now, at any rate!"

DISCOURSE (<u>dihs</u> kohrs) *n.*
the verbal interchange of ideas; a formal, orderly, and extended expression of thought
Synonyms: dialogue, conversation; speech

REPULSIVE (rih <u>puhl</u> sihv) *adj.*
repellant; sickening, disgusting
Synonyms: offensive; nauseating

AVERSION (uh <u>vuhr</u> zhuhn) *n.*
intense dislike
Synonyms: antagonism, antipathy, abhorrence, repulsion, repugnance

DETAINER (dih <u>tayn</u> uhr) (dee <u>tayn</u> uhr) *n.*
one that holds; one that restrains
Synonyms: apprehender, keeper; inhibitor

TALON (<u>taa</u> luhn) *n.*
claw of an animal, especially a bird of prey
Synonyms: nail, hook

EXECUTION (ehk sih <u>kyoo</u> shuhn) *n.*
1. the act of putting to death
Synonyms: killing, suicide, murder
2. the act of performing or carrying out a task
Synonyms: accomplishment, achievement

DELUGE (<u>dehl</u> yooj) (<u>dehl</u> yoozh) (<u>day</u> looj) (<u>day</u> loozh) (dih <u>looj</u>) (dih <u>loozh</u>) *n.*
something that overwhelms; a great flood or rain
· Synonyms: submergence, immersion, inundation; downpour

MITIGATE (<u>miht</u> ih gayt) *v.* **-ing,-ed.**
to soften, make milder
Synonyms: moderate, alleviate, assuage, lighten, palliate

MAWKISH (<u>maw</u> kihsh) *adj.*
sickeningly sentimental
Synonyms: maudlin, insipid, bathetic, saccharine, weepy

DETESTABLY (dee <u>tehst</u> uh blee) *adv.*
in a manner deserving of intense and violent hatred
Synonyms: disgustingly, despicably, grossly

210

And he stared hard at the object of **discourse**, as one might do at a strange **repulsive** animal: a centipede from the Indies, for instance, which curiosity leads one to examine in spite of the **aversion** it raises. The poor thing couldn't bear that. She grew white and red in rapid succession, and, while tears beaded her lashes, bent the strength of her small fingers to loosen the firm clutch of Catherine; and perceiving that as fast as she raised one finger off her arm another closed down, and she could not remove the whole together, she began to make use of her nails; and their sharpness presently ornamented the **detainer's** with crescents of red.

"There's a tigress!" exclaimed Mrs. Linton, setting her free, and shaking her hand with pain. "Begone, for God's sake, and hide your vixen face! How foolish to reveal those **talons** to *him*. Can't you fancy the conclusions he'll draw? Look, Heathcliff! They are instruments that will do **execution**—you must beware of your eyes."

"I'd wrench them off her fingers, if they ever menaced me," he answered brutally, when the door had closed after her. "But what did you mean by teasing the creature in that manner, Cathy? You were not speaking the truth, were you?"

"I assure you I was," she returned. "She has been dying for your sake several weeks; and raving about you this morning, and pouring forth a **deluge** of abuse, because I represented your failings in a plain light, for the purpose of **mitigating** her adoration. But don't notice it further: I wished to punish her sauciness, that's all. I like her too well, my dear Heathcliff, to let you absolutely seize and devour her up."

"And I like her too ill to attempt it," said he, "except in a very ghoulish fashion. You'd hear of odd things if I lived alone with that **mawkish**, waxen face: the most ordinary would be painting on its white the colours of the rainbow, and turning the blue eyes black, every day or two: they **detestably** resemble Linton's."

DELECTABLY (dih <u>lehkt</u> uh blee) *adv.*
appetizingly, deliciously, pleasantly
Synonyms: delightfully, succulently, palatably

COVET (<u>kuh</u> viht) *v.* **-ing,-ed.**
to desire strongly (something possessed by another)
Synonyms: envy, crave

OMINOUS (<u>ah</u> mihn uhs) *adj.*
menacing, threatening, indicating misfortune
Synonyms: inauspicious, unpropitious, sinister, dire, baleful

CLEAVE (kleev) *v.* **-ing,-ed.**
to stick, cling, adhere; to split or separate
Synonyms: cohere, bond; sunder, dissever

FORSAKE (fohr <u>sayk</u>) *v.* **-saking,-sook,-saken.**
to abandon, withdraw from
Synonyms: desert, renounce, leave, quit

"**Delectably!**" observed Catherine. "They are dove's eyes—angel's!"

"She's her brother's heir, is she not?" he asked, after a brief silence.

"I should be sorry to think so," returned his companion. "Half-a-dozen nephews shall erase her title, please Heaven! Abstract your mind from the subject at present. You are too prone to **covet** your neighbour's goods. Remember *this* neighbour's goods are mine."

"If they were *mine*, they would be none the less that," said Heathcliff. "But though Isabella Linton may be silly, she is scarcely mad; and, in short, we'll dismiss the matter, as you advise."

From their tongues they did dismiss it; and Catherine, probably, from her thoughts. The other, I felt certain, recalled it often in the course of the evening. I saw him smile to himself—grin rather—and lapse into **ominous** musing whenever Mrs. Linton had occasion to be absent from the apartment.

I determined to watch his movements. My heart invariably **cleaved** to the master's, in preference to Catherine's side: with reason I imagined, for he was kind, and trustful, and honourable; and she—she could not be called the *opposite*, yet she seemed to allow herself such wide latitude, that I had little faith in her principles, and still less sympathy for her feelings. I wanted something to happen which might have the effect of freeing both Wuthering Heights and the Grange of Mr. Heathcliff, leaving us as we had been prior to his <u>advent</u>. His visits were a continual nightmare to me; and, I suspected, to my master also. His <u>abode</u> at the Heights was an oppression past explaining. I felt that God had **forsaken** the stray sheep there to its own wicked wanderings, and an evil beast prowled between it and the <u>fold</u>, waiting his time to spring and destroy.

COMPLY (kuhm <u>plie</u>) *v.* **-ing,-ied.**
  to yield or agree, to go along with
    Synonyms: accord, submit, acquiesce, obey, respect
IMPULSE (<u>ihm</u> puhls) *n.*
  sudden tendency, inclination
    Synonyms: urge, whim

Chapter 11

Sometimes, while meditating on these things in solitude, I've got up in a sudden terror, and put on my bonnet to go see how all was at the farm. I've persuaded my conscience that it was a duty to warn him how people talked regarding his ways; and then I've recollected his confirmed bad habits, and, hopeless of benefiting him, have flinched from re-entering the dismal house, doubting if I could bear to be taken at my word.

One time I passed the old gate, going out of my way, on a journey to Gimmerton. It was about the period that my narrative has reached: a bright frosty afternoon; the ground bare, and the road hard and dry. I came to a stone where the highway branches off on to the moor at your left hand; a rough sand-pillar, with the letters W. H. cut on its north side, on the east, G., and on the southwest, T. G. It serves as a guide-post to the Grange, the Heights, and village. The sun shone yellow on its grey head, reminding me of summer, and I cannot say why, but all at once, a gush of child's sensations flowed into my heart. Hindley and I held it a favourite spot twenty years before. I gazed long at the weather-worn block, and, stooping down, perceived a hole near the bottom still full of snail-shells and pebbles, which we were fond of storing there with more perishable things; and, as fresh as reality, it appeared that I beheld my early playmate seated on the withered turf: his dark, square head bent forward, and his little hand scooping out the earth with a piece of slate. "Poor Hindley!" I exclaimed involuntarily. I started: my bodily eye was cheated into a momentary belief that the child lifted its face and stared straight into mine! It vanished in a twinkling; but immediately I felt an irresistible yearning to be at the Heights. Superstition urged me to **comply** with this **impulse**.

215

AGITATED (<u>aa</u> gih tay tihd) *adj.*
    upset or uneasy
        Synonyms: disturbed, flustered, bothered

APPARITION (aa puh <u>rih</u> shuhn) *n.*
    a ghostly figure; an unexpected or unusual sight
        Synonyms: spirit, specter; illusion

RUDDY (<u>ruh</u> dee) *adj.*
    healthily reddish or rosy
        Synonyms: flushed, sanguine, fresh, pinkish

COUNTENANCE (<u>kown</u> tuh nuhns) *n.*
    appearance, facial expression
        Synonyms: face, features, visage

MALIGNITY (muh <u>lihg</u> nih tee) *n.*
    evil or aggressive malice; something that produces death
        Synonyms: bitterness, resentment; malevolence

PROPITIATE (pruh <u>pih</u> shee ayt) *v.* **-ing,-ed.**
    to make peace with or appease
        Synonyms: conciliate, content, alleviate, ease

Supposing he should be dead! I thought—or should die soon! Supposing it were a sign of death! The nearer I got to the house the more **agitated** I grew; and on catching sight of it I trembled in every limb. The **apparition** had outstripped me: it stood looking through the gate. That was my first idea on observing an elf-locked, brown-eyed boy setting his **ruddy countenance** against the bars. Further reflection suggested this must be Hareton, *my* Hareton, not altered greatly since I left him, ten months since.

"God bless thee, darling!" I cried, forgetting instantaneously my foolish fears. "Hareton, it's Nelly! Nelly, thy nurse."

He retreated out of arm's length, and picked up a large flint.

"I am come to see thy father, Hareton," I added, guessing from the action that Nelly, if she lived in his memory at all, was not recognised as one with me.

He raised his missile to hurl it. I commenced a soothing speech, but could not stay his hand. The stone struck my bonnet; and then <u>ensued</u>, from the stammering lips of the little fellow, a string of curses, which, whether he comprehended them or not, were delivered with practised emphasis, and distorted his baby features into a shocking expression of **malignity**. You may be certain this grieved more than angered me. Fit to cry, I took an orange from my pocket, and offered it to **propitiate** him. He hesitated, and then snatched it from my hold; as if he fancied I only intended to tempt and disappoint him. I showed another, keeping it out of his reach.

"Who has taught you those fine words, my <u>bairn</u>?" I inquired. "The <u>curate</u>?"

"Damn the <u>curate</u>, and thee! Gie me that," he replied.

"Tell us where you got your lessons, and you shall have it," said I. "Who's your master?"

"Devil daddy," was his answer.

"And what do you learn from daddy?" I continued.

GAIT (gayt) *n.*
    the way one moves on foot, a manner of walking
        Synonyms: tread, walk, march, pace

RESOLVE (rih <u>sahlv</u>) *v.* **-ing,-ed.**
    to determine or to make a firm decision about
        Synonyms: solve, decide
VIGILANT (<u>vih</u> juh lehnt) *adj.*
    attentive, watchful
        Synonyms: alert, aware, careful, wary, guarded
THWART (thwahrt) *v.* **-ing,-ed.**
    to block or prevent from happening; to frustrate
        Synonyms: oppose, defeat, foil, balk; hinder, baffle

He jumped at the fruit; I raised it higher. "What does he teach you?" I asked.

"<u>Naught</u>," said he, "but to keep out of his **gait**. Daddy cannot bide me, because I swear at him."

"Ah! And the devil teaches you to swear at daddy?" I observed.

"Ah—nay," he drawled.

"Who then?"

"Heathcliff."

I asked if he liked Mr. Heathcliff.

"Ay!" he answered again.

Desiring to have his reasons for liking him, I could only gather the sentences—"I known't: he pays dad back what he gies to me—he curses daddy for cursing me. He says I mun do as I will."

"And the <u>curate</u> does not teach you to read and write then?" I pursued.

"No, I was told the <u>curate</u> should have his—teeth dashed down his—throat, if he stepped over the threshold—Heathcliff had promised that!"

I put the orange in his hand, and bade him tell his father that a woman called Nelly Dean was waiting to speak with him, by the garden gate. He went up the walk, and entered the house; but, instead of Hindley, Heathcliff appeared on the door stones; and I turned directly and ran down the road as hard as ever I could race, making no halt till I gained the guide-post, and feeling as scared as if I had raised a goblin. This is not much connected with Miss Isabella's affair: except that it urged me to **resolve** further on mounting **vigilant** guard, and doing my utmost to check the spread of such bad influence at the Grange: even though I should wake a domestic storm, by **thwarting** Mrs. Linton's pleasure.

The next time Heathcliff came, my young lady chanced to be feeding some pigeons in the court. She had never spoken a word to her sister-in-law for three days; but she had likewise dropped her fretful complaining, and we found it a great comfort. Heathcliff had not

BESTOW (bih <u>stoh</u>) *v.* **-ing,-ed.**
  to give as a gift; to apply or devote, as in time or effort
    Synonyms: endow, confer, present; allocate, dedicate

CIVILITY (sih <u>vihl</u> ih tee) *n.*
  a courteous behavior or politeness
    Synonyms: compliment, pleasantry

AVERT (uh <u>vuhrt</u>) *v.* **-ing,-ed.**
  to turn away; avoid
    Synonyms: deflect, parry; deter, forestall, preclude

IMPUDENCE (<u>ihm</u> pyuh duhnts) *n.*
  arrogance, audacity
    Synonyms: insolence, impertinence, boldness

EJACULATE (ih <u>jaak</u> yuh layt) *v.* **-ing,-ed.**
  to exclaim suddenly
    Synonyms: blurt, shout, declare

HYPOCRITE (<u>hih</u> puh kriht) *n.*
  person claiming beliefs or virtues he or she doesn't
  really possess
    Synonyms: fraud, liar, sham, fake, phony

PLAUSIBLE (<u>plaw</u> zih buhl) *adj.*
  believable and valid
    Synonyms: probable, likely, credible

INDIGNATION (ihn dihg <u>nay</u> shun) *n.*
  anger caused by something mean or unjust
    Synonyms: fury, ire, wrath

PRESUMPTUOUS (pree <u>suhmp</u> chyoo uhs) *adj.*
  rude, improperly bold
    Synonyms: brash, familiar, sassy, impertinent

INSOLENT (<u>ihn</u> suh luhnt) *adj.*
  insulting, arrogant
    Synonyms: audacious, rude, presumptuous,
    impertinent

DRAW *v.* **drawing, drew, drawn**
  to pull, drag; to attract or be attracted to; to lead, to
  bring about on purpose
    Synonyms: haul, tow, yank; lure, entice; provoke, elicit

DETEST (dee <u>tehst</u>) (dih <u>tehst</u>) *v.* **-ing,-ed.**
  to feel intense and violent hatred toward
    Synonyms: dislike, loathe

the habit of **bestowing** a single unnecessary **civility** on Miss Linton, I knew. Now, as soon as he beheld her, his first precaution was to take a sweeping survey of the house-front. I was standing by the kitchen window, but I drew out of sight. He then stepped across the pavement to her, and said something. She seemed embarrassed and desirous of getting away. To prevent it, he laid his hand on her arm. She **averted** her face: he apparently put some question which she had no mind to answer. There was another rapid glance at the house, and supposing himself unseen, the scoundrel had the **impudence** to embrace her.

"Judas! Traitor!" I **ejaculated**. "You are a **hypocrite**, too, are you? A deliberate deceiver."

"Who is, Nelly?" said Catherine's voice at my elbow. I had been over intent on watching the pair outside to mark her entrance.

"Your worthless friend!" I answered warmly. "The sneaking rascal yonder. Ah, he has caught a glimpse of us—he is coming in! I wonder will he have the heart to find a **plausible** excuse for making love to Miss, when he told you he hated her?"

Mrs. Linton saw Isabella tear herself free, and run into the garden; and a minute after, Heathcliff opened the door. I couldn't withhold giving some loose to my **indignation**; but Catherine angrily insisted on silence, and threatened to order me out of the kitchen, if I dared to be so **presumptuous** as to put in my **insolent** tongue.

"To hear you, people might think you were the mistress!" she cried. "You want setting down in your right place! Heathcliff, what are you about, raising this stir? I said you must let Isabella alone!—I beg you will, unless you are tired of being received here, and wish Linton to **draw** the bolts against you!"

"God forbid that he should try!" answered the black villain. I **detested** him just then. "God keep him meek and patient! Every day I grow madder after sending him to heaven!"

VEX (vehks) *v.* **-ing,-ed.**
   to irritate, annoy; confuse, puzzle
      Synonyms: bother, plague, afflict, irk; perplex, perturb

APPROBATION (aa pruh <u>bay</u> shuhn) *n.*
   praise, official approval
      Synonyms: acclaim, accolade, encomium, applause,
      homage
INFERNALLY (ihn <u>fuhr</u> nuh lee) *adv.*
   in the manner of the devil, demonically
      Synonyms: diabolically, awfully, maliciously
CONSOLE (kuhn <u>sohl</u>) *v.* **-ing,-ed.**
   to alleviate grief and raise the spirits of, provide solace
      Synonyms: relieve, comfort, soothe

VEHEMENTLY (<u>vee</u> huh muhnt lee) *adv.*
   strongly, urgently
      Synonyms: intensely, passionately, ardently

"Hush!" said Catherine, shutting the inner door. "Don't **vex** me. Why have you disregarded my request? Did she come across you on purpose?"

"What is it to you?" he growled. "I have a right to kiss her, if she chooses; and you have no right to object. I am not *your* husband. *You* needn't be jealous of me!"

"I'm not jealous *of* you," replied the mistress, "I'm jealous *for* you. Clear your face: you shan't scowl at me! If you like Isabella, you shall marry her. But do you like her? Tell the truth, Heathcliff! There, you won't answer. I'm certain you don't!"

"And would Mr. Linton approve of his sister marrying that man?" I inquired.

"Mr. Linton should approve," returned my lady, decisively.

"He might spare himself the trouble," said Heathcliff. "I could do as well without his **approbation**. And as to you, Catherine, I have a mind to speak a few words now, while we are at it. I want you to be aware that I *know* you have treated me **infernally—infernally**! Do you hear? And if you flatter yourself that I don't perceive it, you are a fool; and if you think I can be **consoled** by sweet words, you are an idiot; and if you fancy I'll suffer unrevenged, I'll convince you of the contrary, in a very little while! Meantime, thank you for telling me your sister-in-law's secret: I swear I'll make the most of it. And stand you aside!"

"What new phase of his character is this?" exclaimed Mrs. Linton, in amazement. "I've treated you **infernally**—and you'll take your revenge! How will you take it, ungrateful <u>brute</u>? How have I treated you **infernally**?"

"I seek no revenge on you," replied Heathcliff less **vehemently**. "That's not the plan. The tyrant grinds down his slaves and they don't turn against him; they crush those beneath them. You are welcome to torture me to death for your amusement, only allow me to amuse myself a little in the same style, and refrain from insult as much as you are able. Having levelled my palace, don't

COMPLACENTLY (kuhm <u>play</u> sihnt lee) *adv.*
with an air of self-satisfaction
Synonyms: contentedly, confidently, self-righteously

RESOLVED (rih <u>sahlvd</u>) *adj.*
determined, resolute
Synonyms: decisive, firm, intractable

INTRACTABLE (ihn <u>traak</u> tuh buhl) *adj.*
not easily managed
Synonyms: unruly, stubborn, refractory,
recalcitrant, headstrong

BROOD *v.* **-ing,-ed.**
to think about in a gloomy or serious way
Synonyms: ponder, worry, obsess

SUBSEQUENT (<u>suhb</u> suh kwehnt) *adj.*
following in time or order
Synonyms: succeeding, next, afterward

erect a <u>hovel</u> and **complacently** admire your own charity in giving me that for a home. If I imagined you really wished me to marry Isabel, I'd cut my throat!"

"Oh, the evil is that I am *not* jealous, is it?" cried Catherine. "Well, I won't repeat my offer of a wife. It is as bad as offering Satan a lost soul. Your bliss lies, like his, in inflicting misery. You prove it. Edgar is restored from the ill-temper he gave way to at your coming; I begin to be secure and tranquil; and you, restless to know us at peace, appear **resolved** on exciting a quarrel. Quarrel with Edgar, if you please, Heathcliff, and deceive his sister: you'll hit on exactly the most efficient method of revenging yourself on me."

The conversation ceased. Mrs. Linton sat down by the fire, flushed and gloomy. The spirit which served her was growing **intractable**: she could neither lay nor control it. He stood on the hearth with folded arms, **brooding** on his evil thoughts; and in this position I left them to seek the master, who was wondering what kept Catherine below so long.

"Ellen," said he, when I entered, "have you seen your mistress?"

"Yes; she's in the kitchen, sir," I answered. "She's sadly put out by Mr. Heathcliff's behaviour: and, indeed, I do think it's time to arrange his visits on another footing. There's harm in being too soft, and now it's come to this—" And I related the scene in the court, and, as near as I dared, the whole **subsequent** dispute. I fancied it could not be very prejudicial to Mrs. Linton; unless she made it so afterwards, by assuming the defensive for her guest. Edgar Linton had difficulty in hearing me to the close. His first words revealed that he did not clear his wife of blame.

"This is <u>insufferable</u>!" he exclaimed. "It is disgraceful that she should own him for a friend, and force his company on me! Call me two men out of the hall, Ellen. Catherine shall linger no longer to argue with the low <u>ruffian</u>—I have humoured her enough."

DESCEND (dih <u>sehnd</u>) (dee <u>sehnd</u>) *v.* **-ing,-ed.**
  to pass from a higher place to a lower place
    Synonyms: fall, dismount, gravitate
INTIMATION (ihn tuh <u>may</u> shuhn) *n.*
  clue, suggestion
    Synonyms: implication, allusion, insinuation
BASENESS (<u>bays</u> nehs) *n.*
  the quality of being contemptible, wretched, and
  unworthy
    Synonyms: vulgarity, corruption, immorality
PROVOKE (proh <u>vohk</u>) *v.* **-ing,-ed.**
  to cause a response, e.g., anger or disagreement
    Synonyms: aggravate, stimulate, vex, incite
CONTEMPT (kuhn <u>tehmpt</u>) *n.*
  disrespect, scorn
    Synonyms: derision, disdain
DRAW *v.* **drawing, drew, drawn**
  to attract or be attracted to; to pull, drag; to lead, to
  bring about on purpose
    Synonyms: provoke, elicit; haul, tow, yank; lure, entice
FORBEAR (fohr <u>bayr</u>) *v.* **-ing,-bore.**
  to tolerate or put up with; to refrain or resist
    Synonym: endure, suffer; avoid, withhold, inhibit
DEGRADED (dih <u>gray</u> dihd) (dee <u>gray</u> dihd) *adj.*
  having little moral or intellectual character; low in
  rank or status
    Synonyms: shameful, demeaned, weakened;
    demoted
ACQUIESCE (aak wee <u>ehs</u>) *v.* **-ing,-ed.**
  to agree; comply quietly
    Synonyms: accede, consent; submit
IGNOMINIOUS (ihg nuh <u>mih</u> nee uhs) *adj.*
  disgraceful and dishonorable
    Synonyms: despicable, degrading, debasing
DERISION (dih <u>rih</u> zhuhn) *n.*
  mockery, ridicule
    Synonyms: taunting, jeering, insults, teasing, scorn

He **descended**, and bidding the servants wait in the passage, went, followed by me, to the kitchen. Its occupants had recommenced their angry discussion: Mrs. Linton, at least, was scolding with renewed vigour. Heathcliff had moved to the window, and hung his head, somewhat <u>cowed</u> by her violent rating apparently. He saw the master first, and made a hasty motion that she should be silent; which she obeyed, abruptly, on discovering the reason of his **intimation**.

"How is this?" said Linton, addressing her, "What notion of propriety must you have to remain here, after the language which has been held to you by that blackguard? I suppose, because it is his ordinary talk, you think nothing of it; you are habituated to his **baseness**, and, perhaps, imagine I can get used to it too!"

"Have you been listening at the door, Edgar?" asked the mistress, in a tone particularly calculated to **provoke** her husband, implying both carelessness and **contempt** of his irritation. Heathcliff, who had raised his eyes at the former speech, gave a sneering laugh at the latter; on purpose, it seemed, to **draw** Mr. Linton's attention to him. He succeeded; but Edgar did not mean to entertain him with any high flights of passion.

"I have been so far **forbearing** with you, sir," he said quietly, "not that I was ignorant of your miserable, **degraded** character, but I felt you were only partly responsible for that; and Catherine wishing to keep up your acquaintance, I **acquiesced**—foolishly. Your presence is a moral poison that would contaminate the most virtuous: for that cause, and to prevent worse consequences, I shall deny you hereafter admission into this house, and give notice now that I require your instant departure. Three minutes' delay will render it involuntary and **ignominious**."

Heathcliff measured the height and breadth of the speaker with an eye full of **derision**.

"Cathy, this lamb of yours threatens like a bull!" he said. "It is in danger of splitting its skull against my

FEIGN (fayn) *v.* **-ing,-ed**
  to pretend or fake
    Synonyms: imitate, fabricate, bluff, simulate
VALOUR or VALOR (<u>vaa</u> luhr) *n.*
  bravery, courage
    Synonyms: heroism, intrepidity, gallantry, valliance
INDULGENCE (ihn <u>duhl</u> jehns) *n.*
  lenience, the act of giving into desires
    Synonyms: gratification, tolerance, pampering

COUNTENANCE (<u>kown</u> tuh nuhns) *n.*
  appearance, facial expression
    Synonyms: face, features, visage
AVERT (uh <u>vuhrt</u>) *v.* **-ing,-ed.**
  to avoid; to turn away
    Synonyms: deter, forestall, preclude; deflect, parry
VANQUISH (<u>vaan</u> kwihsh) *v.* **-ing,-ed.**
  to conquer, defeat
    Synonyms: subjugate, overcome, subdue, suppress,
    trounce

knuckles. By God! Mr. Linton, I'm mortally sorry that you are not worth knocking down!"

My master glanced towards the passage, and signed me to fetch the men: he had no intention of hazarding a personal encounter. I obeyed the hint; but Mrs. Linton, suspecting something, followed; and when I attempted to call them, she pulled me back, slammed the door to, and locked it.

"Fair means!" she said, in answer to her husband's look of angry surprise. "If you have not courage to attack him, make an apology, or allow yourself to be beaten. It will correct you of **feigning** more **valour** than you possess. No. I'll swallow the key before you shall get it! I'm delightfully rewarded for my kindness to each! After constant **indulgence** of one's weak nature, and the other's bad one, I earn for thanks two samples of blind ingratitude, stupid to absurdity! Edgar, I was defending you and yours; and I wish Heathcliff may flog you sick, for daring to think an evil thought of me!"

It did not need the medium of a flogging to produce that effect on the master. He tried to wrest the key from Catherine's grasp, and for safety she flung it into the hottest pan of the fire; whereupon Mr. Edgar was taken with a nervous trembling, and his **countenance** grew deadly pale. For his life he could not **avert** that excess of emotion; mingled anguish and humiliation overcame him completely. He leant on the back of a chair, and covered his face.

"Oh, heavens! In old days, this would win you knighthood!" exclaimed Mrs. Linton. "We are **vanquished**! We are **vanquished**! Heathcliff would as soon lift a finger at you as a king would march his army against a colony of mice. Cheer up! You shan't be hurt! Your type is not a lamb, it's a suckling leveret."

"I wish you joy of the milk-blooded coward, Cathy!" said her friend. "I compliment you on your taste. And that is the slavering, shivering thing you preferred to me! I would not strike him with my fist, but I'd kick him with

RESOLVE (rih <u>sahlv</u>) *v.* **-ing,-ed.**
to determine or to make a firm decision about
Synonyms: solve, decide

my foot, and experience considerable satisfaction. Is he weeping, or is he going to faint for fear?"

The fellow approached and gave the chair on which Linton rested a push. He'd better have kept his distance; my master quickly sprang erect, and struck him full on the throat a blow that would have levelled a slighter man. It took his breath for a minute; and while he choked, Mr. Linton walked out by the back door into the yard, and from thence to the front entrance.

"There! You've done with coming here," cried Catherine. "Get away, now; he'll return with a brace of pistols, and half-a-dozen assistants. If he did overhear us, of course he'd never forgive you. You've played him an ill turn, Heathcliff! But go—make haste! I'd rather see Edgar at bay than you."

"Do you suppose I'm going with that blow burning in my gullet?" he thundered. "By hell, no! I'll crush his ribs in like a rotten hazel-nut before I cross the threshold! If I don't floor him now, I shall murder him sometime; so, as you value his existence, let me get at him!"

"He's not coming," I <u>interposed</u>, framing a bit of a lie. "There's the coachman and the two gardeners; you'll surely not wait to be thrust into the road by them! Each has a <u>bludgeon</u>; and master will, very likely, be watching from the parlour windows, to see that they fulfill his orders."

The gardeners and coachman *were* there; but Linton was with them. They had already entered the court. Heathcliff, on second thought, **resolved** to avoid a struggle against the three underlings; he seized the poker, smashed the lock from the inner door, and made his escape as they tramped in.

Mrs. Linton, who was very much excited, bade me accompany her upstairs. She did not know my share in contributing to the disturbance, and I was anxious to keep her in ignorance.

"I'm nearly distracted, Nelly!" she exclaimed, throwing herself on the sofa. "A thousand smiths' hammers are beating in my head! Tell Isabella to shun me. This

UPROAR (<u>uhp</u> rohr) *n.*
a situation of loud and confusing excitement
Synonyms: noise, hubbub, commotion, fracas

RECRIMINATE (rih <u>krihm</u> ih nayt) *v.* **-ing,-ed.**
to accuse an accuser
Synonyms: blame, denounce, implicate

DIVERT (die <u>vuhrt</u>) *v.* **-ing,-ed.**
to distract or amuse; to move in different directions
from a particular point
Synonyms: deter, occupy, entertain; deviate, separate

FORLORN (fohr <u>lohrn</u>) *adj.*
hopeless, despairing; dreary, deserted; unhappy
Synonyms: dejected, despondent; desolate;
downcast, depressed

PROVOKE (proh <u>vohk</u>) *v.* **-ing,-ed.**
to cause a response, e.g., anger or disagreement
Synonyms: aggravate, stimulate, vex, incite

PERIL (<u>pehr</u> ihl) *n.*
danger
Synonyms: trouble, hazard, vulnerability, risk

KINDLE (<u>kihn</u> duhl) *v.* **-ing,-ed.**
to set fire to or ignite; excite or inspire
Synonyms: light, spark; arouse, awaken

APATHY (<u>aa</u> pah thee) *n.*
lack of feeling or emotion
Synonyms: indifference, insouciance, disregard,
unconcern

COUNTENANCE (<u>kown</u> tuh nuhns) *n.*
appearance, facial expression
Synonyms: face, features, visage

STOLIDITY (stah <u>lih</u> dih tee) *n.*
the quality of having or showing little emotion
Synonyms: impassivity, stoicism

EXASPERATING (ihg <u>zaas</u> puhr ay tihng) *adj.*
irritating
Synonyms: frustrating, annoying, vexing

uproar is owing to her; and should she or any one else aggravate my anger at present, I shall get wild. And, Nelly, say to Edgar, if you see him again to-night, that I'm in danger of being seriously ill. I wish it may prove true. He has startled and distressed me shockingly! I want to frighten him. Besides, he might come and begin a string of abuse or complainings; I'm certain I should **recriminate**, and God knows where we should end! Will you do so, my good Nelly? You are aware that I am in no way blameable in this matter. What possessed him to turn listener? Heathcliff's talk was outrageous, after you left us; but I could soon have **diverted** him from Isabella, and the rest meant nothing. Now all is dashed wrong; by the fool's craving to hear evil of self, that haunts some people like a demon! Had Edgar never gathered our conversation, he would never have been the worse for it. Really, when he opened on me in that unreasonable tone of displeasure after I had scolded Heathcliff till I was hoarse for *him*, I did not care, hardly, what they did to each other, especially as I felt that, however the scene closed, we should all be driven asunder for nobody knows how long! Well, if I cannot keep Heathcliff for my friend—if Edgar will be mean and jealous, I'll try to break their hearts by breaking my own. That will be a prompt way of finishing all, when I am pushed to extremity! But it's a deed to be reserved for a **forlorn** hope; I'd not take Linton by surprise with it. To this point he has been discreet in dreading to **provoke** me; you must represent the **peril** of quitting that policy, and remind him of my passionate temper, verging, when **kindled**, on frenzy. I wish you could dismiss that **apathy** out of that **countenance**, and look rather more anxious about me."

The **stolidity** with which I received these instructions was, no doubt, rather **exasperating**: for they were delivered in perfect sincerity; but I believed a person who could plan the turning of her fits of passion to account, beforehand, might, by exerting her will, manage to con-

DESPONDENCY (dih <u>spahn</u> duhn see) *n.*
discouragement, dejection
Synonyms: sadness, depression, desolation
RECONCILE (<u>reh</u> kuhn siel) *v.* **-ing,-ed.**
1. to resolve a dispute
Synonyms: agree, accommodate, rectify, reunite
2. to bring to accept
Synonyms: resign, submit, placate, pacify, appease
PERSEVERE (pehr suh veer) *v.* **-ing,-ed.**
to continue with determination, remain steadfast
Synonyms: persist, endure, plod
STOICAL (<u>stoh</u> ih kuhl) *adj.*
indifferent to or unaffected by emotions
Synonyms: impassive, stolid

COMPUNCTION (kuhm <u>puhnk</u> shuhn) *n.*
feeling of uneasiness caused by guilt or regret
Synonyms: dubiety, qualm, scruple

trol herself tolerably, even while under their influence; and I did not wish to "frighten" her husband, as she said, and multiply his annoyances for the purpose of serving her selfishness. Therefore I said nothing when I met the master coming towards the parlour, but I took the liberty of turning back to listen whether they would resume their quarrel together. He began to speak first.

"Remain where you are, Catherine," he said, without any anger in his voice but with much sorrowful **despondency**. "I shall not stay. I am neither come to wrangle nor be **reconciled**; but I wish just to learn whether, after this evening's events, you intend to continue your intimacy with—"

"Oh, for mercy's sake," interrupted the mistress, stamping her foot, "for mercy's sake, let us hear no more of it now! Your cold blood cannot be worked into a fever. Your veins are full of ice-water, but mine are boiling, and the sight of such dullness makes them dance."

"To get rid of me, answer my question," **persevered** Mr. Linton. "You *must* answer it; and that violence does not alarm me. I have found that you can be as **stoical** as any one, when you please. Will you give up Heathcliff hereafter, or will you give up me? It is impossible for you to be *my* friend and *his* at the same time; and I absolutely *require* to know which you choose."

"I require to be let alone!" exclaimed Catherine furiously. "I demand it! Don't you see I can scarcely stand? Edgar, you—you leave me!"

She rang the bell till it broke with a twang; I entered leisurely. It was enough to try the temper of a saint, such senseless, wicked rages! There she lay dashing her head against the arm of the sofa, and grinding her teeth, so that you might fancy she would crash them to splinters! Mr. Linton stood looking at her in sudden **compunction** and fear. He told me to fetch some water. She had no breath for speaking. I brought a glass full; and as she would not drink, I sprinkled it on her face. In a few seconds she stretched herself out stiff, and turned up her

BLANCHED (blaanchd) *adj.*
   pale, lacking color
      Synonyms: faded, lightened, bleached

LIVID (<u>lih</u> vihd) *adj.*
   pale; discolored from a bruise; reddened with anger
      Synonyms: ashen, pallid; black-and-blue; furious

RESOLVE (rih <u>sahlv</u>) *v.* **-ing,-ed.**
   to determine or to make a firm decision about
      Synonyms: solve, decide

PRETERNATURALLY (pree tuhr <u>naach</u> uh ruh lee) *adv.*
   in an extraordinary or unnatural manner
      Synonyms: abnormally, mysteriously, oddly,
      unearthly

HINDER (<u>hihn</u> duhr) *v.* **-ing,-ed.**
   to prevent action; to delay or impede
      Synonyms: restrain; hamper, inhibit, obstruct

DESCEND (dih <u>sehnd</u>) (dee <u>sehnd</u>) *v.* **-ing,-ed.**
   to pass from a higher place to a lower place
      Synonyms: fall, dismount, gravitate

PEREMPTORILY (puhr <u>ehm</u> tohr uh lee) *adv.*
   absolutely, in a commanding manner
      Synonyms: urgently, imperatively, decisively

ELICIT (ih <u>lih</u> siht) *v.* **-ing,-ed.**
   to draw out, provoke
      Synonyms: evoke, educe, wring, extract, tap

SENTIMENT (<u>sehn</u> tuh muhnt) *n.*
   an attitude, thought, or judgement prompted by
   feeling; a romantic or nostalgic feeling
      Synonyms: idea; emotion

EVASIVE (ih <u>vay</u> sihv) *adj.*
   deliberately ambiguous or vague, deceitful
      Synonyms: misleading, elusive, unclear, indirect

OBLIGE (uh <u>bliej</u>) *v.* **-ing,-ed.**
   to be obligated, to require or force someone to obey
      Synonyms: compel, constrain, bind, favor

SOLEMN (<u>sah</u> luhm) *adj.*
   quiet, deeply serious; somberly impressive
      Synonyms: earnest, brooding; dignified, ceremonial

eyes, while her cheeks, at once **blanched** and **livid**, assumed the aspect of death. Linton looked terrified.

"There is nothing in the world the matter," I whispered. I did not want him to yield, though I could not help being afraid in my heart.

"She has blood on her lips!" he said, shuddering.

"Never mind!" I answered tartly. And I told him how she had **resolved**, previous to his coming, on exhibiting a fit of frenzy. I incautiously gave the account aloud, and she heard me; for she started up—her hair flying over her shoulders, her eyes flashing, the muscles of her neck and arms standing out **preternaturally**. I made up my mind for broken bones, at least; but she only glared about her for an instant, and then rushed from the room. The master directed me to follow; I did, to her chamber door: she **hindered** me from going further by securing it against me.

As she never offered to **descend** to breakfast next morning, I went to ask whether she would have some carried up. "No!" she replied **peremptorily**. The same question was repeated at dinner and tea; and again on the morrow after, and received the same answer. Mr. Linton, on his part, spent his time in the library, and did not inquire concerning his wife's occupations. Isabella and he had had an hour's interview, during which he tried to **elicit** from her some **sentiment** of proper horror for Heathcliff's advances: but he could make nothing of her **evasive** replies, and was **obliged** to close the examination unsatisfactorily; adding, however, a **solemn** warning, that if she were so insane as to encourage that worthless suitor, it would dissolve all bonds of relationship between herself and him.

REPENT (rih <u>pehnt</u>) *v.* **-ing,-ed.**
  to regret a past action
    Synonyms: rue, atone, apologize
RECONCILIATION (reh kuhn sihl ee <u>ay</u> shuhn) *n.*
  the act of agreement after a quarrel, the resolution of
  a dispute
    Synonyms: rapprochement, settlement, accord
PERTINACIOUSLY (puhr tihn <u>ay</u> shuhs lee) *adv.*
  stubbornly, persistently
    Synonyms: obstinately, tenaciously, steadily,
    doggedly
CONDOLENCE (kuhn <u>doh</u> lehnts) *n.*
  an expression of sympathy for one who grieves or is
  in pain
    Synonyms: commiseration, comfort, compassion
EXPOSTULATION (ihk spahs chuh <u>lay</u> shuhn) *n.*
  reasoning; an expression of opposition
    Synonyms: assertion; argument, dissuasion,
    remonstration

Chapter 12

While Miss Linton moped about the park and garden, always silent, and almost always in tears; and her brother shut himself up among books that he never opened—wearying, I guessed, with a continual vague expectation that Catherine, **repenting** her conduct, would come of her own accord to ask pardon, and seek a **reconciliation**—and *she* fasted **pertinaciously**, under the idea, probably, that at every meal, Edgar was ready to choke for her absence, and pride alone held him from running to cast himself at her feet: I went about my household duties, convinced that the Grange had but one sensible soul in its walls, and that lodged in my body. I wasted no **condolences** on Miss, nor any **expostulations** on my mistress; nor did I pay much attention to the sighs of my master, who yearned to hear his lady's name, since he might not hear her voice. I determined they should come about as they pleased for me; and though it was a tiresomely slow process, I began to rejoice at length in a faint dawn of its progress: as I thought at first.

Mrs. Linton, on the third day, unbarred her door, and having finished the water in her pitcher and decanter, desired a renewed supply, and a basin of gruel, for she believed she was dying. That I set down as a speech meant for Edgar's ears; I believed no such thing, so I kept it to myself and brought her some tea and dry toast. She ate and drank eagerly; and sank back on her pillow again, clenching her hands and groaning. "Oh, I will die," she exclaimed, "since no one cares anything about me. I wish I had not taken that." Then a good while after I heard her murmur, "No, I'll not die—he'd be glad—he does not love me at all—he would never miss me!"

COUNTENANCE (<u>kown</u> tuh nuhns) *n.*
appearance, facial expression
Synonyms: face, features, visage

APATHETIC (aa pah <u>theh</u> tihk) *adj.*
showing a lack of feeling or emotion
Synonyms: indifferent, disinterested, unconcerned

LETHARGY (<u>lehth</u> uhr jee) *n.*
indifferent inactivity
Synonyms: lassitude, torpor, stupor, languor,
sluggishness

CONFOUNDED (kuhn <u>fown</u> dihd) *adj.*
baffled, perplexed
Synonyms: overwhelmed, confused, disconcerted,
entangled, muddled

INDIFFERENT (ihn <u>dihf</u> ruhnt) (ihn <u>dihf</u> uhr uhnt) *adj.*
uncaring, unbiased
Synonyms: unconcerned, uncurious, detached,
uninterested, apathetic

DERANGED (dih <u>raynjd</u>) *adj.*
insane, functionally or mentally disturbed
Synonyms: crazed, demented, unbalanced, lunatic

"Did you want anything, ma'am?" I inquired, still preserving my external composure, in spite of her ghastly **countenance** and strange exaggerated manner.

"What is that **apathetic** being doing?" she demanded, pushing her thick entangled locks from her wasted face. "Has he fallen into a **lethargy**, or is he dead?"

"Neither," replied I, "if you mean Mr. Linton. He's tolerably well, I think, though his studies occupy him rather more than they ought: he is continually among his books, since he has no other society."

I should not have spoken so, if I had known her true condition, but I could not get rid of the notion that she acted a part of her disorder.

"Among his books!" she cried, **confounded**. "And I dying, I on the brink of the grave! My God! Does he know how I'm altered?" continued she, staring at her reflection in a mirror hanging against the opposite wall. "Is that Catherine Linton! He imagines me in a pet—in play, perhaps. Cannot you inform him that it is in frightful earnest? Nelly, if it be not too late, as soon as I learn how he feels, I'll choose between these two; either to starve at once—that would be no punishment unless he had a heart—or to recover, and leave the country. Are you speaking the truth about him now? Take care. Is he actually so utterly **indifferent** for my life?"

"Why, ma'am," I answered, "the master has no idea of your being **deranged**; and of course he does not fear that you will let yourself die of hunger."

"You think not? Cannot you tell him I will?" she returned. "Persuade him! Speak of your own mind: say you are certain I will!"

"No, you forget, Mrs. Linton," I suggested, "that you have eaten some food with a relish this evening, and tomorrow you will perceive its good effects."

"If I were only sure it would kill him," she interrupted, "I'd kill myself directly! These three awful nights, I've never closed my lids—and oh, I've been tormented! I've been haunted, Nelly! But I begin to fancy you don't like me.

241

REPEL (rih <u>pehl</u>) *v.* **-ling,-led.**
 to rebuff, repulse; disgust, offend
  Synonyms: reject, spurn, parry; nauseate, revolt
SOLEMNLY (<u>sah</u> luhm lee) *adv.*
 seriously or somberly
  Synonyms: quietly, earnestly, ceremonially

INJUNCTION (ihn <u>juhnk</u> shuhn) *n.*
 command, order
  Synonyms: directive, behest, mandate, edict, decree

DIVERSION (dih <u>vuhr</u> zhuhn) (die <u>vuhr</u> zhuhn) *n.*
 an amusing or relaxing activity; a distraction
  Synonyms: entertainment, recreation; deviation

How strange! I thought, though everybody hated and despised each other, they could not avoid loving me. And they have all turned to enemies in a few hours: *they* have, I'm positive; the people *here*. How dreary to meet death, surrounded by their cold faces. Isabella terrified and **repelled**, afraid to enter the room, it would be so dreadful to watch Catherine go. And Edgar standing **solemnly** by to see it over; then offering prayers of thanks to God for restoring peace to his house, and going back to his *books*! What in the name of all that feels has he to do with *books*, when I am dying?"

She could not bear the notion which I had put into her head of Mr. Linton's philosophical resignation. Tossing about, she increased her feverish bewilderment to madness, and tore the pillow with her teeth; then raising herself up all burning, desired that I would open the window. We were in the middle of winter, the wind blew strong from the north-east, and I objected. Both the expressions flitting over her face, and the changes of her moods, began to alarm me terribly; and brought to my recollection her former illness, and the doctor's **injunction** that she should not be crossed. A minute previously she was violent; now supported on one arm, and not noticing my refusal to obey her, she seemed to find childish **diversion** in pulling the feathers from the <u>rents</u> she had just made, and ranging them on the sheet according to their different species: her mind had strayed to other associations.

"That's a turkey's," she murmured to herself, "and this is a wild duck's; and this is a pigeon's. Ah, they put pigeons' feathers in the pillows—no wonder I couldn't die! Let me take care to throw it on the floor when I lie down. And here is a moor-cock's; and this—I should know it among a thousand—it's a lapwing's. <u>Bonny</u> bird; wheeling over our heads in the middle of the moor. It wanted to get to its nest, for the clouds had touched the swells, and it felt rain coming. This feather was picked up from the <u>heath</u>, the bird was not shot: we saw its nest in

the winter, full of little skeletons. Heathcliff set a trap over it, and the old ones dare not come. I made him promise he'd never shoot a lapwing after that, and he didn't. Yes, here are more! Did he shoot my lapwings, Nelly? Are they red, any of them! Let me look."

"Give over with the baby-work!" I interrupted, dragging the pillow away, and turning the holes towards the mattress, for she was removing its contents by handfuls. "Lie down and shut your eyes: you're wandering. There's a mess! The down is flying about like snow."

I went here and there collecting it.

"I see in you, Nelly," she continued dreamily, "an aged woman: you have grey hair and bent shoulders. This bed is the fairy cave under Peniston Crag, and you are gathering <u>elf-bolts</u> to hurt our <u>heifers</u>; pretending, while I am near, that they are only locks of wool. That's what you'll come to fifty years hence: I know you are not so now. I'm not wandering. You're mistaken, or else I should believe you really *were* that withered hag, and I should think I *was* under Peniston Crag; and I'm conscious it's night, and there are two candles on the table making the black press shine like jet."

"The black press? Where is that?" I asked. "You are talking in your sleep!"

"It's against the wall, as it always is," she replied. "It does appear odd—I see a face in it!"

"There's no press in the room, and never was," said I, resuming my seat, and looping up the curtain that I might watch her.

"Don't *you* see that face?" she inquired, gazing earnestly at the mirror.

And say what I could, I was incapable of making her comprehend it to be her own; so I rose and covered it with a shawl.

"It's behind there still!" she pursued anxiously. "And it stirred. Who is it? I hope it will not come out when you are gone! Oh! Nelly, the room is haunted! I'm afraid of being alone!"

COUNTENANCE (<u>kown</u> tuh nuhns) *n.*
   appearance, facial expression
      Synonyms: face, features, visage

APPALL (uh <u>pahl</u>) *v.* **-ing,-ed.**
   to overcome with shock or dismay
      Synonyms: horrify, astound, petrify

PACIFY (<u>paa</u> suh fie) *v.* **-ing,-ied.**
   to restore calm, bring peace
      Synonyms: mollify, conciliate, appease, placate

I took her hand in mine, and bid her be composed: for a succession of shudders convulsed her frame, and she *would* keep straining her gaze towards the glass.

"There's nobody here!" I insisted. "It was *yourself*. Mrs. Linton: you knew it a while since."

"Myself!" she gasped, "And the clock is striking twelve! It's true, then! That's dreadful!"

Her fingers clutched the clothes, and gathered them over her eyes. I attempted to steal to the door with an intention of calling her husband; but I was summoned back by a piercing shriek—the shawl had dropped from the frame.

"Why, what *is* the matter?" cried I. "Who is coward now? Wake up! That is the glass—the mirror, Mrs. Linton; and you see yourself in it, and there am I too, by your side."

Trembling and bewildered, she held me fast, but the horror gradually passed from her **countenance**; its paleness gave place to a glow of shame.

"Oh, dear! I thought I was at home," she sighed. "I thought I was lying in my chamber at Wuthering Heights. Because I'm weak, my brain got confused, and I screamed unconsciously. Don't say anything; but stay with me. I dread sleeping: my dreams **appall** me."

"A sound sleep would do you good, ma'am," I answered, "and I hope this suffering will prevent your trying starving again."

"Oh, if I were but in my own bed in the old house!" she went on bitterly, wringing her hands. "And that wind sounding in the firs by the lattice. Do let me feel it—it comes straight down the moor—do let me have one breath!"

To **pacify** her, I held the casement ajar for a few seconds. A cold blast rushed through; I closed it, and returned to my post. She lay still now, her face bathed in tears. Exhaustion of body had entirely subdued her spirit: our fiery Catherine was no better than a wailing child.

PROVOKE (proh <u>vohk</u>) *v.* **-ing,-ed.**
    to cause a response, e.g., anger or disagreement
      Synonyms: aggravate, stimulate, vex, incite

DISCERN (dihs <u>uhrn</u>) *v.* **-ing,-ed.**
    to perceive or recognize something obscure
      Synonyms: descry, observe, glimpse, distinguish
PONDER (<u>pahn</u> duhr) *v.* **-ing,-ed.**
    to consider or think about something in depth
      Synonyms: contemplate, reflect, ruminate

DERANGEMENT (dih <u>raynj</u> mehnt) *n.*
    insanity, madness
      Synonyms: craziness, dementia, lunacy

"How long is it since I shut myself in here?" she asked, suddenly reviving.

"It was Monday evening," I replied, "and this is Thursday night, or rather Friday morning, at present."

"What! Of the same week?" she exclaimed. "Only that brief time?"

"Long enough to live on nothing but cold water and ill-temper," observed I.

"Well, it seems a weary number of hours," she muttered doubtfully. "It must be more. I remember being in the parlour after they had quarrelled, and Edgar being cruelly **provoking**, and me running into this room desperate. As soon as ever I had barred the door, utter blackness overwhelmed me, and I fell on the floor. I couldn't explain to Edgar how certain I felt of having a fit, or going raging mad, if he persisted in teasing me! I had no command of tongue, or brain, and he did not guess my agony, perhaps: it barely left me sense to try to escape from him and his voice. Before I recovered sufficiently to see and hear, it began to be dawn, and, Nelly, I'll tell you what I thought, and what has kept recurring and recurring till I feared for my reason. I thought as I lay there, with my head against that table leg, and my eyes dimly **discerning** the grey square of the window, that I was enclosed in the oak-panelled bed at home; and my heart ached with some great grief which, just waking, I could not recollect. I **pondered**, and worried myself to discover what it could be, and, most strangely, the whole last seven years of my life grew a blank! I did not recall that they had been at all. I was a child; my father was just buried, and my misery arose from the separation that Hindley had ordered between me and Heathcliff. I was laid alone, for the first time; and, rousing from a dismal doze after a night of weeping, I lifted my hand to push the panels aside: it struck the table-top! I swept it along the carpet, and then memory burst in: my late anguish was swallowed in a <u>paroxysm</u> of despair. I cannot say why I felt so wildly wretched: it must have been temporary **derangement**; for there is scarcely

EXILE (<u>ehg</u> ziel) (<u>ehk</u> siel) *n.*
   one who is forced or volunteers to live outside of their
   country or in isolation
      Synonyms: outcast, fugitive, outlaw, expellee
GROVEL (<u>grah</u> vuhl) *v.* **-ling,-led.**
   to humble oneself in a demeaning way
      Synonyms: cringe, fawn, kowtow, toady, bootlick
COMPEL (kuhm <u>pehl</u>) *v.* **-ling,-led.**
   to urge or force
      Synonyms: coerce, oblige, constrain
HARDY (<u>hahr</u> dee) *adj.*
   robust, vigorous
      Synonyms: healthy, hale, fit, strong, courageous
TUMULT (<u>tuh</u> muhlt) *n.*
   state of confusion, agitation
      Synonyms: disturbance, turmoil, din, commotion

SULLENLY (<u>suh</u> luhn lee) *adv.*
   in a brooding and gloomy manner
      Synonyms: morosely, somberly, glumly
HINDER (<u>hihn</u> duhr) *v.* **-ing,-ed.**
   to prevent action; to delay or impede
      Synonyms: restrain; hamper, inhibit, obstruct
KEEN *adj.*
   having a sharp edge; intellectually sharp, perceptive
      Synonyms: pointed, razorlike; acute, quick, canny
ENTREAT (ehn <u>treet</u>) *v.* **-ing,-ed.**
   to plead, beg
      Synonyms: beseech, implore, importune, request
SURPASS (suhr <u>paas</u>) *v.* **-ing,-ed.**
   to do better than, be superior to
      Synonyms: transcend, exceed, excel, outdo
SUBSEQUENT (<u>suhb</u> suh kwehnt) *adj.*
   following in time or order
      Synonyms: succeeding, next, afterward

cause. But, supposing at twelve years old I had been wrenched from the Heights, and very early association, and my all in all, as Heathcliff was at that time, and been converted at a stroke into Mrs. Linton, the lady at Thrushcross Grange, and the wife of a stranger: an **exile**, and outcast, thenceforth, from what had been my world. You may fancy a glimpse of the abyss where I **grovelled**! Shake your head as you will, Nelly, *you* have helped to unsettle me! You should have spoken to Edgar, indeed you should, and **compelled** him to leave me quiet! Oh, I'm burning! I wish I were out of doors! I wish I were a girl again, half savage and **hardy**, and free; and laughing at injuries, not maddening under them! Why am I so changed? Why does my blood rush into a hell of **tumult** at a few words? I'm sure I should be myself were I once among the heather on those hills. Open the window again wide: fasten it open! Quick, why don't you move?"

"Because I won't give you your death of cold," I answered.

"You won't give me a chance of life, you mean," she said **sullenly**. "However, I'm not helpless, yet: I'll open it myself."

And sliding from the bed before I could **hinder** her, she crossed the room, walking very uncertainly, threw it back, and bent out, careless of the frosty air that cut about her shoulders as **keen** as a knife. I **entreated**, and finally attempted to force her to retire. But I soon found her delirious strength much **surpassed** mine (she *was* delirious, I became convinced by her **subsequent** actions and ravings). There was no moon, and everything beneath lay in misty darkness: not a light gleamed from any house, far or near—all had been extinguished long ago; and those at Wuthering Heights were never visible—still she asserted she caught their shining.

"Look!" she cried eagerly. "That's my room with the candle in it, and the trees swaying before it: and the other candle is in Joseph's <u>garret</u>. Joseph sits up late, doesn't he? He's waiting till I come home that he may lock the gate.

CONSTERNATION (kahn stuhr <u>nay</u> shuhn) *n.*
amazement or distress that leads to confusion
Synonyms: alarm, bewilderment, perplexity

Well, he'll wait a while yet. It's a rough journey, and a sad heart to travel it; and we must pass by Gimmerton <u>Kirk</u>, to go that journey! We've braved its ghosts often together, and dared each other to stand among the graves and ask them to come. But, Heathcliff, if I dare you now, will you venture? If you do, I'll keep you. I'll not lie there by myself: they may bury me twelve feet deep, and throw the church down over me, but I won't rest till you are with me. I never will!"

She paused, and resumed with a strange smile. "He's considering—he'd rather I'd come to him! Find a way, then! Not through that <u>kirkyard</u>. You are slow! Be content, you always followed me!"

Perceiving it vain to argue against her insanity, I was planning how I could reach something to wrap about her, without quitting my hold of herself (for I could not trust her alone by the gaping <u>lattice</u>), when, to my **consternation**, I heard the rattle of the door-handle, and Mr. Linton entered. He had only then come from the library; and, in passing through the lobby, had noticed our talking and been attracted by curiosity, or fear, to examine what it signified, at that late hour.

"Oh, sir!" I cried, checking the exclamation risen to his lips at the sight which met him, and the bleak atmosphere of the chamber. "My poor mistress is ill, and she quite masters me: I cannot manage her at all; pray, come and persuade her to go to bed. Forget your anger, for she's hard to guide any way but her own."

"Catherine ill?" he said, hastening to us. "Shut the window, Ellen! Catherine! Why—"

He was silent. The haggardness of Mrs. Linton's appearance <u>smote</u> him speechless, and he could only glance from her to me in horrified astonishment.

"She's been fretting here," I continued, "and eating scarcely anything, and never complaining; she would admit none of us till this evening, and so we couldn't inform you of her state as we were not aware of it ourselves; but it is nothing."

ANIMATION (aa nih <u>may</u> shuhn) *n.*
enthusiasm, excitement
Synonyms: elation, vivacity, brio, spirit, verve

LAMENTATION (laa mehn <u>tay</u> shuhn) *n.*
an expression of grief or sorrow, a loud cry
Synonyms: moaning, sobbing, tears, complaint

CONSOLATION (kahn suh <u>lay</u> shuhn) *n.*
something providing comfort or solace for a loss or
hardship
Synonym: condolence

RALLY (<u>raa</u> lee) *v.* **-ing,-ied.**
to recover, recuperate; to assemble
Synonyms: heal, convalesce; muster, gather, convene

VEX (vehks) *v.* **-ing,-ed.**
to irritate, annoy; confuse, puzzle
Synonyms: bother, plague, afflict, irk; perplex, perturb

I felt I uttered my explanations awkwardly; the master frowned. "It is nothing, is it, Ellen Dean?" he said sternly. "You shall account more clearly for keeping me ignorant of this!" And he took his wife in his arms, and looked at her with anguish.

At first she gave him no glance of recognition; he was invisible to her abstracted gaze. The delirium was not fixed, however; having weaned her eyes from contemplating the outer darkness, by degrees she centered her attention on him, and discovered who it was that held her.

"Ah! You are come, are you, Edgar Linton?" she said, with angry **animation**. "You are one of those things that are ever found when least wanted, and when you are wanted, never! I suppose we shall have plenty of **lamentations** now—I see we shall—but they can't keep me from my narrow home out yonder: my resting-place, where I'm bound before spring is over! There it is: not among the Lintons, mind, under the chapel-roof, but in the open air, with a headstone; and you may please yourself, whether you go to them or come to me!"

"Catherine, what have you done?" commenced the master. "Am I nothing to you any more? Do you love that wretch Heath—"

"Hush!" cried Mrs. Linton. "Hush, this moment! You mention that name and I end the matter instantly, by a spring from the window! What you touch at present you may have; but my soul will be on that hill-top before you lay hands on me again. I don't want you, Edgar: I'm past wanting you. Return to your books. I'm glad you possess a **consolation**, for all you had in me is gone."

"Her mind wanders, sir," I <u>interposed</u>. "She has been talking nonsense the whole evening; but let her have quiet, and proper attendance, and she'll **rally**. Hereafter, we must be cautious how we **vex** her."

"I desire no further advice from you," answered Mr. Linton. "You know your mistress's nature, and you encouraged me to harass her. And not to give me one hint

DOMINEERING (dahm uh <u>neer</u> ihng) *adj.*
   having an authoritarian and assertive manner
      Synonyms: bossy, tyrannical, oppressive
FOSTER (<u>fah</u> stuhr) (<u>faw</u> stuhr) *v.* **-ing,-ed.**
   to nourish; to cultivate, promote
      Synonyms: nurture, nurse; advance, further

RUE (roo) *v.* **ruing,-ed.**
   to regret
      Synonyms: deplore, repent
RECANTATION (ree kaan <u>tay</u> shuhn) *n.*
   a retracted statement
      Synonyms: disavowal, disclaimer, renouncement,
      repudiation
KINDLE (<u>kihn</u> duhl) *v.* **-ing,-ed.**
   to set fire to or ignite; excite or inspire
      Synonyms: light, spark; arouse, awaken
INCLINATION (ihn cluh <u>nay</u> shuhn) *n.*
   tendency toward
      Synonyms: leaning, trend, preference, disposition,
      propensity
RESOLVE (rih <u>sahlv</u>) *v.* **-ing,-ed.**
   to determine or to make a firm decision about
      Synonyms: solve, decide
SUSPEND (suh <u>spehnd</u>) *v.* **-ing,-ed.**
   to dangle, hang; to delay, interrupt
      Synonyms: swing; defer, cease, disrupt, halt,
      discontinue

of how she has been these three days! It was heartless! Months of sickness could not cause such a change!"

I began to defend myself, thinking it too bad to be blamed for another's wicked waywardness. "I knew Mrs. Linton's nature to be headstrong and **domineering**," cried I, "but I didn't know that you wished to **foster** her fierce temper! I didn't know that, to humour her, I should wink at Mr. Heathcliff. I performed the duty of a faithful servant in telling you, and I have got a faithful servant's wages! Well, it will teach me to be careful next time. Next time you may gather intelligence for yourself!"

"The next time you bring a tale to me, you shall quit my service, Ellen Dean," he replied.

"You'd rather hear nothing about it, I suppose, then, Mr. Linton?" said I. "Heathcliff has your permission to come a-courting to Miss, and to drop in at every opportunity your absence offers, on purpose to poison the mistress against you?"

Confused as Catherine was, her wits were alert at applying our conversation.

"Ah! Nelly has played traitor," she exclaimed passionately. "Nelly is my hidden enemy. You witch! So you do seek elf-bolts to hurt us! Let me go, I'll make her **rue**! I'll make her howl a **recantation**!"

A maniac's fury **kindled** under her brows; she struggled desperately to disengage herself from Linton's arms. I felt no **inclination** to tarry the event; and, **resolving** to seek medical aid on my own responsibility, I quitted the chamber.

In passing the garden to reach the road, at a place where a bridle hook is driven into the wall, I saw something white moved irregularly, evidently by another agent than the wind. Notwithstanding my hurry, I stayed to examine it, lest ever after I should have the conviction impressed on my imagination that it was a creature of the other world. My surprise and perplexity were great on discovering, by touch more than vision, Miss Isabella's springer, Fanny, **suspended** by a handkerchief, and nearly

MALADY (<u>maal</u> uh dee) *n.*
illness
   Synonyms: disease, disorder, ailment, affliction, infirmity
INDUCE (ih <u>doos</u>) (ihn <u>dyoos</u>) *v.* **-ing,-ed.**
to persuade; bring about
   Synonyms: convince, prevail; effect, lead, occasion
SCRUPLE (<u>skroo</u> puhl) *n.*
a hesitation caused by moral conscience; an ethical and moral belief that prevents action
   Synonyms: restraint, qualm, misgiving; principle
TRIFLE (<u>trie</u> fuhl) *n.*
something of slight worth or little importance
   Synonyms: triviality, novelty, trinket
DISPOSITION (dihs puh <u>zih</u> shuhn) *n.*
mood or temperament
   Synonyms: behavior, tendency, inclination, nature
TEMPEST (<u>tehm</u> pehst) *n.*
rage or fury; a storm
   Synonyms: tumult, turbulence, torrent; inclemency

INTERROGATIVELY (ihn tuhr <u>ahg</u> uh tihv lee) *adv.*
in the manner or form of a question, inquisitively
   Synonyms: curiously, doubtfully, quizzically

at its last gasp. I quickly released the animal, and lifted it into the garden. I had seen it follow its mistress upstairs when she went to bed; and wondered much how it could have got out there, and what mischievous person had treated it so. While untying the knot round the hook, it seemed to me that I repeatedly caught the beat of horses' feet galloping at some distance; but there were such a number of things to occupy my reflections that I hardly gave the circumstance a thought: though it was a strange sound, in that place, at two o'clock in the morning.

Mr. Kenneth was fortunately just issuing from his house to see a patient in the village as I came up the street; and my account of Catherine Linton's **malady induced** him to accompany me back immediately. He was a plain rough man; and he made no **scruple** to speak his doubts of her surviving this second attack; unless she were more submissive to his directions than she had shown herself before.

"Nelly Dean," said he, "I can't help fancying there's an extra cause for this. What has there been to do at the Grange? We've odd reports up here. A stout, hearty lass like Catherine, does not fall ill for a **trifle**; and that sort of people should not either. It's hard work bringing them through fevers, and such things. How did it begin?"

"The master will inform you," I answered, "but you are acquainted with the Earnshaws' violent **dispositions**, and Mrs. Linton caps them all. I may say this: it commenced in a quarrel. She was struck during a **tempest** of passion with a kind of fit. That's her account, at least; for she flew off in the height of it, and locked herself up. Afterwards, she refused to eat, and now she alternately raves and remains in a half dream; knowing those about her, but having her mind filled with all sorts of strange ideas and illusions."

"Mr. Linton will be sorry?" observed Kenneth, **interrogatively**.

"Sorry? He'll break his heart should anything happen!" I replied. "Don't alarm him more than necessary."

PRESUMPTUOUS (pree <u>suhmp</u> chyoo uhs) *adj.*
rude, improperly bold
Synonyms: brash, familiar, sassy, impertinent

ASPIRATION (aa spuhr <u>ay</u> shuhn) *n.*
a great hope or goal
Synonyms: intention, purpose, expectation

MANIFEST (<u>maan</u> uh fehst) *v.* **-ing,-ed.**
to make evident or certain by display
Synonyms: exhibit, showcase, expose

ASCEND (uh <u>sehnd</u>) *v.* **-ing,-ed.**
to rise to another level or climb; to move upward
Synonyms: elevate, escalate, mount; hoist, lift

RASH (raash) *adj.*
careless, hasty, reckless
Synonyms: foolhardy, impulsive, precipitate

"Well, I told him to beware," said my companion, "and he must bide the consequences of neglecting my warning! Hasn't he been intimate with Mr. Heathcliff, lately?"

"Heathcliff frequently visits at the Grange," answered I, "though more on the strength of the mistress having known him when a boy, than because the master likes his company. At present, he's discharged from the trouble of calling; owing to some **presumptuous aspirations** after Miss Linton which he **manifested**. I hardly think he'll be taken in again."

"And does Miss Linton turn a cold shoulder on him?" was the doctor's next question.

"I'm not in her confidence," returned I, reluctant to continue the subject.

"No, she's a sly one," he remarked, shaking his head. "She keeps her own counsel! But she's a real little fool. I have it from good authority, that, last night (and a pretty night it was!) she and Heathcliff were walking in the plantation at the back of your house, above two hours; and he pressed her not to go in again, but just mount his horse and away with him! My informant said she could only put him off by pledging her word of honour to be prepared on their first meeting after that: when it was to be, he didn't hear; but you urge Mr. Linton to look sharp!"

This news filled me with fresh fears: I outstripped Kenneth, and ran most of the way back. The little dog was yelping in the garden yet. I spared a minute to open the gate for it, but instead of going to the house door, it coursed up and down <u>snuffing</u> the grass, and would have escaped to the road, had I not seized and conveyed it in with me. On **ascending** to Isabella's room, my suspicions were confirmed: it was empty. Had I been a few hours sooner, Mrs. Linton's illness might have arrested her **rash** step. But what could be done now? There was a bare possibility of overtaking them if pursued instantly. *I* could not pursue them, however; and I dare not rouse the family, and fill the place with confusion; still less unfold the business to my master, absorbed as he was in his present

CALAMITY (kuh <u>laam</u> ih tee) *n.*
state of despair; misfortune
Synonyms: misery; disaster, cataclysm
COUNTENANCE (<u>kown</u> tuh nuhns) *n.*
appearance, facial expression
Synonyms: face, features, visage

ALIENATION (ay lee uhn <u>ay</u> shuhn)
(ayl yuhn <u>ay</u> shuhn) *n.*
derangement of the mind; separation or isolation
Synonyms: madness, insanity; estrangement,
disaffection
STEALTHY (<u>stehl</u> thee) *adj.*
sly and cautious, sneaky
Synonyms: furtive, secretive, unperceived

CLAMOROUS (<u>klaa</u> muhr uhs) *adj.*
demanding attention; loud
Synonyms: bothersome, insistent; uproarious, noisy,
obstreperous
AGITATION (aa gih <u>tay</u> shuhn) *n.*
commotion, excitement; uneasiness
Synonyms: disturbance; restlessness, anxiety

calamity, and having no heart to spare for a second grief! I saw nothing for it but to hold my tongue, and suffer matters to take their course; and Kenneth being arrived, I went with a badly composed **countenance** to announce him. Catherine lay in a troubled sleep: her husband had succeeded in soothing the excess of frenzy: he now hung over her pillow, watching every shade, and every change of her painfully expressive features.

The doctor, on examining the case for himself, spoke hopefully to him of its having a favourable termination, if we could only preserve around her perfect and constant tranquillity. To me, he signified the threatening danger was not so much death, as permanent **alienation** of intellect.

I did not close my eyes that night, nor did Mr. Linton: indeed, we never went to bed; and the servants were all up long before the usual hour, moving through the house with **stealthy** tread, and exchanging whispers as they encountered each other in their <u>vocations</u>. Every one was active, but Miss Isabella; and they began to remark how sound she slept: her brother, too, asked if she had risen, and seemed impatient for her presence, and hurt that she showed so little anxiety for her sister-in-law. I trembled lest he should send me to call her, but I was spared the pain of being the first proclamation of her flight. One of the maids, a thoughtless girl, who had been on an early errand to Gimmerton, came panting upstairs, open mouthed, and dashed into the chamber, crying:

"Oh, dear, dear! What mun we have next? Master, master, our young lady—"

"Hold your noise!" cried I hastily, enraged at her **clamorous** manner.

"Speak lower, Mary— What is the matter?" said Mr. Linton. "What ails your young lady?"

"She's gone, she's gone! Yon' Heathcliff's run off wi' her!" gasped the girl.

"That is not true!" exclaimed Linton, rising in **agitation**. "It cannot be: how has the idea entered your

head? Ellen Dean, go and seek her. It is incredible: it cannot be."

As he spoke he took the servant to the door, and then repeated his demand to know her reasons for such an assertion.

"Why, I met on the road a lad that fetches milk here," she stammered, "and he asked whether we weren't in trouble at the Grange. I thought he meant for Missis's sickness, so I answered, yes. Then says he, 'There's somebody gone after 'em, I guess!' I stared. He saw I knew <u>nought</u> about it, and he told how a gentleman and lady had stopped to have a horse's shoe fastened at a blacksmith's shop, two miles out of Gimmerton, not very long after midnight! And how the blacksmith's lass had got up to spy who they were: she knew them both directly. And she noticed the man—Heathcliff it was, she felt certain: nob'dy could mistake him besides—put a <u>sovereign</u> in her father's hand for payment. The lady had a cloak about her face; but having desired a sup of water, while she drank, it fell back, and she saw her very plain. Heathcliff held both bridles as they rode on, and they set their faces from the village, and went as fast as the rough roads would let them. The lass said nothing to her father, but she told it all over Gimmerton this morning."

I ran and peeped, for form's sake, into Isabella's room; confirming, when I returned, the servant's statement. Mr. Linton had resumed his seat by the bed; on my re-entrance, he raised his eyes, read the meaning of my blank aspect, and dropped them without giving an order, or uttering a word.

"Are we to try any measures for overtaking and bringing her back?" I inquired. "How should we do?"

"She went of her own accord," answered the master. "She had a right to go if she pleased. Trouble me no more about her. Hereafter she is only my sister in name: not because I disown her, but because she has disowned me."

And that was all he said on the subject: he did not make a single inquiry further, or mention her in any way,

RECOMPENSE (<u>reh</u> kuhm pehns) *v.* **-ing,-ed.**
to give something to as a means of compensation; to
return in kind
Synonyms: repay, reward; indemnify, reciprocate

SANGUINE (<u>saan</u> gwuhn) *adj.*
cheerfully optimistic; ruddy
Synonyms: confident, positive, hopeful; rosy,
rubicund

except directing me to send what property she had in the house to her fresh home, wherever it was, when I knew it.

Chapter 13

For two months the fugitives remained absent; in those two months, Mrs. Linton encountered and conquered the worst shock of what was <u>denominated</u> a brain fever. No mother could have nursed an only child more devotedly than Edgar tended her. Day and night he was watching, and patiently enduring all the annoyances that irritable nerves and a shaken reason could inflict; and, though Kenneth remarked that what he saved from the grave would only **recompense** his care by forming the source of constant future anxiety—in fact, that his health and strength were being sacrificed to preserve a mere ruin of humanity—he knew no limits in gratitude and joy when Catherine's life was declared out of danger; and hour after hour he would sit beside her, tracing the gradual return to bodily health, and flattering his too **sanguine** hopes with the illusion that her mind would settle back to its right balance also, and she would soon be entirely her former self.

The first time she left her chamber was at the commencement of the following March. Mr. Linton had put on her pillow, in the morning, a handful of golden crocuses; her eye, long stranger to any gleam of pleasure, caught them in waking, and shone delighted as she gathered them eagerly together.

"These are the earliest flowers at the Heights," she exclaimed. "They remind me of soft thaw winds, and warm sunshine, and nearly melted snow. Edgar, is there not a south wind, and is not the snow almost gone?"

"The snow is quite gone down here, darling," replied her husband, "and I only see two white spots on the whole range of moors: the sky is blue, and the larks are

LAVISH (<u>laa</u> vihsh) *v.* **-ing,-ed.**
  to shower with abundance or extravagance; to waste
  or spend excessively
    Synonyms: cram, overflow, saturate, teem; squander

DESPONDENCY (dih <u>spahn</u> duhn see) *n.*
  discouragement, dejection
    Synonyms: sadness, depression, desolation

GENIAL (<u>jeen</u> yuhl) (<u>jee</u> nee uhl) *adj.*
  favorable to growth or comfort; pleasant and friendly
    Synonyms: productive, generative; nice, amiable

OBVIATE (<u>ahb</u> vee ayt) *v.* **-ing,-ed.**
  to make unnecessary; to anticipate and prevent
    Synonyms: preclude; avert, forestall, deter
DESCEND (dih <u>sehnd</u>) (dee <u>sehnd</u>) *v.* **-ing,-ed.**
  to pass from a higher place to a lower place
    Synonyms: fall, dismount, gravitate

singing, and the becks and brooks are all brim full. Catherine, last spring at this time, I was longing to have you under this roof, now, I wish you were a mile or two up those hills: the air blows so sweetly, I feel it would cure you."

"I shall never be there but once more," said the invalid, "and then you'll leave me, and I shall remain for ever. Next spring you'll long again to have me under this roof, and you'll look back and think you were happy to-day."

Linton **lavished** on her the kindest caresses, and tried to cheer her by the fondest words; but, vaguely regarding the flowers, she let the tears collect on her lashes and stream down her cheeks unheeding. We knew she was really better, and, therefore, decided that long confinement to a single place produced much of this **despondency**, and it might be partially removed by a change of scene. The master told me to light a fire in the many-weeks-deserted parlour, and to set an easy-chair in the sunshine by the window; and then he brought her down, and she sat a long while enjoying the **genial** heat, and, as we expected, revived by the objects round her: which, though familiar, were free from the dreary associations investing her hated sick chamber. By evening, she seemed greatly exhausted: yet no arguments could persuade her to return to that apartment, and I had to arrange the parlour sofa for her bed, till another room could be prepared. To **obviate** the fatigue of mounting and **descending** the stairs, we fitted up this, where you lie at present: on the same floor with the parlour, and she was soon strong enough to move from one to the other, leaning on Edgar's arm. Ah, I thought myself she might recover, so waited on as she was. And there was double cause to desire it, for on her existence depended that of another: we cherished the hope that in a little while, Mr. Linton's heart would be gladdened, and his lands secured from a stranger's gripe, by the birth of an heir.

I should mention that Isabella sent to her brother, some six weeks from her departure, a short note,

OBSCURE (uhb <u>skyoor</u>) *adj.*
    dim, unclear; not well known
        Synonyms: dark, faint; remote, minor
ENTREATY (ehn <u>tree</u> tee) *n.*
    a plea or request
        Synonyms: imploration, prayer, petition
RECONCILIATION (reh kuhn sihl ee <u>ay</u> shuhn) *n.*
    the act of agreement after a quarrel, the resolution of
    a dispute
        Synonyms: rapprochement, settlement, accord
REPEAL (rih <u>peel</u>) *v.* **-ing,-ed.**
    to revoke or formally withdraw (often a law)
        Synonyms: rescind, nullify, annul, cancel, negate
RELIC (<u>rehl</u> ihk) *n.*
    an object or idea that is special because of its
    connection to the past
        Synonyms: memento, treasure, token

DRAW *v.* **drawing, drew, drawn**
    to lead, to bring about on purpose; to pull, drag;
    to attract or be attracted to
        Synonyms: provoke, elicit; haul, tow, yank; lure, entice
CONTRIVE (kuhn <u>triev</u>) *v.* **-ing,-ed.**
    to devise, plan, or manage; to form in an artistic manner
        Synonyms: concoct, scheme; create, design
SENTIMENT (<u>sehn</u> tuh muhnt) *n.*
    an attitude, thought, or judgement prompted by
    feeling; a romantic or nostalgic feeling
        Synonyms: idea; emotion
BESEECH (bih <u>seech</u>) *v.* **-ing,-ed.**
    to beg, plead, implore
        Synonyms: petition, supplicate, entreat

announcing her marriage with Heathcliff. It appeared dry and cold; but at the bottom was dotted in with pencil an **obscure** apology, and an **entreaty** for kind remembrance and **reconciliation**, if her proceeding had offended him: asserting that she could not help it then, and being done, she had now no power to **repeal** it. Linton did not reply to this, I believe; and, in a <u>fortnight</u> more, I got a long letter which I considered odd, coming from the pen of a bride just out of the honeymoon. I'll read it: for I keep it yet. Any **relic** of the dead is precious, if they were valued living.

DEAR ELLEN, it begins—

I came last night to Wuthering Heights, and heard, for the first time, that Catherine has been, and is yet, very ill. I must not write to her, I suppose, and my brother is either too angry or too distressed to answer what I sent him. Still, I must write to somebody, and the only choice left me is you.

Inform Edgar that I'd give the world to see his face again—that my heart returned to Thrushcross Grange in twenty-four hours after I left it, and is there at this moment, full of warm feelings for him, and Catherine! *I can't follow it, though*—(those words are underlined) they need not expect me, and they may **draw** what conclusions they please; taking care, however, to lay nothing at the door of my weak will or deficient affection.

The remainder of the letter is for yourself alone. I want to ask you two questions: the first is—How did you **contrive** to preserve the common sympathies of human nature when you resided here? I cannot recognise any **sentiment** which those around share with me.

The second question, I have great interest in: it is this— Is Mr. Heathcliff a man? If so, is he mad? And if not, is he a devil? I shan't tell my reasons for making this inquiry; but, I **beseech** you to explain, if you can, what I have married: that is, when you call to see me; and you

MALIGNANTLY (muh <u>lihg</u> nehnt lee) *adv.*
in an evil way; aggressively, maliciously
Synonyms: sinisterly, menacingly; destructively

JARGON (<u>jahr</u> guhn) *n.*
nonsensical talk; specialized language
Synonyms: gibberish, blather; dialect, cant, argot,
idiom, slang

must call, Ellen, very soon. Don't write, but come, and bring me something from Edgar.

Now, you shall hear how I have been received in my new home, as I am led to imagine the Heights will be. It is to amuse myself that I dwell on such subjects as the lack of external comforts: they never occupy my thoughts, except at the moment when I miss them. I should laugh and dance for joy, if I found their absence was the total of my miseries, and the rest was an unnatural dream!

The sun set behind the Grange, as we turned on to the moors; by that, I judged it to be six o'clock; and my companion halted half-an-hour, to inspect the park, and the gardens, and, probably, the place itself, as well as he could so it was dark when we dismounted in the paved yard of the farm-house, and your old fellow-servant, Joseph, issued out to receive us by the light of a dip candle. He did it with a courtesy that <u>redounded</u> to his credit. His first act was to elevate his torch to a level with my face, squint **malignantly**, project his under lip, and turn away. Then he took the two horses, and led them into the stables; reappearing for the purpose of locking the outer gate, as if we lived in an ancient castle.

Heathcliff stayed to speak to him, and I entered the kitchen—a dingy, untidy hole; I daresay you would not know it, it is so changed since it was in your charge. By the fire stood a <u>ruffianly</u> child, strong in limb and dirty in garb, with a look of Catherine in his eyes and about his mouth.

"This is Edgar's legal nephew," I reflected—"mine in a manner; I must shake hands, and—yes—I must kiss him. It is right to establish a good understanding at the beginning."

I approached, and, attempting to take his chubby fist, said:

"How do you do, my dear?"

He replied in a **jargon** I did not comprehend.

"Shall you and I be friends, Hareton?" was my next <u>essay</u> at conversation.

PERSEVERANCE (pehr suh <u>veer</u> ihns) *n.*
resolve, determination
Synonyms: persistence, tenacity, pertinacity,
steadfastness

AUTHORITATIVELY (aw thohr ih <u>tay</u> tihv lee) *adv.*
strictly, in an official and commanding way
Synonyms: despotically, autocratically, imperiously,
tyrannically

COMPLIANCE (kuhm <u>plie</u> uhnts) *n.*
submission, yielding
Synonyms: malleability, complacency, acquiescence

COUNTENANCE (<u>kown</u> tuh nuhns) *n.*
appearance, facial expression
Synonyms: face, features, visage

SOVEREIGN (<u>sah</u> vuhrn) *adj.*
unlimited, absolute; having supreme power
Synonyms: effective, highest; regal, monarchical

CONTEMPT (kuhn <u>tehmpt</u>) *n.*
disrespect, scorn
Synonyms: derision, disdain

CIVIL (<u>sih</u> vuhl) *adj.*
polite; involving the public
Synonyms: courteous; communal

SUSPENSE (suh <u>spents</u>) *n.*
a period of anxiety caused by a mysterious situation
Synonyms: apprehension, anticipation, waiting

GAUNT (gawnt) *adj.*
thin and bony
Synonyms: lean, spare, skinny, scrawny, lank

SLOVENLY (<u>slah</u> vuhn lee) *adj.*
untidy, messy
Synonyms: negligent, slipshod, sloppy, unkempt

An oath, and a threat to set Throttler on me if I did not "<u>frame</u> off," rewarded my **perseverance**.

"Hey, Throttler, lad!" whispered the little wretch, rousing a half-bred bull-dog from its lair in a corner. "Now wilt thou be ganging?" he asked **authoritatively**.

Love for my life urged a **compliance**; I stepped over the threshold to wait till the others should enter. Mr. Heathcliff was nowhere visible; and Joseph, whom I followed to the stables, and requested to accompany me in, after staring and muttering to himself, screwed up his nose, and replied:

"Mim! Mim! Mim! Did iver Christian body hear aught like it? Minching un' munching! How can I tell whet ye say?"

"I say, I wish you to come with me into the house!" I cried, thinking him deaf, yet highly disgusted at his rudeness.

"None o' me! I getten summut else to do," he answered, and continued his work; moving his lantern jaws meanwhile, and surveying my dress and **countenance** (the former a great deal too fine, but the latter, I'm sure, as sad as he could desire) with **sovereign contempt**.

I walked round the yard, and through a <u>wicket</u>, to another door, at which I took the liberty of knocking, in hopes some more **civil** servant might show himself. After a short **suspense**, it was opened by a tall, **gaunt** man, without neckerchief, and otherwise extremely **slovenly**; his features were lost in masses of shaggy hair that hung on his shoulders; and *his* eyes, too, were like a ghostly Catherine's with all their beauty annihilated.

"What's your business here?" he demanded grimly. "Who are you?"

"My name *was* Isabella Linton," I replied. "You've seen me before, sir. I'm lately married to Mr. Heathcliff, and he has brought me here—I suppose by your permission."

"Is he come back, then?" asked the hermit, glaring like a hungry wolf.

SENTINEL (<u>sehn</u> tih nuhl) *n.*
  a watch guard; surveillance, patrol, watch
    Synonyms: scout, protector; lookout, vigilance

INDULGE (ihn <u>duhlj</u>) *v.* **-ing,-ed.** *(See page 194.)*

SOLILOQUY (suh <u>lih</u> luh kwee) *n.*
  literary or dramatic speech by one character, not
  addressed to others
    Synonyms: monologue, solo

EXECRATION (ehk sih <u>kray</u> shun) *n.* *(See page 94.)*

REPENT (rih <u>pehnt</u>) *v.* **-ing,-ed.**
  to regret a past action
    Synonyms: rue, atone, apologize

INCLINE (ihn <u>klien</u>) *v.* **-ing,-ed.** *(See page 206.)*

EXECUTE (<u>ehk</u> sih kyoot) *v.* **-ing,-ed.** *(See page 44.)*

UNIFORM (<u>yoo</u> nuh fohrm) *adj.*
  consistent and unchanging; identical
    Synonyms: unvarying, steady, even, homogeneous;
    indistinguishable

OBSCURITY (uhb <u>skyoor</u> ih tee) *n.*
  dimness, lack of clarity; the state of being unknown
    Synonyms: darkness, faintness; privacy

TARNISH (<u>tahr</u> nihsh) *n.*
  corrosion, discoloration; discredit, disgrace
    Synonyms: stain, blemish; dishonor, defect

VOUCHSAFE (<u>vowch</u> sayf) (vowch <u>sayf</u>) *v.* **-ing,-ed.**
  to grant condescendingly, to give to someone or
  something on a lower level
    Synonyms: deign, endow, allow, accommodate

MISANTHROPICAL (mihs uhn <u>thrahp</u> ih kuhl) *adj.*
  having hatred for human nature or mankind
    Synonyms: cynical, pessimistic, nonbelieving

PRE-EMINENT or PREEMINENT
(pree <u>ehm</u> uh nuhnt) *adj.*
  outstanding, superior
    Synonyms: notable, prominent, important,
    illustrious, supreme

INTERMEDDLING (ihn tuhr <u>mehd</u> lihng) *v.* **-ing,-ed.**
  interference in others' affairs, imposing
    Synonyms: interloping, tampering, snooping,
    encroachment

"Yes—we came just now," I said, "but he left me by the kitchen door; and when I would have gone in, your little boy played **sentinel** over the place, and frightened me off by the help of a bull-dog."

"It's well the hellish villain has kept his word!" growled my future host, searching the darkness beyond me in expectation of discovering Heathcliff; and then he **indulged** in a **soliloquy** of **execrations**, and threats of what he would have done had the "fiend" deceived him.

I **repented** having tried this second entrance, and was almost **inclined** to slip away before he finished cursing, but ere I could **execute** that intention, he ordered me in, and shut and re-fastened the door. There was a great fire, and that was all the light in the huge apartment, whose floor had grown a **uniform** grey; and the once brilliant pewter dishes, which used to attract my gaze when I was a girl, partook of a similar **obscurity**, created by **tarnish** and dust. I inquired whether I might call the maid, and be conducted to a bedroom? Mr. Earnshaw **vouchsafed** no answer. He walked up and down, with his hands in his pockets, apparently quite forgetting my presence; and his abstraction was evidently so deep, and his whole aspect so **misanthropical**, that I shrank from disturbing him again.

You'll not be surprised, Ellen, at my feeling particularly cheerless, seated in worse than solitude on that inhospitable hearth, and remembering that four miles distant lay my delightful home, containing the only people I loved on earth; and there might as well be the Atlantic to part us, instead of those four miles: I could not overpass them! I questioned with myself—where must I turn for comfort? And—mind you, don't tell Edgar, or Catherine—above every sorrow beside, this rose **pre-eminent**: despair at finding nobody who could or would be my ally against Heathcliff! I had sought shelter at Wuthering Heights, almost gladly, because I was secured by that arrangement from living alone with him; but he knew the people we were coming amongst, and he did not fear **intermeddling**.

DOLEFUL (<u>dohl</u> fuhl) *adj.*
  sad, mournful
    Synonyms: funereal, somber, lugubrious, dismal, woeful
EJACULATION (ih <u>jaak</u> yuh lay shuhn) *n.*
  a sudden exclamation
    Synonyms: chatter, vociferation, expletive
AUDIBLY (<u>aw</u> dih blee) *adv.*
  in a manner capable of being heard, aloud
    Synonyms: detectably, perceptibly, loudly, plainly

DRAW *v.* **drawing, drew, drawn**
  to pull, drag; to lead, to bring about on purpose;
  to attract or be attracted to
    Synonyms: haul, tow, yank; provoke, elicit; lure, entice
RELISH (<u>reh</u> lihsh) *v.* **-ing,-ed.**
  to enjoy greatly
    Synonyms: savor, love, fancy

THWART (thwahrt) *v.* **-ing,-ed.**
  to block or prevent from happening; to frustrate
    Synonyms: oppose, defeat, foil, balk; hinder, baffle

I sat and thought a **doleful** time: the clock struck eight, and nine, and still my companion paced to and fro, his head bent on his breast, and perfectly silent, unless a groan or a bitter **ejaculation** forced itself out at intervals. I listened to detect a woman's voice in the house, and filled the interim with wild regrets and dismal anticipations, which, at last, spoke **audibly** in irrepressible sighing and weeping. I was not aware how openly I grieved, till Earnshaw halted opposite, in his measured walk, and gave me a stare of newly-awakened surprise. Taking advantage of his recovered attention, I exclaimed:

"I'm tired with my journey, and I want to go to bed! Where is the maid-servant? Direct me to her, as she won't come to me!"

"We have none," he answered. "You must wait on yourself!"

"Where must I sleep, then?" I sobbed: I was beyond regarding self-respect, weighed down by fatigue and wretchedness.

"Joseph will show you Heathcliff's chamber," said he. "Open that door—he's in there."

I was going to obey, but he suddenly arrested me, and added in the strangest tone:

"Be so good as to turn your lock, and **draw** your bolt—don't omit it!"

"Well!" I said. "But why, Mr. Earnshaw?" I did not **relish** the notion of deliberately fastening myself in with Heathcliff.

"Look here!" he replied, pulling from his waist-coat a curiously constructed pistol, having a double-edged spring knife attached to the barrel. "That's a great tempter to a desperate man, is it not? I cannot resist going up with this every night, and trying his door. If once I find it open he's done for! I do it invariably, even though the minute before I have been recalling a hundred reasons that should make me refrain: it is some devil that urges me to **thwart** my own schemes by killing him. You fight

COVETOUSNESS (<u>kuh</u> vih tuhs nehs) *n.*
   the strong desire to possess something had by another
      Synonyms: envy, craving

APPALLING (uh <u>pahl</u> lihng) *adj.*
   shocking, dismaying
      Synonyms: horrifying, dreadful, astounding

RETRIEVAL (rih <u>tree</u> vuhl) *n.*
   recovery, regain; the act of bringing
      Synonyms: salvage, redemption; fetching

MOROSENESS (muh <u>rohs</u> nehs) (maw <u>rohs</u> nehs) *n.*
   gloom, sadness, surliness
      Synonym: sullenness

CONJECTURE (kuhn <u>jehk</u> shuhr) *v.* **-ing,-ed.**
   to infer, predict, guess
      Synonyms: postulate, hypothesize, suppose, surmise
RESOLVE (rih <u>sahlv</u>) *v.* **-ing,-ed.**
   to determine or to make a firm decision about
      Synonyms: solve, decide

against that devil for love as long as you may; when the time comes, not all the angels in heaven shall save him!"

I surveyed the weapon inquisitively. A hideous notion struck me: how powerful I should be possessing such an instrument! I took it from his hand, and touched the blade. He looked astonished at the expression my face assumed during a brief second; it was not horror, it was **covetousness**. He snatched the pistol back, jealously; shut the knife, and returned it to its concealment.

"I don't care if you tell him," said he. "Put him on his guard, and watch for him. You know the terms we are on, I see: his danger does not shock you."

"What has Heathcliff done to you?" I asked. "In what has he wronged you, to warrant this **appalling** hatred? Wouldn't it be wiser to bid him quit the house?"

"No!" thundered Earnshaw. "Should he offer to leave me, he's a dead man: persuade him to attempt it, and you are a murderess! Am I to lose *all*, without a chance of **retrieval**? Is Hareton to be a beggar? Oh, damnation! I *will* have it back; and I'll have *his* gold too; and then his blood; and hell shall have his soul! It will be ten times blacker with that guest than ever it was before!"

You've acquainted me, Ellen, with your old master's habits. He is clearly on the verge of madness: he was so last night at least. I shuddered to be near him, and thought on the servant's ill-bred **moroseness** as comparatively agreeable. He now recommenced his moody walk, and I raised the latch, and escaped into the kitchen. Joseph was bending over the fire, peering into a large pan that swung above it; and a wooden bowl of oatmeal stood on the <u>settle</u> close by. The contents of the pan began to boil, and he turned to plunge his hand into the bowl; I **conjectured** that this preparation was probably for our supper, and, being hungry, I **resolved** it should be eatable; so, crying out sharply, "*I'll* make the porridge!" I removed the vessel out of his reach, and proceeded to take off my hat and riding <u>habit</u>. "Mr. Earnshaw," I continued,

LAMENTATION (laa mehn <u>tay</u> shuhn) *n.*
  an expression of grief or sorrow, a loud cry
    Synonyms: complaint, moaning, sobbing, tears
COMPEL (kuhm <u>pehl</u>) *v.* **-ling,-led.**
  to urge or force
    Synonyms: coerce, oblige, constrain
PERIL (<u>pehr</u> ihl) *n.*
  danger
    Synonyms: trouble, hazard, vulnerability, risk
CONJURE (<u>kahn</u> juhr) *v.* **-ing,-ed.**
  to summon a devil or spirit by invocation; to affect or
  effect as if by magic; to bring to mind
    Synonyms: materialize; invoke, arouse; recollect
APPARITION (aa puh <u>rih</u> shuhn) *n.*
  an unexpected or unusual sight; a ghostly figure
    Synonyms: illusion; spirit, specter
INDIGNATION (ihn dihg <u>nay</u> shun) *n.*
  anger caused by something mean or unjust
    Synonyms: fury, ire, wrath
EJACULATE (ih <u>jaak</u> yuh layt) *v.* **-ing,-ed.**
  to exclaim suddenly
    Synonyms: blurt, shout, declare

EXPOSTULATE (ihk <u>spahs</u> chuh layt) *v.* **-ing,-ed.**
  to reason earnestly with another; to discuss or examine
    Synonyms: argue, protest, dissuade; debate
AFFIRM (uh <u>fihrm</u>) *v.* **-ing,-ed.**
  to state positively, to assert as valid or confirmed
    Synonyms: declare, avow, maintain
CYNIC (<u>sih</u> nihk) *n.*
  person who distrusts the motives of others
    Synonyms: skeptic, scoffer, doubter
GLOWER (<u>glow</u> uhr) *v.* **-ing,-ed.**
  to glare, stare angrily and intensely
    Synonyms: frown, scowl

"directs me to wait on myself. I will: I'm not going to act the lady among you, for fear I should starve."

"Gooid Lord!" he muttered, sitting down, and stroking his ribbed stockings from the knee to the ankle. "If there's to be fresh ortherings—just when I getten used to two maisters, if I mun hev a *mistress* set oe'r my head, it's like time to be flitting. I niver *did* think to see t' day that I mud lave th' owld place—but I doubt it's nigh at hand!"

This **lamentation** drew no notice from me: I went briskly to work, sighing to remember a period when it would have been all merry fun; but **compelled** speedily to drive off the remembrance. It racked me to recall past happiness, and the greater **peril** there was of **conjuring** up its **apparition**, the quicker the thible ran round, and the faster the handfuls of meal fell into the water. Joseph beheld my style of cookery with growing **indignation**.

"Thear!" he **ejaculated**. "Hareton, thou willn't sup thy porridge to-neeght: they'll be naught but lumps as big as my neive. Thear, agean! I'd fling in bowl un all, if I wer ye! There, pale t' gulip off, un' then ye'll hae done wi't. Bang, bang. It's a mercy t' bothom isn't deaved out!"

It was rather a rough mess, I own, when poured into the basins; four had been provided, and a gallon pitcher of new milk was brought from the dairy, which Hareton seized and commenced drinking and spilling from the expansive tip. I **expostulated**, and desired that he should have his in a mug; **affirming** that I could not taste the liquid treated so dirtily. The old **cynic** chose to be vastly offended at this nicety; assuring me, repeatedly, that "the bairn was every bit as good" as I, "and every bit as wollsome," and wondering how I could fashion to be so conceited. Meanwhile, the infant ruffian continued sucking; and **glowered** at me defyingly, as he slavered into the jug.

"I shall have my supper in another room," I said. "Have you no place you call a parlour?"

ASCENT (uh <u>sehnt</u>) *n.*
   a climb or rising to another level; movement upward;
   an upward slope
      Synonyms: mounting; scaling, escalation; incline,
      upgrade

RETORT (rih <u>tohrt</u>) *v.* **-ing,-ed.**
   to make a cutting response
      Synonyms: retaliate, talk back, counter

"*Parlour!*" he echoed sneeringly. "*Parlour!* Nay, we've noa *parlours*. If yah dunnut loike wer company, there's maister's; un' if yah dunnut loike maister, there's us."

"Then I shall go upstairs!" I answered. "Show me a chamber."

I put my basin on a tray, and went myself to fetch some more milk. With great grumblings, the fellow rose, and preceded me in my **ascent**: we mounted to the <u>garrets</u>; he opened a door, now and then, to look into the apartments we passed.

"Here's a rahm," he said, at last, flinging back a cranky board on hinges. "It's weel eneugh to ate a few porridge in. There's a pack o' corn i' t' corner, thear, meeterly clane; if ye're feared o' muckying yer grand silk cloes, spread yer handkerchir o' top on't."

The "rahm" was a kind of lumber-hole smelling strong of malt and grain; various sacks of which articles were piled around, leaving a wide, bare space in the middle.

"Why, man!" I exclaimed, facing him angrily. "This is not a place to sleep in. I wish to see my bedroom."

"*Bed-rume!*" he repeated, in a tone of mockery. "Yah's see all t' *bed-rumes* thear is—yon's mine."

He pointed into the second <u>garret</u>, only differing from the first in being more naked about the walls, and having a large low, curtainless bed, with an indigo-coloured quilt at one end.

"What do I want with yours?" I **retorted**. "I suppose Mr. Heathcliff does not lodge at the top of the house, does he?"

"Oh! It's Maister *Hathecliff's* ye're wanting!" cried he, as if making a new discovery. "Couldn't ye ha' said soa, at onst? Un then, I mud ha' telled ye, baht all this wark, that that's just one ye cannot see—he allus keeps it locked, un nob'dy iver mells on't but hisseln."

"You've a nice house, Joseph," I could not refrain from observing, "and pleasant inmates; and I think the concentrated essence of all the madness in the world took up its <u>abode</u> in my brain the day I linked my fate with theirs!

DOGGEDLY (<u>daw</u> guhd lee) *adv.*
stubbornly or persistently
Synonyms: tenaciously, obstinately, pertinaciously

CONJECTURE (kuhn <u>jehk</u> shuhr) *v.* **-ing,-ed.**
to infer, predict, guess
Synonyms: postulate, hypothesize, suppose, surmise

AMPLE (<u>aam</u> puhl) *adj.*
abundant, plentiful
Synonyms: substantial, generous

DEFORM (dih <u>fohrm</u>) *v.* **-ing,-ed.**
to disfigure, spoil
Synonyms: contort, twist, mar, misshape

RESOLUTION (reh suh <u>loo</u> shuhn) *n.*
a firm decision
Synonyms: determination, will, explanation

REPOSE (rih <u>pohz</u>) *n.*
relaxation, leisure; a state of peace or tranquility
Synonyms: rest, ease, idleness; calmness, serenity

VEX (vehks) *v.* **-ing,-ed.**
to irritate, annoy; confuse, puzzle
Synonyms: bother, plague, afflict, irk; perplex, perturb

However, that is not to the present purpose—there are other rooms. For heaven's sake be quick, and let me settle somewhere!"

He made no reply to this <u>adjuration</u>; only plodding **doggedly** down the wooden steps, and halting before an apartment which, from that halt and the superior quality of its furniture, I **conjectured** to be the best one. There was a carpet: a good one, but the pattern was obliterated by dust; a fireplace hung with cut paper, dropping to pieces, a handsome oak bedstead with **ample** crimson curtains of rather expensive material and modern make; but they had evidently experienced rough usage: the valances hung in <u>festoons</u>, wrenched from their rings, and the iron rod supporting them was bent in an arc on one side causing the drapery to trail upon the floor. The chairs were also damaged, many of them severely; and deep indentations **deformed** the panels of the walls. I was endeavouring to gather **resolution** for entering and taking possession, when my fool of a guide announced, "This here is t' maister's." My supper by this time was cold, my appetite gone, and my patience exhausted. I insisted on being provided instantly with a place of refuge, and means of **repose**.

"Whear the divil?" began the religious elder. "The Lord bless us! The Lord forgie us! Wheaer the *hell* wold ye gang? Ye marred, wearisome nowt! Ye've seen all but Hareton's bit of a cham'er. There's not another hoile to lig down in th' hahse!"

I was so **vexed**, I flung my tray and its contents on the ground; and then seated myself at the stairs-head, hid my face in my hands, and cried.

"Ech! Ech!" exclaimed Joseph. "Weel done, Miss Cathy! Weel done, Miss Cathy! Howsiver, t' maister sall just tum'le o'er them brocken pots; un' then we's hear summut; we's hear how it's to be. Gooid-for-<u>naught</u> madling! ye desarve pining fro' this to Churstmas, flinging t' precious gifts o' God under fooit i' ver flaysome rages! But, I'm mista'en if ye show yer sperrit lang. Will

COMPEL (kuhm <u>pehl</u>) *v.* **-ling,-led.**
  to urge or force
    Synonyms: coerce, oblige, constrain

WRATH (raath) *n.*
  anger, rage
    Synonyms: fury, ire, resentment, indignation

INTIMATION (ihn tuh <u>may</u> shuhn) *n.*
  clue, suggestion
    Synonyms: implication, allusion, insinuation

INGENIOUS (ih <u>jeen</u> yuhs) *adj.*
  original, clever, inventive
    Synonyms: shrewd, cunning, imaginative

Hathecliff bide sich <u>bonny</u> ways, think ye? I nobbut wish he may catch ye i' that plisky. I nobbut wish he may."

And so he went on scolding to his den beneath, taking the candle with him; and I remained in the dark. The period of reflection succeeding this silly action, **compelled** me to admit the necessity of smothering my pride and choking my **wrath**, and bestirring myself to remove its effects. An unexpected aid presently appeared in the shape of Throttler, whom I now recognized as a son of our old Skulker: it had spent its <u>whelphood</u> at the Grange, and was given by my father to Mr. Hindley. I fancy it knew me: it pushed its nose against mine by way of salute, and then hastened to devour the porridge; while I groped from step to step, collecting the shattered earthenware, and drying the spatters of milk from the banister with my pocket-handkerchief. Our labours were scarcely over when I heard Earnshaw's tread in the passage; my assistant tucked in his tail, and pressed to the wall; I stole into the nearest doorway. The dog's endeavour to avoid him was unsuccessful; as I guessed by a scutter downstairs, and a prolonged, piteous yelping. I had better luck! He passed on, entered his chamber, and shut the door. Directly after Joseph came up with Hareton, to put him to bed. I had found shelter in Hareton's room, and the old man, on seeing me, said:

"They's rahm for boath ye un yer pride, now, I sud think, i' the hahse. It's empty; ye may hev it all to yerseln, un Him as allas maks a third, i' sich ill company!"

Gladly did I take advantage of this **intimation**; and the minute I flung myself into a chair, by the fire, I nodded, and slept. My slumber was deep and sweet, though over far too soon. Mr. Heathcliff awoke me; he had just come in, and demanded, in his loving manner, what I was doing there? I told him the cause of my staying up so late—that he had the key of our room in his pocket. The adjective *our* gave mortal offence. He swore it was not, nor ever should be, mine; and he'd—but I'll not repeat his language, nor describe his habitual conduct: he is **ingenious**

ABHORRENCE (uhb <u>hohr ehnts</u>) *n.*
  loathing, detestation
    Synonyms: hatred, condemnation, abomination
VENOMOUS (<u>vehn</u> uh muhs) *adj.*
  poisonous; malicious or spiteful
    Synonyms: noxious, deadly; harmful
PROXY (<u>prahk</u> see) *n.*
  a person who acts for another; the authority to act for
  another
    Synonyms: agent, substitute, stand-in; permission

PERUSE (puh <u>rooz</u>) *v.* **-ing,-ed.**
  to examine closely
    Synonyms: scrutinize, inspect, study; browse
EPISTLE (ih <u>pihs</u> uhl) *n.*
  a formal letter
    Synonyms: message, missive, note
ARDENT (<u>ahr</u> dihnt) *adj.*
  passionate, enthusiastic, fervent
    Synonyms: intense, vehement, fervid

OBLIGE (uh <u>bliej</u>) *v.* **-ing,-ed.**
  to be obligated, to require or force someone to obey
    Synonyms: compel, constrain, bind, favor
IMPLORINGLY (ihm <u>plohr</u> ihng lee) *adv.*
  in the manner of begging or beseeching
    Synonyms: pleadingly

and unresting in seeking to gain my **abhorrence**! I sometimes wonder at him with an intensity that deadens my
fear; yet, I assure you, a tiger or a **venomous** serpent could
not rouse terror in me equal to that which he wakens. He
told me of Catherine's illness, and accused my brother of
causing it; promising that I should be Edgar's **proxy** in
suffering, till he could get hold of him.

I do hate him—I am wretched—I have been a fool!
Beware of uttering one breath of this to any one at
the Grange. I shall expect you every day—don't disappoint me!

ISABELLA.

Chapter 14

As soon as I had **perused** this **epistle**, I went to the master,
and informed him that his sister had arrived at the
Heights, and sent me a letter expressing her sorrow for
Mrs. Linton's situation, and her **ardent** desire to see him;
with a wish that he would transmit to her, as early as possible, some token of forgiveness by me.

"Forgiveness!" said Linton. "I have nothing to forgive
her, Ellen. You may call at Wuthering Heights this afternoon, if you like, and say that I am not *angry*, but I'm
sorry to have lost her; especially as I can never think she'll
be happy. It is out of the question my going to see her,
however: we are eternally divided; and should she really
wish to **oblige** me, let her persuade the villain she has married to leave the country."

"And you won't write her a little note, sir?" I asked
imploringly.

"No," he answered. "It is needless. My communication
with Heathcliff's family shall be as sparing as his with
mine. It shall not exist!"

Mr. Edgar's coldness depressed me exceedingly; and all
the way from the Grange I puzzled my brains how to put

CONSOLE (kuhn <u>sohl</u>) *v.* **-ing,-ed.**
   to alleviate grief and raise the spirits of, provide solace
     Synonyms: relieve, comfort, soothe

PERVADE (puhr <u>vayd</u>) *v.* **-ing,-ed.**
   to become diffused throughout every part of
     Synonyms: penetrate, permeate, spread

ENCOMPASS (ehn <u>kuhm</u> puhs) *v.* **-ing,-ed.**
   to cover; to include
     Synonyms: surround, enclose, envelop; constitute

WAN (wahn) *adj.*
   sickly pale
     Synonyms: ashen, pallid, blanched, pasty, sickly

LISTLESS (<u>lihst</u> lihs) *adj.*
   lacking energy and enthusiasm
     Synonyms: lethargic, sluggish, languid, indolent

IMPORTUNE (ihm puhr <u>toon</u>) *v.* **-ing,-ed.**
   to ask repeatedly, beg
     Synonyms: beseech, entreat, implore, supplicate

more heart into what he said, when I repeated it; and how to soften his refusal of even a few lines to **console** Isabella. I dare say she had been on the watch for me since morning: I saw her looking through the <u>lattice</u>, as I came up the garden causeway, and I nodded to her; but she drew back, as if afraid of being observed. I entered without knocking. There never was such a dreary, dismal scene as the formerly cheerful house presented! I must confess, that if I had been in the young lady's place, I would, at least, have swept the hearth, and wiped the tables with a duster. But she already partook of the **pervading** spirit of neglect which **encompassed** her. Her pretty face was **wan** and **listless**; her hair uncurled: some locks hanging lankly down, and some carelessly twisted round her head. Probably she had not touched her dress since yester evening. Hindley was not there. Mr. Heathcliff sat at a table, turning over some papers in his pocketbook; but he rose when I appeared, asked me how I did, quite friendly, and offered me a chair. He was the only thing there that seemed decent: and I thought he never looked better. So much had circumstances altered their positions, that he would certainly have struck a stranger as a born and bred gentleman; and his wife a thorough little <u>slattern</u>! She came forward eagerly to greet me; and held out one hand to take the expected letter. I shook my head. She wouldn't understand the hint, but followed me to a sideboard, and **importuned** me in a whisper to give her directly what I had brought. Heathcliff guessed the meaning of her manoeuvres, and said:

"If you have got anything for Isabella (as no doubt you have, Nelly), give it to her. You needn't make a secret of it! We have no secrets between us."

"Oh, I have nothing," I replied, thinking it best to speak the truth at once. "My master bid me tell his sister that she must not expect either a letter or a visit from him at present. He sends his love, ma'am, and his wishes for your happiness, and his pardon for the grief you have occasioned; but he thinks that after this time, his house-

EXTORT (ihk <u>stohrt</u>) *v.* **-ing,-ed.**
to obtain something by threats or force
Synonyms: wring, coerce, blackmail, bludgeon,
bully

COMPEL (kuhm <u>pehl</u>) *v.* **-ling,-led.**
to urge or force
Synonyms: coerce, oblige, constrain
SUSTAIN (suh <u>stayn</u>) *v.* **-ing,-ed.**
to support, uphold; endure, undergo
Synonyms: maintain, prop, confirm, encourage;
withstand

hold and the household here should drop intercommunication, as nothing could come of keeping it up."

Mrs. Heathcliff's lip quivered slightly, and she returned to her seat in the window. Her husband took his stand on the hearthstone, near me, and began to put questions concerning Catherine. I told him as much as I thought proper of her illness, and he **extorted** from me, by cross-examination, most of the facts connected with its origin. I blamed her, as she deserved, for bringing it all on herself; and ended by hoping that he would follow Mr. Linton's example and avoid future interference with his family, for good or evil.

"Mrs. Linton is now just recovering," I said. "She'll never be like she was, but her life is spared; and if you really have a regard for her, you'll shun crossing her way again: nay, you'll move out of this country entirely; and that you may not regret it, I'll inform you Catherine Linton is as different now from your old friend Catherine Earnshaw, as that young lady is different from me. Her appearance is changed greatly, her character much more so; and the person who is **compelled**, of necessity, to be her companion, will only **sustain** his affection hereafter by the remembrance of what she once was, by common humanity, and a sense of duty!"

"That is quite possible," remarked Heathcliff, forcing himself to seem calm, "quite possible that your master should have nothing but common humanity and a sense of duty to fall back upon. But do you imagine that I shall leave Catherine to his *duty* and *humanity*? And can you compare my feelings respecting Catherine to his? Before you leave this house, I must exact a promise from you, that you'll get me an interview with her: consent or refuse, I *will* see her! What do you say?"

"I say, Mr. Heathcliff," I replied, "you must not: you never shall, through my means. Another encounter between you and the master would kill her altogether."

"With your aid, that may be avoided," he continued, "and should there be danger of such an event—should he

RESTRAIN (rih <u>strayn</u>) *v.* **-ing,-ed.**
  to control, repress, restrict, hold back
    Synonyms: hamper, bridle, curb, check
GALL (gahl) *n.*
  1. bitterness, resentment; careless nerve
    Synonyms: rancor; audacity, effrontery, temerity
  2. a bitter fluid secreted by the liver that aids digestion
    Synonym: bile
INCREDULOUS (ihn <u>krehj</u> uh luhs) *adj.*
  skeptical, doubtful
    Synonyms: disbelieving, suspicious
BANISH (<u>baan</u> ish) *v.* **-ing,-ed.**
  to force to leave, exile
    Synonyms: expel, deport
SCRUPLE (<u>skroo</u> puhl) *n.*
  an ethical and moral belief that prevents action; a
  hesitation caused by moral conscience
    Synonyms: principle; restraint, qualm, misgiving
TUMULT (<u>tuh</u> muhlt) *n.*
  state of confusion, agitation
    Synonyms: disturbance, turmoil, din, commotion,
    chaos
DISCORD (<u>dihs</u> kohrd) *n.*
  disagreement or variance in opinion
    Synonyms: dissonance, strife, dissension, clash

be the cause of adding a single trouble more to her existence—why, I think I shall be justified in going to extremes! I wish you had sincerity enough to tell me whether Catherine would suffer greatly from his loss: the fear that she would **restrains** me. And there you see the distinctions between our feelings: had he been in my place, and I in his, though I hated him with a hatred that turned my life to **gall**, I never would have raised a hand against him. You may look **incredulous**, if you please! I never would have **banished** him from her society as long as she desired his. The moment her regard ceased, I would have torn his heart out, and drunk his blood! But, till then—if you don't believe me, you don't know me—till then, I would have died by inches before I touched a single hair of his head!"

"And yet," I interrupted, "you have no **scruples** in completely ruining all hopes of her perfect restoration, by thrusting yourself into her remembrance now, when she has nearly forgotten you, and involving her in a new **tumult** of **discord** and distress."

"You suppose she has nearly forgotten me?" he said. "Oh, Nelly! You know she has not! You know as well as I do, that for every thought she spends on Linton, she spends a thousand on me! At a most miserable period of my life, I had a notion of the kind: it haunted me on my return to the neighbourhood last summer; but only her own assurance could make me admit the horrible idea again. And then, Linton would be nothing, nor Hindley, nor all the dreams that ever I dreamt. Two words would comprehend my future—*death* and *hell*—existence, after losing her, would be hell. Yet I was a fool to fancy for a moment that she valued Edgar Linton's attachment more than mine. If he loved with all the powers of his puny being, he couldn't love as much in eighty years as I could in a day. And Catherine has a heart as deep as I have: the sea could be as readily contained in that horse-trough, as her whole affection be monopolised by him! Tush! He is scarcely a degree dearer to her than her dog, or her horse.

VIVACITY (vih vahs ih tee) *n.*
  liveliness, spiritedness
    Synonyms: vibrance, zest
DEPRECIATE (dih pree shee ayt) *v.* **-ing,-ed.**
  to belittle; to decrease in value or worth
    Synonyms: deprecate, disparage; lessen, lower,
    devalue
ALACRITY (uh laak crih tee) *n.*
  cheerful willingness, eagerness; speed
    Synonyms: enthusiasm, fervor; dispatch, celerity,
    briskness

DEGENERATE (dih jehn uhr ayt) *v.* **-ing,-ed.**
  to deteriorate or decline in quality
    Synonyms: worsen, degrade, fall, decay

It is not in him to be loved like me: how can she love in him what he has not?"

"Catherine and Edgar are as fond of each other as any two people can be," cried Isabella, with sudden **vivacity**. "No one has a right to talk in that manner, and I won't hear my brother **depreciated** in silence!"

"Your brother is wondrous fond of you too, isn't he?" observed Heathcliff scornfully. "He turns you adrift on the world with surprising **alacrity**."

"He is not aware of what I suffer," she replied. "I didn't tell him that."

"You have been telling him something, then: you have written, have you?"

"To say that I was married, I did write—you saw the note."

"And nothing since?"

"No."

"My young lady is looking sadly the worse for her change of condition," I remarked. "Somebody's love comes short in her case, obviously: whose, I may guess; but, perhaps, I shouldn't say."

"I should guess it was her own," said Heathcliff. "She **degenerates** into a mere slut! She is tired of trying to please me uncommonly early. You'd hardly credit it, but the very morrow of our wedding, she was weeping to go home. However, she'll suit this house so much the better for not being over nice, and I'll take care she does not disgrace me by rambling abroad."

"Well, sir," returned I, "I hope you'll consider that Mrs. Heathcliff is accustomed to be looked after and waited on; and that she has been brought up like an only daughter, whom every one was ready to serve. You must let her have a maid to keep things tidy about her, and you must treat her kindly. Whatever be your notion of Mr. Edgar, you cannot doubt that she has a capacity for strong attachments, or she wouldn't have abandoned the elegances, and comforts, and friends of her former home, to fix contentedly, in such a wilderness as this, with you."

INDULGENCE (ihn <u>duhl</u> jehns) *n.*
lenience, the act of giving into desires
Synonyms: gratification, tolerance, pampering

CHIVALROUS (<u>shih</u> vuhl ruhs) *adj.*
having the qualities of the ideal knight: honor,
courtesy, and generosity
Synonyms: gallant, considerate, protective

OBSTINATELY (<u>ahb</u> stih nuht lee) *adv.*
stubbornly
Synonyms: tenaciously, persistently, firmly

GRIMACE (<u>grih</u> muhs) (grih <u>mays</u>) *n.*
facial expression showing pain or disgust
Synonyms: scowl, leer, glare

PROVOKE (proh <u>vohk</u>) *v.* **-ing,-ed.**
to cause a response, e.g., anger or disagreement
Synonyms: aggravate, stimulate, vex, incite

DISCERN (dihs <u>uhrn</u>) *v.* **-ing,-ed.**
to perceive or recognize something obscure
Synonyms: descry, observe, glimpse, distinguish

INFATUATION (ihn faach oo <u>ay</u> shuhn) *n.*
strong or foolish attachment to something or
someone, foolish passion or love
Synonyms: adoration, idolatry, reverence, crush

PERSPICACITY (puhr spih <u>kaa</u> sih tee) *n.*
shrewdness, astuteness
Synonyms: sagacity, insight, intelligence

APPALLING (uh <u>pahl</u> lihng) *adj.*
shocking, dismaying
Synonyms: horrifying, dreadful, astounding

WHEEDLE (<u>weed</u> uhl) *v.* **-ing,-ed.**
to use flattery and charm in order to persuade
Synonyms: entice, coax, cajole, sweet-talk

INNATE (ih <u>nayt</u>) (<u>ihn</u> ayt) *adj.*
natural, inborn
Synonyms: congenital, inherent, essential, intrinsic

ABJECT (aab <u>jehkt</u>) *adj.*
miserable, pitiful
Synonyms: pathetic, lamentable, sorry

"She abandoned them under a delusion," he answered, "picturing in me a hero of romance, and expecting unlimited **indulgences** from my **chivalrous** devotion. I can hardly regard her in the light of a rational creature, so **obstinately** has she persisted in forming a fabulous notion of my character and acting on the false impressions she cherished. But, at last, I think she begins to know me: I don't perceive the silly smiles and **grimaces** that **provoked** me at first; and the senseless incapability of **discerning** that I was in earnest when I gave her my opinion of her **infatuation** and herself. It was a marvellous effort of **perspicacity** to discover that I did not love her. I believed, at one time, no lessons could teach her that! And yet it is poorly learnt; for this morning she announced, as a piece of **appalling** intelligence, that I had actually succeeded in making her hate me! A positive labour of Hercules, I assure you! If it be achieved, I have cause to return thanks. Can I trust your assertion, Isabella? Are you sure you hate me? If I let you alone for half a day, won't you come sighing and **wheedling** to me again? I dare say she would rather I had seemed all tenderness before you: it wounds her vanity to have the truth exposed. But I don't care who knows that the passion was wholly on one side; and I never told her a lie about it. She cannot accuse me of showing one bit of deceitful softness. The first thing she saw me do, on coming out of the Grange, was to hang up her little dog; and when she pleaded for it, the first words I uttered were a wish that I had the hanging of every being belonging to her, except one: possibly she took that exception for herself. But no brutality disgusted her: I suppose she has an **innate** admiration of it, if only her precious person were secure from injury! Now, was it not the depth of absurdity—of genuine idiocy, for that pitiful, <u>slavish</u>, mean-minded <u>brach</u> to dream that I could love her? Tell your master, Nelly, that I never, in all my life, met with such an **abject** thing as she is. She even disgraces the name of Linton; and I've sometimes relented, from pure lack of invention, in my experiments on what

DERIVE (dih <u>riev</u>) *v.* **-ing,-ed.**
  to receive from a source, to originate
    Synonyms: infer, descend, deduce, come (from)
AVAIL (uh <u>vayl</u>) *v.* **-ing,-ed.**
  to be of use or advantage to; to result in; to make use of
    Synonyms: help, serve, benefit; transpire, eventuate;
    employ
IREFULLY (<u>ier</u> fuhl lee) *adv.*
  wrathfully, angrily
    Synonyms: peevishly, acidly, spitefully
DETEST (dee <u>tehst</u>) (dih <u>tehst</u>) *v.* **-ing,-ed.**
  to feel intense and violent hatred toward
    Synonyms: dislike, loathe
INFAMOUS (<u>ihn</u> fuh muhs) *adj.*
  having a bad reputation for committing detestable
  actions
    Synonyms: notorious, scandalous, disgraceful
PROVOKE (proh <u>vohk</u>) *v.* **-ing,-ed.**
  to cause a response, e.g., anger or disagreement
    Synonyms: aggravate, stimulate, vex, incite
DIABOLICAL (die uh <u>bah</u> lih kuhl) *adj.*
  characteristic of the devil
    Synonyms: fiendish, wicked, evil
PRUDENCE (<u>proo</u> dehnts) *n.*
  carefulness, caution
    Synonyms: circumspection, deliberation,
    thoughtfulness
COUNTENANCE (<u>kown</u> tuh nuhns) *n.*
  appearance, facial expression
    Synonyms: face, features, visage
DETAIN (dih <u>tayn</u>) (dee <u>tayn</u>) *v.* **-ing,-ed.**
  to hold; to restrain from continuing on
    Synonyms: apprehend, keep; delay, inhibit

she could endure, and still creep shamefully cringing back! But tell him, also, to set his fraternal and <u>magisterial</u> heart at ease: that I keep strictly within the limits of the law. I have avoided, up to this period, giving her the slightest right to claim a separation; and, what's more, she'd thank nobody for dividing us. If she desired to go, she might: the nuisance of her presence outweighs the gratification to be **derived** from tormenting her!"

"Mr. Heathcliff," said I, "this is the talk of a madman; your wife, most likely, is convinced you are mad; and, for that reason, she has borne with you hitherto: but now that you say she may go, she'll doubtless **avail** herself of the permission. You are not so bewitched, ma'am, are you, as to remain with him of your own accord?"

"Take care, Ellen!" answered Isabella, her eyes sparkling **irefully**; there was no misdoubting by their expression the full success of her partner's endeavours to make himself **detested**. "Don't put faith in a single word he speaks. He's a lying fiend! A monster, and not a human being! I've been told I might leave him before; and I've made the attempt, but I dare not repeat it! Only, Ellen, promise you'll not mention a syllable of his **infamous** conversation to my brother or Catherine. Whatever he may pretend, he wishes to **provoke** Edgar to desperation: he says he has married me on purpose to obtain power over him; and he shan't obtain it—I'll die first! I just hope, I pray, that he may forget his **diabolical prudence** and kill me! The single pleasure I can imagine is to die or see him dead!"

"There—that will do for the present!" said Heathcliff. "If you are called upon in a court of law, you'll remember her language, Nelly! And take a good look at that **countenance**: she's near the point which would suit me. No; you're not fit to be your own guardian, Isabella, now; and I, being your legal protector, must **detain** you in my custody, however distasteful the obligation may be. Go upstairs; I have something to say to Ellen Dean in private.

COMPEL (kuhm <u>pehl</u>) *v.* **-ling,-led.**
   to urge or force
      Synonyms: coerce, oblige, constrain
EXASPERATE (ihg <u>zaas</u> puhr ayt) *v.* **-ing,-ed.**
   to irritate
      Synonyms: frustrate, annoy, vex, pique

QUIESCENCE (kwie <u>eh</u> sihns) *n.*
   inactivity, stillness
      Synonyms: calm, repose, dormancy, idleness

HINDER (<u>hihn</u> duhr) *v.* **-ing,-ed.**
   to prevent action; to delay or impede
      Synonyms: restrain; hamper, inhibit, obstruct
TREACHEROUS (<u>treh</u> chuhr uhs) *adj.*
   untrustworthy, deceitful
      Synonyms: perfidious, treasonous, disloyal, false

That's not the way: upstairs, I tell you! Why, this is the road upstairs, child!"

He seized, and thrust her from the room: and returned muttering:

"I have no pity! I have no pity! The more the worms writhe, the more I yearn to crush out their <u>entrails</u>! It is a moral teething; and I grind with greater energy, in proportion to the increase of pain."

"Do you understand what the word pity means?" I said, hastening to resume my bonnet. "Did you ever feel a touch of it in your life?"

"Put that down!" he interrupted, perceiving my intention to depart. "You are not going yet. Come here now, Nelly; I must either persuade or **compel** you to aid me in fulfilling my determination to see Catherine, and that without delay. I swear that I meditate no harm; I don't desire to cause any disturbance, or to **exasperate** or insult Mr. Linton; I only wish to hear from herself how she is, and why she has been ill; and to ask if anything that I could do would be of use to her. Last night, I was in the Grange garden six hours, and I'll return there to-night; and every night I'll haunt the place, and every day, till I find an opportunity of entering. If Edgar Linton meets me, I shall not hesitate to knock him down, and give him enough to insure his **quiescence** while I stay. If his servants oppose me, I shall threaten them off with these pistols. But wouldn't it be better to prevent my coming in contact with them, or their master? And you could do it so easily. I'd warn you when I came, and then you might let me in unobserved, as soon as she was alone, and watch till I departed, your conscience quite calm: you would be **hindering** mischief."

I protested against playing that **treacherous** part in my employer's house: and, besides, I urged the cruelty and selfishness of his destroying Mrs. Linton's tranquillity for his satisfaction. "The commonest occurrence startles her painfully," I said. "She's all nerves, and she couldn't bear the surprise, I'm positive. Don't persist, sir! Or else, I shall

OBLIGE (uh <u>bliej</u>) *v.* **-ing,-ed.**
 to be obligated, to require or force someone to obey
  Synonyms: compel, constrain, bind, favor

INSIPID (ihn <u>sihp</u> ihd) *adj.*
 bland, lacking flavor; lacking excitement
  Synonyms: flat, unappetizing; lackluster, dull, weak
PALTRY (<u>pahl</u> tree) *adj.*
 pitifully small or worthless
  Synonyms: trivial, trifling, petty, picayune, meager

EXPEDIENT (ihk <u>spee</u> dee uhnt) *adj.*
 convenient, efficient, practical
  Synonyms: appropriate, useful, sensible
COMPLIANCE (kuhm <u>plie</u> uhnts) *n.*
 submission, yielding
  Synonyms: malleability, complacency, acquiescence

be **obliged** to inform my master of your designs; and he'll take measures to secure his house and its inmates from any such unwarrantable intrusions!"

"In that case, I'll take measures to secure you, woman!" exclaimed Heathcliff. "You shall not leave Wuthering Heights till to-morrow morning. It is a foolish story to assert that Catherine could not bear to see me; and as to surprising her, I don't desire it: you must prepare her—ask her if I may come. You say she never mentions my name, and that I am never mentioned to her. To whom should she mention me if I am a forbidden topic in the house? She thinks you are all spies for her husband. Oh, I've no doubt she's in hell among you! I guess by her silence, as much as anything, what she feels. You say she is often restless, and anxious-looking; is that a proof of tranquillity? You talk of her mind being unsettled. How the devil could it be otherwise in her frightful isolation? And that **insipid**, **paltry** creature attending her from *duty* and *humanity*! From *pity* and *charity*! He might as well plant an oak in a flowerpot, and expect it to thrive, as imagine he can restore her to vigour in the soil of his shallow cares! Let us settle it at once: will you stay here, and am I to fight my way to Catherine over Linton and his footman? Or will you be my friend, as you have been hitherto, and do what I request? Decide! Because there is no reason for my lingering another minute, if you persist in your stubborn ill-nature!"

Well, Mr. Lockwood, I argued and complained, and flatly refused him fifty times; but in the long run he forced me to an agreement. I engaged to carry a letter from him to my mistress; and should she consent, I promised to let him have intelligence of Linton's next absence from home, when he might come, and get in as he was able: I wouldn't be there, and my fellow-servants should be equally out of the way. Was it right or wrong? I fear it was wrong, though **expedient**. I thought I prevented another explosion by my **compliance**; and I thought, too, it might create a favourable crisis in Catherine's mental illness: and then I

REBUKE (ree <u>byook</u>) *n.*
reprimand, scolding
  Synonyms: admonition, disapproval, rebuff, censure
DISQUIETUDE (dihs <u>kwie</u> eh tood) *n.*
anxiety; lack of peace or tranquility
  Synonyms: edginess; uneasiness
AFFIRM (uh <u>fihrm</u>) *v.* **-ing,-ed.**
to state positively, to assert as valid or confirmed
  Synonyms: declare, avow, maintain
ITERATION (ih tuhr <u>ay</u> shuhn) *n.*
the act of saying or doing again, repetition
  Synonyms: regularity, rehashing, recurrence,
  retelling
MERIT (<u>mehr</u> iht) *v.* **-ing,-ed.**
to deserve, usually a reward or praise
  Synonyms: be worthy, earn, warrant
APPELLATION (aa puhl <u>ay</u> shuhn) *n.*
a title or name
  Synonyms: denomination, designation, moniker, tag
MISGIVING (mihs <u>gihv</u> ihng) *n.*
a feeling of apprehension, doubt, sense of foreboding
  Synonyms: distrust, presentiment, qualm, disquiet
PREVAIL (prih <u>vayl</u>) *v.* **-ing,-ed.**
to overcome; to succeed lastingly
  Synonyms: dominate, triumph; persist, endure
MISSIVE (<u>mihs</u> ihv) *n.*
note or letter
  Synonyms: bulletin, dispatch, epistle,
  memorandum, message
DESCEND (dih <u>sehnd</u>) (dee <u>sehnd</u>) *v.* **-ing,-ed.**
to pass from a higher place to a lower place
  Synonyms: fall, dismount, gravitate
LURK (<u>luhrk</u>) *v.* **-ing,-ed.**
to hide, to lie hidden or unsuspected; to prowl, sneak
  Synonyms: conceal; stalk, creep, skulk, slink

remembered Mr. Edgar's stern **rebuke** of my carrying tales; and I tried to smooth away all **disquietude** on the subject, by **affirming**, with frequent **iteration**, that that betrayal of trust, if it **merited** so harsh an **appellation**, should be the last. Notwithstanding, my journey homeward was sadder than my journey thither; and many **misgivings** I had, ere I could **prevail** on myself to put the **missive** into Mrs. Linton's hand.

But here is Kenneth; I'll go down, and tell him how much better you are. My history is _dree_, as we say, and will serve to while away another morning.

Dree, and dreary! I reflected as the good woman **descended** to receive the doctor, and not exactly of the kind which I should have chosen to amuse me. But never mind! I'll extract wholesome medicines from Mrs. Dean's bitter herbs; and firstly, let me beware the fascination that **lurks** in Catherine Heathcliff's brilliant eyes. I should be in a curious taking if I surrendered my heart to that young person, and the daughter turned out a second edition of the mother!

Chapter 15

Another week over—and I am so many days nearer health, and spring! I have now heard all my neighbour's history, at different sittings, as the housekeeper could spare time from more important occupations. I'll continue it in her own words, only a little condensed. She is, on the whole, a very fair narrator, and I don't think I could improve her style.

In the evening, she said, the evening of my visit to the Heights, I knew, as well as if I saw him, that Mr. Heathcliff was about the place; and I shunned going out, because I still carried his letter in my pocket, and didn't want to be threatened or teased any more. I had made up my mind not to give it till my master went somewhere, as

MELANCHOLY (<u>mehl</u> uhn kahl ee) *adj.*
   sad, gloomy
   Synonyms: depressed, despondent, woeful, sorrowful

REFUTE (rih <u>fyoot</u>) *v.* **-ing,-ed.**
   to contradict, discredit
   Synonyms: deny, controvert, confute, debunk,
   disprove

TANGIBLE (<u>taan</u> juh buhl) *adj.*
   perceptible, measurable, able to be seen or touched
   Synonyms: palpable, real, concrete, factual, corporeal

CONVALESCENCE (kahn vuhl <u>ehs</u> uhns) *n.*
   a gradual recovery after an illness
   Synonyms: healing, recuperation

DIVERT (die <u>vuhrt</u>) *v.* **-ing,-ed.**
   to distract or amuse; to move in different directions
   from a particular point
   Synonyms: deter, occupy, entertain; deviate, separate

I could not guess how its receipt would affect Catherine. The consequence was, that it did not reach her before the lapse of three days. The fourth was Sunday, and I brought it into her room after the family were gone to church. There was a man-servant left to keep the house with me, and we generally made a practice of locking the doors during the hours of service; but on that occasion the weather was so warm and pleasant that I set them wide open, and, to fulfil my engagement, as I knew who would be coming, I told my companion that the mistress wished very much for some oranges, and he must run over to the village and get a few, to be paid for on the morrow. He departed, and I went upstairs.

Mrs. Linton sat in a loose, white dress, with a light shawl over her shoulders, in the recess of the open window, as usual. Her thick, long hair had been partly removed at the beginning of her illness, and now she wore it simply combed in its natural tresses over her temples and neck. Her appearance was altered, as I had told Heathcliff; but when she was calm, there seemed unearthly beauty in the change. The flash of her eyes had been succeeded by a dreamy and **melancholy** softness; they no longer gave the impression of looking at the objects around her: they appeared always to gaze beyond, and far beyond—you would have said out of this world. Then the paleness of her face—its haggard aspect having vanished as she recovered flesh—and the peculiar expression arising from her mental state, though painfully suggestive of their causes, added to the touching interest which she awakened; and—invariably to me, I know, and to any person who saw her, I should think—**refuted** more **tangible** proofs of **convalescence**, and stamped her as one doomed to decay.

A book lay spread on the sill before her, and the scarcely perceptible wind fluttered its leaves at intervals. I believe Linton had laid it there: for she never endeavoured to **divert** herself with reading, or occupation of any kind, and he would spend many an hour in trying to entice her

PLACIDLY (<u>plaa</u> sihd) *adv.*
    calmly
        Synonyms: tranquilly, serenely, peacefully,
        complacently

SUPPRESS (suh <u>prehs</u>) *v.* **-ing,-ed.**
    to hold back, restrain
        Synonyms: subdue, stifle, muffle, quell, curb

PETULANTLY (<u>peh</u> chuh luhnt lee) *adv.*
    rudely, peevishly
        Synonyms: irritably, testily, fretfully

PERUSE (puh <u>rooz</u>) *v.* **-ing,-ed.**
    to examine closely
        Synonyms: scrutinize, inspect, study; browse

attention to some subject which had formerly been her amusement. She was conscious of his aim, and in her better moods endured his efforts **placidly**, only showing their uselessness by now and then **suppressing** a wearied sigh, and checking him at last with the saddest of smiles and kisses. At other times, she would turn **petulantly** away, and hide her face in her hands, or even push him off angrily; and then he took care to let her alone, for he was certain of doing no good.

Gimmerton chapel bells were still ringing; and the full, mellow flow of the <u>beck</u> in the valley came soothingly on the ear. It was a sweet substitute for the yet absent murmur of the summer foliage, which drowned that music about the Grange when the trees were in leaf. At Wuthering Heights it always sounded on quiet days following a great thaw or a season of steady rain. And of Wuthering Heights Catherine was thinking as she listened: that is, if she thought or listened at all; but she had the vague, distant look I mentioned before, which expressed no recognition of material things either by ear or eye.

"There's a letter for you, Mrs. Linton," I said, gently inserting it in one hand that rested on her knee. "You must read it immediately, because it wants an answer. Shall I break the seal?"

"Yes," she answered, without altering the direction of her eyes.

I opened it—it was very short.

"Now," I continued, "read it."

She drew away her hand, and let it fall. I replaced it in her lap, and stood waiting till it should please her to glance down; but that movement was so long delayed that at last I resumed:

"Must I read it, ma'am? It is from Mr. Heathcliff."

There was a start and a troubled gleam of recollection, and a struggle to arrange her ideas. She lifted the letter, and seemed to **peruse** it; and when she came to the signature she sighed; yet still I found she had not gathered its import, for, upon my desiring to hear her reply, she

TRAVERSE (truh <u>vuhrs</u>) (traa <u>vuhrs</u>) *v.* **-ing,-ed.**
to travel or move across; to turn or move laterally
Synonyms: cross, intersect, pass through; swivel, zigzag

INCLINE (ihn <u>klien</u>) *v.* **-ing,-ed.**
to have a specific tendency, to be predisposed
Synonyms: lean to, influence, impel, prefer

SHIRK (shuhrk) *v.* **-ing,-ed.**
to avoid a task due to laziness or fear
Synonyms: neglect, loaf, skip, skulk, escape

RESOLVE (rih <u>sahlv</u>) *v.* **-ing,-ed.**
to determine or to make a firm decision about
Synonyms: solve, decide

AUDACITY (aw <u>daa</u> sih tee) *n.*
boldness, daring
Synonyms: courage, bravery, recklessness

BESTOW (bih <u>stoh</u>) *v.* **-ing,-ed.**
to give as a gift; to apply or devote, as in time or effort
Synonyms: endow, confer, present; allocate, dedicate

CAPRICE (kuh <u>prees</u>) *n.*
an impulsive change of mind, fickleness
Synonym: whim

merely pointed to the name, and gazed at me with mournful and questioning eagerness.

"Well, he wishes to see you," said I, guessing her need of an interpreter. "He's in the garden by this time, and impatient to know what answer I shall bring."

As I spoke, I observed a large dog lying on the sunny grass beneath raise its ears as if about to bark, and then smoothing them back, announce, by a wag of the tail, that some one approached whom it did not consider a stranger. Mrs. Linton bent forward, and listened breathlessly. The minute after a step **traversed** the hall; the open house was too tempting for Heathcliff to resist walking in: most likely he supposed that I was **inclined** to **shirk** my promise, and so **resolved** to trust to his own **audacity**. With straining eagerness Catherine gazed towards the entrance of her chamber. He did not hit the right room directly, she motioned me to admit him, but he found it out ere I could reach the door, and in a stride or two was at her side, and had her grasped in his arms.

He neither spoke nor loosed his hold for some five minutes, during which period he **bestowed** more kisses than ever he gave in his life before, I dare say: but then my mistress had kissed him first, and I plainly saw that he could hardly bear, for downright agony, to look into her face! The same conviction had stricken him as me, from the instant he beheld her, that there was no prospect of ultimate recovery there—she was fated, sure to die.

"Oh, Cathy! Oh, my life! How can I bear it?" was the first sentence he uttered, in a tone that did not seek to disguise his despair. And now he stared at her so earnestly that I thought the very intensity of his gaze would bring tears into his eyes; but they burned with anguish: they did not melt.

"What now?" said Catherine, leaning back, and returning his look with a suddenly clouded brow: her humour was a mere vane for constantly varying **caprices**. "You and Edgar have broken my heart, Heathcliff! And you both came to bewail the deed to me, as if *you* were the people to be pitied! I shall not pity you, not I. You have

EXILE (<u>ehg</u> ziel) (<u>ehk</u> siel) *n.*
    the state or period of time where one is forced or
    volunteers to live outside of their country or in isolation
        Synonyms: banishment, displacement, ostracism

COUNTENANCE (<u>kown</u> tuh nuhns) *n.*
    appearance, facial expression
        Synonyms: face, features, visage

VINDICTIVENESS (vihn <u>dihk</u> tihv nehs) *n.*
    the desire to seek revenge
        Synonyms: spitefulness, vengefulness

SCINTILLATING (<u>sihn</u> tuhl ay tihng) *adj.*
    sparkling, flashing
        Synonyms: gleaming, glistening, glittering,
        shimmering, twinkling

RETAIN (rih <u>tayn</u>) *v.* **-ing,-ed.**
    to hold, keep possession of
        Synonyms: withhold, reserve, maintain, remember

INFERNAL (ihn <u>fuhr</u> nuhl) *adj.*
    devilish; relating to the dead or hell
        Synonyms: fiendish, awful, malicious; damned, accursed

killed me—and thriven on it, I think. How strong you are! How many years do you mean to live after I am gone?"

Heathcliff had knelt on one knee to embrace her; he attempted to rise, but she seized his hair, and kept him down.

"I wish I could hold you," she continued bitterly, "till we were both dead! I shouldn't care what you suffered. I care nothing for your sufferings. Why shouldn't *you* suffer? I do! Will you forget me? Will you be happy when I am in the earth? Will you say twenty years hence, 'That's the grave of Catherine Earnshaw. I loved her long ago, and was wretched to lose her; but it is past. I've loved many others since: my children are dearer to me than she was; and at death, I shall not rejoice that I am going to her; I shall be sorry that I must leave them!' Will you say so, Heathcliff?"

"Don't torture me till I am as mad as yourself," cried he, wrenching his head free, and grinding his teeth.

The two, to a cool spectator, made a strange and fearful picture. Well might Catherine deem that heaven would be a land of **exile** to her, unless with her mortal body she cast away her moral character also. Her present **countenance** had a wild **vindictiveness** in its white cheek, and a bloodless lip and **scintillating** eye; and she **retained** in her closed fingers a portion of the locks she had been grasping. As to her companion, while raising himself with one hand, he had taken her arm with the other, and so inadequate was his stock of gentleness to the requirements of her condition, that on his letting go I saw four distinct impressions left blue in the colourless skin.

"Are you possessed with a devil," he pursued savagely, "to talk in that manner to me when you are dying? Do you reflect that all those words will be branded on my memory, and eating deeper eternally after you have left me? You know you lie to say I have killed you: and, Catherine, you know that I could as soon forget you as my existence! Is it not sufficient for your **infernal** selfish-

AUDIBLY (<u>aw</u> dih blee) *adv.*
  in a manner capable of being heard, aloud
    Synonyms: detectably, perceptibly, loudly, plainly

AGITATION (aa gih <u>tay</u> shuhn) *n.*
  commotion, excitement; uneasiness
    Synonyms: disturbance; restlessness, anxiety

LIVID (<u>lih</u> vihd) *adj.*
  reddened with anger; discolored from a bruise; pale
    Synonyms: furious; black-and-blue; ashen, pallid

SENTIMENT (<u>sehn</u> tuh muhnt) *n.*
  an attitude, thought, or judgement prompted by
  feeling; a romantic or nostalgic feeling
    Synonyms: idea; emotion

INDIGNANT (ihn <u>dihg</u> nuhnt) *adj.*
  angry, incensed, offended
    Synonyms: furious, irate, mad, wrathful, ireful

ness, that while you are at peace I shall writhe in the torments of hell?"

"I shall not be at peace," moaned Catherine, recalled to a sense of physical weakness by the violent, unequal throbbing of her heart, which beat visibly and **audibly** under this excess of **agitation**. She said nothing further till the <u>paroxysm</u> was over, then she continued, more kindly—

"I'm not wishing you greater torment than I have, Heathcliff. I only wish us never to be parted: and should a word of mine distress you hereafter, think I feel the same distress underground, and for my own sake, forgive me! Come here and kneel down again! You never harmed me in your life. Nay, if you nurse anger, that will be worse to remember than my harsh words! Won't you come here again? Do!"

Heathcliff went to the back of her chair, and leant over, but not so far as to let her see his face, which was **livid** with emotion. She bent round to look at him; he would not permit it: turning abruptly, he walked to the fireplace, where he stood, silent, with his back towards us. Mrs. Linton's glance followed him suspiciously: every movement woke a new **sentiment** in her. After a pause and a prolonged gaze, she resumed; addressing me in accents of **indignant** disappointment—

"Oh, you see, Nelly, he would not relent a moment to keep me out of the grave. *That* is how I'm loved! Well, never mind. That is not *my* Heathcliff. I shall love mine yet; and take him with me: he's in my soul. And," added she, musingly, "the thing that irks me most is this shattered prison, after all. I'm tired of being enclosed here. I'm wearying to escape into that glorious world, and to be always there: not seeing it dimly through tears, and yearning for it through the walls of an aching heart; but really with it, and in it. Nelly, you think you are better and more fortunate than I; in full health and strength: you are sorry for me—very soon that will be altered. I shall be sorry for *you*. I shall be incomparably beyond and above you all. I

SULLEN (<u>suh</u> luhn) *adj.*
  brooding, gloomy
    Synonyms: morose, sulky, somber, glum

ASCERTAIN (aa suhr <u>tayn</u>) *v.* **-ing,-ed.**
  to determine, discover, make certain of
    Synonyms: verify, calculate, detect

BLIGHT (bliet) *v.* **-ing,-ed.**
  to afflict, destroy
    Synonyms: damage, plague

DEGRADATION (day greh <u>day</u> shuhn) *n.*
  the act of losing moral or intellectual character; the
  act of falling in rank or status
    Synonyms: abasement, disgrace, shame; demotion

wonder he won't be near me!" She went on to herself. "I thought he wished it. Heathcliff, dear! You should not be **sullen** now. Do come to me, Heathcliff."

In her eagerness she rose and supported herself on the arm of the chair. At that earnest appeal he turned to her, looking absolutely desperate. His eyes, wide and wet, at last flashed fiercely on her; his breast heaved convulsively. An instant they held asunder, and then how they met I hardly saw, but Catherine made a spring, and he caught her, and they were locked in an embrace from which I thought my mistress would never be released alive: in fact, to my eyes, she seemed directly insensible. He flung himself into the nearest seat, and on my approaching hurriedly to **ascertain** if she had fainted, he gnashed at me, and foamed like a mad dog, and gathered her to him with greedy jealousy. I did not feel as if I were in the company of a creature of my own species: it appeared that he would not understand, though I spoke to him; so I stood off, and held my tongue, in great <u>perplexity</u>.

A movement of Catherine's relieved me a little presently: she put up her hand to clasp his neck, and bring her cheek to his as he held her, while he, in return, covering her with frantic caresses, said wildly—

"You teach me now how cruel you've been—cruel and false. *Why* did you despise me? *Why* did you betray your own heart, Cathy? I have not one word of comfort. You deserve this. You have killed yourself. Yes, you may kiss me, and cry; and wring out my kisses and tears: they'll **blight** you—they'll damn you. You loved me—then what *right* had you to leave me? What right—answer me—for the poor fancy you felt for Linton? Because misery and **degradation**, and death, and nothing that God or Satan could inflict would have parted us, *you*, of your own will, did it. I have not broken your heart—*you* have broken it; and in breaking it, you have broken mine. So much the worse for me, that I am strong. Do I want to live? What kind of living will it be when you—oh, God! Would *you* like to live with your soul in the grave?"

UPBRAID (uhp <u>brayd</u>) *v.* **-ing,-ed.**
   to scold sharply
      Synonyms: berate, tax, reproach, rebuke, chide

SAUNTER (<u>sawn</u> tuhr) *v.* **-ing,-ed.**
   to walk leisurely or amble
      Synonyms: stroll, ramble, perambulate

EXTRICATE (<u>ehk</u> strih kayt) *v.* **-ing,-ed.**
   to free from, disentangle
      Synonyms: disengage, release, disencumber

"Let me alone. Let me alone," sobbed Catherine. "If I have done wrong, I'm dying for it. It is enough! You left me too: but I won't **upbraid** you! I forgive you. Forgive me!"

"It is hard to forgive, and to look at those eyes, and feel those wasted hands," he answered. "Kiss me again; and don't let me see your eyes! I forgive what you have done to me. I love *my* murderer—but *yours*! How can I?"

They were silent—their faces hid against each other, and washed by each other's tears. At least, I suppose the weeping was on both sides; as it seemed Heathcliff *could* weep on a great occasion like this.

I grew very uncomfortable, meanwhile; for the afternoon wore fast away, the man whom I had sent off returned from his errand, and I could distinguish, by the shine of the western sun up the valley, a <u>concourse</u> thickening outside Gimmerton chapel porch.

"Service is over," I announced. "My master will be here in half-an-hour."

Heathcliff groaned a curse, and strained Catherine closer: she never moved.

Ere long I perceived a group of the servants passing up the road towards the kitchen wing. Mr. Linton was not far behind; he opened the gate himself and **sauntered** slowly up, probably enjoying the lovely afternoon that breathed as soft as summer.

"Now he is here," I exclaimed. "For Heaven's sake, hurry down! You'll not meet any one on the front stairs. Do be quick; and stay among the trees till he is fairly in."

"I must go, Cathy," said Heathcliff, seeking to **extricate** himself from his companion's arms. "But if I live, I'll see you again before you are asleep. I won't stray five yards from your window."

"You must not go!" she answered, holding him as firmly as her strength allowed. "You *shall* not, I tell you."

"For one hour," he pleaded earnestly.

"Not for one minute," she replied.

"I *must*—Linton will be up immediately," persisted the alarmed intruder.

RESOLUTION (reh suh <u>loo</u> shuhn) *n.*
a firm decision
    Synonyms: determination, will, explanation

EXPIRE (ehk <u>spier</u>) *v.* **-ing,-ed.**
die; to come to an end; breathe out
    Synonyms: perish; terminate; exhale

DIABOLICAL (die uh <u>bah</u> lih kuhl) *adj.*
characteristic of the devil
    Synonyms: fiendish, wicked, evil

AGITATION (aa gih <u>tay</u> shuhn) *n.*
commotion, excitement; uneasiness
    Synonyms: disturbance; restlessness, anxiety

BLANCH (blaanch) *v.* **-ing,-ed.**
to pale; take the color out of
    Synonyms: to lose color; fade, lighten, bleach

He would have risen, and unfixed her fingers by the act—she clung fast, grasping; there was mad **resolution** in her face.

"No!" she shrieked. "Oh, don't, don't go. It is the last time! Edgar will not hurt us. Heathcliff, I shall die! I shall die!"

"Damn the fool! There he is," cried Heathcliff, sinking back into his seat. "Hush, my darling! Hush, hush, Catherine! I'll stay. If he shot me so, I'd **expire** with a blessing on my lips."

And there they were fast again. I heard my master mounting the stairs—the cold sweat ran from my forehead: I was horrified.

"Are you going to listen to her ravings?" I said passionately. "She does not know what she says. Will you ruin her, because she has not wit to help herself? Get up! You could be free instantly. That is the most **diabolical** deed that ever you did. We are all done for—master, mistress, and servant."

I wrung my hands, and cried out; and Mr. Linton hastened his step at the noise. In the midst of my **agitation**, I was sincerely glad to observe that Catherine's arms had fallen relaxed and her head hung down.

She's fainted or dead, I thought, so much the better. Far better that she should be dead, than lingering a burden and a misery-maker to all about her.

Edgar sprang to his unbidden guest, **blanched** with astonishment and rage. What he meant to do, I cannot tell; however, the other stopped all demonstrations, at once, by placing the lifeless-looking form in his arms.

"Look there!" he said. "Unless you be a fiend, help her first—then you shall speak to me!"

He walked into the parlour, and sat down. Mr. Linton summoned me, and with great difficulty, and after resorting to many means, we managed to restore her to sensation; but she was all bewildered; she sighed, and moaned, and knew nobody. Edgar, in his anxiety for her, forgot her hated friend. I did not. I went, at the earliest

.. no

AFFIRM (uh <u>fihrm</u>) *v.* **-ing,-ed.**
to state positively, to assert as valid or confirmed
Synonyms: declare, avow, maintain

ASCERTAIN (aa suhr <u>tayn</u>) *v.* **-ing,-ed.**
to determine, discover, make certain of
Synonyms: verify, calculate, detect

PARTIALITY (pahr shee <u>aal</u> ih tee) *n.*
favoritism or favorable bias; a special liking for
something
Synonyms: preference, inclination; fondness, fancy

opportunity, and besought him to depart; **affirming** that Catherine was better, and he should hear from me in the morning how she passed the night.

"I shall not refuse to go out of doors," he answered, "but I shall stay in the garden: and, Nelly, mind you keep your word to-morrow. I shall be under those larch trees. Mind! Or I pay another visit, whether Linton be in or not."

He sent a rapid glance through the half-open door of the chamber, and, **ascertaining** that what I stated was apparently true, delivered the house of his luckless presence.

Chapter 16

About twelve o'clock that night, was born the Catherine you saw at Wuthering Heights: a puny, seven months' child; and two hours after the mother died, having never recovered sufficient consciousness to miss Heathcliff, or know Edgar. The latter's distraction at his bereavement is a subject too painful to be dwelt on; its after effects showed how deep the sorrow sunk. A great addition, in my eyes, was his being left without an heir. I bemoaned that, as I gazed on the feeble orphan; and I mentally abused old Linton for (what was only natural **partiality**) the securing his estate to his own daughter, instead of his son's. An unwelcomed infant it was, poor thing! It might have wailed out of life, and nobody cared a morsel, during those first hours of existence. We redeemed the neglect afterwards; but its beginning was as friendless as its end is likely to be.

Next morning—bright and cheerful out of doors— stole softened in through the blinds of the silent room, and suffused the couch and its occupant with a mellow, tender glow. Edgar Linton had his head laid on the pillow, and his eyes shut. His young and fair features were almost

REPOSE (rih <u>pohz</u>) *n.*
    a state of peace or tranquility; relaxation, leisure
        Synonyms: calmness, serenity; rest, ease, idleness

MERIT (<u>mehr</u> iht) *v.* **-ing,-ed.**
    to deserve, usually a reward or praise
        Synonyms: be worthy, earn, warrant

PROTRACTED (proh <u>traak</u> tihd) *adj.*
    prolonged, drawn out, extended
        Synonyms: lengthy, elongated, stretched

as deathlike as those of the form beside him, and almost as fixed: but *his* was the hush of exhausted anguish, and *hers* of perfect peace. Her brow smooth, her lids closed, her lips wearing the expression of a smile; no angel in heaven could be more beautiful than she appeared. And I partook of the infinite calm in which she lay: my mind was never in a holier frame than while I gazed on that untroubled image of Divine rest. I instinctively echoed the words she had uttered a few hours before: "Incomparably beyond and above us all! Whether still on earth or now in heaven, her spirit is at home with God."

I don't know if it be a peculiarity in me, but I am seldom otherwise than happy while watching in the chamber of death, should no frenzied or despairing mourner share the duty with me. I see a **repose** that neither earth nor hell can break, and I feel an assurance of the endless and shadowless hereafter—the Eternity they have entered—where life is boundless in its duration, and love in its sympathy, and joy in its fulness. I noticed on that occasion how much selfishness there is even in a love like Mr. Linton's, when he so regretted Catherine's blessed release! To be sure, one might have doubted, after the wayward and impatient existence she had led, whether she **merited** a haven of peace at last. One might doubt in seasons of cold reflection; but not then, in the presence of her corpse. It asserted its own tranquillity, which seemed a pledge of equal quiet to its former inhabitant.

Do you believe such people *are* happy in the other world, sir? I'd give a great deal to know.

I declined answering Mrs. Dean's question, which struck me as something <u>heterodox</u>. She proceeded—

Retracing the course of Catherine Linton, I fear we have no right to think she is; but we'll leave her with her Maker.

The master looked asleep, and I ventured soon after sunrise to quit the room and steal out to the pure refreshing air. The servants thought me gone to shake off the drowsiness of my **protracted** watch; in reality, my chief

QUELL (kwehl) *v.* **-ing,-ed.**
    to crush; to subdue
        Synonyms: quash, stifle; suppress, pacify, quiet

motive was seeing Mr. Heathcliff. If he had remained among the larches all night, he would have heard nothing of the stir at the Grange; unless, perhaps, he might catch the gallop of the messenger going to Gimmerton. If he had come nearer, he would probably be aware, from the lights flitting to and fro, and the opening and shutting of the outer doors, that all was not right within. I wished, yet feared, to find him. I felt the terrible news must be told, and I longed to get it over; but *how* to do it, I did not know. He was there—at least a few yards further in the park; leant against an old ash tree, his hat off, and his hair soaked with the dew that had gathered on the budded branches, and fell pattering round him. He had been standing a long time in that position, for I saw a pair of <u>ousels</u> passing and repassing scarcely three feet from him, busy in building their nest, and regarding his proximity no more than that of a piece of timber. They flew off at my approach, and he raised his eyes and spoke—

"She's dead!" he said. "I've not waited for you to learn that. Put your handkerchief away—don't snivel before me. Damn you all! She wants none of *your* tears!"

I was weeping as much for him as her; we do sometimes pity creatures that have none of the feeling either for themselves or others. When I first looked into his face, I perceived that he had got intelligence of the catastrophe; and a foolish notion struck me that his heart was **quelled** and he prayed, because his lips moved and his gaze was bent on the ground.

"Yes, she's dead!" I answered, checking my sobs and drying my cheeks. "Gone to heaven, I hope; where we may, every one, join her, if we take due warning and leave our evil ways to follow good!"

"Did *she* take due warning, then?" asked Heathcliff, attempting a sneer. "Did she die like a saint? Come, give me a true history of the event. How did—"

He endeavoured to pronounce the name, but could not manage it; and compressing his mouth he held a silent combat with his inward agony, defying, meanwhile, my

VEHEMENCE (<u>vee</u> huh muhnts) *n.*
  strength, urgency
    Synonyms: fervor, intensity, ferocity, passion, ardor

sympathy with an unflinching ferocious stare. "How did she die?" he resumed at last—<u>fain</u>, notwithstanding his hardihood, to have a support behind him; for, after the struggle, he trembled, in spite of himself, to his very finger-ends.

Poor wretch! I thought. You have a heart and nerves the same as your brother men! Why should you be anxious to conceal them? Your pride cannot blind God! You tempt Him to wring them, till He forces a cry of humiliation.

"Quietly as a lamb!" I answered aloud. "She drew a sigh, and stretched herself, like a child reviving, and sinking again to sleep; and five minutes after I felt one little pulse at her heart, and nothing more!"

"And—did she ever mention me?" he asked, hesitating, as if he dreaded the answer to his question would introduce details that he could not bear to hear.

"Her senses never returned; she recognized nobody from the time you left her," I said. "She lies with a sweet smile on her face; and her latest ideas wandered back to pleasant early days. Her life closed in a gentle dream—may she wake as kindly in the other world!"

"May she wake in torment!" he cried, with frightful **vehemence**, stamping his foot, and groaning in a sudden <u>paroxysm</u> of ungovernable passion. "Why, she's a liar to the end! Where is she? Not *there*—not in heaven—not perished—where? Oh, you said you cared nothing for my sufferings! And I pray one prayer—I repeat it till my tongue stiffens—Catherine Earnshaw, may you not rest as long as I am living! You said I killed you—haunt me, then! The murdered *do* haunt their murderers, I believe. I know that ghosts *have* wandered on earth. Be with me always—take any form—drive me mad! Only *do* not leave me in this abyss, where I cannot find you! Oh, God! It is unutterable! I *cannot* live without my life! I *cannot* live without my soul!"

He dashed his head against the knotted trunk; and, lifting up his eyes, howled, not like a man, but like a sav-

GOAD (gohd) *v.* **-ing,-ed.**
  to prod or urge
    Synonyms: impel, incite, stimulate, provoke, rouse

APPALL (uh pahl) *v.* **-ing,-ed.**
  to overcome with shock or dismay
    Synonyms: horrify, astound, petrify

CONSOLE (kuhn sohl) *v.* **-ing,-ed.**
  to alleviate grief and raise the spirits of, provide solace
    Synonyms: relieve, comfort, soothe

REPOSE (rih pohz) *n.*
  relaxation, leisure; a state of peace or tranquility
    Synonyms: rest, ease, idleness; calmness, serenity

COMPEL (kuhm pehl) *v.* **-ling,-led.**
  to urge or force
    Synonyms: coerce, oblige, constrain

PERSEVERANCE (pehr suh veer ihns) *n.*
  resolve, determination
    Synonyms: persistence, tenacity, pertinacity,
    steadfastness

BESTOW (bih stoh) *v.* **-ing,-ed.**
  to give as a gift; to apply or devote, as in time or effort
    Synonyms: endow, confer, present; allocate, dedicate

AVAIL (uh vayl) *v.* **-ing,-ed.**
  to make use of; to be of use or advantage to; to result in
    Synonyms: employ; help, serve, benefit; transpire,
    eventuate

ASCERTAIN (aa suhr tayn) *v.* **-ing,-ed.**
  to determine, discover, make certain of
    Synonyms: verify, calculate, detect

age beast being **goaded** to death with knives and spears. I observed several splashes of blood about the bark of the tree, and his hand and forehead were both stained; probably the scene I witnessed was a repetition of others acted during the night. It hardly moved my compassion—it **appalled** me: still, I felt reluctant to quit him so. But the moment he recollected himself enough to notice me watching, he thundered a command for me to go, and I obeyed. He was beyond my skill to quiet or **console**!

Mrs. Linton's funeral was appointed to take place on the Friday following her decease; and till then her coffin remained uncovered, and strewn with flowers and scented leaves, in the great drawing-room. Linton spent his days and nights there, a sleepless guardian; and—a circumstance concealed from all but me—Heathcliff spent his nights, at least, outside, equally a stranger to **repose**. I held no communication with him; still, I was conscious of his design to enter, if he could; and on the Tuesday, a little after dark, when my master, from sheer fatigue, had been **compelled** to retire a couple of hours, I went and opened one of the windows; moved by his **perseverance**, to give him a chance of **bestowing** on the faded image of his idol one final adieu. He did not omit to **avail** himself of the opportunity, cautiously and briefly: too cautiously to betray his presence by the slightest noise. Indeed, I shouldn't have discovered that he had been there, except for the disarrangement of the drapery about the corpse's face, and for observing on the floor a curl of light hair, fastened with a silver thread; which, on examination, I **ascertained** to have been taken from a locket hung round Catherine's neck. Heathcliff had opened the trinket and cast out its contents, replacing them by a black lock of his own. I twisted the two, and enclosed them together.

Mr. Earnshaw was, of course, invited to attend the remains of his sister to the grave; he sent no excuse, but he never came; so that, besides her husband, the mourners were wholly composed of tenants and servants. Isabella was not asked.

INTERMENT (ihn <u>tuhr</u> mehnt) *n.*
  burial
      Synonyms: entombment, inhumation

The place of Catherine's **interment**, to the surprise of the villagers, was neither in the chapel under the carved monument of the Lintons, nor yet by the tombs of her own relations, outside. It was dug on a green slope in a corner of the <u>kirkyard</u>, where the wall is so low that <u>heath</u> and bilberry plants have climbed over it from the moor; and peat mould almost buries it. Her husband lies in the same spot now; and they have each a simple headstone above, and a plain grey block at their feet, to mark the graves.

Chapter 17

That Friday made the last of our fine days for a month. In the evening, the weather broke: the wind shifted from south to north-east, and brought rain first, and then sleet and snow. On the morrow one could hardly imagine that there had been three weeks of summer: the primroses and crocuses were hidden under wintry drifts; the larks were silent, the young leaves of the early trees smitten and blackened. And dreary, and chill, and dismal, that morrow did creep over! My master kept his room; I took possession of the lonely parlour, converting it into a nursery: and there I was, sitting with the moaning doll of a child laid on my knee; rocking it to and fro, and watching, meanwhile, the still driving flakes build up the uncurtained window, when the door opened, and some person entered, out of breath and laughing! My anger was greater than my astonishment for a minute. I supposed it one of the maids, and I cried—

"Have done! How dare you show your giddiness here? What would Mr. Linton say if he heard you?"

"Excuse me!" answered a familiar voice. "But I know Edgar is in bed, and I cannot stop myself."

With that the speaker came forward to the fire, panting and holding her hand to her side.

PROFUSELY (proh <u>fyoos</u> lee) *adv.*
   excessively, lavishly, extravagantly
     Synonyms: plentifully, copiously, abundantly,
     riotously
ALLAY (uh <u>lay</u>) *v.* **-ing,-ed.**
   to lessen, ease, or soothe
     Synonyms: alleviate, assuage, quell, mitigate,
     palliate

"I have run the whole way from Wuthering Heights!" she continued, after a pause. "Except where I've flown. I couldn't count the number of falls I've had. Oh, I'm aching all over! Don't be alarmed! There shall be an explanation as soon as I can give it; only just have the goodness to step out and order the carriage to take me on to Gimmerton, and tell a servant to seek up a few clothes in my wardrobe."

The intruder was Mrs. Heathcliff. She certainly seemed in no laughing predicament. Her hair streamed on her shoulders, dripping with snow and water; she was dressed in the girlish dress she commonly wore, befitting her age more than her position: a low frock with short sleeves, and nothing on either head or neck. The frock was of light silk, and clung to her with wet, and her feet were protected merely by thin slippers; add to this a deep cut under one ear, which only the cold prevented from bleeding **profusely**, a white face scratched and bruised, and a frame hardly able to support itself, through fatigue; and you may fancy my first fright was not much **allayed** when I had had leisure to examine her.

"My dear young lady," I exclaimed, "I'll stir nowhere, and hear nothing, till you have removed every article of your clothes, and put on dry things; and certainly you shall not go to Gimmerton to-night, so it is needless to order the carriage."

"Certainly, I shall," she said, "walking or riding: yet I've no objection to dress myself decently. And—ah, see how it flows down my neck now! The fire does make it smart."

She insisted on my fulfilling her directions, before she would let me touch her; and not till after the coachman had been instructed to get ready, and a maid set to pack up some necessary attire, did I obtain her consent for binding the wound and helping to change her garments.

"Now, Ellen," she said, when my task was finished and she was seated in an easy chair on the hearth, with a cup of tea before her, "you sit down opposite me, and put

UNRECONCILED (uhn <u>reh</u> kuhn sield) *adj.*
    unresolved, in disagreement
        Synonyms: conflicting, unrectified, clashing

COMPEL (kuhm <u>pehl</u>) *v.* **-ling,-led.**
    to urge or force
        Synonyms: coerce, oblige, constrain

INCARNATE (ihn <u>kahr</u> niht) *adj.*
    having human or bodily form; personified
        Synonyms: embodied, corporal, physical; typefied

poor Catherine's baby away: I don't like to see it! You mustn't think I care little for Catherine, because I behaved so foolishly on entering. I've cried, too, bitterly—yes, more than any one else has reason to cry. We parted **unreconciled**, you remember, and I shan't forgive myself. But, for all that, I was not going to sympathize with him—the <u>brute</u> beast! Oh, give me the poker! This is the last thing of his I have about me." She slipped the gold ring from her third finger, and threw it on the floor. "I'll smash it!" she continued, striking it with childish spite, "And then I'll burn it!" and she took and dropped the misused article among the coals. "There! He shall buy another, if he gets me back again. He'd be capable of coming to seek me, to tease Edgar. I dare not stay, lest that notion should possess his wicked head! And besides, Edgar has not been kind, has he? And I won't come suing for his assistance; nor will I bring him into more trouble. Necessity **compelled** me to seek shelter here; though, if I had not learned he was out of the way, I'd have halted at the kitchen, washed my face, warmed myself, got you to bring what I wanted, and departed again to anywhere out of the reach of my <u>accursed</u>—of that **incarnate** goblin! Ah! He was in such a fury! If he had caught me! It's a pity Earnshaw is not his match in strength: I wouldn't have run till I'd seen him all but demolished, had Hindley been able to do it!"

"Well, don't talk so fast, Miss!" I interrupted. "You'll disorder the handkerchief I have tied round your face, and make that cut bleed again. Drink your tea, and take breath, and give over laughing: laughter is sadly out of place under this roof, and in your condition!"

"An undeniable truth," she replied. "Listen to that child! It maintains a constant wail—send it out of my hearing for an hour, I shan't stay any longer."

I rang the bell, and committed it to a servant's care; and then I inquired what had urged her to escape from Wuthering Heights in such an unlikely plight, and where she meant to go, as she refused remaining with us.

RESOLVE (rih <u>sahlv</u>) *v.* **-ing,-ed.**
 to determine or to make a firm decision about
  Synonyms: solve, decide
DETEST (dee <u>tehst</u>) (dih <u>tehst</u>) *v.* **-ing,-ed.**
 to feel intense and violent hatred toward
  Synonyms: dislike, loathe
COUNTENANCE (<u>kown</u> tuh nuhns) *n.*
 appearance, facial expression
  Synonyms: face, features, visage
SENTIMENT (<u>sehn</u> tuh muhnt) *n.*
 an attitude, thought, or judgement prompted by
 feeling; a romantic or nostalgic feeling
  Synonyms: idea; emotion
AVERSION (uh <u>vuhr</u> zhuhn) *n.*
 intense dislike
  Synonyms: antagonism, antipathy, abhorrence,
  repulsion, repugnance
CONTRIVE (kuhn <u>triev</u>) *v.* **-ing,-ed.**
 to devise, plan, or manage; to form in an artistic manner
  Synonyms: concoct, scheme; create, design
DOTE (doht) *v.* **-ing,-ed.**
 to lavish attention, to love to excess
  Synonyms: adore, cherish, tender
PERVERTED (puhr <u>vuhrt</u> ihd) *adj.*
 1. misguided
  Synonyms: distorted, false
 2. immoral
  Synonyms: corrupt, depraved, debased, debauched
RETORT (rih <u>tohrt</u>) *v.* **-ing,-ed.**
 to make a cutting response
  Synonyms: retaliate, talk back, counter
COMPEL (kuhm <u>pehl</u>) *v.* **-ling,-led.**
 to urge or force
  Synonyms: coerce, oblige, constrain

"I ought, and I wish to remain," answered she, "to cheer Edgar and take care of the baby, for two things, and because the Grange is my right home. But I tell you he wouldn't let me! Do you think he could bear to see me grow fat and merry—could bear to think that we were tranquil, and not **resolve** on poisoning our comfort? Now, I have the satisfaction of being sure that he **detests** me, to the point of its annoying him seriously to have me within earshot or eyesight: I notice, when I enter his presence, the muscles of his **countenance** are involuntarily distorted into an expression of hatred; partly arising from his knowledge of the good causes I have to feel that **sentiment** for him, and partly from original **aversion**. It is strong enough to make me feel pretty certain that he would not chase me over England, supposing I **contrived** a clear escape; and therefore I must get quite away. I've recovered from my first desire to be killed by him: I'd rather he'd kill himself! He has extinguished my love effectually, and so I'm at my ease. I can recollect yet how I loved him; and can dimly imagine that I could still be loving him, if—no, no! Even if he had **doted** on me, the devilish nature would have revealed its existence somehow. Catherine had an awfully **perverted** taste to esteem him so dearly, knowing him so well. Monster! Would that he could be blotted out of creation, and out of my memory!"

"Hush, Hush! He's a human being," I said. "Be more charitable: there are worse men than he is yet!"

"He's not a human being," she **retorted**, "and he has no claim on my charity. I gave him my heart, and he took and pinched it to death, and flung it back to me. People feel with their hearts, Ellen: and since he has destroyed mine, I have not power to feel for him: and I would not, though he groaned from this to his dying day, and wept tears of blood for Catherine. No, indeed, indeed, I wouldn't." And here Isabella began to cry; but, immediately dashing the water from her lashes, she recommenced. "You asked, what has driven me to flight at last? I was **compelled** to attempt it, because I had

MALIGNITY (muh <u>lihg</u> nih tee) *n.*
evil or aggressive malice; something that produces death
  Synonyms: bitterness, resentment; malevolence

PRUDENCE (<u>proo</u> dehnts) *n.*
carefulness, caution
  Synonyms: circumspection, deliberation, thoughtfulness

EXASPERATE (ihg <u>zaas</u> puhr ayt) *v.* **-ing,-ed.**
to irritate
  Synonyms: frustrate, annoy, vex, pique

SOBER (<u>soh</u> buhr) *adj.*
not intoxicated; self-controlled; serious
  Synonyms: dry, not drunk; subdued, sedate; grave

COVET (<u>kuh</u> viht) *v.* **-ing,-ed.**
to desire strongly (something possessed by another)
  Synonyms: envy, crave

IMPLORE (ihm <u>plohr</u>) *v.* **-ing,-ed.**
to call upon in supplication, beg
  Synonyms: plead, entreat, solicit

CONFOUND (kuhn <u>fownd</u>) *v.* **-ing,-ed.**
  1. to baffle, perplex; to mistake something for another
    Synonyms: overwhelm, disconcert, entangle, muddle; confuse, misidentify
  2. to damn or condemn
    Synonyms: doom, jinx, revile, punish

DEGRADE (dih <u>grayd</u>) (dee <u>grayd</u>) *v.* **-ing,-ed.**
to lower in rank or status; to drag down in moral or intellectual character
  Synonyms: demote; shame, demean, dishonor, weaken

succeeded in rousing his rage a <u>pitch</u> above his **malignity**. Pulling out the nerves with red-hot pincers requires more coolness than knocking on the head. He was worked up to forget the fiendish **prudence** he boasted of, and proceeded to murderous violence. I experienced pleasure in being able to **exasperate** him; the sense of pleasure woke my instinct of self-preservation, so I fairly broke free; and if ever I come into his hands again he is welcome to a signal revenge.

"Yesterday, you know, Mr. Earnshaw should have been at the funeral. He kept himself **sober** for the purpose— tolerably **sober**; not going to bed mad at six o'clock and getting up drunk at twelve. Consequently he rose, in suicidal low spirits, as fit for the church as for a dance; and instead, he sat down by the fire and swallowed gin or brandy by tumblerfuls.

"Heathcliff—I shudder to name him—has been a stranger in the house from last Sunday till to-day. Whether the angels have fed him, or his kin beneath, I cannot tell; but he has not eaten a meal with us for nearly a week. He has just come home at dawn, and gone upstairs to his chamber, locking himself in—as if anybody dreamt of **coveting** his company! There he has continued, praying like a Methodist: only the deity he **implored** is senseless dust and ashes; and God, when addressed, was curiously **confounded** with his own black father! After concluding these precious <u>orisons</u>—and they lasted generally till he grew hoarse and his voice was strangled in his throat—he would be off again; always straight down to the Grange! I wonder Edgar did not send for a <u>constable</u>, and give him into custody! For me, grieved as I was about Catherine, it was impossible to avoid regarding this season of deliverance from **degrading** oppression as a holiday.

"I recovered spirits sufficient to hear Joseph's eternal lectures without weeping, and to move up and down the house less with the foot of a frightened thief than formerly. You wouldn't think that I should cry at anything

DETESTABLE (dee <u>tehst</u> uh buhl) *adj.*
  deserving of intense and violent hatred
    Synonyms: disgusting, despicable, loathsome
ODIOUS (<u>oh</u> dee uhs) *adj.*
  hateful, contemptible
    Synonyms: detestable, obnoxious, offensive,
    repellent, loathsome
OBLIGE (uh <u>bliej</u>) *v.* **-ing,-ed.**
  to be obligated, to require or force someone to obey
    Synonyms: compel, constrain, bind, favor
PROVOKE (proh <u>vohk</u>) *v.* **-ing,-ed.**
  to cause a response, e.g., anger or disagreement
    Synonyms: aggravate, stimulate, vex, incite
SULLEN (<u>suh</u> luhn) *adj.*
  brooding, gloomy
    Synonyms: morose, sulky, somber, glum
AFFIRM (uh <u>fihrm</u>) *v.* **-ing,-ed.**
  to state positively, to assert as valid or confirmed
    Synonyms: declare, avow, maintain
REVERT (rih <u>vuhrt</u>) *v.* **-ing,-ed.**
  to backslide; regress
    Synonyms: return, recur; degenerate, deteriorate
MELANCHOLY (<u>mehl</u> uhn kahl ee) *adj.*
  sad, gloomy
    Synonyms: depressed, despondent, woeful, sorrowful
USURP (yoo <u>suhrp</u>) *v.* **-ing,-ed.**
  to occupy instead, to assume a position; to seize by force
    Synonyms: preempt, displace; arrogate, appropriate

DOLEFUL (<u>dohl</u> fuhl) *adj.*
  sad, mournful
    Synonyms: funereal, somber, lugubrious, dismal,
    woeful

Joseph could say; but he and Hareton are **detestable** companions. I'd rather sit with Hindley, and hear his awful talk, than with 't' little maister' and his staunch supporter, that **odious** old man! When Heathcliff is in, I'm often **obliged** to seek the kitchen with their society, or starve among the damp uninhabited chambers; when he is not, as was the case this week, I establish a table and chair at one corner of the house fire, and never mind how Mr. Earnshaw may occupy himself; and he does not interfere with my arrangements. He is quieter now than he used to be, if no one **provokes** him: more **sullen** and depressed, and less furious. Joseph **affirms** he's sure he's an altered man: that the Lord has touched his heart, and he is saved 'so as by fire.' I'm puzzled to detect signs of the favourable change: but it is not my business.

"Yester-evening I sat in my nook reading some old books till late on towards twelve. It seemed so dismal to go upstairs, with the wild snow blowing outside, and my thoughts continually **reverting** to the kirkyard and the new-made grave! I dared hardly lift my eyes from the page before me, that **melancholy** scene so instantly **usurped** its place. Hindley sat opposite, his head leant on his hand; perhaps meditating on the same subject. He had ceased drinking at a point below irrationality, and had neither stirred nor spoken during two or three hours. There was no sound through the house but the moaning wind, which shook the windows every now and then, the faint crackling of the coals, and the click of my snuffers as I removed at intervals the long wick of the candle. Hareton and Joseph were probably fast asleep in bed. It was very, very sad: and while I read I sighed, for it seemed as if all joy had vanished from the world, never to be restored.

"The **doleful** silence was broken at length by the sound of the kitchen latch: Heathcliff had returned from his watch earlier than usual; owing, I suppose, to the sudden storm. That entrance was fastened, and we heard him coming round to get in by the other. I rose with an irrepressible expression of what I felt on my lips, which

347

INDUCE (ih <u>doos</u>) (ihn <u>dyoos</u>) *v.* **-ing,-ed.**
to persuade; bring about
Synonyms: convince, prevail; effect, lead, occasion

DRAW *v.* **drawing, drew, drawn**
to pull, drag; to lead, to bring about on purpose;
to attract or be attracted to
Synonyms: haul, tow, yank; provoke, elicit; lure, entice

TREACHERY (<u>treh</u> chuhr ee) *n.*
betrayal of trust, deceit
Synonyms: perfidy, treason, disloyalty, falseness,
infidelity

induced my companion, who had been staring towards the door, to turn and look at me.

"'I'll keep him out five minutes,' he exclaimed. 'You won't object?'

"'No, you may keep him out the whole night for me,' I answered. 'Do! Put the key in the lock, and **draw** the bolts.'

"Earnshaw accomplished this ere his guest reached the front; he then came and brought his chair to the other side of my table, leaning over it, and searching in my eyes for a sympathy with the burning hate that gleamed from his: as he both looked and felt like an assassin, he couldn't exactly find that; but he discovered enough to encourage him to speak.

"'You and I,' he said, 'have each a great debt to settle with the man out yonder! If we were neither of us cowards, we might combine to discharge it. Are you as soft as your brother? Are you willing to endure to the last, and not once attempt a repayment?'

"'I'm weary of enduring now,' I replied, 'and I'd be glad of a retaliation that wouldn't recoil on myself; but **treachery** and violence are spears pointed at both ends: they wound those who resort to them worse than their enemies.'

"'**Treachery** and violence are a just return for **treachery** and violence!' cried Hindley. 'Mrs. Heathcliff, I'll ask you to do nothing; but sit still and be dumb. Tell me now, can you? I'm sure you would have as much pleasure as I in witnessing the conclusion of the fiend's existence; he'll be *your* death unless you overreach him; and he'll be *my* ruin. Damn the hellish villain! He knocks at the door as if he were master here already! Promise to hold your tongue, and before that clock strikes—it wants three minutes of one—you're a free woman!'

"He took the implements which I described to you in my letter from his breast, and would have turned down the candle. I snatched it away, however, and seized his arm.

RESOLUTION (reh suh <u>loo</u> shuhn) *n.*
a firm decision
Synonyms: determination, will, explanation
EXECUTE (<u>ehk</u> sih kyoot) *v.* **-ing,-ed.**
to carry out fully; to make or produce
Synonyms: accomplish, achieve; perform, effectuate
MEDDLE (<u>meh</u> duhl) *v.* **-ing,-ed.**
to interfere in others' affairs, to impose
Synonyms: interlope, tamper, snoop, encroach
RETORT (rih <u>tohrt</u>) *v.* **-ing,-ed.**
to make a cutting response
Synonyms: retaliate, talk back, counter
HYPOCRISY (hih <u>pah</u> krih see) *n.*
the practice of claiming beliefs or virtues that one
doesn't really possess
Synonyms: fraud, falseness, fakeness, lip service
AFFIRM (uh <u>fihrm</u>) *v.* **-ing,-ed.**
to state positively, to assert as valid or confirmed
Synonyms: declare, avow, maintain
BASE (bays) *adj.*
lacking qualities of higher mind or spirit
Synonyms: vulgar, corrupt, immoral, menial
EVINCE (ih <u>vihns</u>) *v.* **-ing,-ed.**
to show clearly or display
Synonyms: express, exhibit, demonstrate, manifest
REPROACH (rih <u>prohch</u>) *v.* **-ing,-ed.**
to express disappointment or displeasure; to disgrace
Synonyms: blame, rebuke, admonish; discredit
COUNTENANCE (<u>kown</u> tuh nuhns) *n.*
appearance, facial expression
Synonyms: face, features, visage
BLIGHTINGLY (<u>blie</u> tihng lee) *adv.*
in an afflicted way, piercingly
Synonyms: harshly, penetratingly, bitingly
EXULT (ihg <u>suhlt</u>) *v.* **-ing,-ed.**
to be extremely joyful, to rejoice
Synonyms: celebrate, delight, jubilate

"'I'll not hold my tongue!' I said. 'You mustn't touch him. Let the door remain shut, and be quiet!'

"'No! I've formed my **resolution**, and by God I'll **execute** it!' cried the desperate being. 'I'll do you a kindness in spite of yourself, and Hareton justice! And you needn't trouble your head to screen me; Catherine is gone. Nobody alive would regret me, or be ashamed, though I cut my throat this minute—and it's time to make an end!'

"I might as well have struggled with a bear, or reasoned with a lunatic. The only resource left me was to run to a <u>lattice</u> and warn his intended victim of the fate which awaited him.

"'You'd better seek shelter somewhere else to-night!' I exclaimed in rather a triumphant tone. 'Mr. Earnshaw has a mind to shoot you, if you persist in endeavouring to enter.'

"'You'd better open the door, you—' he answered, addressing me by some elegant term that I don't care to repeat.

"'I shall not **meddle** in the matter,' I **retorted** again. 'Come in and get shot, if you please! I've done my duty.'

"With that I shut the window and returned to my place by the fire; having too small a stock of **hypocrisy** at my command to pretend any anxiety for the danger that menaced him. Earnshaw swore passionately at me: **affirming** that I loved the villain yet; and calling me all sorts of names for the **base** spirit I **evinced**. And I, in my secret heart (and conscience never **reproached** me), thought what a blessing it would be for *him* should Heathcliff put him out of misery; and what a blessing for *me* should he send Heathcliff to his right <u>abode</u>! As I sat nursing these reflections, the <u>casement</u> behind me was banged on to the floor by a blow from the latter individual, and his black **countenance** looked **blightingly** through. The <u>stanchions</u> stood too close to suffer his shoulders to follow, and I smiled, **exulting** in my fancied security. His hair and clothes were whitened with snow,

WRATH (raath) *n.*
   anger, rage
      Synonyms: fury, ire, resentment, indignation
REPENT (rih <u>pehnt</u>) *v.* **-ing,-ed.**
   to regret a past action
      Synonyms: rue, atone, apologize
SENTINEL (<u>sehn</u> tih nuhl) *n.*
   surveillance, patrol, watch; a watch guard
      Synonyms: lookout, vigilance; scout, protector

ABET (uh <u>beht</u>) *v.* **-ting,-ted.**
   to act as an accomplice
      Synonyms: assist, collaborate

ADVERSARY (<u>aad</u> vuhr saa ree) *n.*
   an opponent or enemy
      Synonyms: antagonist, foe, opposition

and his sharp cannibal teeth, revealed by cold and **wrath**, gleamed through the dark.

"'Isabella, let me in, or I'll make you **repent**!' he 'girned,' as Joseph calls it.

"'I cannot commit murder,' I replied. 'Mr. Hindley stands **sentinel** with a knife and loaded pistol.'

"'Let me in by the kitchen door,' he said.

"'Hindley will be there before you,' I answered, 'and that's a poor love of yours that cannot bear a shower of snow! We were left at peace on our beds as long as the summer moon shone, but the moment a blast of winter returns, you must run for shelter! Heathcliff, if I were you, I'd go stretch myself over her grave and die like a faithful dog. The world is surely not worth living in now, is it? You had distinctly impressed on me the idea that Catherine was the whole joy of your life: I can't imagine how you think of surviving her loss.'

"'He's there, is he?' exclaimed my companion, rushing to the gap. 'If I can get my arm out, I can hit him!'

"I'm afraid, Ellen, you'll set me down as really wicked; but you don't know all, so don't judge. I wouldn't have aided or **abetted** an attempt on even *his* life for anything. Wish that he were dead, I must; and therefore I was fearfully disappointed, and unnerved by terror for the consequences of my taunting speech, when he flung himself on Earnshaw's weapon and wrenched it from his grasp.

"The charge exploded, and the knife, in springing back, closed into its owner's wrist. Heathcliff pulled it away by main force, slitting up the flesh as it passed on, and thrust it dripping into his pocket. He then took a stone, struck down the division between two windows, and sprang in. His **adversary** had fallen senseless with excessive pain and the flow of blood that gushed from an artery or a large vein. The <u>ruffian</u> kicked and trampled on him, and dashed his head repeatedly against the flags, holding me with one hand, meantime, to prevent me summoning Joseph. He exerted <u>preterhuman</u> self-denial in

ABSTAIN (uhb <u>stayn</u>) *v.* **-ing,-ed.**
to forgo an activity or action
Synonyms: forbear, refrain
DESIST (dih <u>sihst</u>) (dih <u>zihst</u>) *v.* **-ing,-ed.**
to stop doing something
Synonyms: cease, abort, discontinue, end, quit
INANIMATE (ihn <u>aan</u> ih miht) *adj.*
not alive, lacking energy
Synonyms: dead, lifeless, dull, inactive, soulless
PURPORT (puhr <u>pohrt</u>) *n.*
intention, purpose
Synonyms: importance, meaning
DESCEND (dih <u>sehnd</u>) (dee <u>sehnd</u>) *v.* **-ing,-ed.**
to pass from a higher place to a lower place
Synonyms: fall, dismount, gravitate
ASYLUM (uh <u>sie</u> luhm) *n.*
mental hospital; refuge, sanctuary
Synonyms: institution; haven, shelter
MALEFACTOR (<u>maal</u> uh faak tuhr) *n.*
evil-doer, culprit
Synonyms: criminal, offender, felon
SUPPLICATION (suh plih <u>kay</u> shun) *n.*
a humble and earnest request
Synonyms: petition, appellation, application
MAGISTRATE (<u>maa</u> juh strayt) *n.*
an official who can administrate laws
Synonyms: judge, arbiter, authority, marshal
OBSTINATE (<u>ahb</u> stih nuht) *adj.*
stubborn
Synonyms: headstrong, stiff-necked, bullheaded,
pigheaded, mulish
RESOLUTION (reh suh <u>loo</u> shuhn) *n. (See page 350.)*
EXPEDIENT (ihk <u>spee</u> dee uhnt) *adj.*
convenient, efficient, practical
Synonyms: appropriate, useful, sensible
COMPEL (kuhm <u>pehl</u>) *v.* **-ing,-ed.** *(See page 342.)*
RECAPITULATION (ree kuh pih chyoo <u>lay</u> shuhn) *n.*
a brief summary
Synonyms: synopsis, digest, encapsulation, abstract

abstaining from finishing him completely; but getting out of breath he finally **desisted**, and dragged the apparently **inanimate** body on to the settle. There he tore off the sleeve of Earnshaw's coat, and bound up the wound with brutal roughness; spitting and cursing during the operation as energetically as he had kicked before. Being at liberty, I lost no time in seeking the old servant; who, having gathered by degrees the **purport** of my hasty tale, hurried below, gasping, as he **descended** the steps two at once.

"'What is ther to do, now? What is ther to do, now?'

"'There's this to do,' thundered Heathcliff, 'that your master's mad; and should he last another month, I'll have him to an **asylum**. And how the devil did you come to fasten me out, you toothless hound? Don't stand muttering and mumbling there. Come, I'm not going to nurse him. Wash that stuff away; and mind the sparks of your candle—it is more than half brandy!'

"'And so, ye've been murthering on him?' exclaimed Joseph, lifting his hands and eyes in horror. 'If iver I seed a seeght loike this! May the Lord—'

"Heathcliff gave him a push on to his knees in the middle of the blood, and flung a towel to him; but instead of proceeding to dry it up, he joined his hands and began a prayer, which excited my laughter from its odd phraseology. I was in the condition of mind to be shocked at nothing: in fact, I was as reckless as some **malefactors** show themselves at the foot of the gallows.

"'Oh, I forgot you,' said the tyrant. 'You shall do that. Down with you. And you conspire with him against me, do you, viper? There, that is work fit for you!'

"He shook me till my teeth rattled, and pitched me beside Joseph, who steadily concluded his **supplications** and then rose, vowing he would set off for the Grange directly. Mr. Linton was a **magistrate**, and though he had fifty wives dead, he should inquire into this. He was so **obstinate** in his **resolution**, that Heathcliff deemed it **expedient** to **compel** from my lips a **recapitulation** of what

MALEVOLENCE (muh <u>lehv</u> uh luhnts) *n.*
ill-will; evil or harm done to hurt others
  Synonyms: spite; malice, malignance

SUCCOUR or SUCCOR (<u>suh</u> kuhr) *n.*
relief; a thing that furnishes relief
  Synonyms: aid, help, support; salve, remedy
ATROCIOUS (uh <u>troh</u> shuhs) *adj.*
revolting, shockingly bad, wicked
  Synonyms: horrible, appalling, deplorable, direful
JUDICIOUS (joo <u>dih</u> shuhs) *adj.*
sensible, showing good judgment
  Synonyms: prudent, sagacious, sapient, circumspect

GAUNT (gawnt) *adj.*
thin and bony
  Synonyms: lean, spare, skinny, scrawny, lank
INCLINED (ihn <u>kliend</u>) *adj.*
predisposed, having a certain tendency
  Synonyms: likely, prone
HINDER (<u>hihn</u> duhr) *v.* **-ing,-ed.**
to prevent action; to delay or impede
  Synonyms: restrain; hamper, inhibit, obstruct
DRAW *v.* **drawing, drew, drawn**
to attract or be attracted to; to pull, drag; to lead, to
bring about on purpose
  Synonyms: lure, entice; haul, tow, yank; provoke, elicit
DIABOLICAL (die uh <u>bah</u> lih kuhl) *adj.*
characteristic of the devil
  Synonyms: fiendish, wicked, evil
DEVOID (dih <u>voyd</u>) *adj.*
being without, lacking
  Synonyms: destitute, empty, vacant, null, bare

had taken place; standing over me, heaving with **malevolence**, as I reluctantly delivered the account in answer to his questions. It required a great deal of labour to satisfy the old man that Heathcliff was not the aggressor; especially with my hardly-wrung replies. However, Mr. Earnshaw soon convinced him that he was alive still; Joseph hastened to administer a dose of spirits, and by their **succour** his master presently regained motion and consciousness. Heathcliff, aware that his opponent was ignorant of the treatment received while insensible, called him deliriously intoxicated; and said he should not notice his **atrocious** conduct further, but advised him to get to bed. To my joy, he left us, after giving this **judicious** counsel, and Hindley stretched himself on the hearthstone. I departed to my own room, marvelling that I had escaped so easily.

"This morning, when I came down, about half-an-hour before noon, Mr. Earnshaw was sitting by the fire, deadly sick; his evil genius, almost as **gaunt** and ghastly, leant against the chimney. Neither appeared **inclined** to dine, and, having waited till all was cold on the table, I commenced alone. Nothing **hindered** me from eating heartily, and I experienced a certain sense of satisfaction and superiority, as, at intervals, I cast a look towards my silent companions, and felt the comfort of a quiet conscience within me. After I had done, I ventured on the unusual liberty of **drawing** near the fire, going round Earnshaw's seat, and kneeling in the corner beside him.

"Heathcliff did not glance my way, and I gazed up, and contemplated his features almost as confidently as if they had been turned to stone. His forehead, that I once thought so manly, and that I now think so **diabolical**, was shaded with a heavy cloud; his <u>basilisk</u> eyes were nearly quenched by sleeplessness, and weeping, perhaps, for the lashes were wet then; his lips **devoid** of their ferocious sneer, were sealed in an expression of unspeakable sadness. Had it been another, I would have covered my face in the presence of such grief. In *his* case, I was gratified;

IGNOBLE (ihg <u>noh</u> buhl) *adj.*
dishonorable, not noble in character
Synonyms: mean, low, base, disreputable, sordid

AFFLICT (uh <u>flihkt</u>) *v.* **-ing,-ed.**
to distress severely so as to cause persistent anguish
Synonyms: harm, torment, trouble, pain

PRESUMPTUOUS (pree <u>suhmp</u> chyoo uhs) *adj.*
rude, improperly bold
Synonyms: brash, familiar, sassy, impertinent

IMPLORE (ihm <u>plohr</u>) *v.* **-ing,-ed.**
to call upon in supplication, beg
Synonyms: plead, entreat, solicit

REPULSIVE (rih <u>puhl</u> sihv) *adj.*
repellant; sickening, disgusting
Synonyms: offensive; nauseating

and, **ignoble** as it seems to insult a fallen enemy, I couldn't miss this chance of sticking in a dart: his weakness was the only time when I could taste the delight of paying wrong for wrong."

"Fie, fie, Miss!" I interrupted. "One might suppose you had never opened a Bible in your life. If God **afflict** your enemies, surely that ought to suffice you. It is both mean and **presumptuous** to add your torture to His!"

"In general I'll allow that it would be, Ellen," she continued, "but what misery laid on Heathcliff could content me, unless I have a hand in it? I'd rather he suffered *less*, if I might cause his sufferings and he might *know* that I was the cause. Oh, I owe him so much. On only one condition can I hope to forgive him. It is, if I may take an eye for an eye, a tooth for a tooth; for every wrench of agony return a wrench: reduce him to my level. As he was the first to injure, make him the first to **implore** pardon; and then— why then, Ellen, I might show you some generosity. But it is utterly impossible I can ever be revenged, and therefore I cannot forgive him. Hindley wanted some water, and I handed him a glass, and asked him how he was.

"'Not as ill as I wish,' he replied. 'But leaving out my arm, every inch of me is as sore as if I had been fighting with a legion of imps!'

"'Yes, no wonder,' was my next remark. 'Catherine used to boast that she stood between you and bodily harm: she meant that certain persons would not hurt you for fear of offending her. It's well people don't *really* rise from their grave, or, last night, she might have witnessed a **repulsive** scene! Are not you bruised and cut over your chest and shoulders?'

"'I can't say,' he answered, 'but what do you mean? Did he dare to strike me when I was down?'

"'He trampled on and kicked you, and dashed you on the ground,' I whispered. 'And his mouth watered to tear you with his teeth; because he's only half man: not so much, and the rest fiend.'

COUNTENANCE (<u>kown</u> tuh nuhns) *n.*
appearance, facial expression
Synonyms: face, features, visage

DERISION (dih <u>rih</u> zhuhn) *n.*
mockery, ridicule
Synonyms: taunting, jeering, insults, teasing

"Mr. Earnshaw looked up, like me, to the **countenance** of our mutual foe; who, absorbed in his anguish, seemed insensible to anything around him: the longer he stood, the plainer his reflections revealed their blackness through his features.

"'Oh, if God would but give me strength to strangle him in my last agony, I'd go to hell with joy,' groaned the impatient man, writhing to rise, and sinking back in despair, convinced of his inadequacy for the struggle.

"'Nay, it's enough that he has murdered one of you,' I observed aloud. 'At the Grange, every one knows your sister would have been living now, had it not been for Mr. Heathcliff. After all, it is preferable to be hated than loved by him. When I recollect how happy we were—how happy Catherine was before he came—I'm fit to curse the day.'

"Most likely, Heathcliff noticed more the truth of what was said, than the spirit of the person who said it. His attention was roused, I saw, for his eyes rained down tears among the ashes, and he drew his breath in suffocating sighs. I stared full at him, and laughed scornfully. The clouded windows of hell flashed a moment towards me; the fiend which usually looked out, however, was so dimmed and drowned that I did not fear to hazard another sound of **derision**.

"'Get up, and begone out of my sight,' said the mourner.

"I guessed he uttered those words, at least, though his voice was hardly intelligible.

"'I beg your pardon,' I replied. 'But I loved Catherine too; and her brother requires attendance, which, for her sake, I shall supply. Now that she's dead, I see her in Hindley: Hindley has exactly her eyes, if you had not tried to gouge them out, and made them black and red; and her—'

"'Get up, wretched idiot, before I stamp you to death!' he cried, making a movement that caused me to make one also.

CONTEMPTIBLE (kuhn <u>tehmpt</u> ih buhl) *adj.*
  disrespectful, worthy of scorn
    Synonyms: shameful, disdainful, despicable
DEGRADING (dih <u>grayd</u> ihng) (dee <u>grayd</u> ihng) *adj.*
  belittling and humiliating; unfavorable
    Synonyms: shameful, demeaning, weakening;
    negative, unfortunate
ABOMINABLE (uh <u>bah</u> mihn uh buhl) *adj.*
  loathsome, detestable
    Synonyms: abhorrent, terrible, beastly, deplorable
DETESTATION (dee tehs <u>tay</u> shuhn) *n.*
  intense and violent hatred
    Synonyms: disgust, loathing, abhorrence

PRECIPITATE (preh <u>sih</u> puh tayt) *v.* **-ing,-ed.**
  to move rapidly, to bring about abruptly
    Synonyms: speed, launch, accelerate, quicken
PERPETUAL (puhr <u>peht</u> chyoo uhl) *adj.*
  endless, lasting
    Synonyms: continuous, constant, ceaseless, eternal,
    perennial
INFERNAL (ihn <u>fuhr</u> nuhl) *adj.*
  relating to the dead or hell; devilish
    Synonyms: damned, accursed; fiendish, awful, malicious
ENTREATY (ehn <u>tree</u> tee) *n.*
  a plea or request
    Synonyms: imploration, prayer, petition
BESTOW (bih <u>stoh</u>) *v.* **-ing,-ed.**
  to give as a gift; to apply or devote, as in time or effort
    Synonyms: endow, confer, present; allocate, dedicate
DESCEND (dih <u>sehnd</u>) (dee <u>sehnd</u>) *v.* **-ing,-ed.**
  to pass from a higher place to a lower place
    Synonyms: fall, dismount, gravitate

"'But then,' I continued, holding myself ready to flee, 'if poor Catherine had trusted you, and assumed the ridiculous, **contemptible**, **degrading** title of Mrs. Heathcliff, she would soon have presented a similar picture! *She* wouldn't have borne your **abominable** behaviour quietly: her **detestation** and disgust must have found voice.'

"The back of the settle and Earnshaw's person interposed between me and him: so instead of endeavouring to reach me, he snatched a dinner knife from the table and flung it at my head. It struck beneath my ear, and stopped the sentence I was uttering; but, pulling it out, I sprang to the door and delivered another; which I hope went a little deeper than his missile. The last glimpse I caught of him was a furious rush on his part, checked by the embrace of his host; and both fell locked together on the hearth. In my flight through the kitchen I bid Joseph speed to his master; I knocked over Hareton, who was hanging a litter of puppies from a chair-back in the doorway; and, blest as a soul escaped from purgatory, I bounded, leaped, and flew down the steep road; then, quitting its windings, shot direct across the moor, rolling over banks, and wading through marshes: **precipitating** myself, in fact, towards the beacon light of the Grange. And far rather would I be condemned to a **perpetual** dwelling in the **infernal** regions, than, even for one night, abide beneath the roof of Wuthering Heights again."

Isabella ceased speaking, and took a drink of tea; then she rose, and bidding me put on her bonnet, and great shawl I had brought, and turning a deaf ear to my **entreaties** for her to remain another hour, she stepped on to a chair, kissed Edgar's and Catherine's portraits, **bestowed** a similar salute on me, and **descended** to the carriage, accompanied by Fanny, who yelped wild with joy at recovering her mistress. She was driven away, never to revisit this neighbourhood: but a regular correspondence was established between her and my master when things were more settled. I believe her new abode was in

SUBSEQUENT (<u>suhb</u> suh kwehnt) *adj*.
  following in time or order
    Synonyms: succeeding, next, afterward

FORBEARANCE (fohr <u>baar</u> uhns) *n*.
  patience, restraint, leniency
    Synonyms: resignation, tolerance
AVERSION (uh <u>vuhr</u> zhuhn) *n*.
  intense dislike
    Synonyms: antagonism, antipathy, abhorrence,
    repulsion, repugnance

ABHOR (uhb <u>hohr</u>) *v*. **-ring,-red.**
  to loathe, detest, despise
    Synonyms: hate, condemn, abominate, execrate

MAGISTRATE (<u>maa</u> juh strayt) *n*.
  an official who can administrate laws
    Synonyms: judge, arbiter, authority, marshal
SECLUSION (sih <u>cloo</u> zhuhn) *n*.
  isolation, detachment
    Synonyms: separation, privacy, solitude

the south, near London; there she had a son born, a few months **subsequent** to her escape. He was christened Linton, and, from the first, she reported him to be an ailing, <u>peevish</u> creature.

Mr. Heathcliff, meeting me one day in the village, inquired where she lived. I refused to tell. He remarked that it was not of any moment, only she must beware of coming to her brother: she should not be with him, if he had to keep her himself. Though I would give no information, he discovered, through some of the other servants, both her place of residence and the existence of the child. Still he didn't molest her: for which **forbearance** she might thank his **aversion**, I suppose. He often asked about the infant, when he saw me; and on hearing its name, smiled grimly, and observed:

"They wish me to hate it too, do they?"

"I don't think they wish you to know anything about it," I answered.

"But I'll have it," he said, "when I want it. They may reckon on that!"

Fortunately, its mother died before the time arrived; some thirteen years after the decease of Catherine, when Linton was twelve, or a little more.

On the day succeeding Isabella's unexpected visit, I had no opportunity of speaking to my master: he shunned conversation, and was fit for discussing nothing. When I could get him to listen, I saw it pleased him that his sister had left her husband; whom he **abhorred** with an intensity which the mildness of his nature would scarcely seem to allow. So deep and sensitive was his **aversion**, that he refrained from going anywhere where he was likely to see or hear of Heathcliff. Grief, and that together, transformed him into a complete hermit: he threw up his office of **magistrate**, ceased even to attend church, avoided the village on all occasions, and spent a life of entire **seclusion** within the limits of his park and grounds; only varied by solitary rambles on the moors, and visits to the grave of his wife, mostly at evening, or early morning

MELANCHOLY (<u>mehl</u> uhn kahl ee) *n.*
  sadness, depression
    Synonyms: dejection, despondency, woe, sorrow
ARDENT (<u>ahr</u> dihnt) *adj.*
  passionate, enthusiastic, fervent
    Synonyms: intense, vehement, fervid
ASPIRING (uh <u>spier</u> ihng) *n.*
  hoping or hopes, (the idea of) aiming for a goal
    Synonyms: desiring, intentions, purpose, expectations
CONSOLATION (kahn suh <u>lay</u> shuhn) *n.*
  something providing comfort or solace for a loss or
  hardship
    Synonym: condolence
TOTTER (<u>tah</u> tuhr) *v.* **-ing,-ed.**
  to stand with unsteadiness
    Synonyms: wobble, sway, stagger
DESPOT (<u>dehs</u> puht) (<u>dehs</u> paht) *n.*
  tyrannical ruler
    Synonyms: authoritarian, autocrat, dictator,
    totalitarian

before other wanderers were abroad. But he was too good to be thoroughly unhappy long. *He* didn't pray for Catherine's soul to haunt him. Time brought resignation, and a **melancholy** sweeter than common joy. He recalled her memory with **ardent**, tender love, and hopeful **aspiring** to the better world; where he doubted not she was gone.

And he had earthly **consolation** and affections also. For a few days, I said, he seemed regardless of the puny successor to the departed: the coldness melted as fast as snow in April, and ere the tiny thing could stammer a word or **totter** a step, it wielded a **despot's** <u>sceptre</u> in his heart. It was named Catherine; but he never called it the name in full, as he had never called the first Catherine short; probably because Heathcliff had a habit of doing so. The little one was always Cathy; it formed to him a distinction from the mother, and yet a connection with her; and his attachment sprang from its relation to her, far more than from its being his own.

I used to draw a comparison between him and Hindley Earnshaw, and <u>perplex</u> myself to explain satisfactorily why their conduct was so opposite in similar circumstances. They had both been fond husbands, and were both attached to their children; and I could not see how they shouldn't both have taken the same road, for good or evil. But, I thought in my mind—Hindley, with apparently the stronger head, has shown himself sadly the worse and the weaker man. When his ship struck, the captain abandoned his post; and the crew, instead of trying to save her, rushed into riot and confusion, leaving no hope for their luckless vessel. Linton, on the contrary, displayed the true courage of a loyal and faithful soul: he trusted God; and God comforted him. One hoped, and the other despaired: they chose their own lots, and were righteously doomed to endure them. But you'll not want to hear my moralising, Mr. Lockwood: you'll judge as well as I can, all these things: at least, you'll think you will, and that's the same. The end of Earnshaw was what might have been expected; it followed fast on his sister's:

SUCCINCT (suh <u>sihnkt</u>) *adj.*
   terse, brief, concise
      Synonyms: laconic, pithy

PRESENTIMENT (prih <u>sehn</u> tih mehnt) *n.*
   the anticipation or sense that something may happen
      Synonyms: expectation, premonition

HINDER (<u>hihn</u> duhr) *v.* **-ing,-ed.**
   to prevent action; to delay or impede
      Synonyms: restrain; hamper, inhibit, obstruct
PONDER (<u>pahn</u> duhr) *v.* **-ing,-ed.**
   to consider or think about something in depth
      Synonyms: contemplate, reflect, ruminate
PERTINACIOUS (puhr tih <u>ay</u> shuhs) *adj.*
   stubborn and persistently unyielding
      Synonyms: unrelenting, obstinate, tenacious
RESOLVE (rih <u>sahlv</u>) *v.* **-ing,-ed.**
   to determine or to make a firm decision about
      Synonyms: solve, decide

there was scarcely six months between them. We, at the Grange, never got a very **succinct** account of his state preceding it; all that I did learn, was on occasion of going to aid in the preparations for the funeral. Mr. Kenneth came to announce the event to my master.

"Well, Nelly," said he, riding into the yard one morning, too early not to alarm me with an instant **presentiment** of bad news, "it's yours and my turn to go into mourning at present. Who's given us the slip now, do you think?"

"Who?" I asked in a flurry.

"Why, guess!" he returned, dismounting, and slinging his bridle on a hook by the door. "And nip up the corner of your apron: I'm certain you'll need it."

"Not Mr. Heathcliff, surely?" I exclaimed.

"What! Would you have tears for him?" said the doctor. "No, Heathcliff's a tough young fellow: he looks blooming to-day. I've just seen him. He's rapidly regaining flesh since he lost his better half."

"Who is it then, Mr. Kenneth?" I repeated impatiently.

"Hindley Earnshaw! Your old friend Hindley," he replied, "and my wicked gossip: though he's been too wild for me this long while. There! I said we should draw water. But cheer up. He died true to his character: drunk as a lord. Poor lad! I'm sorry, too. One can't help missing an old companion: though he had the worst tricks with him that ever man imagined, and has done me many a rascally turn. He's barely twenty-seven, it seems; that's your own age: who would have thought you were born in one year?"

I confess this blow was greater to me than the shock of Mrs. Linton's death: ancient associations lingered round my heart; I sat down in the porch and wept as for a blood relation, desiring Mr. Kenneth to get another servant to introduce him to the master. I could not **hinder** myself from **pondering** on the question—"Had he had fair play?" Whatever I did, that idea would bother me: it was so tiresomely **pertinacious** that I **resolved** on requesting leave to

ELOQUENTLY (<u>eh</u> luh kwuhnt lee) *adv.*
  persuasively and effectively, with regards to speech
    Synonyms: expressively, fluently

AFFIRM (uh <u>fihrm</u>) *v.* **-ing,-ed.**
  to state positively, to assert as valid or confirmed
    Synonyms: declare, avow, maintain
INCLINE (ihn <u>klien</u>) *v.* **-ing,-ed.**
  to have a specific tendency, to be predisposed
    Synonyms: lean to, influence, impel, prefer
LENIENTLY (<u>lee</u> nee uhnt lee) (<u>leen</u> yuhnt lee) *adv.*
  permissively, in an easygoing manner
    Synonyms: mercifully, generously, indulgently,
    tolerantly

go to Wuthering Heights, and assist in the last duties to the dead. Mr. Linton was extremely reluctant to consent, but I pleaded **eloquently** for the friendless condition in which he lay; and I said my old master and foster-brother had a claim on my services as strong as his own. Besides, I reminded him that the child Hareton was his wife's nephew, and, in the absence of nearer kin, he ought to act as its guardian; and he ought to and must inquire how the property was left, and look over the concerns of his brother-in-law. He was unfit for attending to such matters then, but he bid me speak to his lawyer; and at length permitted me to go. His lawyer had been Earnshaw's also: I called at the village, and asked him to accompany me. He shook his head, and advised him that Heathcliff should be let alone; **affirming**, if the truth were known, Hareton would be found little else than a beggar.

"His father died in debt," he said. "The whole property is mortgaged, and the sole chance for the natural heir is to allow him an opportunity of creating some interest in the creditor's heart, that he may be **inclined** to deal **leniently** towards him."

When I reached the Heights, I explained that I had come to see everything carried on decently; and Joseph, who appeared in sufficient distress, expressed satisfaction at my presence. Mr. Heathcliff said he did not perceive that I was wanted; but I might stay and order the arrangements for the funeral, if I chose.

"Correctly," he remarked, "that fool's body should be buried at the cross-roads, without ceremony of any kind. I happened to leave him ten minutes yesterday afternoon, and in that interval he fastened the two doors of the house against me, and he has spent the night in drinking himself to death deliberately! We broke in this morning, for we heard him snorting like a horse; and there he was, laid over the <u>settle</u>; flaying and scalping would not have wakened him. I sent for Kenneth, and he came; but not till the beast had changed into <u>carrion</u>: he was both dead

STARK (stahrk) *adj.*
  bare; empty, vacant
    Synonyms: naked; austere, barren, bleak, grim, dismal

EXECUTE (<u>ehk</u> sih kyoot) *v.* **-ing,-ed.**
  to carry out fully; to make or produce
    Synonyms: accomplish, achieve; perform, effectuate
EXULTATION (ihg suhl <u>tay</u> shuhn) *n.*
  the act of being extremely joyful
    Synonyms: celebration, delight, jubilation
HYPOCRISY (hih <u>pah</u> krih see) *n.*
  the practice of claiming beliefs or virtues that one doesn't really possess
    Synonyms: fraud, falseness, fakeness, lip service

DIVINE (dih <u>vien</u>) *v.* **-ing,-ed.**
  to foretell or know by inspiration
    Synonyms: predict, intuit, auger, foresee, presage

INTIMATE (<u>ihn</u> tuh mayt) *v.* **-ing,-ed.**
  to hint or suggest obscurely
    Synonyms: implicate, allude, insinuate

and cold, and **stark**; and so you'll allow it was useless making more stir about him!"

The old servant confirmed this statement, but muttered:

"I'd rayther he'd goan hisseln for t' doctor! I sud ha' taen tent o' t' maister better nor him—and he warn't deead when I left, <u>naught</u> o' t' soart!"

I insisted on the funeral being respectable. Mr. Heathcliff said I might have my own way there too; only, he desired me to remember that the money for the whole affair came out of his pocket. He maintained a hard, careless deportment, indicative of neither joy nor sorrow; if anything, it expressed a flinty gratification at a piece of difficult work successfully **executed**. I observed once, indeed, something like **exultation** in his aspect: it was just when the people were bearing the coffin from the house. He had the **hypocrisy** to represent a mourner: and previous to following with Hareton, he lifted the unfortunate child on to the table and muttered, with peculiar gusto, "Now, my <u>bonny</u> lad, you are *mine*! And we'll see if one tree won't grow as crooked as another, with the same wind to twist it!" The unsuspecting thing was pleased at this speech: he played with Heathcliff's whiskers, and stroked his cheek; but I **divined** its meaning, and observed tartly, "That boy must go back with me to Thrushcross Grange, sir. There is nothing in the world less yours than he is!"

"Does Linton say so?" he demanded.

"Of course—he has ordered me to take him," I replied.

"Well," said the scoundrel, "we'll not argue the subject now: but I have a fancy to try my hand at rearing a young one; so **intimate** to your master that I must supply the place of this with my own, if he attempt to remove it. I don't engage to let Hareton go undisputed; but I'll be pretty sure to make the other come! Remember to tell him."

This hint was enough to bind my hands. I repeated its substance on my return; and Edgar Linton, little inter-

INVETERATE (ihn <u>veht</u> uhr iht) *adj.*
   confirmed, long-standing, deeply rooted
      Synonyms: habitual, chronic

TRIFLING (<u>trie</u> fling) *adj.*
   of slight worth, trivial, insignificant
      Synonyms: paltry, petty, picayune, frivolous, idle

DESOLATE (<u>deh</u> soh liht) *adj.*
   devoid of warmth or comfort; showing the effects of
   abandonment or neglect
      Synonyms: dreary, dismal; barren, bleak, vacant
QUALIFY (<u>kwah</u> lih fie) *v.* **-ing,-ied.**
   to make less harsh, modify, limit; to provide or have
   needed skills
      Synonyms: moderate, differentiate, distinguish; pass
PENSIVE (<u>pehn</u> sihv) *adj.*
   thoughtful
      Synonyms: contemplative, reflective, meditative

ested at the commencement, spoke no more of interfering. I'm not aware that he could have done it to any purpose, had he been ever so willing.

The guest was now the master of Wuthering Heights: he held firm possession, and proved to the attorney—who in his turn, proved it to Mr. Linton—that Earnshaw had mortgaged every yard of land he owned, for cash to supply his mania for gaming; and he, Heathcliff, was the mortgagee. In that manner Hareton, who should now be the first gentleman in the neighbourhood, was reduced to a state of complete dependence on his father's **inveterate** enemy; and lives in his own house as a servant, deprived of the advantage of wages: quite unable to right himself, because of his friendlessness, and his ignorance that he has been wronged.

Chapter 18

The twelve years, continued Mrs. Dean, following that dismal period, were the happiest of my life: my greatest troubles in their passage rose from our little lady's **trifling** illnesses, which she had to experience in common with all children, rich and poor. For the rest, after the first six months, she grew like a larch and could walk and talk too, in her own way, before the <u>heath</u> blossomed a second time over Mrs. Linton's dust. She was the most winning thing that ever brought sunshine into a **desolate** house: a real beauty in face, with the Earnshaws' handsome dark eyes, but the Lintons' fair skin and small features, and yellow curling hair. Her spirit was high, though not rough, and **qualified** by a heart sensitive and lively to excess in its affections. That capacity for intense attachments reminded me of her mother: still she did not resemble her, for she could be soft and mild as a dove, and she had a gentle voice and **pensive** expression: her anger was never furious; her love never fierce: it was deep and tender.

FOIL (foyl) *v.* **-ing,-ed.**
to defeat or overcome, frustrate
Synonyms: thwart, balk, check, baffle
PROPENSITY (pruh <u>pehn</u> suh tee) *n.*
inclination, tendency
Synonyms: predilection, bias, leaning, penchant,
proclivity
PERVERSE (puhr <u>vuhrs</u>) *adj.*
1. having the tendency to oppose or contradict
Synonyms: contrary, improper, obstinate
2. immoral, mean
Synonyms: corrupted, disobedient, depraved
INDULGED (ihn <u>duhlj</u>) *adj.*
spoiled; privileged
Synonyms: pampered; advantaged
VEX (vehks) *v.* **-ing,-ed.**
to irritate, annoy; confuse, puzzle
Synonyms: bother, plague, afflict, irk; perplex, perturb
REPROVE (rih <u>proov</u>) *v.* **-ing,-ed.**
to criticize or correct
Synonyms: rebuke, admonish, reprimand, chide,
reproach
RECLUSE (<u>rehk</u> kloos) (rih <u>kloos</u>) *n.*
a person who is shut off from the world
Synonyms: solitaire, hermit

DESCENT (dih <u>sehnt</u>) (dee <u>sehnt</u>) *n.*
a downward slope; the passing from a higher place to
a lower place
Synonyms: drop, incline; dismount, gravitation
STUNTED (<u>stuhn</u> tehd) *adj.*
having arrested growth or development
Synonyms: little, petite, dwarfish, undersized, runty

However, it must be acknowledged, she had faults to **foil** her gifts. A **propensity** to be saucy was one; and a **perverse** will, that **indulged** children invariably acquire, whether they be good-tempered or cross. If a servant chanced to **vex** her, it was always—"I shall tell Papa!" And if he **reproved** her, even by a look, you would have thought it a heart-breaking business: I don't believe he ever did speak a harsh word to her. He took her education entirely on himself, and made it an amusement. Fortunately, curiosity and a quick intellect made her an apt scholar: she learned rapidly and eagerly, and did honour to his teaching.

Till she reached the age of thirteen, she had not once been beyond the range of the park by herself. Mr. Linton would take her with him a mile or so outside, on rare occasions; but he trusted her to no one else. Gimmerton was an unsubstantial name in her ears; the chapel, the only building she had approached or entered, except her own home. Wuthering Heights and Mr. Heathcliff did not exist for her: she was a perfect **recluse**; and, apparently, perfectly contented. Sometimes, indeed, while surveying the country from her nursery window, she would observe:

"Ellen, how long will it be before I can walk to the top of those hills? I wonder what lies on the other side—is it the sea?"

"No, Miss Cathy," I would answer, "it is hills again, just like these."

"And what are those golden rocks like when you stand under them?" she once asked.

The abrupt **descent** of Penistone Crags particularly attracted her notice; especially when the setting sun shone on it and the topmost heights, and the whole extent of landscape besides lay in shadow. I explained that they were bare masses of stone, with hardly enough earth in their clefts to nourish a **stunted** tree.

"And why are they bright so long after it is evening here?" she pursued.

CONSTITUTION (kahn stih <u>too</u> shuhn) *n.*
the physical structure or health of something or
someone; the sum of components, composition
> Synonyms: disposition, nature, stature; formation,
> design, architecture, make-up

RUDDY (<u>ruh</u> dee) *adj.*
healthily reddish or rosy
> Synonyms: flushed, sanguine, fresh, pinkish

CONJECTURE (kuhn <u>jehk</u> shuhr) *v.* **-ing,-ed.**
to infer, predict, guess
> Synonyms: postulate, hypothesize, suppose, surmise

INDISPOSITION (ihn dihs puh <u>zih</u> shuhn) *n.*
minor illness; unwillingness
> Synonyms: ailment, sickness; reluctance, hesitancy

ENTREAT (ehn <u>treet</u>) *v.* **-ing,-ed.**
to plead, beg
> Synonyms: beseech, implore, importune, request

"Because they are a great deal higher up than we are,"
replied I. "You could not climb them, they are too high
and steep. In winter the frost is always there before it
comes to us; and deep into summer I have found snow
under that black hollow on the north-east side!"

"Oh, you have been on them!" she cried gleefully.
"Then I can go, too, when I am a woman. Has Papa been,
Ellen?"

"Papa would tell you, Miss," I answered hastily, "that
they are not worth the trouble of visiting. The moors,
where you ramble with him, are much nicer; and
Thrushcross Park is the finest place in the world."

"But I know the park, and I don't know those," she
murmured to herself. "And I should delight to look round
me from the brow of that tallest point: my little pony
Minny shall take me some time."

One of the maids mentioning the Fairy Cave, quite
turned her head with a desire to fulfill this project: she
teased Mr. Linton about it; and he promised she should
have the journey when she got older. But Miss Catherine
measured her age by months, and, "Now, am I old
enough to go to Penistone Crags?" was the constant question in her mouth. The road thither wound close by
Wuthering Heights. Edgar had not the heart to pass it; so
she received as constantly the answer, "Not yet, love: not
yet."

I said Mrs. Heathcliff lived about a dozen years after
quitting her husband. Her family were of a delicate
constitution: she and Edgar both lacked the **ruddy** health
that you will generally meet in these parts. What her last
illness was, I am not certain: I **conjecture**, they died of the
same thing, a kind of fever, slow at its commencement,
but incurable, and rapidly consuming life towards the
close. She wrote to inform her brother of the probable
conclusion of a four months' **indisposition** under which
she had suffered, and **entreated** him to come to her, if possible; for she had much to settle, and she wished to bid
him <u>adieu</u>, and deliver Linton safely into his hands. Her

SAT Vocabulary

COMPLY (kuhm <u>plie</u>) *v.* **-ing,-ied.**
  to yield or agree, to go along with
    Synonyms: accord, submit, acquiesce, obey, respect
COMMEND (kuh <u>mehnd</u>) *v.* **-ing,-ed.**
  to entrust or hand over in care; to praise or show
  respect
    Synonyms: assign, relegate; flatter, compliment
VIGILANCE (<u>vih</u> juh lehnts) *n.*
  attentiveness, watchfulness
    Synonyms: alertness, awareness, care, diligence
REITERATE (ree <u>ih</u> tuhr ayt) *v.* **-ing,-ed.**
  to say or do again, repeat
    Synonyms: echo, rehash, restate, retell

INDULGE (ihn <u>duhlj</u>) *v.* **-ing,-ed.**
  to give in to a craving or desire
    Synonyms: humor, gratify, allow, pamper
CONTRIVE (kuhn <u>triev</u>) *v.* **-ing,-ed.**
  to devise, plan, or manage; to form in an artistic manner
    Synonyms: concoct, scheme; create, design

PROVISION (pruh <u>vih</u> zhuhn) *n.*
  a stock of needed materials or supplies; a preparatory
  measure
    Synonyms: equipment, necessities; precaution,
    carefulness

hope was, that Linton might be left with him, as he had been with her: his father, she would <u>fain</u> convince herself, had no desire to assume the burden of his maintenance or education. My master hesitated not a moment in **complying** with her request: reluctant as he was to leave home at ordinary calls, he flew to answer this; **commending** Catherine to my peculiar **vigilance**, in his absence, with **reiterated** orders that she must not wander out of the park, even under my escort: he did not calculate on her going unaccompanied.

He was away three weeks. The first day or two, my charge sat in a corner of the library, too sad for either reading or playing: in that quiet state she caused me little trouble; but it was succeeded by an interval of impatient fretful weariness; and being too busy, and too old then, to run up and down amusing her, I hit on a method by which she might entertain herself. I used to send her on her travels round the grounds—now on foot, and now on a pony; **indulging** her with a patient audience of all her real and imaginary adventures, when she returned.

The summer shone in full prime; and she took such a taste for this solitary rambling that she often **contrived** to remain out from breakfast till tea; and then the evenings were spent in recounting her fanciful tales. I did not fear her breaking bounds; because the gates were generally locked, and I thought she would scarcely venture forth alone, if they had stood wide open. Unluckily, my confidence proved misplaced. Catherine came to me, one morning, at eight 'clock, and said she was that day an Arabian merchant, going to cross the Desert with his caravan; and I must give her plenty of **provision** for herself and beasts: a horse, and three camels, personated by a large hound and a couple of pointers. I got together a good store of dainties, and slung them in a basket on one side of the saddle; and she sprang up as gay as a fairy, sheltered by her wide-brimmed hat and gauze veil from the July sun, and trotted off with a merry laugh, mocking my cautious counsel to avoid galloping, and come back

HAUGHTY (<u>haw</u> tee) (<u>hah</u> tee) *adj.*
 arrogant and condescending
  Synonyms: proud, disdainful, supercilious, scornful,
  vainglorious

EJACULATE (ih <u>jaak</u> yuh layt) *v.* **-ing,-ed.**
 to exclaim suddenly
  Synonyms: blurt, shout, declare

SUSPENSE (suh <u>spents</u>) *n.*
 a feeling of anxiety caused by a mysterious situation
  Synonyms: apprehension, anticipation, waiting

VEHEMENTLY (<u>vee</u> huh muhnt lee) *adv.*
 strongly, urgently
  Synonyms: intensely, passionately, ardently

early. The **haughty** thing never made her appearance at tea. One traveller, the hound, being an old dog and fond of its ease, returned; but neither Cathy, nor the pony, nor the two pointers were visible in any direction: I <u>despatched</u> emissaries down this path, and that path, and at last went wandering in search of her myself. There was a labourer working at a fence round a plantation, on the borders of the grounds. I inquired of him if he had seen our young lady.

"I saw her at morn," he replied. "She would have me to cut her a hazel switch, and then she leapt her Galloway over the hedge yonder, where it is lowest, and galloped out of sight."

You may guess how I felt at hearing this news. It struck me directly she must have started for Penistone Crags. "What will become of her?" I **ejaculated**, pushing through a gap which the man was repairing, and making straight to the highroad. I walked as if for a wager, mile after mile, till a turn brought me in view of the Heights; but no Catherine could I detect far or near. The Crags lie about a mile and a half beyond Mr. Heathcliff's place, and that is four from the Grange, so I began to fear night would fall ere I could reach them. "And what if she should have slipped in clambering among them?" I reflected. "And been killed, or broken some of her bones?" My **suspense** was truly painful; and, at first, it gave me delightful relief to observe, in hurrying by the farmhouse, Charlie, the fiercest of the pointers, lying under a window, with swelled head and bleeding ear. I opened the <u>wicket</u> and ran to the door, knocking **vehemently** for admittance. A woman whom I knew, and who formerly lived at Gimmerton answered: she had been servant there since the death of Mr. Earnshaw.

"Ah," said she, "you are come a seeking your little mistress! Don't be frightened. She's here safe: but I'm glad it isn't the master."

"He is not at home then, is he?" I panted, quite breathless with quick walking and alarm.

COUNTENANCE (<u>kown</u> tuh nuhns) *n.*
appearance, facial expression
Synonyms: face, features, visage

PETULANCE (<u>peh</u> chuh luhnts) *n.*
rudeness, peevishness
Synonyms: irritability, querulousness, testiness,
fretfulness

"No, no," she replied, "both he and Joseph are off, and I think they won't return this hour or more. Step in and rest you a bit."

I entered, and beheld my stray lamb seated on the hearth, rocking herself in a little chair that had been her mother's when a child. Her hat was hung against the wall, and she seemed perfectly at home, laughing and chattering, in the best spirits imaginable, to Hareton—now a great, strong lad of eighteen—who stared at her with considerable curiosity and astonishment: comprehending precious little of the fluent succession of remarks and questions which her tongue never ceased pouring forth.

"Very well, Miss!" I exclaimed, concealing my joy under an angry **countenance**. "This is your last ride, till Papa comes back. I'll not trust you over the threshold again, you naughty, naughty girl!"

"Aha, Ellen!" she cried gaily, jumping up and running to my side. "I shall have a pretty story to tell to-night: and so you've found me out. Have you ever been here in your life before?"

"Put that hat on, and home at once," said I. "I'm dreadfully grieved at you, Miss Cathy: you've done extremely wrong. It's no use pouting and crying: that won't repay the trouble I've had, scouring the country after you. To think how Mr. Linton charged me to keep you in; and you stealing off so! It shows you are a cunning little fox, and nobody will put faith in you any more."

"What have I done?" sobbed she, instantly checked. "Papa charged me nothing: he'll not scold me, Ellen—he's never cross, like you!"

"Come, come!" I repeated. "I'll tie the riband. Now, let us have no **petulance**. Oh, for shame! You thirteen years old, and such a baby!"

This exclamation was caused by her pushing the hat from her head, and retreating to the chimney out of my reach.

"Nay," said the servant, "don't be hard on the <u>bonny</u> lass, Mrs. Dean. We made her stop: she'd <u>fain</u> have ridden

RELISH (<u>reh</u> lihsh) *v.* **-ing,-ed.**
  to enjoy greatly
    Synonyms: savor, love, fancy

WAX (waaks) *v.* **-ing,-ed.**
  to begin to be; to increase gradually
    Synonyms: become, grow; enlarge, expand, swell
IMPERTINENT (ihm <u>puhr</u> tuh nuhnt) *adj.*
  rude, audacious; improper
    Synonyms: forward, bold; impolite, discourteous

forwards, afeared you should be uneasy. Hareton offered to go with her, and I thought he should: it's a wild road over the hills."

Hareton, during the discussion, stood with his hands in his pockets, too awkward to speak; though he looked as if he did not **relish** my intrusion.

"How long am I to wait?" I continued, disregarding the woman's interference. "It will be dark in ten minutes. Where is the pony, Miss Cathy? And where is Phoenix? I shall leave you, unless you be quick; so please yourself."

"The pony is in the yard," she replied, "and Phoenix is shut in there. He's bitten—and so is Charlie. I was going to tell you all about it; but you are in a bad temper, and don't deserve to hear."

I picked up her hat, and approached to reinstate it; but perceiving that the people of the house took her part, she commenced capering round the room; and on my giving chase, ran like a mouse over and under and behind the furniture, rendering it ridiculous for me to pursue. Hareton and the woman laughed, and she joined them, and **waxed** more **impertinent** still; till I cried, in great irritation:

"Well, Miss Cathy, if you were aware whose house this is, you'd be glad enough to get out."

"It's *your* father's, isn't it?" said she, turning to Hareton.

"Nay," he replied, looking down, and blushing bashfully. He could not stand a steady gaze from her eyes, though they were just his own.

"Whose then—your master's?" she asked.

He coloured deeper, with a different feeling, muttered an oath, and turned away.

"Who is his master?" continued the tiresome girl, appealing to me. "He talked about 'our house,' and 'our folk.' I thought he had been the owner's son. And he never said, 'Miss'; he should have done, shouldn't he, if he's a servant?"

INDIGNATION (ihn dihg <u>nay</u> shun) *n.*
anger caused by something mean or unjust
Synonyms: fury, ire, wrath

CIVIL (<u>sih</u> vuhl) *adj.*
polite
Synonyms: courteous, communal

REPROVER (rih <u>proo</u> vuhr) *n.*
one who criticizes or corrects
Synonyms: rebuker, critic, scolder, advisor

Hareton grew black as a thundercloud, at this childish speech. I silently shook my questioner, and at last succeeded in equipping her for departure.

"Now, get my horse," she said, addressing her unknown kinsman as she would one of the stable-boys at the Grange. "And you may come with me. I want to see where the goblin-hunter rises in the marsh, and to hear about the *fairishes*, as you call them: but make haste! What's the matter? Get my horse, I say."

"I'll see thee damned before I be *thy* servant!" growled the lad.

"You'll see me *what*?" asked Catherine in surprise.

"Damned—thou saucy witch!" he replied.

"There, Miss Cathy! You see you have got into pretty company," I <u>interposed</u>. "Nice words to be used to a young lady! Pray don't begin to dispute with him. Come, let us seek for Minny ourselves, and begone."

"But, Ellen," cried she, staring, fixed in astonishment. "How dare he speak so to me? Mustn't he be made to do as I ask him? You wicked creature, I shall tell Papa what you said.—Now, then!"

Hareton did not appear to feel this threat; so the tears sprang into her eyes with **indignation**. "You bring the pony," she exclaimed, turning to the woman, "and let my dog free this moment!"

"Softly, Miss," answered she addressed: "You'll lose nothing by being **civil**. Though Mr. Hareton, there, be not the master's son, he's your cousin; and I was never hired to serve you."

"*He* my cousin!" cried Cathy, with a scornful laugh.

"Yes, indeed," responded her **reprover**.

"Oh, Ellen! Don't let them say such things," she pursued, in great trouble. "Papa is gone to fetch my cousin from London: my cousin is a gentleman's son. That my—" she stopped, and wept outright; upset at the bare notion of relationship with such a clown.

"Hush, hush!" I whispered. "People can have many cousins, and of all sorts, Miss Cathy, without being any

VEX (vehks) *v.* **-ing,-ed.**
   to irritate, annoy; confuse, puzzle
      Synonyms: bother, plague, afflict, irk; perplex, perturb

PROPITIATE (pruh <u>pih</u> shee ayt) *v.* **-ing,-ed.**
   to appease or satisfy
      Synonyms: conciliate, pacify, ease, placate
LAMENTATION (laa mehn <u>tay</u> shuhn) *n.*
   an expression of grief or sorrow, a loud cry
      Synonyms: moaning, sobbing, tears, complaint
ANTIPATHY (aan <u>tih</u> puh thee) *n.*
   dislike, hostility; extreme opposition or aversion
      Synonyms: antagonism; enmity, malice

LUXURIANT (luhg <u>zhoor</u> ee ehnt) *adj.*
   elegant, lavish
      Synonyms: rich, abundant, profuse
SUSCEPTIBILITY (suh sehp tuh <u>bihl</u> ih tee) *n.*
   vulnerability, defenselessness
      Synonyms: sensitivity, exposure, risk
MALEVOLENCE (muh <u>lehv</u> uh luhnts) *n.*
   ill-will; evil or harm done to hurt others
      Synonyms: spite; malice, malignance
REBUKE (ree <u>byook</u>) *v.* **-ing,-ed.**
   to reprimand, scold
      Synonyms: admonish, reprove, reproach, chide

the worse for it; only they needn't keep their company, if they be disagreeable and bad."

"He's not—he's not my cousin, Ellen!" she went on, gathering fresh grief from reflection, and flinging herself into my arms for refuge from the idea.

I was much **vexed** at her and the servant for their mutual revelations; having no doubt of Linton's approaching arrival, communicated by the former, being reported to Mr. Heathcliff; and feeling as confident that Catherine's first thought on her father's return, would be to seek an explanation of the latter's assertion concerning her rude-bred kindred. Hareton, recovering from his disgust at being taken for a servant, seemed moved by her distress; and, having fetched the pony round to the door, he took, to **propitiate** her, a fine crooked-legged terrier-whelp from the kennel, and putting it into her hand bid her wisht! for he meant nought. Pausing in her **lamentations**, she surveyed him with a glance of awe and horror, then burst forth anew.

I could scarcely refrain from smiting at this **antipathy** to the poor fellow; who was a well-made, athletic youth, good-looking in features, and stout and healthy, but attired in garments befitting his daily occupations of working on the farm, and lounging among the moors after rabbits and game. Still, I thought I could detect in his physiognomy a mind owning better qualities than his father ever possessed. Good things lost amid a wilderness of weeds, to be sure, whose rankness far overtopped their neglected growth; yet, notwithstanding, evidence of a wealthy soil, that might yield **luxuriant** crops under other and favourable circumstances. Mr. Heathcliff, I believe, had not treated him physically ill; thanks to his fearless nature, which offered no temptation to that course of oppression. He had none of the timid **susceptibility** that would have given zest to ill-treatment, in Heathcliff's judgment. He appeared to have bent his **malevolence** on making him a brute: he was never taught to read or write; never **rebuked** for any bad habit which did not annoy his

PRECEPT (<u>pree</u> sehpt) *n.*
a command or principle intended as a general rule of action
> Synonyms: law, tenet, edict, axiom

PARTIALITY (pahr shee <u>aal</u> ih tee) *n.*
favoritism or favorable bias; a special liking for something
> Synonyms: preference, inclination; fondness, fancy

COMPEL (kuhm <u>pehl</u>) *v.* **-ling,-led.**
to urge or force
> Synonyms: coerce, oblige, constrain

SOLACE (<u>sah</u> lihs) *n.*
comfort in distress, consolation
> Synonyms: succor, balm, cheer, condolence

USURPER (yoo <u>suhrp</u> uhr) *n.*
one who seizes by force or without right
> Synonyms: preemptor, hijacker, thief

CULPABLY (<u>kuhl</u> puh blee) *adv.*
guiltily, wrongly
> Synonyms: sinfully, reprehensibly

PERDITION (puhr <u>dih</u> shuhn) *n.*
eternal misery or damnation; a huge loss or total destruction
> Synonyms: nightmare, inferno; catastrophe, ruin

CONSOLATION (kahn suh <u>lay</u> shuhn) *n.*
something providing comfort or solace for a loss or hardship
> Synonym: condolence

FOSTER (<u>fah</u> stuhr) (<u>faw</u> stuhr) *v.* **-ing,-ed.**
to cultivate, promote; to nourish
> Synonyms: advance, further; nurture, nurse

INNUENDO (ihn yoo <u>ehn</u> doh) *n.*
indirect and subtle criticism, insinuation
> Synonyms: implication, aspersion, imputation, reflection, intimation

AFFIRM (uh <u>fihrm</u>) *v.* **-ing,-ed.**
to state positively, to assert as valid or confirmed
> Synonyms: declare, avow, maintain

keeper; never led a single step towards virtue, or guarded by a single **precept** against vice. And from what I heard, Joseph contributed much to his deterioration, by a narrow-minded **partiality** which prompted him to flatter and pet him, as a boy, because he was the head of the old family. And as he had been in the habit of accusing Catherine Earnshaw and Heathcliff, when children, of putting the master past his patience, and **compelling** him to seek **solace** in drink by what he termed their "offalld ways," so at present he laid the whole burden of Hareton's faults on the shoulders of the **usurper** of his property. If the lad swore, he wouldn't correct him; nor however **culpably** he behaved. It gave Joseph satisfaction, apparently, to watch him go the worst lengths. He allowed that the lad was ruined: that his soul was abandoned to **perdition**; but then, he reflected that Heathcliff must answer for it. Hareton's blood would be required at his hands; and there lay immense **consolation** in that thought. Joseph had instilled into him a pride of name, and of his lineage; he would, had he dared, have **fostered** hate between him and the present owner of the Heights: but his dread of that owner amounted to superstition; and he confined his feelings regarding him to muttered **innuendoes** and private <u>comminations</u>. I don't pretend to be intimately acquainted with the mode of living customary in those days at Wuthering Heights: I only speak from hearsay; for I saw little. The villagers **affirmed** Mr. Heathcliff was near, and a cruel hard landlord to his tenants; but the house, inside, had regained its ancient aspect of comfort under female management, and the scenes of riot common in Hindley's time were not now enacted within its walls. The master was too gloomy to seek companionship with any people, good or bad; and he is yet.

This, however, is not making progress with my story. Miss Cathy rejected the peace-offering of the terrier, and demanded her own dogs, Charlie and Phoenix. They came limping, and hanging their heads; and we set out for home, sadly out of sorts, every one of us. I could not

BEGUILE (buh <u>giel</u>) *v.* **-ing,-ed.**
to charm; to deceive, mislead; to pass time
Synonyms: enchant, inveigle; lure, coax, cozen;
amuse, occupy

NEGLIGENCE (<u>nehg</u> lih jehnts) *n.*
carelessness, inattention
Synonyms: indifference, casualness, disinterest

wring from my little lady how she had spent the day; except that, as I supposed, the goal of her pilgrimage was Penistone Crags; and she arrived without adventure to the gate of the farmhouse, when Hareton happened to issue forth, attended by some canine followers, who attacked her train. They had a smart battle, before their owners could separate them: that formed an introduction. Catherine told Hareton who she was, and where she was going; and asked him to show her the way: finally, **beguiling** him to accompany her. He opened the mysteries of the Fairy Cave, and twenty other queer places. But, being in disgrace, I was not favoured with a description of the interesting objects she saw. I could gather, however, that her guide had been a favourite till she hurt his feelings by addressing him as a servant; and Heathcliff's housekeeper hurt hers by calling him her cousin. Then the language he had held to her <u>rankled</u> in her heart; she who was always "love," and "darling," and "queen," and "angel," with everybody at the Grange, to be insulted so shockingly by a stranger! She did not comprehend it, and hard work I had to obtain a promise that she would not lay the grievance before her father. I explained how he objected to the whole household at the Heights, and how sorry he would be to find she had been there; but I insisted most on the fact, that if she revealed my **negligence** of his orders, he would perhaps be so angry, that I should have to leave; and Cathy couldn't bear that prospect: she pledged her word, and kept it, for my sake. After all, she was a sweet little girl.

Chapter 19

A letter, edged with black, announced the day of my master's return. Isabella was dead; and he wrote to bid me get mourning for his daughter, and arrange a room, and other accommodations, for his youthful nephew.

INDULGE (ihn <u>duhlj</u>) *v*. **-ing,-ed.**
　to give in to a craving or desire
　　Synonyms: humor, gratify, allow, pamper
SANGUINE (<u>saan</u> gwuhn) *adj*.
　cheerfully optimistic; ruddy
　　Synonyms: confident, positive, hopeful; rosy,
　　rubicund
INNUMERABLE (ih <u>noo</u> muhr uh buhl)
(ih <u>nyoo</u> muhr uh buhl) *adj*.
　too many to be counted
　　Synonyms: incalculable, immeasurable, infinite,
　　inestimable
OBLIGE (uh <u>bliej</u>) *v*. **-ing,-ed.**
　to be obligated, to require or force someone to obey
　　Synonyms: compel, constrain, bind, favor

SOBER (<u>soh</u> buhr) *adj*.
　self-controlled; serious; not intoxicated
　　Synonyms: subdued, sedate; grave; dry, not drunk

SUSPENSE (suh <u>spents</u>) *n*.
　a feeling of anxiety caused by a mysterious situation
　　Synonyms: apprehension, anticipation, waiting

DESCEND (dih <u>sehnd</u>) (dee <u>sehnd</u>) *v*. **-ing,-ed.**
　to pass from a higher place to a lower place
　　Synonyms: fall, dismount, gravitate

Catherine ran wild with joy at the idea of welcoming her father back; and indulged most **sanguine** anticipations of the **innumerable** excellences of her "real" cousin. The evening of their expected arrival came. Since early morning, she had been busy ordering her own small affairs; and now, attired in her new black frock—poor thing! her aunt's death impressed her with no definite sorrow—she **obliged** me, by constant worrying, to walk with her down through the grounds to meet them.

"Linton is just six months younger than I am," she chattered, as we strolled leisurely over the swells and hollows of mossy turf, under shadow of the trees. "How delightful it will be to have him for a play-fellow. Aunt Isabella sent Papa a beautiful lock of his hair; it was lighter than mine—more flaxen, and quite as fine. I have it carefully preserved in a little glass box: and I've often thought what pleasure it would be to see its owner. Oh! I am happy—and Papa, dear, dear Papa! Come, Ellen, let us run! Come, run."

She ran, and returned and ran again many times before my **sober** footsteps reached the gate, and then she seated herself on the grassy bank beside the path, and tried to wait patiently; but that was impossible: she couldn't be still a minute.

"How long they are!" she exclaimed. "Ah, I see some dust on the road—they are coming? No! When will they be here? May not go a little way—half a mile, Ellen, only just half a mile? Do say yes, to that clump of birches at the turn!"

I refused <u>staunchly</u>. At length her **suspense** was ended: the travelling carriage rolled in sight. Miss Cathy shrieked and stretched out her arms, as soon as she caught her father's face looking from the window. He **descended**, nearly as eager as herself: and a considerable interval elapsed ere they had a thought to spare for any but themselves. While they exchanged caresses, I took a peep in to see after Linton. He was asleep in a corner, wrapped in a warm, fur-lined cloak, as if it had been winter. A pale,

INCIPIENT (ihn <u>sihp</u> ee uhnt) *adj.*
   beginning to exist or appear, in an initial stage
     Synonyms: dawning, nascent, inchoate

COUNTENANCE (<u>kown</u> tuh nuhns) *n.*
   appearance, facial expression
     Synonyms: face, features, visage

delicate, effeminate boy, who might have been taken for my master's younger brother so strong was the resemblance: but there was a sickly <u>peevishness</u> in his aspect, that Edgar Linton never had. The latter saw me looking; and having shaken hands, advised me to close the door, and leave him undisturbed; for the journey had fatigued him. Cathy would <u>fain</u> have taken one glance, but her father told her to come, and they walked together up the park, while I hastened before to prepare the servants.

"Now, darling," said Mr. Linton, addressing his daughter, as they halted at the bottom of the front steps, "your cousin is not so strong or so merry as you are, and he has lost his mother, remember, a very short time since; therefore, don't expect him to play and run about with you directly. And don't harass him much by talking: let him be quiet this evening, at least, will you?"

"Yes, yes, Papa," answered Catherine, "but I do want to see him; and he hasn't once looked out."

The carriage stopped; and the sleeper being roused, was lifted to the ground by his uncle.

"This is your cousin Cathy, Linton," he said, putting their little hands together. "She's fond of you already; and mind you don't grieve her by crying to-night. Try to be cheerful now; the travelling is at an end, and you have nothing to do but rest and amuse yourself as you please."

"Let me go to bed, then," answered the boy, shrinking from Catherine's salute; and he put up his fingers to remove **incipient** tears.

"Come, come, there's a good child," I whispered, leading him in. "You'll make her weep too—see how sorry she is for you!"

I do not know whether it was sorrow for him, but his cousin put on as sad a **countenance** as himself, and returned to her father. All three entered, and mounted to the library, where tea was laid ready. I proceeded to remove Linton's cap and <u>mantle</u>, and placed him on a chair by the table; but he was no sooner seated than he

RESOLVE (rih <u>sahlv</u>) *v.* **-ing,-ed.**
    to determine or to make a firm decision about
        Synonyms: solve, decide

MISGIVING (mihs <u>gihv</u> ihng) *n.*
    a feeling of apprehension, doubt, sense of foreboding
        Synonyms: distrust, presentiment, qualm, disquiet

TREPIDATION (treh pih <u>day</u> shuhn) *n.*
    fear, anxiety
        Synonyms: alarm, dread, apprehension, fright

began to cry afresh. My master inquired what was the matter.

"I can't sit on a chair," sobbed the boy.

"Go to the sofa, then, and Ellen shall bring you some tea," answered his uncle patiently.

He had been greatly tried during the journey, I felt convinced, by his fretful ailing charge. Linton slowly trailed himself off, and lay down. Cathy carried a foot-stool and her cup to his side. At first she sat silent; but that could not last: she had **resolved** to make a pet of her little cousin, as she would have him to be; and she commenced stroking his curls, and kissing his cheek, and offering him tea in her saucer, like a baby. This pleased him, for he was not much better: he dried his eyes, and lightened into a faint smile.

"Oh, he'll do very well," said the master to me, after watching them a minute. "Very well, if we can keep him, Ellen. The company of a child of his own age will instill new spirit into him soon, and by wishing for strength he'll gain it."

"Ay, if we can keep him!" I mused to myself; and sore **misgivings** came over me that there was slight hope of that. And then, I thought, however will that weakling live at Wuthering Heights? Between his father and Hareton, what playmates and instructors they'll be. Our doubts were presently decided—even earlier than I expected. I had just taken the children upstairs, after tea was finished and seen Linton asleep—he would not suffer me to leave him till that was the case—I had come down, and was standing by the table in the hall, lighting a bedroom candle for Mr. Edgar, when a maid stepped out of the kitchen and informed me that Mr. Heathcliff's servant Joseph was at the door, and wished to speak with the master.

"I shall ask him what he wants first," I said, in considerable **trepidation**. "A very unlikely hour to be troubling people, and the instant they have returned from a long journey. I don't think the master can see him."

SANCTIMONIOUS (saangk tih <u>moh</u> nee uhs) *adj.*
excessively devout or hypocritically pious
Synonyms: self-righteous, preachy, false

DISDAINFULLY (dihs <u>dayn</u> fuh lee) *adv.*
scornfully, contemptuously
Synonyms: disrespectfully, disparagingly

COMMENDATION (kah mehn <u>day</u> shuhn) *n.*
the act of entrusting into someone's care; an act of
praise or a show of respect; an award
Synonyms: relegation, assignment; acclaim,
approval, flattery; tribute, reward
PEREMPTORY (puhr <u>ehmp</u> tuh ree) *adj.*
absolute and final; commanding
Synonyms: conclusive, decisive; self-assured,
dominating

Joseph had advanced through the kitchen as I uttered these words, and now presented himself in the hall. He was donned in his Sunday garments, with his most **sanctimonious** and sourest face, and, holding his hat in one hand and his stick in the other, he proceeded to clean his shoes on the mat.

"Good evening, Joseph," I said coldly. "What business brings you here to-night?"

"It's Maister Linton I mun spake to," he answered, waving me **disdainfully** aside.

"Mr. Linton is going to bed; unless you have something particular to say, I'm sure he won't hear it now," I continued. "You had better sit down in there, and entrust your message to me."

"Which is his rahm?" pursued the fellow, surveying the range of closed doors.

I perceived he was bent on refusing my mediation, so very reluctantly I went up to the library, and announced the unseasonable visitor, advising that he should be dismissed till next day. Mr. Linton had not time to empower me to do so, for Joseph mounted close at my heels, and, pushing into the apartment, planted himself at the far side of the table, with his two fists clapped on the head of his stick, and began in an elevated tone, as if anticipating opposition:

"Hathecliff has sent me for his lad, and I munn't goa back 'bout him."

Edgar Linton was silent a minute; an expression of exceeding sorrow overcast his features: he would have pitied the child on his own account; but, recalling Isabella's hopes and fears, and anxious wishes for her son, and her **commendations** of him to his care, he grieved bitterly at the prospect of yielding him up, and searched in his heart how it might be avoided. No plan offered itself. The very exhibition of any desire to keep him would have rendered the claimant more **peremptory**: there was nothing left but to resign him. However, he was not going to rouse him from his sleep.

PRECARIOUS (prih <u>caa</u> ree uhs) *adj.*
uncertain
Synonyms: insecure, unstable, hazardous, perilous

AUTHORITATIVE (aw <u>thohr</u> ih tay tihv) *adj.*
strict, in an official and commanding way
Synonyms: despotic, autocratic, imperious, tyrannical

INDIGNANT (ihn <u>dihg</u> nuhnt) *adj.*
angry, incensed, offended
Synonyms: furious, irate, mad, wrathful, ireful

OBVIATE (<u>ahb</u> vee ayt) *v.* **-ing,-ed.**
to make unnecessary; to anticipate and prevent
Synonyms: preclude; avert, forestall, deter

OBLIGE (uh <u>bliej</u>) *v.* **-ing,-ed.**
to be obligated, to require or force someone to obey
Synonyms: compel, constrain, bind, favor

"Tell Mr. Heathcliff," he answered calmly, "that his son shall come to Wuthering Heights to-morrow. He is in bed, and too tired to go the distance now. You may also tell him that the mother of Linton desired him to remain under my guardianship; and, at present, his health is very **precarious**."

"Noa!" said Joseph, giving a thud with his prop on the floor, and assuming an **authoritative** air. "Noa! That means <u>naught</u>. Hathecliff maks noa 'count o' t' mother, nor ye norther; but he'll hev his lad; und I mun tak him—soa now ye knaw!"

"You shall not tonight!" answered Linton decisively. "Walk downstairs at once, and repeat to your master what I have said. Ellen, show him down. Go—"

And, aiding the **indignant** elder with a lift by the arm, he rid the room of him, and closed the door.

"Varrah weell!" shouted Joseph, as he slowly drew off. "To-morn, he's come hisseln, and *thrust* him out, if ye darr!"

Chapter 20

To **obviate** the danger of this threat being fulfilled, Mr. Linton commissioned me to take the boy home early, on Catherine's pony; and, said he, "As we shall now have no influence over his destiny, good or bad, you must say nothing of where he is gone, to my daughter. She cannot associate with him hereafter, and it is better for her to remain in ignorance of his proximity; lest she should be restless, and anxious to visit the Heights. Merely tell her his father sent for him suddenly, and he has been **obliged** to leave us."

Linton was very reluctant to be roused from his bed at five o'clock, and astonished to be informed that he must prepare for further travelling; but I softened off the matter by stating that he was going to spend some time with

DEFER (dih <u>fuhr</u>) *v.* **-ring,-red.**
to delay; to delegate to another
Synonyms: extend, impede, postpone, stall; submit, yield

PERSEVERE (pehr suh <u>veer</u>) *v.* **-ing,-ed.**
to continue with determination, remain steadfast
Synonyms: persist, endure, plod

OBSTINATELY (<u>ahb</u> stih nuht lee) *adv.*
stubbornly
Synonyms: tenaciously, persistently, firmly

his father, Mr. Heathcliff, who wished to see him so much, he did not like to **defer** the pleasure till he should recover from his late journey.

"My father!" he cried, in strange <u>perplexity</u>. "Mamma never told me I had a father. Where does he live? I'd rather stay with uncle."

"He lives a little distance from the Grange," I replied, "just beyond those hills: not so far, but you may walk over here when you get hearty. And you should be glad to go home, and to see him. You must try to love him, as you did your mother, and then he will love you."

"But why have I not heard of him before?" asked Linton. "Why didn't Mamma and he live together, as other people do?"

"He had business to keep him in the north," I answered, "and your mother's health required her to reside in the south."

"And why didn't Mamma speak to me about him?" **persevered** the child. "She often talked of Uncle, and I learnt to love him long ago. How am I to love Papa? I don't know him."

"Oh, all children love their parents," I said. "Your mother, perhaps, thought you would want to be with him if she mentioned him often to you. Let us make haste. An early ride on such a beautiful morning is much preferable to an hour's more sleep."

"Is *she* to go with us," he demanded, "the little girl I saw yesterday?"

"Not now," replied I.

"Is Uncle?" he continued.

"No, I shall be your companion there," I said.

Linton sank back on his pillow and fell into a brown study.

"I won't go without Uncle," he cried at length. "I can't tell where you mean to take me."

I attempted to persuade him of the naughtiness of showing reluctance to meet his father; still he **obstinately** resisted any progress towards dressing, and I had to call

REITERATE (ree <u>ih</u> tuhr ayt) *v.* **-ing,-ed.**
to say or do again, repeat
    Synonyms: echo, rehash, restate, retell

DESPONDENCY (dih <u>spahn</u> duhn see) *n.*
discouragement, dejection
    Synonyms: sadness, depression, desolation

for my master's assistance in coaxing him out of bed. The poor thing was finally got off, with several delusive assurances that his absence should be short; that Mr. Edgar and Cathy would visit him, and other promises, equally ill-founded, which I invented and **reiterated** at intervals throughout the way. The pure heather-scented air, the bright sunshine, and the gentle canter of Minny, relieved his **despondency** after a while. He began to put questions concerning his new home, and its inhabitants, with greater interest and liveliness.

"Is Wuthering Heights as pleasant a place as Thrushcross Grange?" he inquired, turning to take a last glance into the valley, whence a light mist mounted and formed a fleecy cloud on the skirts of the blue.

"It is not so buried in trees," I replied, "and it is not quite so large, but you can see the country beautifully all round; and the air is healthier for you—fresher and dryer. You will, perhaps, think the building old and dark at first; though it is a respectable house, the next best in the neighbourhood. And you will have such nice rambles on the moors. Hareton Earnshaw—that is Miss Cathy's other cousin, and so yours in a manner—will show you all the sweetest spots; and you can bring a book in fine weather, and make a green hollow your study; and, now and then, your uncle may join you in a walk: he does, frequently, walk out on the hills."

"And what is my father like?" he asked. "Is he as young and handsome as uncle?"

"He's as young," said I, "but he has black hair and eyes, and looks sterner; and he is taller and bigger altogether. He'll not seem to you so gentle and kind at first, perhaps, because it is not his way: still, mind you, be frank and cordial with him; and naturally he'll be fonder of you than any uncle, for you are his own."

"Black hair and eyes!" mused Linton. "I can't fancy him. Then I am not like him, am I?"

"Not much," I answered. Not a morsel, I thought, surveying with regret the white complexion and slim frame

LANGUID (<u>laang</u> gwihd) *adj.*
  lacking energy, indifferent, slow
    Synonyms: weak, listless, lackadaisical, sluggish
MORBID (<u>mohr</u> bihd) *adj.*
  relating to disease; gruesome; abnormally gloomy
    Synonyms: pathological, unhealthy; grisly, macabre,
    unwholesome; dismal
KINDLE (<u>kihn</u> duhl) *v.* **-ing,-ed.**
  to excite or inspire; to set fire to or ignite
    Synonyms: arouse, awaken; light, spark
VESTIGE (<u>veh</u> stihj) *n.*
  trace, remnant
    Synonyms: relic, remains, token, sign, spoor

COGITATION (kah jih <u>tay</u> shuhn) *n.*
  careful thought
    Synonyms: reflection, consideration, deliberation
COUNTENANCE (<u>kown</u> tuh nuhns) *n.*
  appearance, facial expression
    Synonyms: face, features, visage
SOLEMN (<u>sah</u> luhm) *adj.*
  quiet, deeply serious; somberly impressive
    Synonyms: earnest, brooding; dignified, ceremonial
COMPENSATION (kahm pehn <u>say</u> shuhn) *n.*
  something that makes up for the faults of something
  else; repayment, reimbursement
    Synonyms: balance, counteraction; indemnity,
    retribution

of my companion, and his large **languid** eyes—his mother's eyes, save that, unless a **morbid** touchiness **kindled** them a moment, they had not a **vestige** of her sparkling spirit.

"How strange that he should never come to see Mamma and me!" he murmured. "Has he ever seen me? If he has, I must have been a baby. I remember not a single thing about him!"

"Why, Master Linton," said I, "three hundred miles is a great distance; and ten years seem very different in length to a grown-up person compared with what they do to you. It is probable Mr. Heathcliff proposed going from summer to summer, but never found a convenient opportunity; and now it is too late. Don't trouble him with questions on the subject: it will disturb him, for no good."

The boy was fully occupied with his own **cogitations** for the remainder of the ride, till we halted before the farmhouse garden gate. I watched to catch his impressions in his **countenance**. He surveyed the carved front and low-browed <u>lattices</u>, the straggling gooseberry bushes and crooked firs, with **solemn** intentness, and then shook his head: his private feelings entirely disapproved of the exterior of his new <u>abode</u>. But he had sense to postpone complaining: there might be **compensation** within. Before he dismounted, I went and opened the door. It was half-past six; the family had just finished breakfast; the servant was clearing and wiping down the table. Joseph stood by his master's chair telling some tale concerning a lame horse; and Hareton was preparing for the hay field.

"Hallo, Nelly!" said Mr. Heathcliff, when he saw me. "I feared I should have to come down and fetch my property myself. You've brought it, have you? Let us see what we can make of it."

He got up and strode to the door. Hareton and Joseph followed in gaping curiosity. Poor Linton ran a frightened eye over the faces of the three.

"Sure-ly," said Joseph, after a grave inspection, "he's swopped wi' ye, maister, an' yon's his lass!"

SANGUINE (<u>saan</u> gwuhn) *adj.*
cheerfully optimistic; ruddy
Synonyms: confident, positive, hopeful; rosy, rubicund

TREPIDATION (treh pih <u>day</u> shuhn) *n.*
fear, anxiety
Synonyms: alarm, dread, apprehension, fright

FILIAL (<u>fih</u>l ee uhl) *adj.*
relating to a sequence of generations or family
connection, particularly that of a child and parent
Synonyms: familial, faithful, reverential

WINCE (wihns) *v.* **-ing,-ed.**
to flinch, to shrink away from pain or fear
Synonyms: cringe, recoil, grimace, cower

Heathcliff having stared his son into an <u>ague</u> of confusion, uttered a scornful laugh.

"God! What a beauty! What a lovely, charming thing!" he exclaimed. "Haven't they reared it on snails and sour milk, Nelly? Oh, damn my soul but that's worse than I expected—and the devil knows I was not **sanguine**!"

I bid the trembling and bewildered child get down, and enter. He did not thoroughly comprehend the meaning of his father's speech, or whether it were intended for him: indeed, he was not yet certain that the grim, sneering stranger was his father. But he clung to me with growing **trepidation**; and on Mr. Heathcliff's taking a seat and bidding him "come hither," he hid his face on my shoulder and wept.

"Tut, tut!" said Heathcliff, stretching out a hand and dragging him roughly between his knees, and then holding up his head by the chin. "None of that nonsense! We're not going to hurt thee, Linton—isn't that thy name? Thou art thy mother's child, entirely! Where is *my* share in thee, <u>puling</u> chicken?"

He took off the boy's cap and pushed back his thick flaxen curls, felt his slender arms and his small fingers; during which examination, Linton ceased crying, and lifted his great blue eyes to inspect the inspector.

"Do you know me?" asked Heathcliff, having satisfied himself that the limbs were all equally frail and feeble.

"No," said Linton, with a gaze of vacant fear.

"You've heard of me, I dare say?"

"No," he replied again.

"No! What a shame of your mother, never to waken your **filial** regard for me! You are my son, then, I'll tell you; and your mother was a wicked slut to leave you in ignorance of the sort of father you possessed. Now, don't **wince**, and colour up! Though it *is* something to see you have not white blood. Be a good lad; and I'll do for you. Nelly, if you be tired you may sit down; if not, get home again. I guess you'll report what you hear and see to the

INFERNAL (ihn <u>fuhr</u> nuhl) *adj.*
   devilish; relating to the dead or hell
      Synonyms: fiendish, awful, malicious; damned, accursed
DESCENDANT (dih <u>sehn</u> dehnt) *n.*
   an offspring or heir
      Synonyms: child, kin, progeny

AVERSION (uh <u>vuhr</u> zhuhn) *n.*
   intense dislike
      Synonyms: antagonism, antipathy, abhorrence,
      repulsion, repugnance
AFFIRM (uh <u>fihrm</u>) *v.* **-ing,-ed.**
   to state positively, to assert as valid or confirmed
      Synonyms: declare, avow, maintain
COMPEL (kuhm <u>pehl</u>) *v.* **-ling,-led.**
   to urge or force
      Synonyms: coerce, oblige, constrain
RETAIN (rih <u>tayn</u>) *v.* **-ing,-ed.**
   to hold, keep possession of
      Synonyms: withhold, reserve, maintain, remember
SENTIMENT (<u>sehn</u> tuh muhnt) *n.*
   an attitude, thought, or judgment prompted by
   feeling; a romantic or nostalgic feeling
      Synonyms: idea; emotion

cipher at the Grange; and this thing won't be settled while you linger about it."

"Well," replied I, "I hope you'll be kind to the boy, Mr. Heathcliff, or you'll not keep him long; and he's all you have akin in the wide world, that you will ever know—remember."

"I'll be *very* kind to him, you needn't fear," he said, laughing. "Only nobody else must be kind to him: I'm jealous of monopolising his affection. And, to begin my kindness, Joseph, bring the lad some breakfast. Hareton, you **infernal** calf, begone to your work. Yes, Nell," he added, when they had departed, "my son is prospective owner of your place, and I should not wish him to die till I was certain of being his successor. Besides, he's *mine*, and I want the triumph of seeing *my* **descendant** fairly lord of their estates: my child hiring their children to till their father's lands for wages. That is the sole consideration which can make me endure the <u>whelp</u>: I despise him for himself, and hate him for the memories he revives! But that consideration is sufficient: he's as safe with me, and shall be tended as carefully as your master tends his own. I have a room upstairs, furnished for him in handsome style: I've engaged a tutor, also, to come three times a week, from twenty miles distance, to teach him what he pleases to learn. I've ordered Hareton to obey him; and in fact I've arranged everything with a view to preserve the superior and the gentleman in him above his associates. I do regret, however, that he so little deserves the trouble: if I wished any blessing in the world, it was to find him a worthy object of pride; and I'm bitterly disappointed with the whey-faced whining wretch!"

While he was speaking, Joseph returned bearing a basin of milk-porridge, and placed it before Linton; who stirred round the homely mess with a look of **aversion**, and **affirmed** he could not eat it. I saw the old manservant shared largely in his master's scorn of the child; though he was **compelled** to **retain** the **sentiment** in his heart,

INDIGNANTLY (ihn <u>dihg</u> nuhnt lee) *adv.*
  angrily
    Synonyms: furiously, irately, madly, irefully

DAINTY (<u>dayn</u> tee) *adj.*
  delicate, sweet
    Synonyms: fine, graceful

CONSTITUTION (kahn stih <u>too</u> shuhn) *n.*
  the physical structure or health of something or
  someone; the sum of components, composition
    Synonyms: disposition, nature, stature; formation,
    design, architecture, make-up
CONSOLE (kuhn <u>sohl</u>) *v.* **-ing,-ed.**
  to alleviate grief and raise the spirits of, provide solace
    Synonyms: relieve, comfort, soothe
REBUFF (ree <u>buhf</u>) *v.* **-ing,-ed.**
  to reject bluntly
    Synonyms: repel, refuse, snub

because Heathcliff plainly meant his underlings to hold him in honour.

"Cannot ate it?" repeated he, peering in Linton's face, and subduing his voice to a whisper, for fear of being overheard. "But Maister Hareton nivir ate <u>naught</u> else, when he wer a little un; and what wer gooid eneugh for him's gooid eneugh for ye, I's rayther think!"

"I *shan't* eat it!" answered Linton snappishly. "Take it away."

Joseph snatched up the food **indignantly**, and brought it to us.

"Is there aught ails th' <u>victuals</u>?" he asked thrusting the tray under Heathcliff's nose.

"What should ail them?" he said.

"Wah!" answered Joseph. "Yon **dainty** chap says he cannut ate 'em. But I guess it's raight! His mother wer just soa—we wer a'most too mucky to sow t' corn for makking her breead."

"Don't mention his mother to me," said the master angrily. "Get him something that he can eat, that's all. What is his usual food, Nelly?"

I suggested boiled milk or tea; and the housekeeper received instructions to prepare some. Come, I reflected, his father's selfishness may contribute to his comfort. He perceives his delicate **constitution**, and the necessity of treating him tolerably. I'll **console** Mr. Edgar by acquainting him with the turn Heathcliff's humour has taken. Having no excuse for lingering longer I slipped out, while Linton was engaged in timidly **rebuffing** the advances of a friendly sheep-dog. But he was too much on the alert to be cheated: as I closed the door, I heard a cry, and a frantic repetition of the words:

"Don't leave me! I'll not stay here! I'll not stay here!"

Then the latch was raised and fell: they did not suffer him to come forth. I mounted Minny, and urged her to a trot; and so my brief guardianship ended.

LAMENTATION (laa mehn <u>tay</u> shuhn) *n.*
>an expression of grief or sorrow, a loud cry
>>Synonyms: moaning, sobbing, tears, complaint

OBLIGE (uh <u>bliej</u>) *v.* **-ing,-ed.**
>to be obligated, to require or force someone to obey
>>Synonyms: compel, constrain, bind, favor

AFFIRM (uh <u>fihrm</u>) *v.* **-ing,-ed.**
>to state positively, to assert as valid or confirmed
>>Synonyms: declare, avow, maintain

PACIFY (<u>paa</u> suh fie) *v.* **-ing,-ied.**
>to restore calm, bring peace
>>Synonyms: mollify, conciliate, appease, placate

WAX (waaks) *v.* **-ing,-ed.**
>to begin to be; to increase gradually
>>Synonyms: become, grow; enlarge, expand, swell

SECLUDED (sih <u>cloo</u> dihd) *adj.*
>isolated and remote
>>Synonyms: solitary, sequestered, out-of-the-way

ANTIPATHY (aan <u>tih</u> puh thee) *n.*
>dislike, hostility; extreme opposition or aversion
>>Synonyms: antagonism; enmity, malice

Chapter 21

We had sad work with little Cathy that day; she rose in high glee, eager to join her cousin, and such passionate tears and **lamentations** followed the news of his departure, that Edgar himself was **obliged** to soothe her, by **affirming** he should come back soon: he added, however, "if I can get him," and there were no hopes of that. This promise poorly **pacified** her but time was more potent; and though still at intervals she inquired of her father when Linton would return, before she did see him again his features had **waxed** so dim in her memory that she did not recognize him.

When I chanced to encounter the housekeeper of Wuthering Heights in paying business-visits to Gimmerton, I used to ask how the young master got on; for he lived almost as **secluded** as Catherine herself, and was never to be seen. I could gather from her that he continued in weak health, and was a tiresome inmate. She said Mr. Heathcliff seemed to dislike him ever longer and worse, though he took some trouble to conceal it: he had an **antipathy** to the sound of his voice, and could not do at all with his sitting in the same room with him many minutes together. There seldom passed much talk between them. Linton learnt his lessons and spent his evenings in a small apartment they called the parlour or else lay in bed all day: for he was constantly getting coughs, and colds, and aches, and pains of some sort.

"And I never knew such a faint-hearted creature," added the woman, "nor one so careful of hisseln. He *will* go on, if I leave the window open a bit late in the evening. Oh! It's killing! A breath of night air! And he must have a fire in the middle of summer, and Joseph's bacca pipe is poison; and he must always have sweets and dainties, and always milk, milk for ever—heeding <u>naught</u> how the rest

RELISH (<u>reh</u> lihsh) *v.* **-ing,-ed.**
to enjoy greatly
Synonyms: savor, love, fancy

DIVINE (dih <u>vien</u>) *v.* **-ing,-ed.**
to foretell or know by inspiration
Synonyms: predict, intuit, auger, foresee, presage

MANIFEST (<u>maan</u> uh fehst) *v.* **-ing,-ed.**
to make evident or certain by display
Synonyms: exhibit, showcase, expose

of us are pinched in winter; and there he'll sit, wrapped in his furred cloak in his chair by the fire, with some toast and water or other slop on the <u>hob</u> to sip at; and if Hareton, for pity, comes to amuse him—Hareton is not bad-natured, though he's rough—they're sure to part, one swearing and the other crying. I believe the master would **relish** Earnshaw's thrashing him to a mummy, if he were not his son; and I'm certain he would be fit to turn him out of doors, if he knew half the nursing he gives hisseln. But then, he won't go into danger of temptation: he never enters the parlour, and should Linton show those ways in the house where he is, he sends him upstairs directly."

I **divined**, from this account, that utter lack of sympathy had rendered young Heathcliff selfish and disagreeable, if he were not so originally; and my interest in him, consequently, decayed: though still I was moved with a sense of grief at his lot, and a wish that he had been left with us. Mr. Edgar encouraged me to gain information: he thought a great deal about him, I fancy, and would have run some risk to see him; and he told me once to ask the housekeeper whether he ever came into the village? She said he had only been twice, on horseback, accompanying his father, and both times he pretended to be quite knocked up for three or four days afterwards. The housekeeper left, if I recollect rightly, two years after he came; and another, whom I did not know, was her successor: she lives there still.

Time wore on at the Grange in its former pleasant way, till Miss Cathy reached sixteen. On the anniversary of her birth we never **manifested** any signs of rejoicing, because it was also the anniversary of my late mistress's death. Her father invariably spent that day alone in the library; and walked, at dusk, as far as Gimmerton <u>kirkyard</u>, where he would frequently prolong his stay beyond midnight. Therefore Catherine was thrown on her own resources for amusement. This 20th of March was a beautiful spring day, and when her father had retired, my young lady came down dressed for going out, and said

COMPEL (kuhm <u>pehl</u>) *v.* **-ling,-led.**
   to urge or force
      Synonyms: coerce, oblige, constrain

she asked to have a ramble on the edge of the moor with me: Mr. Linton had given her leave, if we went only a short distance and were back within the hour.

"So make haste, Ellen!" she cried. "I know where I wish to go; where a colony of moor-game are settled: I want to see whether they have made their nests yet."

"That must be a good distance up," I answered. "They don't breed on the edge of the moor."

"No, it's not," she said. "I've gone very near with Papa."

I put on my bonnet and <u>sallied</u> out, thinking nothing more of the matter. She bounded before me, and returned to my side, and was off again like a young greyhound; and, at first, I found plenty of entertainment in listening to the larks singing far and near, and enjoying the sweet, warm sunshine; and watching her, my pet, and my delight, with her golden ringlets flying loose behind and her bright cheek, as soft and pure in its bloom as a wild rose, and her eyes radiant with cloudless pleasure. She was a happy creature, and an angel, in those days. It's a pity she could not be content.

"Well," said I, "where are your moor-game, Miss Cathy? We should be at them: the Grange park-fence is a great way off now."

"Oh, a little further—only a little further, Ellen," was her answer continually. "Climb to that hillock, pass that bank, and by the time you reach the other side I shall have raised the birds."

But there were so many hillocks and banks to climb and pass, that, at length, I began to be weary, and told her we must halt, and retrace our steps. I shouted to her as she had outstripped me a long way; she either did not hear or did not regard for she still sprang on, and I was **compelled** to follow. Finally, she dived into a hollow; and before I came in sight of her again, she was two miles nearer Wuthering Heights than her own home; and I beheld a couple of persons arrest her, one of whom I felt convinced was Mr. Heathcliff himself.

REPROVE (rih <u>proov</u>) *v.* **-ing,-ed.**
    to criticize or correct
        Synonyms: rebuke, admonish, reprimand, chide,
        reproach
CORROBORATION (kuh rahb uh <u>ray</u> shuhn) *n.*
    confirmation, verification
        Synonyms: proof, substantiation, support
MALEVOLENCE (muh <u>lehv</u> uh luhnts) *n.*
    ill-will; evil or harm done to hurt others
        Synonyms: spite; malice, malignance

ACCEDE (aak <u>seed</u>) *v.* **-ing,-ed.**
    to agree to; to express approval
        Synonyms: assent, concur; acquiesce, consent

Cathy had been caught in the act of plundering, or, at least, hunting out the nests of the grouse. The Heights were Heathcliff's land, and he was **reproving** the poacher.

"I've neither taken any nor found any," she said, as I toiled to them, expanding her hands in **corroboration** of the statement. "I didn't mean to take them; but Papa told me there were quantities up here, and I wished to see the eggs."

Heathcliff glanced at me with an ill-meaning smile, expressing his acquaintance with the party, and, consequently, his **malevolence** towards it, and demanded who "Papa" was.

"Mr. Linton of Thrushcross Grange," she replied. "I thought you did not know me, or you wouldn't have spoken in that way."

"You suppose Papa is highly esteemed and respected then?" he said sarcastically.

"And what are you?" inquired Catherine, gazing curiously on the speaker. "That man I've seen before. Is he your son?"

She pointed to Hareton, the other individual, who had gained nothing but increased bulk and strength by the addition of two years to his age: he seemed as awkward and rough as ever.

"Miss Cathy," I interrupted, "it will be three hours instead of one that we are out, presently. We really must go back."

"No, that man is not my son," answered Heathcliff, pushing me aside. "But I have one, and you have seen him before too; and, though your nurse is in a hurry, I think both you and she would be the better for a little rest. Will you just turn this <u>nab</u> of heath, and walk into my house? You'll get home earlier for the ease; and you shall receive a kind welcome."

I whispered to Catherine that she mustn't, on my account, **accede** to the proposal: it was entirely out of the question. "Why?" she asked, aloud. "I'm tired of running, and the ground is dewy: I can't sit here. Let us go, Ellen.

RESOLVE (rih sahlv) *v.* **-ing,-ed.**
to determine or to make a firm decision about
Synonyms: solve, decide

Besides, he says I have seen his son. He's mistaken, I think; but I guess where he lives: at the farm-house I visited in coming from Penistone Crags. Don't you?"

"I do. Come, Nelly, hold your tongue—it will be a treat for her to look in on us. Hareton, get forwards with the lass. You shall walk with me, Nelly."

"No, she's not going to any such place," I cried, struggling to release my arm, which he had seized: but she was almost at the door-stones already, scampering round the brow at full speed. Her appointed companion did not pretend to escort her: he shied off by the road-side and vanished.

"Mr. Heathcliff, it's very wrong," I continued. "You know you mean no good. And there she'll see Linton, and all will be told as soon as ever we return; and I shall have the blame."

"I want her to see Linton," he answered. "He's looking better these few days: it's not often he's fit to be seen. And we'll soon persuade her to keep the visit secret: where is the harm of it?"

"The harm of it is, that her father would hate me if he found I suffered her to enter your house; and I am convinced you have a bad design in encouraging her to do so," I replied.

"My design is as honest as possible. I'll inform you of its whole scope," he said. "That the two cousins may fall in love, and get married. I'm acting generously to your master: his young <u>chit</u> has no expectations, and should she second my wishes, she'll be provided for at once as joint successor with Linton."

"If Linton died," I answered, "and his life is quite uncertain, Catherine would be the heir."

"No, she would not," he said. "There is no clause in the will to secure it so: his property would go to me; but, to prevent disputes, I desire their union, and am **resolved** to bring it about."

RESOLVE (rih <u>sahlv</u>) *v.* **-ing,-ed.**
    to determine or to make a firm decision about
        Synonyms: solve, decide

SALUBRIOUS (suh <u>loo</u> bree uhs) *adj.*
    healthful
        Synonyms: curative, medicinal, tonic, therapeutic,
        bracing

GENIAL (<u>jeen</u> yuhl) (<u>jee</u> nee uhl) *adj.*
    favorable to growth or comfort; pleasant and friendly
        Synonyms: productive, generative; nice, amiable

KINDLE (<u>kihn</u> duhl) *v.* **-ing,-ed.**
    to excite or inspire; to set fire to or ignite
        Synonyms: arouse, awaken; light, spark

FERVENTLY (<u>fuhr</u> vehnt lee) *adv.*
    passionately, intensely, zealously
        Synonyms: vehemently, eagerly, enthusiastically,
        avidly

LANGUID (<u>laang</u> gwihd) *adj.*
    lacking energy, indifferent, slow
        Synonyms: weak, listless, lackadaisical, sluggish

MITIGATE (<u>miht</u> ih gayt) *v.* **-ing,-ed.**
    to soften, make milder
        Synonyms: moderate, alleviate, assuage, lighten,
        palliate

"And I'm **resolved** she shall never approach your house with me again," I returned, as we reached the gate, where Miss Cathy waited our coming.

Heathcliff bade me be quiet; and, preceding us up the path, hastened to open the door. My young lady gave him several looks, as if she could not exactly make up her mind what to think of him; but now he smiled when he met her eye, and softened his voice in addressing her; and I was foolish enough to imagine the memory of her mother might disarm him from desiring her injury. Linton stood on the hearth. He had been out walking in the fields, for his cap was on, and he was calling to Joseph to bring him dry shoes. He had grown tall for his age, still wanting some months of sixteen. His features were pretty yet, and his eye and complexion brighter than I remembered them, though with merely temporary lustre borrowed from the **salubrious** air and **genial** sun.

"Now, who is that?" asked Mr. Heathcliff, turning to Cathy. "Can you tell?"

"Your son?" she said, having doubtfully surveyed, first one and then the other.

"Yes, yes," answered he, "but is this the only time you have beheld him? Think! Ah! You have a short memory. Linton, don't you recall your cousin, that you used to tease us so with wishing to see?"

"What, Linton!" cried Cathy, **kindling** into joyful surprise at the name. "Is that little Linton? He's taller than I am! Are you Linton?"

The youth stepped forward, and acknowledged himself: she kissed him **fervently**, and they gazed with wonder at the change time had wrought in the appearance of each. Catherine had reached her full height; her figure was both plump and slender, elastic as steel, and her whole aspect sparkling with health and spirits. Linton's looks and movements were very **languid**, and his form extremely slight; but there was a grace in his manner that **mitigated** these defects, and rendered him not unpleasing. After exchanging numerous marks of fondness with him,

LAVISH (<u>laa</u> vihsh) *adj.*
   abundant and excessive; extravagant
      Synonyms: overgenerous, plentiful; luxuriant,
      sumptuous
HINDER (<u>hihn</u> duhr) *v.* **-ing,-ed.**
   to prevent action; to delay or impede
      Synonyms: restrain; hamper, inhibit, obstruct
SUPPRESSED (suh <u>prehsd</u>) *adj.*
   restrained
      Synonyms: subdued, stifled, muffled, quelled, curbed
GRIMACE (<u>grih</u> muhs) (grih <u>mays</u>) *n.*
   facial expression showing pain or disgust
      Synonyms: scowl, leer, glare
AVERSION (uh <u>vuhr</u> zhuhn) *n.*
   intense dislike
      Synonyms: antagonism, antipathy, abhorrence,
      repulsion, repugnance

his cousin went to Mr. Heathcliff, who lingered by the door, dividing his attention between the objects inside and those that lay without: pretending, that is, to observe the latter, and really noting the former alone.

"And you are my uncle, then!" she cried, reaching up to salute him. "I thought I liked you, though you were cross at first. Why don't you visit at the Grange with Linton? To live all these years such close neighbours, and never see us, is odd: what have you done so for?"

"I visited it once or twice too often before you were born," he answered. "There—damn it! If you have any kisses to spare, give them to Linton: they are thrown away on me."

"Naughty Ellen!" exclaimed Catherine, flying to attack me next with her **lavish** caresses. "Wicked Ellen! To try to **hinder** me from entering. But I'll take this walk every morning in future: may I, Uncle? And sometimes bring Papa. Won't you be glad to see us?"

"Of course!" replied the uncle, with a hardly **suppressed grimace**, resulting from his deep **aversion** to both the proposed visitors. "But stay," he continued, turning towards the young lady. "Now I think of it, I'd better tell you. Mr. Linton has a prejudice against me: we quarrelled at one time of our lives, with unchristian <u>ferocity</u>; and, if you mention coming here to him, he'll put a veto on your visits altogether. Therefore, you must not mention it, unless you be careless of seeing your cousin hereafter: you may come, if you will, but you must not mention it."

"Why did you quarrel?" asked Catherine, considerably crestfallen.

"He thought me too poor to wed his sister," answered Heathcliff, "and was grieved that I got her; his pride was hurt, and he'll never forgive it."

"That's wrong!" said the young lady. "Some time, I'll tell him so. But Linton and I have no share in your quarrel. I'll not come here, then; he shall come to the Grange."

CONTEMPT (kuhn <u>tehmpt</u>) *n.*
  disrespect, scorn
    Synonyms: derision, disdain
COVET (<u>kuh</u> viht) *v.* **-ing,-ed.**
  to desire strongly (something possessed by another)
    Synonyms: envy, crave
DEGRADATION (day greh <u>day</u> shuhn) *n.*
  the act of falling in rank or status; the act of losing
  moral or intellectual character
    Synonyms: demotion; abasement, disgrace, shame
PALTRY (<u>pawl</u> tree) *adj.*
  pitifully small or worthless
    Synonyms: trivial, trifling, petty, picayune, meager
CONFOUND (kuhn <u>fownd</u>) *v.* **-ing,-ed.**
  1. to damn or condemn
    Synonyms: doom, jinx, revile, punish
  2. to baffle, perplex; to mistake something for another
    Synonyms: overwhelm, disconcert, entangle,
    muddle; confuse, misidentify
VAPID (<u>vaa</u> pihd) (<u>vay</u> pihd) *adj.*
  dull, tasteless
    Synonyms: insipid, vacuous, inane

"It will be too far for me," murmured her cousin. "To walk four miles would kill me. No, come here, Miss Catherine, now and then: not every morning, but once or twice a week."

The father launched towards his son a glance of bitter **contempt**.

"I am afraid, Nelly, I shall lose my labour," he muttered to me. "Miss Catherine, as the ninny calls her, will discover his value, and send him to the devil. Now if it had been Hareton!—Do you know that, twenty times a day, I **covet** Hareton, with all his **degradation**? I'd have loved the lad had he been some one else. But I think he's safe from *her* love. I'll pit him against that **paltry** creature, unless it bestir itself briskly. We calculate it will scarcely last till it is eighteen. Oh, **confound** the **vapid** thing! He's absorbed in drying his feet, and never looks at her— Linton!"

"Yes, Father," answered the boy.

"Have you nothing to show your cousin anywhere about? Not even a rabbit or a weasel's nest? Take her into the garden, before you change your shoes; and into the stable to see your horse."

"Wouldn't you rather sit here?" asked Linton, addressing Cathy in a tone which expressed reluctance to move again.

"I don't know," she replied, casting a longing look at the door, and evidently eager to be active.

He kept his seat, and shrank closer to the fire. Heathcliff rose, and went into the kitchen, and from thence to the yard, calling out for Hareton. Hareton responded, and presently the two re-entered. The young man had been washing himself as was visible by the glow on his cheeks and his wetted hair.

"Oh, I'll ask *you*, Uncle," cried Miss Cathy, recollecting the housekeeper's assertion. "That is not my cousin, is he?"

"Yes," he replied, "your mother's nephew. Don't you like him?"

Catherine looked queer.

UNCIVIL (uhn <u>sih</u> vuhl) *adj.*
  impolite
    Synonyms: discourteous, rude, ungracious
SLIGHT (sliet) *n.*
  an insult or unkind remark
    Synonyms: belittlement, snub, disparagement

COUNTENANCE (<u>kown</u> tuh nuhns) *n.*
  appearance, facial expression
    Synonyms: face, features, visage
AVERT (uh <u>vuhrt</u>) *v.* **-ing,-ed.**
  to turn away; avoid
    Synonyms: deflect, parry; deter, forestall, preclude

SULLEN (<u>suh</u> luhn) *adj.*
  brooding, gloomy
    Synonyms: morose, sulky, somber, glum

"Is he not a handsome lad?" he continued.

The **uncivil** little thing stood on tiptoe, and whispered a sentence in Heathcliff's ear. He laughed; Hareton darkened: I perceived he was very sensitive to suspected **slights**, and had obviously a dim notion of his inferiority. But his master or guardian chased the frown by exclaiming:

"You'll be the favourite among us, Hareton! She says you are a—What was it? Well, something very flattering. Here! You go with her round the farm. And behave like a gentleman, mind! Don't use any bad words; and don't stare when the young lady is not looking at you, and be ready to hide your face when she is; and, when you speak, say your words slowly and keep your hands out of your pockets. Be off, and entertain her as nicely as you can."

He watched the couple walking past the window. Earnshaw had his **countenance** completely **averted** from his companion. He seemed studying the familiar landscape with a stranger's and an artist's interest. Catherine took a sly look at him, expressing small admiration. She then turned her attention to seeking out objects of amusement for herself, and tripped merrily on, lilting a tune to supply the lack of conversation.

"I've tied his tongue," observed Heathcliff. "He'll not venture a single syllable, all the time! Nelly, you recollect me at his age—nay, some years younger. Did I ever look so stupid, so 'gaumless,' as Joseph calls it?"

"Worse," I replied, "because more **sullen** with it."

"I've a pleasure in him," he continued, reflecting aloud. "He has satisfied my expectations. If he were a born fool I should not enjoy it half so much. But he's no fool; and I can sympathise with all his feelings, having felt them myself. I know what he suffers now, for instance, exactly: it is merely a beginning of what he shall suffer, though. And he'll never be able to emerge from his <u>bathos</u> of coarseness and ignorance. I've got him faster than his scoundrel of a father secured me, and lower; for he takes a

MERIT (<u>mehr</u> iht) *n.*
an admirable ability or attribute; high quality or
excellence
Synonyms: virtue, capacity, strength; credit, perfection
UNAVAILING (uhn uh <u>vayl</u> ihng) *adj.*
of no use or advantage
Synonyms: futile, ineffectual, worthless

INDIGNANT (ihn <u>dihg</u> nuhnt) *adj.*
angry, incensed, offended
Synonyms: furious, irate, mad, wrathful, ireful
RAIL (rayl) *v.* **-ing,-ed.**
to scold with bitter or abusive language
Synonyms: upbraid, berate, revile, vituperate
EVINCE (ih <u>vihns</u>) *v.* **-ing,-ed.**
to show clearly or display
Synonyms: express, exhibit, demonstrate, manifest
REPENT (rih <u>pehnt</u>) *v.* **-ing,-ed.**
to regret a past action
Synonyms: rue, atone, apologize
IRRESOLUTELY (eer reh suh <u>loot</u> lee) *adv.*
hesitantly; without a clear purpose
Synonyms: indecisively, waveringly; aimlessly

pride in his <u>brutishness</u>. I've taught him to scorn everything extra-animal as silly and weak. Don't you think
Hindley would be proud of his son, if he could see him?
Almost as proud as I am of mine. But there's this difference; one is gold put to the use of paving-stones, and the
other is tin polished to ape a service of silver. *Mine* has
nothing valuable about it; yet I shall have the **merit** of
making it go as far as such poor stuff can go. *His* had
first-rate qualities, and they are lost: rendered worse than
unavailing. *I* have nothing to regret; *he* would have more
than any, but I, are aware of. And the best of it is,
Hareton is damnably fond of me! You'll own that I've
out-matched Hindley there. If the dead villain could rise
from his grave to abuse me for his offspring's wrongs, I
should have the fun of seeing the said offspring fight him
back again, **indignant** that he should dare to **rail** at the
one friend he has in the world!"

Heathcliff chuckled a fiendish laugh at the idea. I
made no reply, because I saw that he expected none.
Meantime, our young companion, who sat too removed
from us to hear what was said, began to **evince** symptoms
of uneasiness, probably **repenting** that he had denied himself the treat of Catherine's society for fear of a little
fatigue. His father remarked the restless glances wandering to the window, and the hand **irresolutely** extended
towards his cap.

"Get up, you idle boy!" he exclaimed, with assumed
heartiness. "Away after them! They are just at the corner,
by the stand of hives."

Linton gathered his energies, and left the hearth. The
<u>lattice</u> was open, and, as he stepped out, I heard Cathy
inquiring of her unsociable attendant, what was that
inscription over the door? Hareton stared up, and
scratched his head like a true clown.

"It's some damnable writing," he answered. "I cannot
read it."

"Can't read it?" cried Catherine. "I can read it: it's
English. But I want to know why it is there."

MIRTH (muhrth) *n.*
  frivolity, gaiety, laughter
    Synonyms: merriment, jollity, hilarity, glee

RETORT (rih <u>tohrt</u>) *v.* **-ing,-ed.**
  to make a cutting response
    Synonyms: retaliate, talk back, counter
BOOR (bohr) *n.*
  crude person, one lacking manners or taste
    Synonyms: lout, clod, oaf, vulgarian, yahoo
AVERSION (uh <u>vuhr</u> zhuhn) *n.*
  intense dislike
    Synonyms: antagonism, antipathy, abhorrence,
    repulsion, repugnance
FLIPPANT (<u>flihp</u> ehnt) *adj.*
  disrespectfully casual or irreverent
    Synonyms: pert, inconsiderate, sassy, glib
ANIMATION (aa nih <u>may</u> shuhn) *n.*
  enthusiasm, excitement
    Synonyms: elation, vivacity, brio, spirit, verve

Linton giggled, the first appearance of **mirth** he had exhibited.

"He does not know his letters," he said to his cousin. "Could you believe in the existence of such a colossal dunce?"

"Is he all as he should be?" asked Miss Cathy seriously; "Or is he simple: not right? I've questioned him twice now, and each time he looked so stupid I think he does not understand me. I can hardly understand *him*, I'm sure!"

Linton repeated his laugh, and glanced at Hareton tauntingly; who certainly did not seem quite clear of comprehension at that moment.

"There's nothing the matter but laziness; is there, Earnshaw?" he said. "My cousin fancies you are an idiot. There you experience the consequences of scorning 'book-larning,' as you would say. Have you noticed, Catherine, his frightful Yorkshire pronunciation?"

"Why, where the devil is the use on't?" growled Hareton, more ready in answering his daily companion. He was about to enlarge further, but the two youngsters broke into a noisy fit of merriment; my giddy miss being delighted to discover that she might turn his strange talk to matter of amusement.

"Where is the use of the devil in that sentence?" tittered Linton. "Papa told you not to say any bad words, and you can't open your mouth without one. Do try to behave like a gentleman, now do!"

"If thou weren't more a lass than a lad, I'd fell thee this minute, I would; pitiful lath of a crater!" **retorted** the angry **boor**, retreating, while his face burnt with mingled rage and mortification; for he was conscious of being insulted, and embarrassed how to resent it.

Mr. Heathcliff having overheard the conversation, as well as I, smiled when he saw him go; but immediately afterwards cast a look of singular **aversion** on the **flippant** pair, who remained chattering in the doorway: the boy finding **animation** enough while discussing Hareton's

ANECDOTE (<u>aa</u> nihk doht) *n.*
  a short, often funny, account of an event
    Synonyms: story, joke
RELISH (<u>reh</u> lihsh) *v.* **-ing,-ed.**
  to enjoy greatly
    Synonyms: savor, love, fancy
EVINCE (ih <u>vihns</u>) *v.* **-ing,-ed.**
  to show clearly or display
    Synonyms: express, exhibit, demonstrate, manifest

PARTIAL (<u>pahr</u> shuhl) *adj.*
  biased; showing favoritism or a fondness
    Synonyms: unfair, one-sided, prejudiced;
    affectionate, sympathetic

RELINQUISH (rih <u>lihn</u> kwihsh) *v.* **-ing,-ed.**
  to renounce or surrender something
    Synonyms: yield, resign, abandon, cede, waive
CHAGRIN (shuh <u>grihn</u>) *n.*
  shame, embarrassment, humiliation
    Synonyms: mortification, discomfiture

RESTRAINT (rih <u>straynt</u>) *n.*
  a rule or limitation; control, repression, restriction
    Synonyms: barrier, order, rein; confinement
SALUTATION (saal yoo <u>tay</u> shuhn) *n.*
  greeting
    Synonyms: regards, welcome, hello

faults and deficiencies, and relating **anecdotes** of his goings-on; and the girl **relishing** his pert and spiteful sayings, without considering the ill-nature they **evinced**. I began to dislike, more than to compassionate Linton, and to excuse his father, in some measure, for holding him cheap.

We stayed till afternoon: I could not tear Miss Cathy away sooner, but happily my master had not quitted his apartment, and remained ignorant of our prolonged absence. As we walked home, I would <u>fain</u> have enlightened my charge on the characters of the people we had quitted; but she got it into her head that I was prejudiced against them.

"Aha!" she cried. "You take Papa's side, Ellen, you are **partial**, I know; or else you wouldn't have cheated me so many years into the notion that Linton lived a long way from here. I'm really extremely angry; only I'm so pleased I can't show it! But you must hold your tongue about my uncle: he's *my* uncle, remember, and I'll scold Papa for quarrelling with him."

And so she ran on, till I **relinquished** the endeavour to convince her of her mistake. She did not mention the visit that night, because she did not see Mr. Linton. Next day it all came out, sadly to my **chagrin**; and still I was not altogether sorry: I thought the burden of directing and warning would be more efficiently borne by him than me. But he was too timid in giving satisfactory reasons for his wish that she should shun connection with the household of the Heights, and Catherine liked good reasons for every **restraint** that harassed her petted will.

"Papa!" she exclaimed, after the morning's **salutations**. "Guess whom I saw yesterday, in my walk on the moors. Ah, Papa, you started! You've not done right, have you, now? I saw—But listen and you shall hear how I found you out; and Ellen, who is in league with you, and yet pretended to pity me so, when I kept hoping, and was always disappointed about Linton's coming back!"

REPROACHFUL (rih prohch fuhl) *adj.*
　　disappointed or critical; disparaging
　　　　Synonyms: disapproving, shameful; reviling, scolding

DIABOLICAL (die uh bah lih kuhl) *adj.*
　　characteristic of the devil
　　　　Synonyms: fiendish, wicked, evil

DETEST (dee tehst) (dih tehst) *v.* **-ing,-ed.**
　　to feel intense and violent hatred toward
　　　　Synonyms: dislike, loathe

DISPOSITION (dihs puh zih shuhn) *n.*
　　mood or temperament
　　　　Synonyms: behavior, tendency, inclination, nature
DISCOURSE (dihs kohrs) *v.* **-ing,-ed.**
　　to talk or converse
　　　　Synonyms: speak, discuss, lecture
DETESTATION (dee tehs tay shuhn) *n.*
　　intense and violent hatred
　　　　Synonyms: disgust, loathing, abhorrence

She gave a faithful account of her excursion and its consequences; and my master, though he cast more than one **reproachful** look at me, said nothing till she had concluded. Then he drew her to him, and asked if she knew why he had concealed Linton's near neighbourhood from her. Could she think it was to deny her a pleasure that she might harmlessly enjoy?

"It was because you disliked Mr. Heathcliff," she answered.

"Then you believe I care more for my own feelings than yours, Cathy?" he said. "No, it was not because I disliked Mr. Heathcliff, but because Mr. Heathcliff dislikes me; and is a most **diabolical** man, delighting to wrong and ruin those he hates, if they give him the slightest opportunity. I knew that you could not keep up an acquaintance with your cousin, without being brought into contact with him; and I knew he would **detest** you on my account; so for your own good, and nothing else, I took precautions that you should not see Linton again. I meant to explain this some time as you grew older, and I'm sorry I delayed it."

"But Mr. Heathcliff was quite cordial, Papa," observed Catherine, not at all convinced, "and *he* didn't object to our seeing each other: he said I might come to his house when I pleased; only I must not tell you, because you had quarrelled with him, and would not forgive him for marrying Aunt Isabella. And you won't. *You* are the one to be blamed: he is willing to let *us* be friends, at least; Linton and I; and you are not."

My master, perceiving that she would not take his word for her uncle-in-law's evil **disposition**, gave a hasty sketch of his conduct to Isabella, and the manner in which Wuthering Heights became his property. He could not bear to **discourse** long upon the topic; for though he spoke little of it, he still felt the same horror and **detestation** of his ancient enemy that had occupied his heart ever since Mrs. Linton's death. "She might have been living yet, if it had not been for him!" was his constant bitter reflection;

REPENT (rih <u>pehnt</u>) *v.* **-ing,-ed.**
    to regret a past action
      Synonyms: rue, atone, apologize
BROOD *v.* **-ing,-ed.**
    to think about in a gloomy or serious way
      Synonyms: ponder, worry, obsess
COVET (<u>kuh</u> viht) *v.* **-ing,-ed.**
    to desire strongly (something possessed by another)
      Synonyms: envy, crave
REMORSE (rih <u>mohrs</u>) *n.*
    a gnawing distress arising from a sense of guilt
      Synonyms: anguish, ruefulness, shame, penitence

AFFLICTION (uh <u>flihk</u> shuhn) *n.*
    severe distress, persistent anguish
      Synonyms: hurt, calamity, suffering, pain

and, in his eyes, Heathcliff seemed a murderer. Miss Cathy—conversant with no bad deeds except her own slight acts of disobedience, injustice, and passion, arising from hot temper and thoughtlessness, and **repented** of on the day they were committed—was amazed at the blackness of spirit that could **brood** on and **covet** revenge for years, and deliberately prosecute its plans without a visitation of **remorse**. She appeared so deeply impressed and shocked at this new view of human nature—excluded from all her studies and all her ideas till now—that Mr. Edgar deemed it unnecessary to pursue the subject. He merely added:

"You will know hereafter, darling, why I wish you to avoid his house and family; now return to your old employments and amusements, and think no more about them."

Catherine kissed her father and sat down quietly to her lessons for a couple of hours, according to custom; then she accompanied him into the grounds, and the whole day passed as usual: but in the evening, when she had retired to her room, and I went to help her undress, I found her crying, on her knees by the bedside.

"Oh, fie, silly child!" I exclaimed. "If you had any real griefs, you'd be ashamed to waste a tear on this little <u>contrariety</u>. You never had one shadow of substantial sorrow, Miss Catherine. Suppose, for a minute, that master and I were dead, and you were by yourself in the world: how would you feel then? Compare the present occasion with such an **affliction** as that, and be thankful for the friends you have, instead of **coveting** more."

"I'm not crying for myself, Ellen," she answered. "It's for him. He expected to see me again to-morrow, and there he'll be so disappointed: and he'll wait for me, and I shan't come!"

"Nonsense," said I, "do you imagine he has thought as much of you as you have of him? Hasn't he Hareton for a companion? Not one in a hundred would weep at losing a relation they had just seen twice, for two afternoons.

CONJECTURE (kuhn <u>jehk</u> shuhr) *v.* **-ing,-ed.**
   to infer, predict, guess
      Synonyms: postulate, hypothesize, suppose, surmise

IMPLORING (ihm <u>plohr</u> ihng) *adj.*
   pitiful, begging
      Synonyms: pleading, supplicating, solicitous

COUNTENANCE (<u>kown</u> tuh nuhns) *n.*
   appearance, facial expression
      Synonyms: face, features, visage

REPENT (rih <u>pehnt</u>) *v.* **-ing,-ed.**
   to regret a past action
      Synonyms: rue, atone, apologize

PETULANT (<u>peh</u> chuh luhnt) *adj.*
   rude, peevish
      Synonyms: irritable, querulous, testy, fretful

Linton will **conjecture** how it is, and trouble himself no further about you."

"But may I not write a note to tell him why I cannot come?" she asked, rising to her feet. "And just send those books I promised to lend him? His books are not as nice as mine, and he wanted to have them extremely, when I told him how interesting they were. May I not, Ellen?"

"No, indeed! No, indeed!" replied I, with decision. "Then he would write to you, and there'd never be an end of it. No, Miss Catherine, the acquaintance must be dropped entirely: so Papa expects, and I shall see that it is done."

"But how can one little note—" she recommenced, putting on an **imploring countenance**.

"Silence!" I interrupted. "We'll not begin with your little notes. Get into bed."

She threw at me a very naughty look, so naughty that I would not kiss her good-night at first. I covered her up, and shut her door, in great displeasure; but, **repenting**, halfway, I returned softly, and lo! there was Miss standing at the table with a bit of blank paper before her and a pencil in her hand, which she guiltily slipped out of sight, on my entrance.

"You'll get nobody to take that, Catherine," I said, "if you write it; and at present I shall put out your candle."

I set the extinguisher on the flame, receiving as I did so a slap on my hand, and a **petulant** "Cross thing!" I then quitted her again, and she drew the bolt in one of her worst, most <u>peevish</u> humours. The letter was finished and forwarded to its destination by a milk-fetcher who came from the village: but that I didn't learn till some time afterwards. Weeks passed on, and Cathy recovered her temper; though she grew wondrous fond of stealing off to corners by herself; and often, if I came near her suddenly while reading, she would start and bend over the book, evidently desirous to hide it; and I detected edges of loose paper sticking out beyond the leaves. She also got a trick of coming down early in the morning and lingering about

TRIFLE (<u>trie</u> fuhl) *v.* **-ing,-ed.**
  to toy around with; to waste time or money
    Synonyms: putter, fidget, lollygag; squander,
    fritter away
TRANSMUTE (traans <u>myoot</u>) *v.* **-ing,-ed.**
  to change in appearance or shape
    Synonyms: transform, convert, metamorphose,
    transfigure, transmogrify

COPIOUS (<u>koh</u> pee uhs) *adj.*
  abundant, plentiful
    Synonyms: ample, abounding
ARDOUR or ARDOR (<u>ahr</u> duhr) *n.*
  passion, enthusiasm
    Synonyms: intensity, vehemence
AFFECTED (uh <u>fehk</u> tihd) *adj.*
  phony, artificial
    Synonyms: feigned, insincere, posed, arty, pretentious
INCORPOREAL (ihn kohr <u>pohr</u> ee uhl) *adj.*
  intangible, immaterial; lacking a body
    Synonyms: imaginary, nonexistent; spiritual
DESCEND (dih <u>sehnd</u>) (dee <u>sehnd</u>) *v.* **-ing,-ed.**
  to pass from a higher place to a lower place
    Synonyms: fall, dismount, gravitate
VALOROUSLY (<u>vaa</u> luhr ihs lee) *adv.*
  bravely, courageously
    Synonyms: heroically, intrepidly, gallantly, valiantly
EPISTLE (ih <u>pihs</u> uhl) *n.*
  a formal letter
    Synonyms: message, missive, note

the kitchen, as if she were expecting the arrival of something: and she had a small drawer in a cabinet in the library, which she would **trifle** over for hours, and whose key she took special care to remove when she left it.

One day, as she inspected this drawer, I observed that the playthings, and trinkets which recently formed its contents, were **transmuted** into bits of folded paper. My curiosity and suspicions were aroused; I determined to take a peep at her mysterious treasures; so, at night, as soon as she and my master were safe upstairs, I searched and readily found among my house-keys one that would fit the lock. Having opened, I emptied the whole contents into my apron, and took them with me to examine at leisure in my own chamber. Though I could not but suspect, I was still surprised to discover that they were a mass of correspondence—daily almost, it must have been—from Linton Heathcliff: answers to documents forwarded by her. The earlier dated were embarrassed and short; gradually, however, they expanded into **copious** love letters, foolish, as the age of the writer rendered natural, yet with touches here and there which I thought were borrowed from a more experienced source. Some of them struck me as singularly odd compounds of **ardour** and flatness; commencing in strong feeling, and concluding in the **affected**, wordy style that a schoolboy might use to a fancied, **incorporeal** sweetheart. Whether they satisfied Cathy, I don't know, but they appeared very worthless trash to me. After turning over as many as I thought proper, I tied them in a handkerchief and set them aside, re-locking the vacant drawer.

Following her habit, my young lady **descended** early, and visited the kitchen: I watched her go to the door, on the arrival of a certain little boy; and, while the dairymaid filled his can, she tucked something into his jacket pocket, and plucked something out. I went round by the garden, and laid wait for the messenger; who fought **valorously** to defend his trust, and we spilt the milk between us; but I succeeded in abstracting the **epistle**; and, threatening seri-

PERUSE (puh <u>roos</u>) *v.* **-ing,-ed.**
    to examine closely
        Synonyms: scrutinize, inspect, study; browse

ELOQUENT (<u>eh</u> luh kwuhnt) *adj.*
    persuasive and effective, with regards to speech
        Synonyms: expressive, fluent

DIVERT (die <u>vuhrt</u>) *v.* **-ing,-ed.**
    to distract or amuse; to move in different directions
    from a particular point
        Synonyms: deter, occupy, entertain; deviate, separate

SOLACE (<u>sah</u> lihs) *n.*
    comfort in distress, consolation
        Synonyms: succor, balm, cheer, condolence

COUNTENANCE (<u>kown</u> tuh nuhns) *n.*
    appearance, facial expression
        Synonyms: face, features, visage

ous consequences if he did not look sharp home, I remained under the wall and **perused** Miss Cathy's affectionate composition. It was more simple and more **eloquent** than her cousin's; very pretty and very silly. I shook my head, and went meditating into the house. The day being wet, she could not **divert** herself with rambling about the park; so, at the conclusion of her morning studies, she resorted to the **solace** of the drawer. Her father sat reading at the table; and I, on purpose, had sought a bit of work in some unripped fringes of the window curtain, keeping my eye steadily fixed on her proceedings. Never did any bird flying back to a plundered nest which it had left brimful of chirping young ones, express more complete despair in its anguished cries and flutterings, than she by her single "Oh!" and the change that transfigured her late happy **countenance**. Mr. Linton looked up.

"What is the matter, love? Have you hurt yourself?" he said.

His tone and look assured her *he* had not been the discoverer of the hoard.

"No, Papa!" she gasped. "Ellen! Ellen! Come upstairs—I'm sick!"

I obeyed her summons, and accompanied her out.

"Oh, Ellen! You have got them," she commenced immediately, dropping on her knees, when we were enclosed alone. "Oh, give them to me, and I'll never, never do so again! Don't tell Papa. You have not told Papa, Ellen? Say you have not? I've been exceedingly naughty, but I won't do it any more!"

With a grave severity in my manner, I bade her stand up.

"So," I exclaimed, "Miss Catherine, you are tolerably far on, it seems: you may well be ashamed of them! A fine bundle of trash you study in your leisure hours, to be sure: why, it's good enough to be printed! And what do you suppose the master will think, when I display it before him? I haven't shown it yet, but you needn't imagine I shall keep your ridiculous secrets. For shame! And

EPISTLE (ih <u>pihs</u> uhl) *n.*
   a formal letter
      Synonyms: message, missive, note
ENTREATY (ehn <u>tree</u> tee) *n.*
   a plea or request
      Synonyms: imploration, prayer, petition
INCLINE (ihn <u>klien</u>) *v.* **-ing,-ed.**
   to have a specific tendency, to be predisposed
      Synonyms: lean to, influence, impel, prefer

SUPPLICATE (<u>suh</u> plih kayt) *v.* **-ing,-ed.**
   to make a humble and earnest request
      Synonyms: petition, pray, beseech, beg

DRAW *v.* **drawing, drew, drawn**
   to pull, drag; to attract or be attracted to; to lead, to
   bring about on purpose
      Synonyms: haul, tow, yank; lure, entice; provoke, elicit

you must have led the way in writing such absurdities: he would not have thought of beginning, I'm certain."

"I didn't! I didn't!" sobbed Cathy, fit to break her heart. "I didn't once think of loving him till—"

"*Loving!*" cried I, as scornfully as I could utter the word. "*Loving!* Did anybody ever hear the like! I might just as well talk of loving the miller who comes once a year to buy our corn. Pretty loving, indeed! And both times together you have seen Linton hardly four hours in your life! Now here is the babyish trash. I'm going with it to the library; and we'll see what your father says to such *loving*."

She sprang at her precious **epistles**, but I held them above my head; and then she poured out further frantic **entreaties** that I would burn them—do anything rather than show them. And being really fully as much **inclined** to laugh as scold—for I esteemed it all girlish vanity—I at length relented in a measure, and asked:

"If I consent to burn them, will you promise faithfully neither to send nor receive a letter again, nor a book (for I perceive you have sent him books), nor locks of hair, nor rings, nor playthings?"

"We don't send playthings!" cried Catherine, her pride overcoming her shame.

"Nor anything at all, then, my lady," I said. "Unless you will, here I go."

"I promise, Ellen!" she cried, catching my dress. "Oh, put them in the fire, do, do!"

But when I proceeded to open a place with the poker, the sacrifice was too painful to be borne. She earnestly **supplicated** that I would spare her one or two.

"One or two, Ellen, to keep for Linton's sake!"

I unknotted the handkerchief, and commenced dropping them in from an angle, and the flame curled up the chimney.

"I will have one, you cruel wretch!" she screamed, darting her hand into the fire, and **drawing** forth some half consumed fragments, at the expense of her fingers.

INTER (ihn <u>tuhr</u>) *v.* **-ring,-red.**
  to bury
    Synonyms: entomb, inhume
DESCEND (dih <u>sehnd</u>) (dee <u>sehnd</u>) *v.* **-ing,-ed.**
  to pass from a higher place to a lower place
    Synonyms: fall, dismount, gravitate

OBSTINATELY (<u>ahb</u> stih nuht lee) *adv.*
  stubbornly
    Synonyms: tenaciously, persistently, firmly

DIURNAL (die <u>uhr</u> nuhl) *adj.*
  existing during the day (as opposed to night), daily
    Synonyms: daylight, daytime

"Very well—and I will have some to exhibit to Papa!" I answered, shaking back the rest into the bundle, and turning anew to the door.

She emptied her blackened pieces into the flames, and motioned me to finish the <u>immolation</u>. It was done; I stirred up the ashes, and **interred** them under a shovelful of coals; and she mutely, and with a sense of intense injury, retired to her private apartment. I **descended** to tell my master that the young lady's <u>qualm</u> of sickness was almost gone, but I judged it best for her to lie down a while. She wouldn't dine; but she reappeared at tea, pale, and red about the eyes, and marvellously subdued in outward aspect. Next morning, I answered the letter by a slip of paper, inscribed, "Master Heathcliff is requested to send no more notes to Miss Linton, as she will not receive them." And, thenceforth, the little boy came with vacant pockets.

Chapter 22

Summer drew to an end, and early autumn: it was past Michaelmas, but the harvest was late that year, and a few of our fields were still uncleared. Mr. Linton and his daughter would frequently walk out among the <u>reapers</u>; at the carrying of the last <u>sheaves</u>, they stayed till dusk, and the evening happening to be chill and damp, my master caught a bad cold, that settled **obstinately** on his lungs, and confined him indoors throughout the whole of the winter, nearly without intermission.

Poor Cathy, frightened from her little romance, had been considerably sadder and duller since its abandonment; and her father insisted on her reading less, and taking more exercise. She had his companionship no longer; I esteemed it a duty to supply its lack, as much as possible, with mine; an inefficient substitute; for I could only spare two or three hours, from my numerous **diurnal**

MELANCHOLY (<u>mehl</u> uhn kahl ee) *n.*
   sadness, depression
      Synonyms: dejection, despondency, woe, sorrow
COUNTENANCE (<u>kown</u> tuh nuhns) *n.*
   appearance, facial expression
      Synonyms: face, features, visage
DIVERT (die <u>vuhrt</u>) *v.* **-ing,-ed.**
   to distract or amuse; to move in different directions
   from a particular point
      Synonyms: deter, occupy, entertain; deviate, separate
STUNTED (<u>stuhn</u> tehd) *adj.*
   having arrested growth or development
      Synonyms: little, petite, dwarfish, undersized, runty
AGILITY (uh <u>jihl</u> ih tee) *n.*
   great coordination, nimbleness
      Synonyms: spryness, dexterity, litheness
DESCEND (dih <u>sehnd</u>) (dee <u>sehnd</u>) *v.* **-ing,-ed.**
   to pass from a higher place to a lower place
      Synonyms: fall, dismount, gravitate

occupations, to follow her footsteps, and then my society was obviously less desirable than his.

On an afternoon in October, or the beginning of November—a fresh watery afternoon, when the turf and paths were rustling with moist, withered leaves, and the cold, blue sky was half hidden by clouds—dark grey streamers, rapidly mounting from the west, and holding abundant rain—I requested my young lady to forego her ramble, because I was certain of showers. She refused; and I unwillingly donned a cloak, and took my umbrella to accompany her on a stroll to the bottom of the park: a formal walk which she generally affected if low-spirited— and that she invariably was when Mr. Edgar had been worse than ordinary, a thing never known from his confession, but guessed both by her and me, from his increased silence and the **melancholy** of his **countenance**. She went sadly on: there was no running or bounding now, though the chill wind might well have tempted her to race. And often, from the side of my eye, I could detect her raising a hand, and brushing something off her cheek. I gazed round for a means of **diverting** her thoughts. On one side of the road rose a high, rough bank, where hazels and **stunted** oaks, with their roots half-exposed, held uncertain tenure: the soil was too loose for the latter; and strong winds had blown some nearly horizontal. In summer, Miss Catherine delighted to climb along these trunks, and sit in the branches, swinging twenty feet above the ground; and I, pleased with her **agility** and her light, childish heart, still considered it proper to scold every time I caught her at such an elevation, but so that she knew there was no necessity for **descending**. From dinner to tea she would lie in her breeze-rocked cradle, doing nothing except singing old songs—my nursery lore—to herself, or watching the birds, joint tenants, feed and entice their young ones to fly: or nestling with closed lids, half thinking, half dreaming, happier than words can express.

"Look, Miss!" I exclaimed, pointing to a nook under the roots of one twisted tree. "Winter is not here yet.

MULTITUDE (<u>muhl</u> tuh tood) *n.*
the state of being many, a great number
Synonyms: mass, myriad, slew, crowd

MELANCHOLY (mehl uhn <u>kahl</u> ee) *adj.*
sad, depressing
Synonyms: dejected, despondent, woeful, sorrowful

SAUNTER (<u>sawn</u> tuhr) *v.* **-ing,-ed.**
to walk leisurely or amble
Synonyms: stroll, ramble, perambulate

BLANCHED (blaanchd) *adj.*
pale, lacking color
Synonyms: faded, lightened, bleached

AVERTED (uh <u>vuhrt</u> ihd) *adj.*
turned away or to the side
Synonyms: shunted, deflected

RESTRAINT (rih <u>straynt</u>) *n.*
control, repression, restriction; a rule or limitation
Synonyms: confinement; barrier, order, rein

STIFLED (<u>stie</u> fuhld) *adj.*
suppressed or held back; smothered or suffocated
Synonyms: muted, muffled, restrained; deadened

CALAMITY (kuh <u>laam</u> ih tee) *n.*
misfortune; state of despair
Synonyms: disaster, cataclysm; misery

There's a little flower up yonder, the last bud from the **multitude** of bluebells that clouded those turf steps in July with a lilac mist. Will you clamber up, and pluck it to show to Papa?"

Cathy stared a long time at the lonely blossom trembling in its earthy shelter, and replied, at length:

"No, I'll not touch it: but it looks **melancholy**, does it not, Ellen?"

"Yes," I observed, "about as starved and sackless as you: your cheeks are bloodless; let us take hold of hands and run. You're so low, I dare say I shall keep up with you."

"No," she repeated, and continued **sauntering** on, pausing at intervals, to muse over a bit of moss, or a tuft of **blanched** grass, or a fungus spreading its bright orange among the heaps of browned foliage; and, ever and anon, her hand was lifted to her **averted** face.

"Catherine, why are you crying, love?" I asked, approaching and putting my arm over her shoulder. "You mustn't cry because Papa has a cold; be thankful it is nothing worse."

She now put no further **restraint** on her tears; her breath was **stifled** by sobs.

"Oh, it *will* be something worse," she said. "And what shall I do when Papa and you leave me, and I am by myself? I can't forget your words, Ellen; they are always in my ear. How life will be changed, how dreary the world will be, when Papa and you are dead."

"None can tell, whether you won't die before us," I replied. "It's wrong to anticipate evil. We'll hope there are years and years to come before any of us go: Master is young, and I am strong, and hardly forty-five. My mother lived till eighty, a <u>canty</u> dame to the last. And suppose Mr. Linton were spared till he saw sixty, that would be more years than you have counted, Miss. And would it not be foolish to mourn a **calamity** above twenty years beforehand?"

CONSOLATION (kahn suh <u>lay</u> shuhn) *n.*
something providing comfort or solace for a loss or
hardship
Synonym: condolence

EXPEDIENT (ihk <u>spee</u> dee uhnt) *adj.*
convenient, efficient, practical
Synonyms: appropriate, useful, sensible

VEX (vehks) *v.* **-ing,-ed.**
to irritate, annoy; confuse, puzzle
Synonyms: bother, plague, afflict, irk; perplex, perturb

RESOLUTION (reh suh <u>loo</u> shuhn) *n.*
a firm decision
Synonyms: determination, will, explanation

"But Aunt Isabella was younger than Papa," she remarked, gazing up with timid hope to seek further **consolation**.

"Aunt Isabella had not you and me to nurse her," I replied. "She wasn't as happy as Master: she hadn't as much to live for. All you need do, is to wait well on your father, and cheer him by letting him see you cheerful; and avoid giving him anxiety on any subject: mind that, Cathy! I'll not disguise but you might kill him, if you were wild and reckless, and cherished a foolish, fanciful affection for the son of a person who would be glad to have him in his grave; and allowed him to discover that you fretted over the separation he has judged it **expedient** to make."

"I fret about nothing on earth except Papa's illness," answered my companion. "I care for nothing in comparison with Papa. And I'll never—never—oh, never, while I have my senses, do an act or say a word to **vex** him. I love him better than myself, Ellen; and I know it by this: I pray every night that I may live after him: because I would rather be miserable than that he should be: that proves I love him better than myself."

"Good words," I replied. "But deeds must prove it also; and after he is well, remember you don't forget **resolutions** formed in the hour of fear."

As we talked, we neared a door that opened on the road; and my young lady, tightening into sunshine again, climbed up and seated herself on the top of the wall, reaching over to gather some hips that bloomed scarlet on the summit branches of the wild rose trees, shadowing the highway side: the lower fruit had disappeared, but only birds could touch the upper, except from Cathy's present station. In stretching to pull them, her hat fell off; and as the door was locked, she proposed scrambling down to recover it. I bid her be cautious lest she get a fall, and she nimbly disappeared. But the return was no such easy matter: the stones were smooth and neatly cemented, and the rose bushes and blackberry stragglers could yield no

ASCEND (uh <u>sehnd</u>) *v.* **-ing,-ed.**
   to rise to another level or climb; to move upward
      Synonyms: elevate, escalate, mount; hoist, lift
SCALE (skayl) *v.* **-ing,-ed.**
   to climb to the top of
      Synonyms: ascend, mount

DESPOND (also DESPONDENCY) (dih <u>spahnd</u>) *n.*
   discouragement, dejection
      Synonyms: sadness, depression, desolation, despair

assistance in re-**ascending**. I, like a fool, didn't recollect that, till I heard her laughing and exclaiming:

"Ellen, you'll have to fetch the key, or else I must run round to the porter's lodge. I can't **scale** the ramparts on this side!"

"Stay where you are," I answered, "I have my bundle of keys in my pocket: perhaps I may manage to open it; if not I'll go."

Catherine amused herself with dancing to and fro before the door, while I tried all the large keys in succession. I had applied the last, and found that none would do; so, repeating my desire that she would remain there, I was about to hurry home as fast as I could, when an approaching sound arrested me. It was the trot of a horse; Cathy's dance stopped also.

"Who is that?" I whispered.

"Ellen, I wish you could open the door," whispered back my companion anxiously.

"Ho, Miss Linton!" cried a deep voice (the rider's). "I'm glad to meet you. Don't be in haste to enter, for I have an explanation to ask and obtain."

"I shan't speak to you, Mr. Heathcliff," answered Catherine. "Papa says you are a wicked man, and you hate both him and me; and Ellen says the same."

"That is nothing to the purpose," said Heathcliff. (He it was.) "I don't hate my son, I suppose; and it is concerning him that I demand your attention. Yes; you have cause to blush. Two or three months since, were you not in the habit of writing to Linton? Making love in play, eh? You deserved, both of you, flogging for that! You especially, the older, and less sensitive, as it turns out. I've got your letters, and if you give me any pertness I'll send them to your father. I presume you grew weary of the amusement and dropped it, didn't you? Well, you dropped Linton with it into a <u>Slough</u> of **Despond**. He was in earnest: in love, really. As true as I live, he's dying for you; breaking his heart at your fickleness: not figuratively, but actually. Though Hareton has made him a standing jest for six

PALTRY (<u>pahl</u> tree) *adj.*
  pitifully small or worthless
    Synonyms: trivial, trifling, petty, picayune, meager

AFFIRM (uh <u>fihrm</u>) *v.* **-ing,-ed.**
  to state positively, to assert as valid or confirmed
    Synonyms: declare, avow, maintain

ENTREAT (ehn <u>treet</u>) *v.* **-ing,-ed.**
  to plead, beg
    Synonyms: beseech, implore, importune, request

weeks, and I have used more serious measures, and attempted to frighten him out of his idiocy, he gets worse daily; and he'll be under the sod before summer, unless you restore him!"

"How can you lie so glaringly to the poor child?" I called from the inside. "Pray ride on! How can you deliberately get up such **paltry** falsehoods? Miss Cathy, I'll knock the lock off with a stone: you won't believe that <u>vile</u> nonsense. You can feel in yourself, it is impossible that a person should die for love of a stranger."

"I was not aware there were eavesdroppers," muttered the detected villain. "Worthy Mrs. Dean, I like you, but I don't like your double-dealing," he added aloud. "How could *you* lie so glaringly, as to **affirm** I hated the 'poor child'? And invent <u>bugbear</u> stories to terrify her from my door-stones? Catherine Linton (the very name warms me), my <u>bonnie</u> lass, I shall be from home all this week; go and see if I have not spoken truth: do, there's a darling! Just imagine your father in my place, and Linton in yours; then think how you would value your careless lover if he refused to stir a step to comfort you, when your father himself **entreated** him; and don't from pure stupidity, fall into the same error. I swear, on my salvation, he's going to his grave, and none but you can save him!"

The lock gave way and I issued out.

"I swear Linton is dying," repeated Heathcliff, looking hard at me. "And grief and disappointment are hastening his death. Nelly, if you won't let her go, you can walk over yourself. But I shall not return till this time next week; and I think your master himself would scarcely object to her visiting her cousin!"

"Come in," said I, taking Cathy by the arm and half-forcing her to re-enter, for she lingered, viewing with troubled eyes the features of the speaker, too stern to express his inward deceit.

He pushed his horse close, and bending down, observed:

CONTRIVE (kuhn <u>triev</u>) *v.* **-ing,-ed.**
    to devise, plan, or manage; to form in an artistic manner
      Synonyms: concoct, scheme; create, design

DIVINE (dih <u>vien</u>) *v.* **-ing,-ed.**
    to foretell or know by inspiration
      Synonyms: predict, intuit, auger, foresee, presage

DIVERSION (dih <u>vuhr</u> zhuhn) (die <u>vuhr</u> zhuhn) *n.*
    an amusing or relaxing activity; a distraction
      Synonyms: entertainment, recreation; deviation
EXPOSTULATE (ihk <u>spahs</u> chuh layt) *v.* **-ing,-ed.**
    to reason earnestly with another; to discuss or examine
      Synonyms: argue, protest, dissuade; debate
DERIDE (dih <u>ried</u>) *v.* **-ing,-ed.**
    to mock, ridicule, make fun of
      Synonyms: taunt, jeer, insult, tease

CREDULITY (kreh <u>doo</u> lih tee) (kreh <u>dyoo</u> lih tee) *n.*
    a tendency to believe anything, gullibility
      Synonyms: naïveté, innocence

"Miss Catherine, I'll own to you that I have little patience with Linton; and Hareton and Joseph have less. I'll own that he's with a harsh set. He pines for kindness, as well as love; and a kind word from you would be his best medicine. Don't mind Mrs. Dean's cruel cautions; but be generous, and **contrive** to see him. He dreams of you day and night, and cannot be persuaded that you don't hate him, since you neither write nor call."

I closed the door, and rolled a stone to assist the loosened lock in holding it; and spreading my umbrella, I drew my charge underneath: for the rain began to drive through the moaning branches of the trees, and warned us to avoid delay. Our hurry prevented any comment on the encounter with Heathcliff, as we stretched towards home; but I **divined** instinctively that Catherine's heart was clouded now in double darkness. Her features were so sad, they did not seem hers: she evidently regarded what she had heard as every syllable true.

The master had retired to rest before we came in. Cathy stole to his room to inquire how he was; he had fallen asleep. She returned, and asked me to sit with her in the library. We took our tea together; and afterwards she lay down on the rug, and told me not to talk, for she was weary. I got a book, and pretended to read. As soon as she supposed me absorbed in my occupation, she recommenced her silent weeping; it appeared, at present, her favourite **diversion**. I suffered her to enjoy it a while; then I **expostulated**: **deriding** and ridiculing all Mr. Heathcliff's assertions about his son, as if I were certain she would coincide. Alas! I hadn't skill to counteract the effect his account had produced: it was just what he intended.

"You may be right, Ellen," she answered, "but I shall never feel at ease till I know. And I must tell Linton it is not my fault that I don't write, and convince him that I shall not change."

What use were anger and protestations against her silly **credulity**? We parted that night—hostile; but next day beheld me on the road to Wuthering Heights, by the side

DEJECTED (dih <u>jehk</u> tihd) (dee <u>jehk</u> tihd) *adj.*
  having low spirits, depressed
    Synonyms: blue, glum, miserable, cheerless

COUNTENANCE (<u>kown</u> tuh nuhns) *n.*
  appearance, facial expression
    Synonyms: face, features, visage

ASCERTAIN (aa suhr <u>tayn</u>) *v.* **-ing,-ed.**
  to determine, discover, make certain of
    Synonyms: verify, calculate, detect

AFFIRMATION (uh fuhr <u>may</u> shuhn) *n.*
  a statement of agreement, a valid confirmation
    Synonyms: assent, nod, yes

RESOLUTE (reh suh <u>loot</u>) *adj.*
  determined; with a clear purpose
    Synonyms: firm, unwavering; intent, resolved

of my wilful young mistress's pony. I couldn't bear to witness her sorrow: to see her pale **dejected countenance**, and heavy eyes: and I yielded, in the faint hope that Linton himself might prove, by his reception of us, how little of the tale was founded on fact.

Chapter 23

The rainy night had ushered in a misty morning—half frost, half-drizzle—and temporary brooks crossed our path—gurgling from the uplands. My feet were thoroughly wetted; I was cross and low; exactly the humour suited for making the most of these disagreeable things. We entered the farmhouse by the kitchen way, to **ascertain** whether Mr. Heathcliff were really absent; because I put slight faith in his own **affirmation**.

Joseph seemed sitting in a sort of <u>Elysium</u> alone, beside a roaring fire; a quart of ale on the table near him, bristling with large pieces of toasted oat-cake; and his black, short pipe in his mouth. Catherine ran to the hearth to warm herself. I asked if the master was in? My question remained so long unanswered, that I thought the old man had grown deaf, and repeated it louder.

"Na—ay!" he snarled, or rather screamed through his nose. "Na—ay! Yah muh goa back whear yah coom frough."

"Joseph!" cried a <u>peevish</u> voice, simultaneously with me, from the inner room. "How often am I to call you? There are only a few red ashes now. Joseph! Come this moment."

Vigorous puffs, and a **resolute** stare into the grate declared he had no ear for this appeal. The housekeeper and Hareton were invisible; one gone on an errand, and the other at his work, probably. We knew Linton's tones, and entered.

NEGLIGENT (<u>nehg</u> lih jehnt) *adj.*
  careless, inattentive
    Synonyms: derelict, lax, remiss, slack, casual

CONTRITE (kuhn <u>triet</u>) *adj.*
  deeply sorrowful and repentant for a wrong
    Synonyms: regretful, apologetic, remorseful
DETESTABLE (dee <u>tehst</u> uh buhl) *adj.*
  deserving of intense and violent hatred
    Synonyms: disgusting, despicable, loathsome
REBUKE (ree <u>byook</u>) *v.* **-ing,-ed.**
  to reprimand, scold
    Synonyms: admonish, reprove, reproach, chide
CORRUGATED (<u>kohr</u> uh gay tihd) *adj.*
  wrinkled or folded
    Synonyms: crumpled, furrowed

OBLIGE (uh <u>bliej</u>) *v.* **-ing,-ed.**
  to be obligated, to require or force someone to obey
    Synonyms: compel, constrain, bind, favor
RESOLVE (rih <u>sahlv</u>) *v.* **-ing,-ed.**
  to determine or to make a firm decision about
    Synonyms: solve, decide

"Oh, I hope you'll die in a <u>garret</u>! starved to death," said the boy, mistaking our approach for that of his **negligent** attendant.

He stopped, on observing his error; his cousin flew to him.

"Is that you, Miss Linton?" he said, raising his head from the arm of the great chair, in which he reclined. "No—don't kiss me: it takes my breath. Dear me! Papa said you would call," continued he, after recovering a little from Catherine's embrace; while she stood by looking very **contrite**. "Will you shut the door, if you please? You left it open; and those—those **detestable** creatures won't bring coals to the fire. It's so cold!"

I stirred up the cinders, and fetched a scuttleful myself. The invalid complained of being covered with ashes; but he had a tiresome cough, and looked feverish and ill, so I did not **rebuke** his temper.

"Well, Linton," murmured Catherine, when his **corrugated** brow relaxed. "Are you glad to see me? Can I do you any good?"

"Why didn't you come before?" he asked. "You should have come, instead of writing. It tired me dreadfully, writing those long letters. I'd far rather have talked to you. Now, I can neither bear to talk, nor anything else. I wonder where Zillah is! Will you (looking at me) step into the kitchen and see?"

I had received no thanks for my other service; and being unwilling to run to and fro at his behest, I replied:

"Nobody is out there but Joseph."

"I want to drink," he exclaimed fretfully, turning away. "Zillah is constantly <u>gadding</u> off to Gimmerton since Papa went: it's miserable! And I'm **obliged** to come down here—they **resolved** never to hear me upstairs."

"Is your father attentive to you, Master Heathcliff?" I asked, perceiving Catherine to be checked in her friendly advances.

"Attentive? He makes *them* a little more attentive at least," he cried. "The wretches! Do you know, Miss

ODIOUS (<u>oh</u> dee uhs) *adj.*
  hateful, contemptible
    Synonyms: detestable, obnoxious, offensive,
    repellent, loathsome

REITERATE (ree <u>ih</u> tuhr ayt) *v.* **-ing,-ed.**
  to say or do again, repeat
    Synonyms: echo, rehash, restate, retell

VEX (vehks) *v.* **-ing,-ed.**
  to irritate, annoy; confuse, puzzle
    Synonyms: bother, plague, afflict, irk; perplex, perturb

PROVOKE (proh <u>vohk</u>) *v.* **-ing,-ed.**
  to cause a response, e.g., anger or disagreement
    Synonyms: aggravate, stimulate, vex, incite

Linton, that <u>brute</u> Hareton laughs at me! I hate him! Indeed, I hate them all: they are **odious** beings."

Cathy began searching for some water; she lighted on a pitcher in the dresser, filled a tumbler, and brought it. He bid her add a spoonful of wine from a bottle on the table; and having swallowed a small portion, appeared more tranquil, and said she was very kind.

"And are you glad to see me?" asked she, **reiterating** her former question, and pleased to detect the faint dawn of a smile.

"Yes, I am. It's something new to hear a voice like yours!" he cried. "But I have been **vexed**, because you wouldn't come. And Papa swore it was owing to me: he called me a pitiful, shuffling, worthless thing; and said you despised me; and if he had been in my place, he would be more the master of the Grange than your father, by this time. But you don't despise me, do you, Miss—"

"I wish you would say Catherine, or Cathy," interrupted my young lady. "Despise you? No! Next to Papa and Ellen, I love you better than anybody living. I don't love Mr. Heathcliff, though; and I dare not come when he returns; will he stay away many days?"

"Not many," answered Linton, "but he goes on to the moors frequently, since the shooting season commenced; and you might spend an hour or two with me in his absence. Do say you will. I think I should not be <u>peevish</u> with you: you'd not **provoke** me, and you'd always be ready to help me, wouldn't you?"

"Yes," said Catherine, stroking his long soft hair, "if I could only get Papa's consent, I'd spend half my time with you. Pretty Linton! I wish you were my brother."

"And then you would like me as well as your father?" observed he, more cheerfully. "But Papa says you would love me better than him and all the world, if you were my wife; so I'd rather you were that."

"No I should never love anybody better than Papa," she returned gravely. "And people hate their wives, some-

AFFIRM (uh <u>fihrm</u>) *v.* **-ing,-ed.**
   to state positively, to assert as valid or confirmed
     Synonyms: declare, avow, maintain
AVERSION (uh <u>vuhr</u> zhuhn) *n.*
   intense dislike
     Synonyms: antagonism, antipathy, abhorrence,
     repulsion, repugnance

RETORT (rih <u>tohrt</u>) *v.* **-ing,-ed.**
   to make a cutting response
     Synonyms: retaliate, talk back, counter

AGITATION (aa gih <u>tay</u> shuhn) *n.*
   uneasiness; commotion, excitement
     Synonyms: restlessness, anxiety; disturbance

times; but not their sisters and brothers: and if you were the latter you would live with us, and Papa would be as fond of you as he is of me."

Linton denied that people ever hated their wives; but Cathy **affirmed** they did, and, in her wisdom, instanced his own father's **aversion** to her aunt. I endeavoured to stop her thoughtless tongue. I couldn't succeed till everything she knew was out. Master Heathcliff, much irritated, asserted her relation was false.

"Papa told me; and Papa does not tell falsehoods," she answered pertly.

"*My* papa scorns yours!" cried Linton. "He calls him a sneaking fool."

"Yours is a wicked man," **retorted** Catherine, "and you are very naughty to dare to repeat what he says. He must be wicked to have made Aunt Isabella leave him as she did."

"She didn't leave him," said the boy. "You shan't contradict me."

"She did," cried the young lady.

"Well, I'll tell *you* something!" said Linton. "Your mother hated your father: now then."

"Oh!" exclaimed Catherine, too enraged to continue.

"And she loved mine," added he.

"You little liar! I hate you now!" she panted, and her face grew red with passion.

"She did! She did!" sang Linton, sinking into the recess of his chair, and leaning back his head to enjoy the **agitation** of the other disputant, who stood behind.

"Hush, Master Heathcliff!" I said. "That's your father's tale, too, I suppose."

"It isn't—you hold your tongue!" he answered. "She did, she did, Catherine! She did, she did!"

Cathy, beside herself, gave the chair a violent push, and caused him to fall against one arm. He was immediately seized by a suffocating cough that soon ended his triumph. It lasted so long that it frightened even me. As to his cousin, she wept, with all her might; aghast at the

QUELL (kwehl) *v.* **-ing,-ed.**
   to subdue; to crush
      Synonyms: suppress, pacify, quiet; quash, stifle
LAMENTATION (laa mehn <u>tay</u> shuhn) *n.*
   an expression of grief or sorrow, a loud cry
      Synonyms: moaning, sobbing, tears, complaint
SOLEMNLY (<u>sah</u> luhm lee) *adv.*
   seriously or somberly
      Synonyms: quietly, earnestly, ceremonially

STIFLED (<u>stie</u> fuhld) *adj.*
   suppressed or held back; smothered or suffocated
      Synonyms: muted, muffled, restrained; deadened
PATHOS (<u>pay</u> thahs) *n.*
   a quality that causes deeply emotional feelings; a
   feeling of deep emotion
      Synonyms: poignancy; suffering, sadness, passion

DOLEFULLY (<u>dohl</u> fuhl lee) *adv.*
   sadly, mournfully
      Synonyms: funereally, somberly, lugubriously,
      dismally, woefully

mischief she had done: though she said nothing. I held him till the fit exhausted itself. Then he thrust me away, and leant his head down silently. Catherine **quelled** her **lamentations** also, took a seat opposite, and looked **solemnly** into the fire.

"How do you feel now, Master Heathcliff?" I inquired, after waiting ten minutes.

"I wish *she* felt as I do," he replied, "spiteful, cruel thing! Hareton never touches me—he never struck me in his life. And I was better to-day: and there—" his voice died in a whimper.

"I didn't strike you!" muttered Cathy, chewing her lip to prevent another burst of emotion.

He sighed and moaned like one under great suffering, and kept it up for a quarter of an hour; on purpose to distress his cousin apparently, for whenever he caught a **stifled** sob from her he put renewed pain and **pathos** into the inflections of his voice.

"I'm sorry I hurt you, Linton," she said at length, racked beyond endurance. "But I couldn't have been hurt by that little push, and I had no idea that you could, either: you're not much, are you, Linton? Don't let me go home thinking I've done you harm. Answer! Speak to me."

"I can't speak to you," he murmured. "You've hurt me so, that I shall lie awake all night choking with this cough. If you had it you'd know what it was; but *you'll* be comfortably asleep while I'm in agony, and nobody near me. I wonder how you would like to pass those fearful nights!" And he began to wail aloud, for very pity of himself.

"Since you are in the habit of passing dreadful nights," I said, "it won't be Miss who spoils your ease: you'd be the same had she never come. However, she shall not disturb you again; and perhaps you'll get quieter when we leave you."

"Must I go?" asked Catherine **dolefully**, bending over him. "Do you want me to go, Linton?"

PERVERSENESS (puhr <u>vuhrs</u> nehs) *n.*
  deliberate disobedience or misbehavior; contrariness
    Synonyms: unruliness; immorality, irrationality
INDULGED (ihn <u>duhlj</u>) *adj.*
  privileged; spoiled
    Synonyms: advantaged; pampered
GRIEVOUS (<u>gree</u> vuhs) *adj.*
  causing grief or sorrow; serious and distressing
    Synonyms: dolorous, mournful; dire, grave
DISPOSITION (dihs puh <u>zih</u> shuhn) *n.*
  mood or temperament
    Synonyms: behavior, tendency, inclination, nature
ENTREAT (ehn <u>treet</u>) *v.* **-ing,-ed.**
  to plead, beg
    Synonyms: beseech, implore, importune, request
COMPUNCTION (kuhm <u>puhnk</u> shuhn) *n.*
  a feeling of uneasiness caused by guilt or regret
    Synonyms: dubiety, qualm, scruple

PROVOKE (proh <u>vohk</u>) *v.* **-ing,-ed.**
  to cause a response, e.g., anger or disagreement
    Synonyms: aggravate, stimulate, vex, incite

"You can't alter what you've done," he replied
<u>pettishly</u>, shrinking from her, "unless you alter it for the
worse by teasing me into a fever."

"Well, then, I must go?" she repeated.

"Let me alone, at least," said he. "I can't bear your
talking."

She lingered, and resisted my persuasions to departure
a tiresome while; but as he neither looked up nor spoke,
she finally made a movement to the door and I followed.
We were recalled by a scream. Linton had slid from his
seat on to the hearthstone, and lay writhing in the mere
perverseness of an **indulged** plague of a child, determined
to be as **grievous** and harassing as it can. I thoroughly
gauged his **disposition** from his behaviour, and saw at
once it would be folly to attempt humouring him. Not so
my companion: she ran back in terror, knelt down, and
cried, and soothed, and **entreated**, till he grew quiet
from lack of breath: by no means from **compunction** at
distressing her.

"I shall lift him on the <u>settle</u>," I said, "and he may roll
about as he pleases: we can't stop to watch him. I hope
you are satisfied, Miss Cathy, that *you* are not the person
to benefit him; and that his condition of health is not
occasioned by attachment to you. Now, then, there he is!
Come away: as soon as he knows there is nobody by to
care for his nonsense, he'll be glad to lie still."

She placed a cushion under his head, and offered him
some water; he rejected the latter, and tossed uneasily on
the former, as if it were a stone or a block of wood. She
tried to put it more comfortably.

"I can't do with that," he said, "it's not high enough."
Catherine brought another to lay above it.

"That's *too* high," murmured the **provoking** thing.

"How must I arrange it, then?" she asked despairingly.

He twined himself up to her, as she half knelt by the
<u>settle</u>, and converted her shoulder into a support.

"No, that won't do," I said. "You'll be content with the
cushion, Master Heathcliff. Miss has wasted too much

time on you already: we cannot remain five minutes longer."

"Yes, yes, we can!" replied Cathy. "He's good and patient now. He's beginning to think I shall have far greater misery than he will to-night, if I believe he is the worse for my visit; then I dare not come again. Tell the truth about it, Linton; for I mustn't come, if I have hurt you."

"You must come, to cure me," he answered. "You ought to come, because you have hurt me: you know you have extremely! I was not as ill when you entered as I am at present—was I?"

"But you've made yourself ill by crying and being in a passion."

"I didn't do it at all," said his cousin. "However, we'll be friends now. And you want me: you would wish to see me sometimes, really?"

"I told you I did," he replied impatiently. "Sit on the settle and let me lean on your knee. That's as Mamma used to do, whole afternoons together. Sit quite still and don't talk: but you may sing a song, if you can sing; or you may say a nice long interesting ballad—one of those you promised to teach me: or a story. I'd rather have a ballad, though: begin."

Catherine repeated the longest she could remember. The employment pleased both mightily. Linton would have another, and after that another, notwithstanding my strenuous objections; and so they went on until the clock struck twelve, and we heard Hareton in the court, returning for his dinner.

"And to-morrow, Catherine, will you be here to-morrow?" asked young Heathcliff, holding her frock as she rose reluctantly.

"No," I answered, "nor next day neither." She, however, gave a different response evidently, for his forehead cleared as she stooped and whispered in his ear.

"You won't go to-morrow, recollect, Miss!" I commenced, when we were out of the house. "You are not dreaming of it, are you?"

CONJECTURE (kuhn <u>jehk</u> shuhr) *v.* **-ing,-ed.**
   to infer, predict, guess
      Synonyms: postulate, hypothesize, suppose, surmise

TEDIOUS (<u>tee</u> dee uhs) (<u>tee</u> djuhs) *adj.*
   tiresome because of length or dullness; very slow
      Synonyms: wearisome, boring; dragging, drudging

WAX (waaks) *v.* **-ing,-ed.**
   to begin to be; to increase gradually
      Synonyms: become, grow; enlarge, expand, swell

PROTRACTED (proh <u>traak</u> tihd) *adj.*
   prolonged, drawn out, extended
      Synonyms: lengthy, elongated, stretched

She smiled.

"Oh, I'll take good care," I continued. "I'll have that lock mended, and you can escape by no way else."

"I can get over the wall," she said, laughing. "The Grange is not a prison, Ellen, and you are not my <u>gaoler</u>. And besides, I'm almost seventeen: I'm a woman. And I'm certain Linton would recover quickly if he had me to look after him. I'm older than he is, you know, and wiser: less childish, am I not? And he'll soon do as I direct him, with some slight coaxing. He's a pretty little darling when he's good. I'd make such a pet of him, if he were mine. We should never quarrel, should we, after we were used to each other? Don't you like him, Ellen?"

"Like him!" I exclaimed. "The worst-tempered bit of a sickly slip that ever struggled into its teens. Happily, as Mr. Heathcliff **conjectured**, he'll not win twenty. I doubt whether he'll see spring, indeed. And small loss to his family whenever he drops off. And lucky it is for us that his father took him: the kinder he was treated, the more **tedious** and selfish he'd be. I'm glad you have no chance of having him for a husband, Miss Catherine."

My companion **waxed** serious at hearing this speech. To speak of his death so regardlessly, wounded her feelings.

"He's younger than I," she answered, after a **protracted** pause of meditation, "and he ought to live the longest: he will—he must live as long as I do. He's as strong now as when he first came into the north; I'm positive of that. It's only a cold that ails him, the same as Papa has. You say Papa will get better, and why shouldn't he?"

"Well, well," I cried, "after all, we needn't trouble ourselves; for listen, Miss, and mind, I'll keep my word,—if you attempt going to Wuthering Heights again, with or without me, I shall inform Mr. Linton, and, unless he allow it, the intimacy with your cousin must not be revived."

"It has been revived," muttered Cathy sulkily.

"Must not be continued, then," I said.

INCAPACITATED (ihn kuh <u>paas</u> ih tay tehd) *adj.*
  disabled, lacking strength or power
    Synonyms: incapable, helpless, defective, impaired
CALAMITY (kuh <u>laam</u> ih tee) *n.*
  state of despair; misfortune
    Synonyms: misery; disaster, cataclysm

USURP (yoo <u>suhrp</u>) *v.* **-ing,-ed.**
  to occupy instead, to assume a position; to seize by force
    Synonyms: preempt, displace; arrogate, appropriate

"We'll see," was her reply, and she set off at a gallop, leaving me to toil in the rear.

We both reached home before our dinner-time; my master supposed we had been wandering through the park, and therefore he demanded no explanation of our absence. As soon as I entered, I hastened to change my soaked shoes and stockings; but sitting such a while at the Heights had done the mischief. On the succeeding morning I was laid up, and during three weeks I remained **incapacitated** for attending to my duties: a **calamity** never experienced prior to that period, and never, I am thankful to say, since.

My little mistress behaved like an angel, in coming to wait on me, and cheer my solitude: the confinement brought me exceedingly low. It is wearisome, to a stirring active body: but few have slighter reasons for complaint than I had. The moment Catherine left Mr. Linton's room, she appeared at my bedside. Her day was divided between us; no amusement **usurped** a minute: she neglected her meals, her studies, and her play; and she was the fondest nurse that ever watched. She must have had a warm heart, when she loved her father so, to give so much to me. I said her days were divided between us; but the master retired early, and I generally needed nothing after six o'clock; thus the evening was her own. Poor thing! I never considered what she did with herself after tea. And though frequently, when she looked in to bid me good-night, I remarked a fresh colour in her cheeks and a pinkness over her slender fingers; instead of fancying the hue borrowed from a cold ride across the moors, I laid it to the charge of a hot fire in the library.

PERUSE (puh <u>roos</u>) *v.* **-ing,-ed.**
   to examine closely
      Synonyms: scrutinize, inspect, study; browse

DISRELISH (dihs <u>reh</u> lihsh) *n.*
   dislike
      Synonyms: distaste, aversion, displeasure

RESOLVE (rih <u>sahlv</u>) *v.* **-ing,-ed.**
   to determine or to make a firm decision about
      Synonyms: solve, decide

AFFIRM (uh <u>fihrm</u>) *v.* **-ing,-ed.**
   to state positively, to assert as valid or confirmed
      Synonyms: declare, avow, maintain

Chapter 24

At the close of three weeks, I was able to quit my chamber, and move about the house. And on the first occasion of my sitting up in the evening, I asked Catherine to read to me, because my eyes were weak. We were in the library, the master having gone to bed: she consented, rather unwillingly, I fancied; and imagining my sort of books did not suit her, I bid her place herself in the choice of what she **perused**. She selected one of her own favourites, and got forward steadily about an hour, then came frequent questions.

"Ellen, are not you tired? Hadn't you better lie down now? You'll be sick, keeping up so long, Ellen."

"No, no, dear, I'm not tired," I returned continually.

Perceiving me immovable, she <u>essayed</u> another method of showing her **disrelish** for her occupation. It changed to yawning, and stretching, and:

"Ellen, I'm tired."

"Give over then and talk," I answered.

That was worse: she fretted and sighed, and looked at her watch till eight, and finally went to her room, completely over-done with sleep; judging by her <u>peevish</u>, heavy look, and the constant rubbing she inflicted on her eyes. The following night she seemed more impatient still; and on the third from recovering my company, she complained of a headache, and left me. I thought her conduct odd; and having remained alone a long while, I **resolved** on going and inquiring whether she were better, and asking her to come and lie on the sofa, instead of upstairs in the dark. No Catherine could I discover upstairs, and none below. The servants **affirmed** they had not seen her. I listened at Mr. Edgar's door; all was silence. I returned

STEALTHILY (<u>stehl</u> thuh lee) *adv.*
 quietly and cautiously
  Synonyms: furtively, secretly, surreptitiously,
  covertly
ESPIONAGE (<u>ehs</u> pee uh nahzh) (<u>ehs</u> pee uh nihj) *n.*
 the act of watching secretly in order to obtain
 information
  Synonyms: spying, investigation, observation
INARTICULATE (ihn ahr <u>tihk</u> yuh liht) *adj.*
 tongue-tied, unable to speak clearly
  Synonyms: incomprehensible, unintelligible

to her apartment, extinguished my candle, and seated myself in the window.

The moon shone bright; a sprinkling of snow covered the ground, and I reflected that she might, possibly, have taken it into her head to walk about the garden, for refreshment. I did detect a figure creeping along the inner fence of the park; but it was not my young mistress: on its merging into the light, I recognized one of the grooms. He stood a considerable period, viewing the carriage-road through the grounds; then started off at a brisk pace, as if he detected something, and reappeared presently, leading Miss's pony; and there she was, just dismounted, and walking by its side. The man took his charge **stealthily** across the grass towards the stable. Cathy entered by the <u>casement</u>-window of the drawing-room, and glided noiselessly up to where I awaited her. She put the door gently to, slipped off her snowy shoes, untied her hat, and was proceeding, unconscious of my **espionage**, to lay aside her <u>mantle</u>, when I suddenly rose and revealed myself. The surprise petrified her an instant: she uttered an **inarticulate** exclamation, and stood fixed.

"My dear Miss Catherine," I began, too vividly impressed by her recent kindness to break into a scold, "where have you been riding out at this hour? And why should you try to deceive me, by telling a tale? Where have you been? Speak."

"To the bottom of the park," she stammered. "I didn't tell a tale."

"And nowhere else?" I demanded.

"No," was the muttered reply.

"Oh, Catherine!" I cried sorrowfully. "You know you have been doing wrong, or you wouldn't be driven to uttering an untruth to me. That does grieve me. I'd rather be three months ill, than hear you <u>frame</u> a deliberate lie."

She sprang forward, and bursting into tears, threw her arms round my neck.

"Well, Ellen, I'm so afraid of you being angry," she said. "Promise not to be angry, and you shall know the very truth: I hate to hide it."

We sat down in the window-seat; I assured her I would not scold, whatever her secret might be, and I guessed it of course; so she commenced:

"I've been to Wuthering Heights, Ellen, and I've never missed going a day since you fell ill; except thrice before, and twice after you left your room. I gave Michael books and pictures to prepare Minny every evening, and to put her back in the stable: you mustn't scold *him* either, mind. I was at the Heights by half-past six, and generally stayed till half-past eight, and then galloped home. It was not to amuse myself that I went: I was often wretched all the time. Now and then I was happy; once in a week perhaps. At first, I expected there would be sad work persuading you to let me keep my word to Linton: for I had engaged to call again next day, when we quitted him; but, as you stayed upstairs on the morrow, I escaped that trouble. While Michael was refastening the lock of the park door in the afternoon, I got possession of the key, and told him how my cousin wished me to visit him, because he was sick, and couldn't come to the Grange; and how Papa would object to my going: and then I negotiated with him about the pony. He is fond of reading, and he thinks of leaving soon to get married; so he offered, if I would lend him books out of the library, to do what I wished: but I preferred giving him my own, and that satisfied him better.

"On my second visit, Linton seemed in lively spirits; and Zillah (that is their housekeeper) made us a clean room and a good fire, and told us that, as Joseph was out at a prayer-meeting and Hareton Earnshaw was off with his dogs—robbing our woods of pheasants, as I heard afterwards—we might do what we liked. She brought me some warm wine and gingerbread, and appeared exceedingly good-natured; and Linton sat in the arm chair, and I in the little rocking-chair on the hearthstone, and we laughed and talked so merrily, and found so much to say:

UNDULATE (<u>uhn</u> dyoo layt) *v.* **-ing,-ed.**
   to roll along in a rippled motion, to move in waves
      Synonyms: oscillate, fluctuate, billow, surge, pulsate
JUBILEE (joo bih <u>lee</u>) *n.*
   a joyous celebration
      Synonyms: party, hoopla, festivity, jamboree

we planned where we would go, and what we would do in summer. I needn't repeat that, because you would call it silly.

"One time, however, we were near quarrelling. He said the pleasantest manner of spending a hot July day was lying from morning till evening on a bank of <u>heath</u> in the middle of the moors, with the bees humming dreamily about among the bloom, and the larks singing high up overhead, and the blue sky and bright sun shining steadily and cloudlessly. That was his most perfect idea of heaven's happiness. Mine was rocking in a rustling green tree, with a west wind blowing, and bright white clouds flitting rapidly above; and not only larks, but throstles, and blackbirds, and linnets, and cuckoos pouring out music on every side, and the moors seen at a distance, broken into cool dusky dells; but close by great swells of long grass **undulating** in waves to the breeze; and woods and sounding water, and the whole world awake and wild with joy. He wanted all to lie in an ecstasy of peace; I wanted all to sparkle and dance in a glorious **jubilee**. I said his heaven would be only half alive; and he said mine would be drunk; I said I should fall asleep in his; and he said he could not breathe in mine, and began to grow very snappish. At last, we agreed to try both, as soon as the right weather came; and then we kissed each other and were friends.

"After sitting still an hour, I looked at the great room with its smooth uncarpeted floor, and thought how nice it would be to play in, if we removed the table; and I asked Linton to call Zillah in to help us, and we'd have a game at blind-man's buff; she should try to catch us: you used to, you know, Ellen. He wouldn't: there was no pleasure in it, he said; but he consented to play at ball with me. We found two in a cupboard, among a heap of old toys, tops, and hoops, and battledores, and shuttlecocks. One was marked C, and the other H.; I wished to have the C., because that stood for Catherine, and the H. might be for Heathcliff, his name; but the bran came out of H., and

OBLIGE (uh <u>bliej</u>) *v.* **-ing,-ed.**
to be obligated, to require or force someone to obey
Synonyms: compel, constrain, bind, favor
ENTREAT (ehn <u>treet</u>) *v.* **-ing,-ed.**
to plead, beg
Synonyms: beseech, implore, importune, request

INCLINE (ihn <u>klien</u>) *v.* **-ing,-ed.**
to have a specific tendency, to be predisposed
Synonyms: lean to, influence, impel, prefer
ELATION (ih <u>lay</u> shuhn) *n.*
exhilaration, joy
Synonyms: happiness, gladness, bliss, felicity,
euphoria

MIRTH (muhrth) *n.*
frivolity, gaiety, laughter
Synonyms: merriment, jollity, hilarity, glee

494

Linton didn't like it. I beat him constantly, and he got cross again, and coughed, and returned to his chair. That night, though, he easily recovered his good humour: he was charmed with two or three pretty songs—*your* songs, Ellen; and when I was **obliged** to go, he begged and **entreated** me to come the following evening; and I promised. Minny and I went flying home as light as air; and I dreamt of Wuthering Heights and my sweet, darling cousin, till morning.

"On the morrow I was sad; partly because you were poorly, and partly that I wished my father knew, and approved of my excursions: but it was beautiful moonlight after tea; and, as I rode on, the gloom cleared. I shall have another happy evening, I thought to myself; and what delights me more, my pretty Linton will. I trotted up their garden, and was turning round to the back, when that fellow Earnshaw met me, took my bridle, and bid me go in by the front entrance. He patted Minny's neck, and said she was a <u>bonny</u> beast, and appeared as if he wanted me to speak to him. I only told him to leave my horse alone, or else it would kick him. He answered in his vulgar accent, 'It wouldn't do mitch hurt if it did'; and surveyed its legs with a smile. I was half **inclined** to make it try; however, he moved off to open the door, and, as he raised the latch, he looked up to the inscription above, and said, with a stupid mixture of awkwardness and **elation**:

"'Miss Catherine! I can read yon, now.'

"'Wonderful,' I exclaimed. 'Pray let us hear you—you *are* grown clever!'

"He spelt, and drawled over by syllables, the name— 'Hareton Earnshaw.'

"'And the figures?' I cried encouragingly, perceiving that he came to a dead halt.

"'I cannot tell them yet,' he answered.

"'Oh, you dunce!' I said, laughing heartily at his failure.

"The fool stared, with a grin hovering about his lips, and a scowl gathering over his eyes, as if uncertain whether he might not join in my **mirth**: whether it were

CONTEMPT (kuhn <u>tehmpt</u>) *n.*
  disrespect, scorn
    Synonyms: derision, disdain
RETRIEVE (rih <u>treev</u>) *v.* **-ing,-ed.**
  to reclaim, recover; to bring
    Synonyms: regain, recoup; fetch
SKULK (skuhlk) *v.* **-ing,-ed.**
  to move in a stealthy or cautious manner, to sneak
    Synonyms: lurk, shirk, hide, evade, prowl
DISCOMFIT (dihs <u>kuhm</u> fiht) *v.* **-ing,-ed.**
  to make uneasy or embarrass
    Synonyms: disconcert, baffle, frustrate, confound

BASE (bays) *adj.*
  lacking qualities of higher mind or spirit
    Synonyms: vulgar, corrupt, immoral, menial

CIVIL (<u>sih</u> vuhl) *adj.*
  polite
    Synonyms: courteous, communal

not pleasant familiarity, or what it really was, **contempt**. I settled his doubts, by suddenly **retrieving** my gravity and desiring him to walk away, for I came to see Linton, not him. He reddened—I saw that by the moonlight— dropped his hand from the latch, and **skulked** off a picture of mortified vanity. He imagined himself to be as accomplished as Linton, I suppose, because he could spell his own name; and was marvellously **discomfited** that I didn't think the same.''

"Stop, Miss Catherine, dear!" I interrupted. "I shall not scold, but I don't like your conduct there. If you had remembered that Hareton was your cousin as much as Master Heathcliff, you would have felt how improper it was to behave in that way. At least, it was praiseworthy ambition for him to desire to be as accomplished as Linton; and probably he did not learn merely to show off: you had made him ashamed of his ignorance before, I have no doubt; and he wished to remedy it and please you. To sneer at his imperfect attempt was very bad breeding. Had *you* been brought up in his circumstances, would you be less rude? He was as quick and as intelligent a child as ever you were; and I'm hurt that he should be despised now, because that **base** Heathcliff has treated him so unjustly.''

"Well, Ellen, you won't cry about it, will you?" she exclaimed, surprised at my earnestness. "But wait, and you shall hear if he conned his A B C to please me; and if it were worth while being **civil** to the brute. I entered; Linton was lying on the settle, and half got up to wel- come me.

"'I'm ill to-night, Catherine, love,' he said, 'and you must have all the talk, and let me listen. Come, and sit by me. I was sure you wouldn't break your word, and I'll make you promise again, before you go.'

"I knew now that I mustn't tease him, as he was ill; and I spoke softly and put no questions, and avoided irritating him in any way. I had brought some of my nicest books for him; he asked me to read a little of one, and I was

497

COMPLY (kuhm <u>plie</u>) *v.* **-ing,-ied.**
  to yield or agree, to go along with
    Synonyms: accord, submit, acquiesce, obey, respect
VENOM (<u>veh</u> nuhm) *n.*
  malice; poison
    Synonyms: spite, rancor; infection, virulence
INARTICULATE (ihn ahr <u>tihk</u> yuh liht) *adj.*
  tongue-tied, unable to speak clearly
    Synonyms: incomprehensible, unintelligible

MALIGNANT (muh <u>lihg</u> nehnt) *adj.*
  evil in influence or effect; aggressively malicious;
  tending to produce death
    Synonyms: vindictive, threatening; destructive,
    harmful; lethal, fatal
ODIOUS (<u>oh</u> dee uhs) *adj.*
  hateful, contemptible
    Synonyms: detestable, obnoxious, offensive,
    repellent, loathsome

about to **comply**, when Earnshaw burst the door open: having gathered **venom** with reflection. He advanced direct to us, seized Linton by the arm, and swung him off the seat.

"'Get to thy own room!' he said, in a voice almost **inarticulate** with passion; and his face looked swelled and furious. 'Take her there if she comes to see thee; thou shalln't keep me out of this. Begone wi' ye both!'

"He swore at us, and left Linton no time to answer, nearly throwing him into the kitchen; and he clenched his fist as I followed, seemingly longing to knock me down. I was afraid for a moment, and I let one volume fall; he kicked it after me, and shut us out. I heard a **malignant** crackly laugh by the fire, and turning, beheld that **odious** Joseph standing rubbing his bony hands, and quivering.

"'I wer sure he'd sarve ye out! He's a grand lad! He's getten t' raight sperrit in him! *He* knaws—Ay, he knaws, as weel as I do, who sud be t' maister yonder—Ech, ech, ech! He made ye skift properly! Ech, ech, ech!'

"'Where must we go?' I asked of my cousin, disregarding the old wretch's mockery.

"Linton was white and trembling. He was not pretty then, Ellen: oh no! he looked frightful; for his thin face and large eyes were wrought into an expression of frantic, powerless fury. He grasped the handle of the door, and shook it: it was fastened inside.

"'If you don't let me in I'll kill you!—if you don't let me in, I'll kill you!' he rather shrieked than said. 'Devil! Devil!—I'll kill you—I'll kill you!'

"Joseph uttered his croaking laugh again.

"'Thear, that's t' father!' he cried. 'That's father! We've allas summut o' either side in us. Niver heed, Hareton, lad—dunnut be 'feared—he cannot get at thee!'

"I took hold of Linton's hands, and tried to pull him away; but he shrieked so shockingly that I dared not proceed. At last his cries were choked by a dreadful fit of coughing; blood gushed from his mouth, and he fell on the ground. I ran into the yard, sick with terror; and

ASCEND (uh <u>sehnd</u>) *v.* **-ing,-ed.**
    to rise to another level or climb; to move upward
        Synonyms: elevate, escalate, mount; hoist, lift

AFFIRM (uh <u>fihrm</u>) *v.* **-ing,-ed.**
    to state positively, to assert as valid or confirmed
        Synonyms: declare, avow, maintain

DIN (dihn) *n.*
    blaring noise
        Synonyms: loudness, clamor, cacophony, commotion

AGITATION (aa gih <u>tay</u> shuhn) *n.*
    uneasiness; commotion, excitement
        Synonyms: restlessness, anxiety; disturbance

COMPEL (kuhm <u>pehl</u>) *v.* **-ling,-led.**
    to urge or force
        Synonyms: coerce, oblige, constrain

called for Zillah, as loud as I could. She soon heard me: she was milking the cows in a shed behind the barn, and hurrying from her work, she inquired what there was to do? I hadn't breath to explain; dragging her in, I looked about for Linton. Earnshaw had come out to examine the mischief he had caused, and he was then conveying the poor thing upstairs. Zillah and I **ascended** after him; but he stopped me at the top of the steps, and said I shouldn't go in: I must go home. I exclaimed that he had killed Linton, and I *would* enter. Joseph locked the door, and declared I should do 'no sich stuff,' and asked me whether I were 'bahn to be as mad as him.' I stood crying, till the housekeeper reappeared. She **affirmed** he would be better in a bit, but he couldn't do with that shrieking and **din**; and she took me, and nearly carried me into the house.

"Ellen, I was ready to tear my hair off my head! I sobbed and wept so that my eyes were almost blind; and the <u>ruffian</u> you have such sympathy with stood opposite: presuming every now and then to bid me 'wisht,' and denying that it was his fault; and, finally, frightened by my assertions that I would tell Papa, and that he should be put in prison and hanged, he commenced blubbering himself, and hurried out to hide his cowardly **agitation**. Still, I was not rid of him: when at length they **compelled** me to depart, and I had gone some hundred yards off the premises, he suddenly issued from the shadow of the roadside, and checked Minny and took hold of me.

"'Miss Catherine, I'm ill grieved,' he began, 'but it's rayther too bad—'

"I gave him a cut with my whip, thinking perhaps he would murder me. He let go, thundering one of his horrid curses, and I galloped home more than half out of my senses.

"I didn't bid you good night that evening, and I didn't go to Wuthering Heights the next: I wished to go exceedingly; but I was strangely excited, and dreaded to hear that Linton was dead, sometimes; and sometimes shuddered at the thought of encountering Hareton. On the

SUSPENSE (suh <u>spents</u>) *n.*
a feeling of anxiety caused by a mysterious situation
Synonyms: apprehension, anticipation, waiting

CONFOUND (kuhn <u>fownd</u>) *v.* **-ing,-ed.**
1. to baffle, perplex; to mistake something for another
Synonyms: overwhelm, disconcert, entangle,
muddle; confuse, misidentify
2. to damn or condemn
Synonyms: doom, jinx, revile, punish

UPROAR (<u>uhp</u> rohr) *n.*
a situation of loud and confusing excitement
Synonyms: noise, hubbub, commotion, fracas

RESOLUTION (reh suh <u>loo</u> shuhn) *n.*
a firm decision
Synonyms: determination, will, explanation

third day I took courage: at least, I couldn't bear longer **suspense**, and stole off once more. I went at five o'clock, and walked; fancying I might manage to creep into the house, and up to Linton's room, unobserved. However, the dogs gave notice of my approach. Zillah received me, and saying, 'the lad was mending nicely,' showed me into a small, tidy, carpeted apartment, where, to my inexpressible joy, I beheld Linton laid on a little sofa, reading one of my books. But he would neither speak to me nor look at me, through a whole hour, Ellen: he has such an unhappy temper. And what quite **confounded** me, when he did open his mouth, it was to utter the falsehood that I had occasioned the **uproar**, and Hareton was not to blame! Unable to reply, except passionately, I got up and walked from the room. He sent after me a faint 'Catherine!' He did not reckon on being answered so— but I wouldn't turn back; and the morrow was the second day on which I stayed at home, nearly determined to visit him no more. But it was so miserable going to bed and getting up, and never hearing anything about him, that my **resolution** melted into air before it was properly formed. It *had* appeared wrong to take the journey once; now it seemed wrong to refrain. Michael came to ask if he must saddle Minny, I said 'Yes,' and considered myself doing a duty as she bore me over the hills.

"I was forced to pass the front windows to get to the court: it was no use trying to conceal my presence.

"'Young master is in the house,' said Zillah, as she saw me making for the parlour. I went in; Earnshaw was there also, but he quitted the room directly. Linton sat in the great arm-chair half asleep; walking up to the fire, I began in a serious tone, partly meaning it to be true:

"'As you don't like me, Linton, and as you think I come on purpose to hurt you, and pretend that I do so every time, this is our last meeting: let us say good-bye; and tell Mr. Heathcliff that you have no wish to see me, and that he mustn't invent any more falsehoods on the subject.'

REPENT (rih <u>pehnt</u>) *v.* **-ing,-ed.**
   to regret a past action
      Synonyms: rue, atone, apologize
RECONCILE (<u>reh</u> kuhn siel) *v.* **-ing,-ed.**
   1. to resolve a dispute
      Synonyms: agree, accommodate, rectify, reunite
   2. to bring to accept
      Synonyms: resign, submit, placate, pacify, appease

PROVOKINGLY (proh <u>voh</u> kihng lee) *adv.*
   in a way that causes a response, e.g. anger or
   disagreement
      Synonyms: aggravatingly, vexingly, incitingly

"'Sit down and take your hat off, Catherine,' he answered. 'You are so much happier than I am, you ought to be better. Papa talks enough of my defects, and shows enough scorn of me, to make it natural I should doubt myself. I doubt whether I am not altogether as worthless as he calls me frequently; and then I feel so cross and bitter, I hate everybody! I *am* worthless, and bad in temper, and bad in spirit, almost always; and, if you choose, you *may* say good-bye: you'll get rid of an annoyance. Only, Catherine, do me this justice: believe that if I might be as sweet, and as kind, and as good as you are, I would be; as willingly, and more so, than as happy and as healthy. And believe that your kindness has made me love you deeper than if I deserved your love: and though I couldn't, and cannot help showing my nature to you, I regret it and **repent** it; and shall regret and **repent** it till I die!'

"I felt he spoke the truth; and I felt I must forgive him: and, though he should quarrel the next moment, I must forgive him again. We were **reconciled**; but we cried, both of us, the whole time I stayed: not entirely for sorrow, yet I *was* sorry Linton had that distorted nature. He'll never let his friends be at ease, and he'll never be at ease himself! I have always gone to his little parlour, since that night; because his father returned the day after.

"About three times, I think, we have been merry and hopeful, as we were the first evening; the rest of my visits were dreary and troubled: now with his selfishness and spite, and now with his sufferings: but I've learned to endure the former with nearly as little resentment as the latter. Mr. Heathcliff purposely avoids me: I have hardly seen him at all. Last Sunday, indeed, coming earlier than usual, I heard him abusing poor Linton, cruelly, for his conduct of the night before. I can't tell how he knew of it, unless he listened. Linton had certainly behaved **provokingly**: however, it was the business of nobody but me, and I interrupted Mr. Heathcliff's lecture by entering and telling him so. He burst into a laugh, and went away, saying he was glad I took that view of the matter. Since

IMPLORE (ihm <u>plohr</u>) *v.* **-ing,-ed.**
  to call upon in supplication, beg
    Synonyms: plead, entreat, solicit
DISPOSITION (dihs puh <u>zih</u> shuhn) *n.*
  mood or temperament
    Synonyms: behavior, tendency, inclination, nature
CONSOLATION (kahn suh <u>lay</u> shuhn) *n.*
  something providing comfort or solace for a loss or
  hardship
    Synonym: condolence

then, I've told Linton he must whisper his bitter things. Now, Ellen, you have heard all. I can't be prevented from going to Wuthering Heights, except by inflicting misery on two people; whereas, if you'll only not tell Papa, my going need disturb the tranquillity of none. You'll not tell, will you? It will be very heartless if you do."

"I'll make up my mind on that point by to-morrow, Miss Catherine," I replied. "It requires some study; and so I'll leave you to your rest, and go think it over."

I thought it over aloud, in my master's presence; walking straight from her room to his, and relating the whole story, with the exception of her conversations with her cousin, and any mention of Hareton. Mr. Linton was alarmed and distressed, more than he would acknowledge to me. In the morning, Catherine learnt my betrayal of her confidence, and she learnt also that her secret visits were to end. In vain she wept and writhed against the <u>interdict</u>, and **implored** her father to have pity on Linton: all she got to comfort her was a promise that he would write and give him leave to come to the Grange when he pleased; but explaining that he must no longer expect to see Catherine at Wuthering Heights. Perhaps, had he been aware of his nephew's **disposition** and state of health, he would have seen fit to withhold even that slight **consolation**.

Chapter 25

"These things happened last winter, sir," said Mrs. Dean, "hardly more than a year ago. Last winter, I did not think, at another twelve months' end, I should be amusing a stranger to the family with relating them! Yet, who knows how long you'll be a stranger? You're too young to rest always contented, living by yourself; and I some way fancy no one could see Catherine Linton and not love her. You smile; but why do you look so lively and interested,

SENTIMENT (<u>sehn</u> tuh muhnt) *n.*
a romantic or nostalgic feeling, an attitude, thought,
or judgment prompted by feeling
Synonyms: idea, emotion

PERIL (<u>pehr</u> ihl) *n.*
danger
Synonyms: trouble, hazard, vulnerability, risk

BEQUEATH (bih <u>kweeth</u>) *v.* **-ing.-ed.**
to give, as in a will; to hand down
Synonyms: bestow; pass on, transmit

INDULGENT (ihn <u>duhl</u> jehnt) *adj.*
lenient, tolerant
Synonyms: gratifying, pleasing

SPARSELY (<u>spahrs</u> lee) *adv.*
in a scattered or thinly spread manner
Synonyms: scarcely, hardly, scantily, sparingly

SOLILOQUIZE (suh <u>lih</u> luh kwiez) *v.* **-ing,-ed.**
to talk to oneself; to make a literary or dramatic speech
Synonyms: express, verbalize; dramatize

when I talk about her? And why have you asked me to hang her picture over your fireplace? And why—"

"Stop, my good friend!" I cried. "It may be very possible that *I* should love her, but would she love me? I doubt it too much to venture my tranquillity by running into temptation: and then my home is not here. I'm of the busy world, and to its arms I must return. Go on. Was Catherine obedient to her father's commands?"

"She was," continued the housekeeper. "Her affection for him was still the chief **sentiment** in her heart; and he spoke without anger: he spoke in the deep tenderness of one about to leave his treasure amid **perils** and foes, where his remembered words would be the only aid that he could **bequeath** to guide her. He said to me, a few days afterwards:

"'I wish my nephew would write, Ellen, or call. Tell me, sincerely, what you think of him: is he changed for the better, or is there a prospect of improvement, as he grows a man?'

"'He's very delicate, sir,' I replied, 'and scarcely likely to reach manhood; but this I can say, he does not resemble his father, and if Miss Catherine had the misfortune to marry him, he would not be beyond her control: unless she were extremely and foolishly **indulgent**. However, master, you'll have plenty of time to get acquainted with him, and see whether he would suit her: it wants four years and more to his being of age.'"

Edgar sighed; and walking to the window, looked out towards Gimmerton <u>Kirk</u>. It was a misty afternoon, but the February sun shone dimly, and we could just distinguish the two fir-trees in the yards, and the **sparsely** scattered gravestones.

"I've prayed often," he half **soliloquized**, "for the approach of what is coming; and now I begin to shrink, and fear it. I thought the memory of the hour I came down that glen a bridegroom would be less sweet than the anticipation that I was soon, in a few months, or, possibly, weeks, to be carried up, and laid in its lonely hollow!

CONSOLE (kuhn <u>sohl</u>) *v.* **-ing,-ed.**
   to alleviate grief and raise the spirits of, provide solace
      Synonyms: relieve, comfort, soothe

BUOYANT (<u>boy</u> ehnt) *adj.*
   lively and cheerful; having the tendency to float or rise
      Synonyms: carefree, jovial; light, airy, bouncy

PERSEVERE (pehr suh <u>veer</u>) *v.* **-ing,-ed.**
   to continue with determination, remain steadfast
      Synonyms: persist, endure, plod

PROVIDENCE (<u>prah</u> vih dehnts) *n.*
   divine control and direction by God; preparation and
   foresight
      Synonyms: fate, destiny, good luck; prudence,
      precaution

CONVALESCENCE (kahn vuhl <u>ehs</u> uhns) *n.*
   a gradual recovery after an illness
      Synonyms: healing, recuperation

DEFER (dih <u>fuhr</u>) *v.* **-ring,-red.**
   to delay; to delegate to another
      Synonyms: extend, impede, postpone, stall; submit,
      yield

INTIMATE (<u>ihn</u> tuh mayt) *v.* **-ing,-ed.**
   to hint or suggest obscurely
      Synonyms: implicate, allude, insinuate

Ellen, I've been very happy with my little Cathy: through winter nights and summer days she was a living hope at my side. But I've been as happy musing by myself among those stones, under that old church: lying, through the long June evenings, on the green mound of her mother's grave, and wishing—yearning for the time when I might lie beneath it. What can I do for Cathy? How must I quit her? I'd not care one moment for Linton being Heathcliff's son; nor for his taking her from me, if he could **console** her for my loss. I'd not care that Heathcliff gained his ends, and triumphed in robbing me of my last blessing! But should Linton be unworthy—only a feeble tool to his father—I cannot abandon her to him! And, hard though it be to crush her **buoyant** spirit, I must **persevere** in making her sad while I live, and leaving her solitary when I die. Darling! I'd rather resign her to God, and lay her in the earth before me."

"Resign her to God as it is, sir," I answered, "and if we should lose you—which may He forbid—under His **providence**, I'll stand her friend and counsellor to the last. Miss Catherine is a good girl: I don't fear that she will go wilfully wrong; and people who do their duty are always finally rewarded."

Spring advanced; yet my master gathered no real strength, though he resumed his walks in the grounds with his daughter. To her inexperienced notions, this itself was a sign of **convalescence**; and then his cheek was often flushed, and his eyes were bright: she felt sure of his recovering. On her seventeenth birthday, he did not visit the churchyard: it was raining, and I observed:

"You'll surely not go out to-night, sir?"

He answered:

"No, I'll **defer** it this year a little longer."

He wrote again to Linton, expressing his great desire to see him; and, had the invalid been presentable, I've no doubt his father would have permitted him to come. As it was, being instructed, he returned an answer, **intimating** that Mr. Heathcliff objected to his calling at the Grange;

ELOQUENTLY (<u>eh</u> luh kwuhnt lee) *adv.*
persuasively and effectively, with regards to speech
Synonyms: expressively, fluently

AFFIRM (uh <u>fihrm</u>) *v.* **-ing,-ed.**
to state positively, to assert as valid or confirmed
Synonyms: declare, avow, maintain

COMPLY (kuhm <u>plie</u>) *v.* **-ing,-ied.**
to yield or agree, to go along with
Synonyms: accord, submit, acquiesce, obey, respect

UNRESTRAINED (uhn rih <u>straynd</u>) *adj.*
uninhibited, lacking control, unrestricted
Synonyms: unbridled, unchecked, outspoken

EPISTLE (ih <u>pihs</u> uhl) *n.*
a formal letter
Synonyms: message, missive, note

LAMENTATION (laa mehn <u>tay</u> shuhn) *n.*
an expression of grief or sorrow, a loud cry
Synonyms: complaint, moaning, sobbing, tears

but his uncle's kind remembrance delighted him, and he hoped to meet him, sometimes, in his rambles, and personally to petition that his cousin and he might not remain long so utterly divided.

That part of his letter was simple, and probably his own. Heathcliff knew he could plead **eloquently** for Catherine's company, then.

"I do not ask," he said, "that she may visit here; but, am I never to see her, because my father forbids me to go to her home, and you forbid her to come to mine? Do, now and then, ride with her towards the Heights; and let us exchange a few words, in your presence! We have done nothing to deserve this separation; and you are not angry with me; you have no reason to dislike me, you allow, yourself. Dear Uncle! Send me a kind note to-morrow, and leave to join you anywhere you please, except at Thrushcross Grange. I believe an interview would convince you that my father's character is not mine: he **affirms** I am more your nephew than his son; and though I have faults which render me unworthy of Catherine, she has excused them, and for her sake, you should also. You inquire after my health—it is better, but while I remain cut off from all hope, and doomed to solitude, or the society of those who never did and never will like me, how can I be cheerful and well?"

Edgar, though he felt for the boy, could not consent to grant his request; because he could not accompany Catherine. He said, in summer, perhaps, they might meet: meantime, he wished him to continue writing at intervals, and engaged to give him what advice and comfort he was able by letter; being well aware of his hard position in his family. Linton **complied**; and had he been **unrestrained**, would probably have spoiled all by filling his **epistles** with complaints and **lamentations**: but his father kept a sharp watch over him; and, of course, insisted on every line that my master sent being shown; so, instead of penning his peculiar personal sufferings and distresses, the themes constantly uppermost in his thoughts, he harped on the

SAT Vocabulary

INTIMATE (<u>ihn</u> tuh mayt) *v.* **-ing,-ed.**
   to hint or suggest obscurely
      Synonyms: implicate, allude, insinuate

ACQUIESCE (aak wee <u>ehs</u>) *v.* **-ing,-ed.**
   to agree; comply quietly
      Synonyms: accede, consent; submit

RETAIN (rih <u>tayn</u>) *v.* **-ing,-ed.**
   to hold, keep possession of
      Synonyms: withhold, reserve, maintain, remember

FOREBODING (fohr <u>boh</u> dihng) *n.*
   an omen, prediction, or presentiment of upcoming
   evil
      Synonyms: inkling, premonition, prophecy, vibe

RALLY (<u>raa</u> lee) *v.* **-ing,-ied.**
   to recover, recuperate; to assemble
      Synonyms: heal, convalesce; muster, gather, convene

COMPEL (kuhm <u>pehl</u>) *v.* **-ling,-led.**
   to urge or force
      Synonyms: coerce, oblige, constrain

AVARICIOUS (aa vuhr <u>ihsh</u> ihs) *adj.*
   greedy
      Synonyms: covetous, rapacious, eager, selfish

ASSENT (uh <u>sehnt</u>) *n.*
   an agreement or consent
      Synonyms: concurrence, acquiescence

ENTREATY (ehn <u>tree</u> tee) *n.*
   a plea or request
      Synonyms: imploration, prayer, petition

DEVOID (dih <u>voyd</u>) *adj.*
   being without, lacking
      Synonyms: destitute, empty, vacant, null, bare

514

cruel obligation of being held asunder from his friend and love; and gently **intimated** that Mr. Linton must allow an interview soon, or he should fear he was purposely deceiving him with empty promises.

Cathy was a powerful ally at home; and, between them, they at length persuaded my master to **acquiesce** in their having a ride or a walk together about once a week, under my guardianship, and on the moors nearest the Grange: for June found him still declining. Though he had set aside yearly a portion of his income for my young lady's fortune, he had a natural desire that she might **retain**—or at least return in a short time to—the house of her ancestors; and he considered her only prospect of doing that was by a union with his heir; he had no idea that the latter was failing almost as fast as himself; nor had any one, I believe: no doctor visited the Heights, and no one saw Master Heathcliff to make report of his condition among us. I, for my part, began to fancy my **forebodings** were false, and that he must be actually **rallying**, when he mentioned riding and walking on the moors, and seemed so earnest in pursuing his object. I could not picture a father treating a dying child as tyrannically and wickedly as I afterwards learned Heathcliff had treated him, to **compel** this apparent eagerness: his efforts redoubling the more imminently his **avaricious** and unfeeling plans were threatened with defeat by death.

Chapter 26

Summer was already past its prime, when Edgar reluctantly yielded his **assent** to their **entreaties**, and Catherine and I set out on our first ride to join her cousin. It was a close, sultry day: **devoid** of sunshine, but with a sky too dappled and hazy to threaten rain; and our place of meeting had been fixed at the guide-stone, by the cross-roads.

INJUNCTION (ihn <u>juhnk</u> shuhn) *n.*
  command, order
    Synonyms: directive, behest, mandate, edict, decree

EJACULATION (ih <u>jaak</u> yuh lay shuhn) *n.*
  a sudden exclamation
    Synonyms: chatter, vociferation, expletive

RETAIN (rih <u>tayn</u>) *v.* **-ing,-ed.**
  to hold, keep possession of
    Synonyms: withhold, reserve, maintain, remember
LANGUID (<u>laang</u> gwihd) *adj.*
  lacking energy, indifferent, slow
    Synonyms: weak, listless, lackadaisical, sluggish

On arriving there, however, a little herd-boy, <u>despatched</u> as a messenger told us that:

"Maister Linton wer just o' this side th' Heights: and he'd be mitch obleeged to us to gang on a bit further."

"Then Master Linton has forgot the first **injunction** of his uncle," I observed. "He bid us keep on the Grange land, and here we are off at once."

"Well, we'll turn our horses' heads round, when we reach him," answered my companion, "our excursion shall lie towards home."

But when we reached him, and that was scarcely a quarter of a mile from his own door, we found he had no horse; and we were forced to dismount, and leave ours to graze. He lay on the heath, awaiting our approach, and did not rise till we came within a few yards. Then he walked so feebly, and looked so pale, that I immediately exclaimed:

"Why, Master Heathcliff, you are not fit for enjoying a ramble, this morning. How ill you do look!"

Catherine surveyed him with grief and astonishment: she changed the **ejaculation** of joy on her lips, to one of alarm; and the congratulation on their long-postponed meeting, to an anxious inquiry, whether he were worse than usual?

"No—better—better!" he panted, trembling, and **retaining** her hand as if he needed its support, while his large blue eyes wandered timidly over her; the hollowness round them transforming to haggard wildness the **languid** expression they once possessed.

"But you have been worse," persisted his cousin, "worse than when I saw you last; you are thinner, and—"

"I'm tired," he interrupted hurriedly. "It is too hot for walking, let us rest here. And, in the morning, I often feel sick—Papa says I grow so fast."

Badly satisfied, Cathy sat down, and he reclined beside her.

"This is something like your paradise," said she, making an effort at cheerfulness. "You recollect the two days we agreed to spend in the place and way each thought

SUSTAIN (suh <u>stayn</u>) *v.* **-ing,-ed.**
  to support, uphold; endure, undergo
    Synonyms: maintain, prop, confirm, encourage;
    withstand
INCAPACITY (ihn kuh <u>paas</u> ih tee) *n.*
  disability, lack of strength or power or ability
    Synonyms: helplessness, handicap, impairment
LISTLESS (<u>lihst</u> lihs) *adj.*
  lacking energy and enthusiasm
    Synonyms: lethargic, sluggish, languid, indolent
APATHY (<u>aa</u> pah thee) *n.*
  lack of feeling or emotion
    Synonyms: indifference, insouciance, disregard,
    unconcern
MOROSENESS (muh <u>rohs</u> nehs) (maw <u>rohs</u> nehs) *n.*
  gloom, sadness, surliness
    Synonym: sullenness
REPEL (rih <u>pehl</u>) *v.* **-ling,-led.**
  to rebuff, repulse; disgust, offend
    Synonyms: reject, spurn, parry; nauseate, revolt
CONSOLATION (kahn suh <u>lay</u> shuhn) *n. (See page 506.)*
MIRTH (muhrth) *n.*
  frivolity, gaiety, laughter
    Synonyms: merriment, jollity, hilarity, glee
SCRUPLE (<u>skroo</u> puhl) *n.*
  a hesitation caused by moral conscience; an ethical
  and moral belief that prevents action
    Synonyms: restraint, qualm, misgiving; principle
LETHARGY (<u>lehth</u> uhr jee) *n.*
  indifferent inactivity
    Synonyms: lassitude, torpor, stupor, languor,
    sluggishness
AGITATION (aa gih <u>tay</u> shuhn) *n. (See page 500.)*
DIVERSION (dih <u>vuhr</u> zhuhn) *n. (See page 466.)*
AFFIRM (uh <u>fihrm</u>) *v.* **-ing,-ed. (See page 512.)**
PERTINACIOUS (puhr tihn <u>ay</u> shuhs) *adj.*
  stubborn and persistently unyielding
    Synonyms: unrelenting, obstinate, tenacious

pleasantest? This is surely yours, only there are clouds: but then they are so soft and mellow: it is nicer than sunshine. Next week, if you can, we'll ride down to the Grange Park, and try mine."

Linton did not appear to remember what she talked of; and he had evidently great difficulty in **sustaining** any kind of conversation. His lack of interest in the subjects she started, and his equal **incapacity** to contribute to her entertainment, were so obvious that she could not conceal her disappointment. An indefinite alteration had come over his whole person and manner. The <u>pettishness</u> that might be caressed into fondness, had yielded to a **listless apathy**; there was less of the <u>peevish</u> temper of a child which frets and teases on purpose to be soothed, and more of the self-absorbed **moroseness** of a confirmed invalid, **repelling consolation**, and ready to regard the good-humoured **mirth** of others as an insult. Catherine perceived, as well as I did, that he held it rather a punishment, than a gratification, to endure our company; and she made no **scruple** of proposing, presently, to depart. That proposal, unexpectedly, roused Linton from his **lethargy**, and threw him into a strange state of **agitation**. He glanced fearfully towards the Heights, begging she would remain another half-hour at least.

"But I think," said Cathy, "you'd be more comfortable at home than sitting here; and I cannot amuse you to-day, I see, by my tales, and songs, and chatter. You have grown wiser than I, in these six months; you have little taste for my **diversions** now: or else, if I could amuse you, I'd willingly stay."

"Stay to rest yourself," he replied. "And Catherine, don't think, or say that I'm *very* unwell: it is the heavy weather and heat that make me dull; and I walked about, before you came, a great deal for me. Tell Uncle I'm in tolerable health, will you?"

"I'll tell him that *you* say so, Linton. I couldn't **affirm** that you are," observed my young lady, wondering at his **pertinacious** assertion of what was evidently an untruth.

PROVOKE (proh <u>vohk</u>) *v.* **-ing,-ed.**
  to cause a response, e.g., anger or disagreement
    Synonyms: aggravate, stimulate, vex, incite
INDULGENCE (ihn <u>duhl</u> jehns) *n.*
  lenience, the act of giving into desires
    Synonyms: gratification, tolerance, pampering

SUPPRESSED (suh <u>prehsd</u>) *adj.*
  restrained
    Synonyms: subdued, stifled, muffled, quelled, curbed
SOLACE (<u>sah</u> lihs) *n.*
  comfort in distress, consolation
    Synonyms: succor, balm, cheer, condolence

COMPEL (kuhm <u>pehl</u>) *v.* **-ling,-led.**
  to urge or force
    Synonyms: coerce, oblige, constrain
PENANCE (<u>peh</u> nihns) *n.*
  voluntary suffering to repent for a wrong
    Synonyms: atonement, reparation, chastening,
    reconciliation

"And be here again next Thursday," continued he, shunning her puzzled gaze. "And give him my thanks for permitting you to come—my best thanks, Catherine. And—and, if you *did* meet my father, and he asked you about me, don't lead him to suppose that I've been extremely silent and stupid: don't look sad and downcast, as you *are* doing—he'll be angry."

"I care nothing for his anger," exclaimed Cathy, imagining she would be its object.

"But I do," said her cousin, shuddering. "*Don't* **provoke** him against me, Catherine, for he is very hard."

"Is he severe to you, Master Heathcliff?" I inquired. "Has he grown weary of **indulgence**, and passed from passive to active hatred?"

Linton looked at me, but did not answer, and, after keeping her seat by his side another ten minutes, during which his head fell drowsily on his breast, and he uttered nothing except **suppressed** moans of exhaustion or pain, Cathy began to seek **solace** in looking for bilberries, and sharing the produce of her researches with me: she did not offer them to him, for she saw further notice would only weary and annoy.

"Is it half-an-hour now, Ellen?" she whispered in my ear, at last. "I can't tell why we should stay. He's asleep, and Papa will be wanting us back."

"Well, we must not leave him asleep," I answered. "Wait till he wakes, and be patient. You were mighty eager to set off, but your longing to see poor Linton has soon evaporated!"

"Why did *he* wish to see me?" returned Catherine. "In his crossest humours, formerly, I liked him better than I do in his present curious mood. It's just as if it were a task he was **compelled** to perform—this interview—for fear his father should scold him. But I'm hardly going to come to give Mr. Heathcliff pleasure; whatever reason he may have for ordering Linton to undergo this **penance**. And, though I'm glad he's better in health, I'm sorry he's so much less pleasant, and so much less affectionate to me."

CONJECTURE (kuhn <u>jehk</u> shuhr) *v.* **-ing,-ed.**
 to infer, predict, guess
  Synonyms: postulate, hypothesize, suppose, surmise

DETAIN (dih <u>tayn</u>) (dee <u>tayn</u>) *v.* **-ing,-ed.**
 to restrain from continuing on; to hold as if in custody
  Synonyms: delay, inhibit; apprehend, keep

"You think *he* is better in health then?" I said.

"Yes," she answered; "because he always made such a great deal of his sufferings, you know. He is not tolerably well, as he told me to tell Papa; but he's better, very likely."

"There you differ with me, Miss Cathy," I remarked. "I should **conjecture** him to be far worse."

Linton here started from his slumber in bewildered terror, and asked if any one had called his name.

"No," said Catherine, "unless in dreams. I cannot conceive how you manage to doze out of doors, in the morning."

"I thought I heard my father," he gasped, glancing up to the frowning <u>nab</u> above us. "You are sure nobody spoke?"

"Quite sure," replied his cousin. "Only Ellen and I were disputing concerning your health. Are you truly stronger, Linton, than when we separated in winter? If you be I'm certain one thing is not stronger—your regard for me: speak—are you?"

The tears gushed from Linton's eyes as he answered, "Yes, yes, I am!" And, still under the spell of the imaginary voice, his gaze wandered up and down to detect its owner.

Cathy rose. "For to-day we must part," she said. "And I won't conceal that I have been sadly disappointed with our meeting; though I'll mention it to nobody but you: not that I stand in awe of Mr. Heathcliff."

"Hush," murmured Linton, "for God's sake, hush! He's coming." And he clung to Catherine's arm, striving to **detain** her, but at that announcement she hastily disengaged herself, and whistled to Minny, who obeyed her like a dog.

"I'll be here next Thursday," she cried, springing to the saddle. "Good-bye. Quick, Ellen!"

And so we left him, scarcely conscious of our departure, so absorbed was he in anticipating his father's approach.

EMULATE (<u>ehm</u> yuh layt) *v.* **-ing,-ed.**
   to copy, imitate; to equal
      Synonyms: ape; rival,vie
DIVINE (dih <u>vien</u>) *v.* **-ing,-ed.**
   to foretell or know by inspiration
      Synonyms: predict, intuit, auger, foresee, presage
BROOD *v.* **-ing,-ed.**
   to think about in a gloomy or serious way
      Synonyms: ponder, worry, obsess
COUNTENANCE (<u>kown</u> tuh nuhns) *n.*
   appearance, facial expression
      Synonyms: face, features, visage
WAN (wahn) *adj.*
   sickly pale
      Synonyms: ashen, pallid, blanched, pasty, sickly
DRAW *v.* **drawing, drew, drawn**
   to lead, to bring about on purpose; to pull, drag;
   to attract
      Synonyms: provoke, elicit; haul, tow, yank; lure, entice

Before we reached home, Catherine's displeasure softened into a <u>perplexed</u> sensation of pity and regret, largely blended with vague, uneasy doubts about Linton's actual circumstances, physical and social; in which I partook, though I counselled her not to say much; for a second journey would make us better judges. My master requested an account of our ongoings. His nephew's offering of thanks was duly delivered, Miss Cathy gently touching on the rest: I also threw little light on his inquiries, for I hardly knew what to hide, and what to reveal.

Chapter 27

Seven days glided away, every one marking its course by the henceforth rapid alteration of Edgar Linton's state. The havoc that months had previously wrought was now **emulated** by the inroads of hours. Catherine, we would <u>fain</u> have deluded yet: but her own quick spirit refused to delude her: it **divined** in secret, and **brooded** on the dreadful probability, gradually ripening into certainty. She had not the heart to mention her ride, when Thursday came round; I mentioned it for her, and obtained permission to order her out of doors: for the library, where her father stopped a short time daily—the brief period he could bear to sit up—and his chamber, had become her whole world. She grudged each moment that did not find her bending over his pillow, or seated by his side. Her **countenance** grew **wan** with watching and sorrow, and my master gladly dismissed her to what he flattered himself would be a happy change of scene and society; **drawing** comfort from the hope that she would not now be left entirely alone after his death.

He had a fixed idea, I guessed by several observations he let fall, that, as his nephew resembled him in person, he would resemble him in mind; for Linton's letters bore few

DEFER (dih <u>fuhr</u>) *v.* **-ring,-red.** *(See page 510.)*
RESPIRE (rih <u>spier</u>) *v.* **-ing,-ed.**
  to breathe
    Synonyms: inhale, exhale
TRANSIENT (<u>traan</u> see uhnt) *adj.*
  temporary, short-lived, fleeting
    Synonyms: transitory, ephemeral, fugitive,
    momentary, evanescent
REPROACH (rih <u>prohch</u>) *v.* **-ing,-ed.**
  to express disappointment or displeasure; to disgrace
    Synonyms: blame, rebuke, admonish; discredit
DISCERN (dihs <u>uhrn</u>) *v.* **-ing,-ed.**
  to perceive or recognize something obscure
    Synonyms: descry, observe, glimpse, distinguish
RESOLVE (rih <u>sahlv</u>) *v.* **-ing,-ed.**
  to determine or to make a firm decision about
    Synonyms: solve, decide
ANIMATION (aa nih <u>may</u> shuhn) *n.*
  enthusiasm, excitement
    Synonyms: elation, vivacity, brio, spirit, verve
CANDID (<u>kaan</u> dihd) *adj.*
  honest
    Synonyms: frank, sincere, blunt
SUPPLICATE (<u>suh</u> plih kayt) *v.* **-ing,-ed.**
  to make a humble and earnest request
    Synonyms: petition, pray, beseech, beg
ENIGMATICAL (eh nihg <u>mah</u> tih kuhl) *adj.*
  puzzling, inexplicable
    Synonyms: mysterious, cryptic, baffling
ABSOLVE (uhb <u>sahlv</u>) *v.* **-ing,-ed.**
  to forgive, free from blame
    Synonyms: acquit, exculpate, exonerate, pardon
TRIFLING (<u>trie</u> flihng) *n.*
  dawdling; the wasting of time or money
    Synonyms: puttering, fidgeting, lollygagging;
    squandering

or no indications of his defective character. And I, through pardonable weakness, refrained from correcting the error, asking myself what good there would be in disturbing his last moments with information that he had neither power nor opportunity to turn to account.

We **deferred** our excursion till the afternoon; a golden afternoon of August: every breath from the hills so full of life, that it seemed whoever **respired** it, though dying, might revive. Catherine's face was just like the landscape—shadows and sunshine flitting over it in rapid succession; but the shadows rested longer, and the sunshine was more **transient**; and her poor little heart **reproached** itself for even that passing forgetfulness of its cares.

We **discerned** Linton watching at the same spot he had selected before. My young mistress alighted, and told me that, as she was **resolved** to stay a very little while, I had better hold the pony and remain on horseback; but I dissented: I wouldn't risk losing sight of the charge committed to me a minute; so we climbed the slope of heath together. Master Heathcliff received us with greater **animation** on this occasion: not the **animation** of high spirits though, nor yet of joy; it looked more like fear.

"It is late!" he said, speaking short and with difficulty. "Is not your father very ill? I thought you wouldn't come."

"*Why* won't you be **candid**?" cried Catherine, swallowing her greeting. "Why cannot you say at once you don't want me? It is strange, Linton, that for the second time you have brought me here on purpose, apparently, to distress us both, and for no reason besides!"

Linton shivered, and glanced at her, half **supplicating**, half ashamed; but his cousin's patience was not sufficient to endure this **enigmatical** behaviour.

"My father *is* very ill," she said, "and why am I called from his bedside? Why didn't you send to **absolve** me from my promise, when you wished I wouldn't keep it? Come! I desire an explanation: playing and **trifling** are completely

BANISH (<u>baan</u> ish) *v.* **-ing,-ed.**
  to force to leave, exile
    Synonyms: expel, deport
AFFECTATION (aaf ehk <u>tay</u> shun) *n.*
  fakeness, phoniness, artificiality, false display
    Synonyms: insincerity, pose, pretension
CONTEMPT (kuhn <u>tehmpt</u>) *n.*
  disrespect, scorn
    Synonyms: derision, disdain
SPONTANEOUSLY (spahn <u>tay</u> nee uhs lee) *adv.*
  at the spur of the moment, impulsively
    Synonyms: instinctively, automatically,
    extemporaneously
SPURN (spuhrn) *v.* **-ing,-ed.**
  to reject or refuse contemptuously, to scorn
    Synonyms: disdain, snub, ostracize, ignore, cut
DEGRADE (dih <u>grayd</u>) (dee <u>grayd</u>) *v.* **-ing,-ed.**
  to lower in rank or status; to drag down in moral or
  intellectual character
    Synonyms: demote; shame, demean, dishonor,
    weaken
ABJECT (aab <u>jehkt</u>) *adj.*
  miserable, pitiful
    Synonyms: pathetic, lamentable, sorry

INDULGENT (ihn <u>duhl</u> jehnt) *adj.*
  lenient, tolerant
    Synonyms: gratifying, pleasing
VEXATION (vehk <u>say</u> shuhn) *n.*
  irritation, annoyance; confusion, puzzlement
    Synonyms: aggravation, affliction; trouble, anxiety

banished out of my mind; and I can't dance attendance on your **affectations** now!"

"My **affectations**!" he murmured. "What are they? For Heaven's sake, Catherine, don't look so angry! Despise me as much as you please; I am a worthless, cowardly wretch: I can't be scorned enough; but I'm too mean for your anger. Hate my father, and spare me for **contempt**."

"Nonsense!" cried Catherine, in a passion. "Foolish, silly boy! And there! He trembles, as if I were really going to touch him! You needn't bespeak **contempt**, Linton: anybody will have it **spontaneously** at your service. Get off! I shall return home: it is folly dragging you from the hearthstone, and pretending—what do we pretend? Let go my frock! If I pitied you for crying and looking so very frightened, you should **spurn** such pity. Ellen, tell him how disgraceful this conduct is. Rise, and don't **degrade** yourself into an **abject** reptile—*don't*!"

With streaming face and an expression of agony, Linton had thrown his nerveless frame along the ground: he seemed convulsed with exquisite terror.

"Oh!" he sobbed, "I cannot bear it! Catherine, Catherine, I'm a traitor, too, and I dare not tell you! But leave me, and I shall be killed! *Dear* Catherine, my life is in your hands: and you have said you loved me, and if you did, it wouldn't harm you. You'll not go, then? Kind, sweet, good Catherine! And perhaps you *will* consent— and he'll let me die with you!"

My young lady, on witnessing his intense anguish, stooped to raise him. The old feeling of **indulgent** tenderness overcame her **vexation**, and she grew thoroughly moved and alarmed.

"Consent to what?" she asked. "To stay? Tell me the meaning of this strange talk, and I will. You contradict your own words, and distract me! Be calm and frank, and confess at once all that weighs on your heart. You wouldn't injure me, Linton, would you? You wouldn't let any enemy hurt me, if you could prevent it? I'll believe

ATTENUATED (uh <u>tehn</u> yoo ay tihd) *adj.*
  thin and weakened
    Synonyms: emaciated, gaunt, skeletal

MAGNANIMITY (maag naan <u>ihm</u> ih tee) *n.*
  generosity, nobility of spirit
    Synonyms: unselfishness, altruism, goodness
PROVOKE (proh <u>vohk</u>) *v.* **-ing,-ed.**
  to cause a response, e.g., anger or disagreement
    Synonyms: aggravate, stimulate, vex, incite
COGITATE (<u>kah</u> jih tayt) *v.* **-ing,-ed.**
  to ponder or think carefully
    Synonyms: reflect, consider, deliberate
DESCEND (dih <u>sehnd</u>) (dee <u>sehnd</u>) *v.* **-ing,-ed.**
  to pass from a higher place to a lower place
    Synonyms: fall, dismount, gravitate
AUDIBLE (<u>aw</u> dih buhl) *adj.*
  capable of being heard
    Synonyms: detectable, perceptible

you are a coward for yourself, but not a cowardly betrayer of your best friend."

"But my father threatened me," gasped the boy, clasping his **attenuated** fingers, "and I dread him—I dread him! I *dare* not tell!"

"Oh, well!" said Catherine, with scornful compassion. "Keep your secret: *I'm* no coward. Save yourself: I'm not afraid."

Her **magnanimity provoked** his tears: he wept wildly, kissing her supporting hands, and yet could not summon courage to speak out. I was **cogitating** what the mystery might be, and determined Catherine should never suffer, to benefit him or any one else, by my good will; when hearing a rustle among the ling, I looked up and saw Mr. Heathcliff almost close upon us, **descending** upon the Heights. He didn't cast a glance towards my companions, though they were sufficiently near for Linton's sobs to be **audible**; but hailing me in the almost hearty tone he assumed to none besides, and the sincerity of which I couldn't avoid doubting, he said:

"It is something to see you so near to my house, Nelly. How are you at the Grange? Let us hear. The rumour goes," he added in a lower tone, "that Edgar Linton is on his deathbed: perhaps they exaggerate his illness!"

"No, my master is dying," I replied. "It is true enough. A sad thing it will be for us all, but a blessing for him!"

"How long will he last, do you think?" he asked.

"I don't know," I said.

"Because," he continued, looking at the two young people, who were fixed under his eye—Linton appeared as if he could not venture to stir or raise his head, and Catherine could not move, on his account—"because that lad yonder seems determined to beat me; and I'd thank his uncle to be quick, and go before him. Hallo! Has the whelp been playing that game long? I *did* give him some lessons about snivelling. Is he pretty lively with Miss Linton generally?"

GROVEL (<u>grah</u> vuhl) *v.* **-ling,-led.**
  to humble oneself in a demeaning way
    Synonyms: cringe, fawn, kowtow, toady, bootlick
PROSTRATE (<u>prah</u> strayt) *adj.*
  lying face downward, lying flat on ground
    Synonyms: horizontal, submissive, overcome

PALTRY (<u>pahl</u> tree) *adj.*
  pitifully small or worthless
    Synonyms: trivial, trifling, petty, picayune, meager

FILIAL (<u>fihl</u> ee uhl) *adj.*
  relating to a sequence of generations or family
  connection, particularly that of a child and parent
    Synonyms: familial, faithful, reverential
SCRUPLE (<u>skroo</u> puhl) *n.*
  an ethical and moral belief that prevents action; a
  hesitation caused by moral conscience
    Synonyms: principle; restraint, qualm, misgiving

"Lively? No—he has shown the greatest distress," I answered. "To see him, I should say, that instead of rambling with his sweetheart on the hills, he ought to be in bed, under the hands of a doctor."

"He shall be in a day or two," muttered Heathcliff. "But first—get up, Linton! Get up!" he shouted. "Don't **grovel** on the ground there: up, this moment!"

Linton had sunk **prostrate** again in another <u>paroxysm</u> of helpless fear, caused by his father's glance towards him, I suppose: there was nothing else to produce such humiliation. He made several efforts to obey, but his little strength was annihilated for the time, and he fell back again with a moan. Mr. Heathcliff advanced, and lifted him to lean against a ridge of turf.

"Now," said he, with curbed <u>ferocity</u>, "I'm getting angry; and if you don't command that **paltry** spirit of yours—*Damn* you! Get up directly!"

"I will, father," he panted. "Only, let me alone, or I shall faint. I've done as you wished, I'm sure. Catherine will tell you that I—that I—have been cheerful. Ah! Keep by me, Catherine; give me your hand."

"Take mine," said his father, "stand on your feet. There now—she'll lend you her arm. That's right, look at *her*. You would imagine I was the devil himself, Miss Linton, to excite such horror. Be so kind as to walk home with him, will you? He shudders if I touch him."

"Linton, dear!" whispered Catherine, "I can't go to Wuthering Heights: Papa has forbidden me. He'll not harm you: why are you so afraid?"

"I can never re-enter that house," he answered. "I'm *not* to re-enter it without you!"

"Stop!" cried his father. "We'll respect Catherine's **filial scruples**. Nelly, take him in, and I'll follow your advice concerning the doctor, without delay."

"You'll do well," replied I. "But I must remain with my mistress: to mind your son is not my business."

"You are very stiff," said Heathcliff. "I know that, but you'll force me to pinch the baby and make it scream

533

IMPLORE (ihm <u>plohr</u>) *v.* **-ing,-ed.**
  to call upon in supplication, beg
    Synonyms: plead, entreat, solicit
IMPORTUNITY (ihm puhr <u>toon</u> ih tee) *n.*
  repeated begging or an urgent request
    Synonyms: entreaty, imploration, supplication
HINDER (<u>hihn</u> duhr) *v.* **-ing,-ed.**
  to prevent action; to delay or impede
    Synonyms: restrain; hamper, inhibit, obstruct
DISCERN (dihs <u>uhrn</u>) *v.* **-ing,-ed.**
  to perceive or recognize something obscure
    Synonyms: descry, observe, glimpse, distinguish

DAINTY (<u>dayn</u> tee) *adj.*
  delicate, sweet
    Synonyms: fine, graceful

RESOLUTION (reh suh <u>loo</u> shuhn) *n.*
  a firm decision
    Synonyms: determination, will, explanation

before it moves your charity. Come, then, my hero. Are you willing to return, escorted by me?"

He approached once more, and made as if he would seize the fragile being; but, shrinking back, Linton clung to his cousin, and **implored** her to accompany him, with a frantic **importunity** that admitted no denial. However I disapproved, I couldn't **hinder** her: indeed, how could she have refused him herself? What was filling him with dread we had no means of **discerning**: but there he was, powerless under its grip, and any addition seemed capable of shocking him into idiocy. We reached the threshold: Catherine walked in, and I stood waiting till she had conducted the invalid to a chair, expecting her out immediately; when Mr. Heathcliff, pushing me forward, exclaimed:

"My house is not stricken with the plague, Nelly; and I have a mind to be hospitable to-day: sit down, and allow me to shut the door."

He shut and locked it also. I started.

"You shall have tea before you go home," he added. "I am by myself. Hareton is gone with some cattle to the Lees, and Zillah and Joseph are off on a journey of pleasure; and, though I'm used to being alone, I'd rather have some interesting company, if I can get it. Miss Linton, take your seat by *him*. I give you what I have. The present is hardly worth accepting, but I have nothing else to offer. It is Linton, I mean. How she does stare! It's odd what a savage feeling I have to anything that seems afraid of me! Had I been born where laws are less strict and tastes less **dainty**, I should treat myself to a slow <u>vivisection</u> of those two, as an evening's amusement."

He drew in his breath, struck the table, and swore to himself, "By hell! I hate them."

"I'm not afraid of you!" exclaimed Catherine, who could not hear the latter part of his speech. She stepped close up; her black eyes flashing with passion and **resolution**. "Give me that key: I will have it!" she said. "I wouldn't eat or drink here, if I were starving."

DIABOLICAL (die uh <u>bah</u> lih kuhl) *adj.*
    characteristic of the devil
        Synonyms: fiendish, wicked, evil

CHASTISE (<u>chaa</u> stiez) *v.* **-ing,-ed.**
    to punish, discipline, scold
        Synonyms: castigate, penalize

Heathcliff had the key in his hand that remained on the table. He looked up, seized with a sort of surprise at her boldness; or, possibly, reminded by her voice and glance, of the person from whom she inherited it. She snatched at the instrument, and half-succeeded in getting it out of his loosened fingers, but her action recalled him to the present; he recovered it speedily.

"Now, Catherine Linton," he said, "stand off, or I shall knock you down; and that will make Mrs. Dean mad."

Regardless of this warning, she captured his closed hand and its contents again. "We *will* go!" she repeated, exerting her utmost efforts to cause the iron muscles to relax; and finding that her nails made no impression, she applied her teeth pretty sharply. Heathcliff glanced at me a glance that kept me from interfering a moment. Catherine was too intent on his fingers to notice his face. He opened them suddenly, and resigned the object of dispute; but, ere she had well secured it, he seized her with the liberated hand, and, pulling her on his knee, administered with the other a shower of terrific slaps on the side of the head, each sufficient to have fulfilled his threat, had she been able to fall.

At this **diabolical** violence I rushed on him furiously. "You villain!" I began to cry. "You villain!" A touch on the chest silenced me. I am stout, and soon put out of breath; and, what with that and the rage, I staggered dizzily back, and felt ready to suffocate, or to burst a blood-vessel. The scene was over in two minutes; Catherine, released, put her two hands to her temples, and looked just as if she were not sure whether her ears were off or on. She trembled like a reed, poor thing, and leant against the table perfectly bewildered.

"I know how to **chastise** children, you see," said the scoundrel grimly, as he stooped to repossess himself of the key, which had dropped to the floor. "Go to Linton now, as I told you; and cry at your ease! I shall be your father, tomorrow—all the father you'll have in a few days—and you shall have plenty of that. You can bear

CONFOUNDED (kuhn <u>fown</u> dihd) *adj.*
    baffled, perplexed
        Synonyms: overwhelmed, confused, disconcerted,
        entangled, muddled
EXPEDITIOUSLY (ehk spih <u>dihsh</u> uhs lee) *adv.*
    in a fast and efficient manner
        Synonyms: speedily, rapidly, promptly

DIABOLICAL (die uh <u>bah</u> lih kuhl) *adj.*
    characteristic of the devil
        Synonyms: fiendish, wicked, evil

WRATH (raath) *n.*
    anger, rage
        Synonyms: fury, ire, resentment, indignation
DECOY (dih <u>koy</u>) *v.* **-ing,-ed.**
    to mislead or trap
        Synonyms: lure, entice, ensnare, tempt

plenty; you're no weakling: you shall have a daily taste, if I catch such a devil of a temper in your eyes again!"

Cathy ran to me instead of Linton, and knelt down and put her burning cheek on my lap, weeping aloud. Her cousin had shrunk into a corner of the settle, as quiet as a mouse, congratulating himself, I dare say, that the correction had lighted on another than him. Mr. Heathcliff, perceiving us all **confounded**, rose, and **expeditiously** made the tea himself. The cups and saucers were laid ready. He poured it out, and handed me a cup.

"Wash away your spleen," he said. "And help your own naughty pet and mine. It is not poisoned, though I prepared it. I'm going out to seek your horses."

Our first thought, on his departure, was to force an exit somewhere. We tried the kitchen door, but that was fastened outside. We looked at the windows—they were too narrow for even Cathy's little figure.

"Master Linton," I cried, seeing we were regularly imprisoned, "you know what your **diabolical** father is after and you shall tell us or I'll box your ears, as he has done your cousin's."

"Yes, Linton, you must tell," said Catherine. "It was for your sake I came, and it will be wickedly ungrateful if you refuse."

"Give me some tea, I'm thirsty, and then I'll tell you," he answered. "Mrs. Dean, go away. I don't like you standing over me. Now, Catherine, you are letting your tears fall into my cup. I won't drink that. Give me another."

Catherine pushed another to him, and wiped her face. I felt disgusted at the little wretch's composure, since he was no longer in terror for himself. The anguish he had exhibited on the moor subsided as soon as ever he entered Wuthering Heights; so I guessed he had been menaced with an awful visitation of **wrath** if he failed in **decoying** us there; and, that accomplished, he had no further immediate fears.

"Papa wants us to be married," he continued, after sipping some of the liquid. "And he knows your papa

CONTEMPTIBLE (kuhn <u>tehmpt</u> ih buhl) *adj.*
disrespectful, worthy of scorn
Synonyms: shameful, disdainful, despicable
TREACHERY (<u>treh</u> chuhr ee) *n.*
betrayal of trust, deceit
Synonyms: perfidy, treason, disloyalty, falseness, infidelity
REBUKE (ree <u>byook</u>) *v.* **-ing,-ed.**
to reprimand, scold
Synonyms: admonish, reprove, reproach, chide
EXECUTION (ehk sih <u>kyoo</u> shuhn) *n.*
1. the act of performing or carrying out a task
Synonyms: accomplishment, achievement
2. the act of putting to death
Synonyms: killing, suicide, murder
SUSPENSE (suh <u>spents</u>) *n.*
a feeling of anxiety caused by a mysterious situation
Synonyms: apprehension, anticipation, waiting
HINDER (<u>hihn</u> duhr) *v.* **-ing,-ed.**
to prevent action; to delay or impede
Synonyms: restrain; hamper, inhibit, obstruct
ELOQUENCE (<u>eh</u> luh kwuhns) *n.*
persuasive and effective speech
Synonyms: expressiveness, fluency
DISTRAUGHT (dih <u>strawt</u>) *adj.*
very worried and emotionally upset
Synonyms: despondent, agitated, mad, insane, abstracted
ENTREATY (ehn <u>tree</u> tee) *n.*
a plea or request
Synonyms: imploration, prayer, petition

wouldn't let us marry now; and he's afraid of my dying, if we wait; so we are to be married in the morning, and you are to stay here all night; and if you do as he wishes, you shall return home next day, and take me with you."

"Take you with her, pitiful <u>changeling</u>?" I exclaimed. "*You* marry? Why, the man is mad; or he thinks us fools, every one. And do you imagine that beautiful young lady, that healthy, hearty girl, will tie herself to a little perishing monkey like you! Are you cherishing the notion that *anybody*, let alone Miss Catherine Linton, would have you for a husband? You want whipping for bringing us in here at all, with your dastardly <u>puling</u> tricks; and—don't look so silly, now! I've a very good mind to shake you severely, for your **contemptible treachery**, and your <u>imbecile</u> conceit."

I did give him a slight shaking; but it brought on the cough, and he took to his ordinary resource of moaning and weeping, and Catherine **rebuked** me.

"Stay all night? No," she said, looking slowly round, "Ellen, I'll burn that door down, but I'll get out."

And she would have commenced the **execution** of her threat directly, but Linton was up in alarm for his dear self again. He clasped her in his two feeble arms, sobbing:

"Won't you have me, and save me? Not let me come to the Grange? Oh, darling Catherine! You mustn't go and leave, after all. You *must* obey my father—you *must*!"

"I must obey my own," she replied, "and relieve him from this cruel **suspense**. The whole night! What would he think? He'll be distressed already. I'll either break or burn a way out of the house. Be quiet! You're in no danger, but if you **hinder** me—Linton, I love Papa better than you!"

The mortal terror he felt of Mr. Heathcliff's anger, restored to the boy his coward's **eloquence**. Catherine was near **distraught**: still, she persisted that she must go home, and tried **entreaty** in her turn, persuading <u>him</u> to subdue his selfish agony. While they were thus occupied, our <u>gaoler</u> re-entered.

CLAMOUR or CLAMOR (<u>klaa</u> muhr) *n.*
noisy outcry; continuous loud noise
Synonyms: exclamation, shout; din, cacophony,
racket, uproar

"Your beasts have trotted off," he said, "and—now, Linton! Snivelling again? What has she been doing to you? Come, come—have done, and get to bed. In a month or two, my lad, you'll be able to pay her back for present tyrannies with a vigorous hand. You're pining for pure love, are you not? Nothing else in the world: and she shall have you! There, to bed! Zillah won't be here to-night; you must undress yourself. Hush! Hold your noise! Once in your own room, I'll not come near you: you needn't fear. By chance you've managed tolerably. I'll look to the rest."

He spoke these words, holding the door open for his son to pass; and the latter achieved his exit exactly as a spaniel might, which suspected the person who attended on it of designing a spiteful squeeze. The lock was re-secured. Heathcliff approached the fire, where my mistress and I stood silent. Catherine looked up, and instinctively raised her hand to her cheek: his neighbourhood revived a painful sensation. Anybody else would have been incapable of regarding the childish act with sternness, but he scowled on her and muttered:

"Oh! You are not afraid of me? Your courage is well disguised: you *seem* damnably afraid!"

"I *am* afraid now," she replied, "because, if I stay, Papa will be miserable; and how can I endure making him miserable—when he—when he—Mr. Heathcliff, *let* me go home! I promise to marry Linton: Papa would like me to: and I love him. Why should you wish to force me to do what I'll willingly do of myself?"

"Let him dare to force you," I cried. "There's a law in the land, thank God, there is; though we be in an out-of-the-way place. I'd inform if he were my own son: and it's felony without benefit of clergy!"

"Silence!" said the ruffian. "To the devil with your **clamour**! I don't want *you* to speak. Miss Linton, I shall enjoy myself remarkably in thinking your father will be miserable: I shall not sleep for satisfaction. You could have hit on no surer way of fixing your residence under my roof for the next twenty-four hours, than informing

543

CONTEMPT (kuhn <u>tehmpt</u>) *n.*
 disrespect, scorn
   Synonyms: derision, disdain
INJUNCTION (ihn <u>juhnk</u> shuhn) *n.*
 command, order
   Synonyms: directive, behest, mandate, edict, decree
DIVERSION (dih <u>vuhr</u> zhuhn) (die <u>vuhr</u> zhuhn) *n.*
 an amusing or relaxing activity; a distraction
   Synonyms: entertainment, recreation; deviation
AMENDS (uh <u>mehnds</u>) *n. pl.*
 compensation for a loss or something that caused harm
   Synonyms: reparations, restitutions, apologies
PROVIDENT (prah vih <u>dehn</u>) *adj.*
 cautious and prepared for future events
   Synonyms: frugal, careful, prudent, economical
CONSOLATION (kahn suh <u>lay</u> shuhn) *n.*
 something providing comfort or solace for a loss or
 hardship
   Synonym: condolence
PATERNAL (puh <u>tuhr</u> nuhl) *adj.*
 fatherly, related to the characteristics of fatherhood;
 inherited from the father
   Synonyms: parental; hereditary
DRAW *v.* **drawing, drew, drawn**
 to pull, drag; to lead, to bring about on purpose;
 to attract
   Synonyms: haul, tow, yank; provoke, elicit; lure, entice
PARE (payr) *v.* **-ing,-ed.**
 to trim, to remove the extremities or excess of something
   Synonyms: cut, skin, peel, clip, shave
AMIABLE (<u>ay</u> mee uh buhl) *adj.*
 friendly, pleasant, likable
   Synonyms: affable, convivial, amicable, agreeable
DETAIN (dih <u>tayn</u>) (dee <u>tayn</u>) *v.* **-ing,-ed.**
 to hold; to restrain from continuing on
   Synonyms: apprehend, keep; delay, inhibit

me that such an event would follow. As to your promise to marry Linton, I'll take care you shall keep it; for you shall not quit this place till it is fulfilled."

"Send Ellen, then, to let Papa know I'm safe!" exclaimed Catherine, weeping bitterly. "Or marry me now. Poor Papa! Ellen, he'll think we're lost. What shall we do?"

"Not he! He'll think you are tired of waiting on him, and run off for a little amusement," answered Heathcliff. "You cannot deny that you entered my house of your own accord, in **contempt** of his **injunctions** to the contrary. And it is quite natural that you should desire amusement at your age; and that you would weary of nursing a sick man, and that man *only* your father. Catherine, his happiest days were over when your days began. He cursed you, I dare say, for coming into the world (I did, at least), and it would just do if he cursed you as *he* went out of it. I'd join him. I don't love you! How should I? Weep away. As far as I can see, it will be your chief **diversion** hereafter; unless Linton make **amends** for other losses: and your **provident** parent appears to fancy he may. His letters of advice and **consolation** entertained me vastly. In his last he recommended my jewel to be careful of his; and kind to her when he got her. Careful and kind—that's **paternal**. But Linton requires his whole stock of care and kindness for himself. Linton can play the little tyrant well. He'll undertake to torture any number of cats, if their teeth be **drawn** and their claws **pared**. You'll be able to tell his uncle fine tales of his *kindness*, when you get home again, I assure you."

"You're right there!" I said. "Explain your son's character. Show his resemblance to yourself; and then, I hope, Miss Cathy will think twice before she takes the cockatrice!"

"I don't much mind speaking of his **amiable** qualities now," he answered, "because she must either accept him or remain a prisoner, and you along with her, till your master dies. I can **detain** you both, quite concealed, here.

RETRACT (rih <u>traakt</u>) *v.* **-ing,-ed.**
to draw in or take back
Synonyms: disavow, recede, retreat, retrogress

MALICE (<u>maal</u> ihs) *n.*
animosity, spite, hatred
Synonyms: malevolence, cruelty, enmity, rancor, hostility

IRREVOCABLY (ih rehv <u>oh</u> kuh blee) *adv.*
conclusively, irreversibly
Synonyms: permanently, indelibly, irreparably

PROVOKE (proh <u>vohk</u>) *v.* **-ing,-ed.**
to cause a response, e.g., anger or disagreement
Synonyms: aggravate, stimulate, vex, incite

REPULSE (rih <u>puhls</u>) *v.* **-ing,-ed.**
to repel; to sicken or disgust
Synonyms: reject; nauseate

FAWN *v.* **-ing,-ed.**
to seek the favor of, to flatter excessively
Synonyms: kowtow, toady, grovel, truckle, applepolish

DETEST (dee <u>tehst</u>) (dih <u>tehst</u>) *v.* **-ing,-ed.**
to feel intense and violent hatred toward
Synonyms: dislike, loathe

AVERSION (uh <u>vuhr</u> zhuhn) *n.*
intense dislike
Synonyms: antagonism, antipathy, abhorrence, repulsion, repugnance

OBLIGE (uh <u>bliej</u>) *v.* **-ing,-ed.**
to be obligated, to require or force someone to obey
Synonyms: compel, constrain, bind, favor

If you doubt, encourage her to **retract** her word, and you'll have an opportunity of judging!"

"I'll not **retract** my word," said Catherine. "I'll marry him within this hour, if I may go to Thrushcross Grange afterwards. Mr. Heathcliff, you're a cruel man, but you're not a fiend; and you won't from *mere* **malice**, destroy **irrevocably** all my happiness. If Papa thought I had left him on purpose, and if he died before I returned, could I bear to live? I've given over crying: but I'm going to kneel here, at your knee; and I'll not get up, and I'll not take my eyes from your face till you look back at me! No, don't turn away! *Do* look! You'll see nothing to **provoke** you. I don't hate you. I'm not angry that you struck me. Have you never loved *anybody* in all your life, Uncle? *Never?* Ah! You must look once. I'm so wretched, you can't help being sorry and pitying me."

"Keep your eft's fingers off; and move, or I'll kick you!" cried Heathcliff, brutally **repulsing** her. "I'd rather be hugged by a snake. How the devil can you dream of **fawning** on me? I **detest** you!"

He shrugged his shoulders: shook himself, indeed, as if his flesh crept with **aversion**; and thrust back his chair; while I got up, and opened my mouth, to commence a downright torrent of abuse. But I was rendered dumb in the middle of the first sentence, by a threat that I should be shown into a room by myself the very next syllable I uttered. It was growing dark—we heard a sound of voices at the garden gate. Our host hurried out instantly: *he* had his wits about him; *we* had not. There was a talk of two or three minutes, and he returned alone.

"I thought it had been your cousin Hareton," I observed to Catherine. "I wish he would arrive! Who knows but he might take our part?"

"It was three servants sent to seek you from the Grange," said Heathcliff, overhearing me. "You should have opened a lattice and called out: but I could swear that chit is glad you didn't. She's glad to be **obliged** to stay, I'm certain."

VENT (vehnt) *n.*
> a way to escape or release from confinement
>> Synonyms: exposure, exit, opening

CONTRIVE (kuhn <u>triev</u>) *v.* **-ing,-ed.**
> to devise, plan, or manage; to form in an artistic manner
>> Synonyms: concoct, scheme; create, design

ENTREATY (ehn <u>tree</u> tee) *n.*
> a plea or request
>> Synonyms: imploration, prayer, petition

DERELICTION (dehr eh <u>lihk</u> shuhn) *n.*
> the act of abandonment; a state of neglect and
> abandonment
>> Synonyms: alienation, desertion, negligence;
>> delinquency, disregard

COMPLY (kuhm <u>plie</u>) *v.* **-ing,-ied.**
> to yield or agree, to go along with
>> Synonyms: accord, submit, acquiesce, obey, respect

DETAIN (dih <u>tayn</u>) (dee <u>tayn</u>) *v.* **-ing,-ed.**
> to hold; to restrain from continuing on
>> Synonyms: apprehend, keep; delay, inhibit

At learning the chance we had missed, we both gave **vent** to our grief without control; and he allowed us to wail on till nine o'clock. Then he bid us go upstairs, through the kitchen, to Zillah's chamber, and I whispered my companion to obey: perhaps we might **contrive** to get through the window there, or into a <u>garret</u>, and out by its skylight. The window, however, was narrow, like those below, and the <u>garret</u> trap was safe from our attempts; for we were fastened in as before. We neither of us lay down: Catherine took her station by the <u>lattice</u>, and watched anxiously for morning; a deep sigh being the only answer I could obtain to my frequent **entreaties** that she would try to rest. I seated myself in a chair, and rocked to and fro, passing harsh judgment on my many **derelictions** of duty, from which, it struck me then, all the misfortunes of my employers sprang. It was not the case, in reality, I am aware; but it was, in my imagination, that dismal night; and I thought Heathcliff himself less guilty than I.

At seven o'clock he came, and inquired if Miss Linton had risen. She ran to the door immediately, and answered, "Yes."

"Here, then," he said, opening it, and pulling her out. I rose to follow, but he turned the lock again. I demanded my release.

"Be patient," he replied. "I'll send up your breakfast in a while."

I thumped on the panels, and rattled the latch angrily, and Catherine asked why I was still shut up? He answered, I must try to endure it another hour, and they went away. I endured it two or three hours; at length, I heard a footstep: not Heathcliff's.

"I've brought you something to eat," said a voice, "oppen t' door!"

Complying eagerly, I beheld Hareton, laden with food enough to last me all day.

"Take it," he added, thrusting the tray into my hand.

"Stay one minute," I began.

"Nay," cried he, and retired, regardless of any prayers I could pour forth to **detain** him.

SURLY (<u>suhr</u> lee) *adj*.
   rude and bad-tempered
      Synonyms: gruff, testy, grumpy

And there I remained enclosed the whole day, and the whole of the next night; and another, and another. Five nights and four · days I remained, altogether, seeing nobody but Hareton, once every morning; and he was a model of a <u>gaoler</u>: **surly**, and dumb, and deaf to every attempt at moving his sense of justice or compassion.

Chapter 28

On the fifth morning, or rather afternoon, a different step approached—lighter and shorter, and, this time, the person entered the room. It was Zillah; donned in her scarlet shawl, with a black silk bonnet on her head, and a willow basket swung to her arm.

"Eh, dear! Mrs. Dean!" she exclaimed. "Well! There is a talk about you at Gimmerton. I never thought but you were sunk in the Blackhorse marsh, and missy with you, till master told me you'd been found, and he'd lodged you here! What! And you must have got on an island, sure? And how long were you in the hole? Did master save you, Mrs. Dean? But you're not so thin—you've not been so poorly, have you?"

"Your master is a true scoundrel!" I replied. "But he shall answer for it. He needn't have raised that tale: it shall all be laid bare!"

"What do you mean?" asked Zillah. "It's not his tale: they tell that in the village—about your being lost in the marsh: and I calls to Earnshaw, when I come in—'Eh, they's queer things, Mr. Hareton, happened since I went off. It's a sad pity of that likely young lass, and <u>cant</u> Nelly Dean.' He stared. I thought he had not heard aught, so I told him the rumour. The master listened, and he just smiled to himself, and said, 'If they have been in the marsh, they are out now, Zillah. Nelly Dean is lodged, at this minute, in your room. You can tell her to flit, when you go up; here is the key. The bog-water got into her

APATHETIC (aa pah <u>theh</u> tihk) *adj*.
   showing a lack of feeling or emotion
      Synonyms: indifferent, disinterested, unconcerned

head, and she would have run home quite flighty, but I fixed her till she came round to her senses. You can bid her go to the Grange at once, if she be able, and carry a message from me, that her young lady will follow in time to attend the squire's funeral.'"

"Mr. Edgar is not dead?" I gasped. "Oh! Zillah, Zillah!"

"No, no; sit down, my good mistress," she replied, "you're right sickly yet. He's not dead; Doctor Kenneth thinks he may last another day. I met him on the road and asked."

Instead of sitting down, I snatched my outdoor things, and hastened below, for the way was free. On entering the house, I looked about for some one to give information of Catherine. The place was filled with sunshine, and the door stood wide open; but nobody seemed at hand. As I hesitated whether to go off at once, or return and seek my mistress, a slight cough drew my attention to the hearth. Linton lay on the <u>settle</u>, sole tenant, sucking a stick of sugar-candy, and pursuing my movements with **apathetic** eyes. "Where is Miss Catherine?" I demanded sternly, supposing I could frighten him into giving intelligence, by catching him thus, alone. He sucked on like an innocent.

"Is she gone?" I said.

"No," he replied, "she's upstairs: she's not to go; we won't let her."

"You won't let her, little idiot!" I exclaimed. "Direct me to her room immediately, or I'll make you sing out sharply."

"Papa would make you sing out, if you attempted to get there," he answered. "He says I'm not to be soft with Catherine: she's my wife, and it's shameful that she should wish to leave me. He says she hates me and wants me to die, that she may have my money; but she shan't have it: and she shan't go home! She never shall!—She may cry, and be sick as much as she pleases!"

He resumed his former occupation, closing his lids, as if he meant to drop asleep.

AFFIRM (uh <u>fihrm</u>) *v.* **-ing,-ed.**
   to state positively, to assert as valid or confirmed
   Synonyms: declare, avow, maintain

DETEST (dee <u>tehst</u>) (dih <u>tehst</u>) *v.* **-ing,-ed.**
   to feel intense and violent hatred toward
   Synonyms: dislike, loathe

VEXATION (vehk <u>say</u> shuhn) *n.*
   irritation, annoyance; confusion, puzzlement
   Synonyms: aggravation, affliction; trouble, anxiety

"Master Heathcliff," I resumed, "have you forgotten all Catherine's kindness to you last winter, when you **affirmed** you loved her, and when she brought you books and sung you songs, and came many a time through wind and snow to see you? She wept to miss one evening, because you would be disappointed; and you felt then that she was a hundred times too good to you: and now you believe the lies your father tells, though you know he **detests** you both. And you join him against her. That's fine gratitude, is it not?"

The corner of Linton's mouth fell, and he took the sugar-candy from his lips.

"Did she come to Wuthering Heights, because she hated you?" I continued. "Think for yourself! As to your money, she does not even know that you will have any. And you say she's sick; and yet, you leave her alone, up there in a strange house! *You* who have felt what it is to be so neglected! You could pity your own sufferings; and she pitied them too; but you won't pity hers! I shed tears, Master Heathcliff, you see—an elderly woman, and a servant merely—and you, after pretending such affection, and having reason to worship her almost, store every tear you have for yourself, and lie there quite at ease. Ah! You're a heartless, selfish boy!"

"I can't stay with her," he answered crossly. "I'll not stay by myself. She cries so I can't bear it. And she won't give over, though I say I'll call my father. I did call him once, and he threatened to strangle her, if she was not quiet; but she began again the instant he left the room, moaning and grieving all night long, though I screamed for **vexation** that I couldn't sleep."

"Is Mr. Heathcliff out?" I inquired, perceiving that the wretched creature had no power to sympathise with his cousin's mental tortures.

"He's in the court," he replied, "talking to Dr. Kenneth, who says Uncle is dying, truly, at last. I'm glad, for I shall be master of the Grange after him. Catherine always spoke of it as *her* house. It isn't hers! It's mine:

Papa says everything she has is mine. All her nice books are mine; she offered to give me them, and her pretty birds, and her pony Minny, if I would get the key to her room, and let her out; but I told her she had nothing to give, they were all, all mine. And then she cried, and took a little picture from her neck, and said I should not have that; two pictures in a gold case, on one side her mother, and on the other, Uncle, when they were young. That was yesterday—I said *they* were mine, too; and tried to get them from her. The spiteful thing wouldn't let me: she pushed me off, and hurt me. I shrieked out—that frightens her—she heard Papa coming, and she broke the hinges and divided the case, and gave me her mother's portrait; the other she attempted to hide: but Papa asked what was the matter, and I explained it. He took the one I had away, and ordered her to resign hers to me; she refused, and he—he struck her down, and wrenched it off the chain, and crushed it with his foot."

"And were you pleased to see her struck?" I asked: having my designs in encouraging his talk.

"I winked," he answered. "I wink to see my father strike a dog or a horse, he does it so hard. Yet I was glad at first—she deserved punishing for pushing me: but when Papa was gone, she made me come to the window and showed me her cheek cut on the inside, against her teeth, and her mouth filling with blood; and then she gathered up the bits of the picture, and went and sat down with her face to the wall, and she has never spoken to me since: and I sometimes think she can't speak for pain. I don't like to think so; but she's a naughty thing for crying continually; and she looks so pale and wild, I'm afraid of her."

"And you can get the key if you choose?" I said.

"Yes, when I'm upstairs," he answered, "but I can't walk upstairs now."

"In what apartment is it?" I asked.

"Oh," he cried, "I shan't tell *you* where it is! It is our secret. Nobody, neither Hareton nor Zillah, is to know.

COMPULSORY (kuhm <u>puhl</u> suh ree) *adj.*
required, not having a choice
Synonyms: mandatory, necessary, obligatory

DIVINE (dih <u>vien</u>) *v.* **-ing,-ed.**
to foretell or know by inspiration
Synonyms: predict, intuit, auger, foresee, presage

There! You've tired me—go away, go away!" And he turned his face on to his arm, and shut his eyes again.

I considered it best to depart without seeing Mr. Heathcliff, and bring a rescue for my young lady from the Grange. On reaching it, the astonishment of my fellow-servants to see me, and their joy also, was intense; and when they heard that their little mistress was safe, two or three were about to hurry up and shout the news at Mr. Edgar's door: but I bespoke the announcement of it, myself. How changed I found him, even in those few days! He lay an image of sadness and resignation waiting his death. Very young he looked; though his actual age was thirty-nine, one would have called him ten years younger, at least. He thought of Catherine; for he murmured her name. I touched his hand, and spoke.

"Catherine is coming, dear master!" I whispered. "She is alive and well; and will be here, I hope, to-night."

I trembled at the first effects of this intelligence: he half rose up, looked eagerly round the apartment, and then sank back in a swoon. As soon as he recovered, I related our **compulsory** visit, and detention at the Heights. I said Heathcliff forced me to go in: which was not quite true. I uttered as little as possible against Linton; nor did I describe all his father's brutal conduct—my intentions being to add no bitterness, if I could help it, to his already overflowing cup.

He **divined** that one of his enemy's purposes was to secure the personal property, as well as the estate, to his son: or rather himself; yet why he did not wait till his decease was a puzzle to my master, because ignorant how nearly he and his nephew would quit the world together. However, he felt that his will had better be altered: instead of leaving Catherine's fortune at her own disposal, he determined to put it in the hands of trustees for her use during life, and for her children, if she had any, after her. By that means, it could not fall to Mr. Heathcliff should Linton die.

RESOLVE (rih <u>sahlv</u>) *v.* **-ing,-ed.**
  to determine or to make a firm decision about
    Synonyms: solve, decide
BEVY (<u>beh</u> vee) *n.*
  group
    Synonyms: band, gang, bunch, pack, troop

IMPORTUNATE (ihm <u>pohr</u> chuh niht) *adj.*
  1. extremely urgent, pleading
    Synonyms: craving, beseeching, earnest, imperative
  2. troublesome, difficult
    Synonyms: annoying, disturbing

COMPEL (kuhm <u>pehl</u>) *v.* **-ling,-led.**
  to urge or force
    Synonyms: coerce, oblige, constrain
IMPLORE (ihm <u>plohr</u>) *v.* **-ing,-ed.**
  to call upon in supplication, beg
    Synonyms: plead, entreat, solicit

Having received his orders, I <u>despatched</u> a man to fetch the attorney, and four more, provided with serviceable weapons, to demand my young lady of her <u>gaoler</u>. Both parties were delayed very late. The single servant returned first. He said Mr. Green, the lawyer, was out when he arrived at his house, and he had to wait two hours for his re-entrance; and then Mr. Green told him he had a little business in the village that must be done; but he would be at Thrushcross Grange before morning. The four men came back unaccompanied also. They brought word that Catherine was ill, too ill to quit her room; and Heathcliff would not suffer them to see her. I scolded the stupid fellows well for listening to that tale, which I would not carry to my master; **resolving** to take a whole **bevy** up to the Heights, at daylight, and storm it literally, unless the prisoner were quietly surrendered to us. Her father *shall* see her, I vowed, and vowed again, if that devil be killed on his own doorstones in trying to prevent it!

Happily, I was spared the journey and the trouble. I had gone downstairs at three o'clock to fetch a jug of water; and was passing through the hall with it in my hand, when a sharp knock at the front door made me jump. "Oh! It is Green," I said, recollecting myself—"only Green," and I went on, intending to send somebody else to open it; but the knock was repeated: not loud, and still **importunate**. I put the jug on the banister and hastened to admit him myself. The harvest moon shone clear outside. It was not the attorney. My own sweet little mistress sprang on my neck, sobbing:

"Ellen! Ellen! Is Papa alive?"

"Yes," I cried. "Yes, my angel, he is. God be thanked, you are safe with us again!"

She wanted to run, breathless as she was, upstairs to Mr. Linton's room; but I **compelled** her to sit down on a chair, and made her drink, and washed her pale face, chafing it into a faint colour with my apron. Then I said I must go first, and tell of her arrival; **imploring** her to say, she should be happy with young Heathcliff. She stared,

561

DILATE (<u>die</u> layt) (die <u>layt</u>) *v.* **-ing,-ed.**
    to enlarge, swell, extend
        Synonyms: expand, spread, distend

RAPT (raapt) *adj.*
    deeply absorbed
        Synonyms: engrossed, immersed, moved, entranced,
        smitten

BROOD *v.* **-ing,-ed.**
    to think about in a gloomy or serious way
        Synonyms: ponder, worry, obsess
REPOSE (rih <u>pohz</u>) *n.*
    relaxation, leisure; a state of peace or tranquility
        Synonyms: rest, ease, idleness; calmness, serenity

DELEGATED (<u>deh</u> lih gay tihd) *adj.*
    assigned (as in power or duties)
        Synonyms: entrusted, committed, appointed,
        authorized
HINDER (<u>hihn</u> duhr) *v.* **-ing,-ed.**
    to prevent action; to delay or impede
        Synonyms: restrain; hamper, inhibit, obstruct
INFRINGEMENT (ihn <u>frihnj</u> mihnt) *n.*
    transgression, violation; encroachment, trespassing
        Synonyms: infraction, offense; overstep

but soon comprehending why I counselled her to utter the falsehood, she assured me she would not complain.

I couldn't abide to be present at their meeting. I stood outside the chamber-door a quarter of an hour, and hardly ventured near the bed, then. All was composed, however: Catherine's despair was as silent as her father's joy. She supported him calmly, in appearance; and he fixed on her features his raised eyes, that seemed **dilating** with ecstasy.

He died blissfully, Mr. Lockwood: he died so. Kissing her cheek, he murmured:

"I am going to her; and you, darling child, shall come to us!" and never stirred or spoke again; but continued that **rapt**, radiant gaze, till his pulse imperceptibly stopped and his soul departed. None could have noticed the exact minute of his death, it was so entirely without a struggle.

Whether Catherine had spent her tears, or whether the grief were too weighty to let them flow, she sat there dry-eyed till the sun rose; she sat till noon, and would still have remained **brooding** over that deathbed, but I insisted on her coming away and taking some **repose**. It was well I succeeded in removing her, for at dinner-time appeared the lawyer, having called at Wuthering Heights to get his instructions how to behave. He had sold himself to Mr. Heathcliff: that was the cause of his delay in obeying my master's summons. Fortunately, no thought of worldly affairs crossed the latter's mind, to disturb him, after his daughter's arrival.

Mr. Green took upon himself to order everything and everybody about the place. He gave all the servants, but me, notice to quit. He would have carried his **delegated** authority to the point of insisting that Edgar Linton should not be buried beside his wife, but in the chapel, with his family. There was the will, however, to **hinder** that, and my loud protestations against any **infringement** of its directions. The funeral was hurried over; Catherine,

INCUR (ihn <u>kuhr</u>) *v.* **-ring,-red.**
    to become liable; to acquire or meet with, usually
    something negative or harmful
        Synonyms: oblige, owe; get, obtain, endure, sustain

ASCEND (uh <u>sehnd</u>) *v.* **-ing,-ed.**
    to rise to another level or climb; to move upward
        Synonyms: elevate, escalate, mount; hoist, lift

CONTRIVANCE (kuhn <u>trie</u> vehnts) *n.*
    something that is devised, such as a scheme, plan, or
    arrangement; an artistic design
        Synonyms: concoction, invention; creation

CONJECTURE (kuhn <u>jehk</u> shuhr) *n.*
    speculation, prediction
        Synonyms: postulation, hypothesis, supposition, guess

RETAIN (rih <u>tayn</u>) *v.* **-ing,-ed.**
    to hold, keep possession of
        Synonyms: withhold, reserve, maintain, remember

Mrs. Linton Heathcliff now, was suffered to stay at the Grange till her father's corpse had quitted it.

She told me that her anguish had at last spurred Linton to **incur** the risk of liberating her. She heard the men I sent disputing at the door, and she gathered the sense of Heathcliff's answer. It drove her desperate. Linton, who had been conveyed up to the little parlour soon after I left, was terrified into fetching the key before his father re-**ascended**. He had the cunning to unlock and re-lock the door, without shutting it; and when he should have gone to bed, he begged to sleep with Hareton, and his petition was granted for once. Catherine stole out before break of day. She dare not try the doors, lest the dogs should raise an alarm; she visited the empty chambers and examined their windows; and, luckily, lighting on her mother's she got easily out of its <u>lattice</u>, and on to the ground, by means of the fir-tree close by. Her accomplice suffered for his share in the escape, notwithstanding his timid **contrivances**.

Chapter 29

The evening after the funeral, my young lady and I were seated in the library; now musing mournfully—one of us despairingly—on our loss, now venturing **conjectures** as to the gloomy future.

We had just agreed the best destiny which could await Catherine, would be a permission to continue resident at the Grange; at least, during Linton's life: he being allowed to join her there, and I to remain as housekeeper. That seemed rather too favourable an arrangement to be hoped for and yet I did hope, and began to cheer up under the prospect of **retaining** my home and my employment, and, above all, my beloved young mistress; when a servant—one of the discarded ones, not yet departed—rushed

AVAIL (uh <u>vayl</u>) *v.* **-ing,-ed.**
to make use of; to be of use or advantage to; to result in
Synonyms: employ; help, serve, benefit; transpire, eventuate

SALLOW (<u>saa</u> loh) *adj.*
sickly yellow in color
Synonyms: ashen, pasty, peaked, wan
IMPULSE (<u>ihm</u> puhls) *n.*
sudden tendency, inclination
Synonyms: urge, whim

hastily in, and said "that devil Heathcliff" was coming through the court: should he fasten the door in his face?

If we had been mad enough to order that proceeding, we had not time. He made no ceremony of knocking or announcing his name: he was master, and **availed** himself of the master's privilege to walk straight in, without saying a word. The sound of our informant's voice directed him to the library: he entered, and motioning him out, shut the door.

It was the same room into which he had been ushered, as a guest, eighteen years before: the same moon shone through the window; and the same autumn landscape lay outside. We had not yet lighted a candle, but all the apartment was visible, even to the portraits on the wall: the splendid head of Mrs. Linton, and the graceful one of her husband. Heathcliff advanced to the hearth. Time had little altered his person either. There was the same man: his dark face rather **sallower** and more composed, his frame a stone or two heavier, perhaps, and no other difference. Catherine had risen, with an **impulse** to dash out, when she saw him.

"Stop!" he said, arresting her by the arm. "No more runnings away! Where would you go? I'm come to fetch you home; and I hope you'll be a dutiful daughter, and not encourage my son to further disobedience. I was embarrassed how to punish him when I discovered his part in the business: he's such a cobweb, a pinch would annihilate him; but you'll see by his look that he has received his due! I brought him down one evening, the day before yesterday, and just set him in a chair, and never touched him afterwards. I sent Hareton out, and we had the room to ourselves. In two hours, I called Joseph to carry him up again; and since then my presence is as potent on his nerves as a ghost; and I fancy he sees me often, though I am not near. Hareton says he wakes and shrieks in the night by the hour together, and calls you to protect him from me; and, whether you like your precious

OBLIGE (uh <u>bliej</u>) *v.* **-ing,-ed.**
    to be obligated, to require or force someone to obey
        Synonyms: compel, constrain, bind, favor
COMPEL (kuhm <u>pehl</u>) *v.* **-ling,-led.**
    to urge or force
        Synonyms: coerce, oblige, constrain

GALL (gahl) *n.*
    1. a bitter fluid secreted by the liver that aids digestion
        Synonym: bile
    2. bitterness, resentment; careless nerve
        Synonyms: rancor; audacity, effrontery, temerity
INCLINATION (ihn cluh <u>nay</u> shuhn) *n.*
    tendency toward
        Synonyms: leaning, trend, preference, disposition,
        propensity

mate or not, you must come: he's your concern now; I yield all my interest in him to you.

"Why not let Catherine continue here," I pleaded, "and send Master Linton to her? As you hate them both, you'd not miss them: they *can* only be a daily plague to your unnatural heart."

"I'm seeking a tenant for the Grange," he answered, "and I want my children about me, to be sure. Besides, that lass owes me her services for her bread. I'm not going to nurture her in luxury and idleness after Linton has gone. Make haste and get ready, now; and don't **oblige** me to **compel** you."

"I shall," said Catherine. "Linton is all I have to love in the world, and though you have done what you could to make him hateful to me, and me to him, you *cannot* make us hate each other. And I defy you to hurt him when I am by, and I defy you to frighten me!"

"You are a boastful champion," replied Heathcliff, "but I don't like you well enough to hurt him: you shall get the full benefit of the torment, as long as it lasts. It is not I who will make him hateful to you—it is his own sweet spirit. He's as bitter as **gall** at your desertion and its consequences: don't expect thanks for this noble devotion. I heard him draw a pleasant picture to Zillah of what he would do if he were as strong as I: the **inclination** is there, and his very weakness will sharpen his wits to find a substitute for strength."

"I know he has a bad nature," said Catherine, "he's your son. But I'm glad I've a better, to forgive it; and I know he loves me, and for that reason I love him. Mr. Heathcliff, *you* have *nobody* to love you; and, however miserable you make us, we shall still have the revenge of thinking that your cruelty arises from your greater misery. You *are* miserable, are you not? Lonely, like the devil, and envious like him? *Nobody* loves you—*nobody* will cry for you when you die. I wouldn't be you!"

Catherine spoke with a kind of dreary triumph: she seemed to have made up her mind to enter into the spirit

DRAW *v.* **drawing, drew, drawn**
to lead, to bring about on purpose; to pull, drag;
to attract
Synonyms: provoke, elicit; haul, tow, yank; lure, entice

INCESSANTLY (ihn <u>sehs</u> uhnt lee) *adv.*
continuously, without cease
Synonyms: constantly, interminably, relentlessly
REMORSELESSLY (rih <u>mohrs</u> lehs lee) *adv.*
without feelings of distress or guilt
Synonym: shamelessly

of her future family, and **draw** pleasure from the griefs of her enemies.

"You shall be sorry to be yourself presently," said her father-in-law, "if you stand there another minute. Begone, witch, and get your things!"

She scornfully withdrew. In her absence, I began to beg for Zillah's place at the Heights, offering to resign mine to her; but he would suffer it on no account. He bid me be silent; and then, for the first time, allowed himself a glance round the room and a look at the pictures. Having studied Mrs. Linton's, he said:

"I shall have that home. Not because I need it, but—" He turned abruptly to the fire, and continued, with what, for lack of a better word, I must call a smile—"I'll tell you what I did yesterday! I got the sexton, who was digging Linton's grave, to remove the earth off her coffin-lid, and I opened it. I thought, once, I would have stayed there: when I saw her face again—it is hers yet!—he had hard work to stir me; but he said it would change if the air blew on it, and so I struck one side of the coffin loose, and covered it up: not Linton's side, damn him! I wish he'd been soldered in lead. And I bribed the sexton to pull it away when I'm laid there, and slide mine out too; I'll have it made so: and then, by the time Linton gets to us he'll not know which is which!"

"You were very wicked, Mr. Heathcliff!" I exclaimed. "Were you not ashamed to disturb the dead?"

"I disturbed nobody, Nelly," he replied, "and I gave some ease to myself. I shall be a great deal more comfortable now; and you'll have a better chance of keeping me underground, when I get there. Disturbed her? No! She has disturbed me, night and day, through eighteen years—**incessantly**—**remorselessly**—till yesternight; and yesternight I was tranquil. I dreamt I was sleeping the last sleep by that sleeper, with my heart stopped and my cheek frozen against hers."

"And if she had been dissolved into earth, or worse, what would you have dreamt of then?" I said.

DELVE (dehlv) *v.* **-ing,-ed.**
to dig; to search or explore intensely
Synonyms: shovel, excavate; probe, examine,
research

DISCERN (dihs <u>uhrn</u>) *v.* **-ing,-ed.**
to perceive or recognize something obscure
Synonyms: descry, observe, glimpse, distinguish
RELINQUISH (rih <u>lihn</u> kwihsh) *v.* **-ing,-ed.**
to renounce or surrender something
Synonyms: yield, resign, abandon, cede, waive
CONSOLE (kuhn <u>sohl</u>) *v.* **-ing,-ed.**
to alleviate grief and raise the spirits of, provide solace
Synonyms: relieve, comfort, soothe

"Of dissolving with her, and being more happy still!" he answered. "Do you suppose I dread any change of that sort? I expected such a transformation on raising the lid: but I'm better pleased that it should not commence till I share it. Besides, unless I had received a distinct impression of her passionless features, that strange feeling would hardly have been removed. It began oddly. You know I was wild after she died; and eternally, from dawn to dawn, praying her to return to me her spirit! I have a strong faith in ghosts: I have a conviction that they can, and do, exist among us! The day she was buried there came a fall of snow. In the evening I went to the churchyard. It blew bleak as winter—all round was solitary. I didn't fear that her fool of a husband would wander up the den so late; and no one else had business to bring them there. Being alone, and conscious two yards of loose earth was the sole barrier between us, I said to myself— 'I'll have her in my arms again! If she be cold, I'll think it is this north wind that chills *me*; and if she be motionless, it is sleep.' I got a spade from the tool-house, and began to **delve** with all my might—it scraped the coffin; I fell to work with my hands; the wood commenced cracking about the screws; I was on the point of attaining my object, when it seemed that I heard a sigh from some one above, close at the edge of the grave, and bending down. 'If I can only get this off,' I muttered, 'I wish they may shovel in the earth over us both!' and I wrenched at it more desperately still. There was another sigh, close at my ear. I appeared to feel the warm breath of it displacing the sleet-laden wind. I knew no living thing in flesh and blood was by; but, as certainly as you perceive the approach to some substantial body in the dark, though it cannot be **discerned**, so certainly I felt that Cathy was there: not under me, but on the earth. A sudden sense of relief flowed from my heart through every limb. I **relinquished** my labour of agony, and turned **consoled** at once: unspeakably **consoled**. Her presence was with me: it remained while I refilled the grave, and led me home. You

FERVOUR or FERVOR (<u>fuhr</u> vuhr) *n.*
passion, intensity, zeal
Synonyms: vehemence, eagerness, enthusiasm
SUPPLICATION (suh plih <u>kay</u> shun) *n.*
a humble and earnest request
Synonyms: petition, appellation, application
INFERNAL (ihn <u>fuhr</u> nuhl) *adj.*
devilish; relating to the dead or hell
Synonyms: fiendish, awful, malicious; damned, accursed

PACIFY (<u>paa</u> suh fie) *v.* **-ing,-ied.**
to restore calm, bring peace
Synonyms: mollify, conciliate, appease, placate
BEGUILE (buh <u>giel</u>) *v.* **-ing,-ed.**
to deceive, mislead; to charm; to pass time
Synonyms: lure, coax, cozen; enchant, inveigle;
amuse, occupy

may laugh, if you will; but I was sure I should see her there. I was sure she was with me, and I could not help talking to her. Having reached the Heights, I rushed eagerly to the door. It was fastened; and, I remember that accursed Earnshaw and my wife opposed my entrance. I remember stopping to kick the breath out of him, and then hurrying upstairs, to my room and hers. I looked round impatiently—I felt her by me—I could *almost* see her, and yet I *could not*! I ought to have sweat blood then, from the anguish of my yearning—from the **fervour** of my **supplications** to have but one glimpse! I had not one. She showed herself, as she often was in life, a devil to me! And, since then, sometimes more and sometimes less, I've been the sport of that intolerable torture! **Infernal**! Keeping my nerves at such a stretch, that, if they had not resembled catgut, they would long ago have relaxed to the feebleness of Linton's. When I sat in the house with Hareton, it seemed that on going out, I should meet her; when I walked on the moors I should meet her coming in. When I went from home, I hastened to return: she *must* be somewhere at the Heights, I was certain! And when I slept in her chamber—I was beaten out of that. I couldn't lie there; for the moment I closed my eyes, she was either outside the window, or sliding back the panels, or entering the room, or even resting her darling head on the same pillow as she did when a child; and I must open my lids to see. And so I opened and closed them a hundred times a night—to be always disappointed! It racked me! I've often groaned aloud, till that old rascal Joseph no doubt believed that my conscience was playing the fiend inside of me. Now, since I've seen her, I'm **pacified**—a little. It was a strange way of killing! Not by inches, but by fractions and hairbreadths, to **beguile** me with the spectre of a hope, through eighteen years!"

Mr. Heathcliff paused and wiped his forehead; his hair clung to it, wet with perspiration; his eyes were fixed on the red embers of the fire, the brows not contracted, but raised next the temples; diminishing the grim aspect of

COUNTENANCE (<u>kown</u> tuh nuhns) *n.*
appearance, facial expression
Synonyms: face, features, visage

IMPART (ihm <u>pahrt</u>) *v.* **-ing,-ed.**
to give or share, to pass on
Synonyms: bestow, contribute, reveal, convey

PRY (prie) *v.* **-ing,-ied.**
to intrude into; force open
Synonyms: snoop, nose, spy, eavesdrop; probe

HAUGHTY (<u>haw</u> tee) (<u>hah</u> tee) *adj.*
arrogant and condescending
Synonyms: proud, disdainful, supercilious, scornful, vainglorious

his **countenance**, but **imparting** a peculiar look of trouble, and a painful appearance of mental tension towards one absorbing subject. He only half addressed me, and I maintained silence. I didn't like to hear him talk! After a short period he resumed his meditation on the picture, took it down and leant it against the sofa to contemplate it at better advantage; and while so occupied Catherine entered, announcing that she was ready, when her pony should be saddled.

"Send that over to-morrow," said Heathcliff to me; then turning to her, he added—"You may do without your pony: it is a fine evening, and you'll need no ponies at Wuthering Heights; for what journeys you take, your own feet will serve you. Come along."

"Good-bye, Ellen!" whispered my dear little mistress. As she kissed me, her lips felt like ice. "Come and see me, Ellen; don't forget."

"Take care you do no such thing, Mrs. Dean!" said her new father. "When I wish to speak to you I'll come here. I want none of your **prying** at my house!"

He signed her to precede him; and casting back a look that cut my heart, she obeyed. I watched them from the window, walk down the garden. Heathcliff fixed Catherine's arm under his: though she disputed the act at first evidently; and with rapid strides he hurried her into the alley, whose trees concealed them.

Chapter 30

I have paid a visit to the Heights, but I have not seen her since she left: Joseph held the door in his hand when I called to ask after her, and wouldn't let me pass. He said Mrs. Linton was "thrang," and the master was not in. Zillah has told me something of the way they go on, otherwise I should hardly know who was dead and who living. She thinks Catherine **haughty**, and does not like

ACQUIESCE (aak wee <u>ehs</u>) *v.* **-ing,-ed.**
    to agree; comply quietly
        Synonyms: accede, consent; submit
EVINCE (ih <u>vihns</u>) *v.* **-ing,-ed.**
    to show clearly or display
        Synonyms: express, exhibit, demonstrate, manifest
CONTEMPT (kuhn <u>tehmpt</u>) *n.*
    disrespect, scorn
        Synonyms: derision, disdain

her, I can guess by her talk. My young lady asked some aid of her when she first came; but Mr. Heathcliff told her to follow her own business, and let his daughter-in-law look after herself; and Zillah willingly **acquiesced**, being a narrow-minded, selfish woman. Catherine **evinced** a child's annoyance at this neglect; repaid it with **contempt**, and thus enlisted my informant among her enemies, as securely as if she had done her some great wrong. I had a long talk with Zillah about six weeks ago, a little before you came, one day when we foregathered on the moor; and this is what she told me.

"The first thing Mrs. Linton did," she said, "on her arrival at the Heights, was to run upstairs, without even wishing good evening to me and Joseph; she shut herself into Linton's room, and remained till morning. Then, while the master and Earnshaw were at breakfast, she entered the house, and asked all in a quiver if the doctor might be sent for? Her cousin was very ill.

"'We know that!' answered Heathcliff. 'But his life is not worth a farthing, and I won't spend a farthing on him.'

"'But I cannot tell how to do,' she said, 'and if nobody will help me, he'll die!'

"'Walk out of the room,' cried the master, 'and let me never hear a word more about him! None here cares what becomes of him; if you do, act the nurse! If you do not, lock him up and leave him.'

"Then she began to bother me, and I said I'd had enough plague with the tiresome thing; we each had our tasks, and hers was to wait on Linton, Mr. Heathcliff bid me leave that labour to her.

"How they managed together, I can't tell. I fancy he fretted a great deal, and moaned hisseln night and day; and she had precious little rest: one could guess by her white face and heavy eyes. She sometimes came into the kitchen all wildered like, and looked as if she would <u>fain</u> beg assistance; but I was not going to disobey the master. I never dare disobey him, Mrs. Dean; and, though I thought it wrong that Kenneth should not be sent for, it

MEDDLE (<u>meh</u> duhl) *v.* **-ing,-ed.**
    to interfere in others' affairs, to impose
        Synonyms: interlope, tamper, snoop, encroach

MARRED (mahrd) *adj.*
    spoiled; damaged, defaced
        Synonyms: impaired, interrupted; injured,
        disfigured, blemished, scarred

was no concern of mine either to advise or complain, and I always refused to **meddle**. Once or twice, after we had gone to bed, I've happened to open my door again and seen her sitting crying on the stairs' top; and then I've shut myself in quick, for fear of being moved to interfere. I did pity her then, I'm sure: still I didn't wish to lose my place, you know.

"At last, one night she came boldly into my chamber, and frightened me out of my wits, by saying:

"'Tell Mr. Heathcliff that his son is dying—I'm sure he is, this time. Get up, instantly, and tell him.'

"Having uttered this speech, she vanished again. I lay a quarter of an hour listening and trembling. Nothing stirred—the house was quiet.

"'She's mistaken,' I said to myself. 'He's got over it. I needn't disturb them.' And I began to doze. But my sleep was **marred** a second time by a sharp ringing of the bell—the only bell we have, put up on purpose for Linton; and the master called to me to see what was the matter, and inform them that he wouldn't have that noise repeated.

"I delivered Catherine's message. He cursed to himself, and in a few minutes came out with a lighted candle, and proceeded to their room. I followed. Mrs. Heathcliff was seated by the bedside, with her hands folded on her knees. Her father-in-law went up, held the light to Linton's face, looked at him, and touched him; afterwards he turned to her.

"'Now—Catherine,' he said, 'how do you feel?'

"She was dumb.

"'How do you feel, Catherine?' he repeated.

"'He's safe, and I'm free,' she answered. 'I should feel well—but,' she continued, with a bitterness she couldn't conceal, 'you have left me so long to struggle against death alone, that I feel and see only death! I feel like death!'

"And she looked like it, too! I gave her a little wine. Hareton and Joseph, who had been wakened by the ringing and the sound of feet, and heard our talk from

REPEL (rih <u>pehl</u>) *v.* **-ling,-led.**
  to rebuff, repulse; disgust, offend
    Synonyms: reject, spurn, parry; nauseate, revolt
BEQUEATH (bih <u>kweeth</u>) *v.* **-ing,-ed.**
  to give, as in a will; to hand down
    Synonyms: bestow; pass on, transmit
MEDDLE (<u>meh</u> duhl) *v.* **-ing,-ed.**
  to interfere in others' affairs, to impose
    Synonyms: interlope, tamper, snoop, encroach
DESTITUTE (<u>dehs</u> tih toot) (<u>dehs</u> tih tyoot) *adj.*
  lacking; very poor, poverty-stricken
    Synonyms: without, wanting, deprived; insolvent,
    impecunious, penurious, needy, broke

HINDER (<u>hihn</u> duhr) *v.* **-ing,-ed.**
  to prevent action; to delay or impede
    Synonyms: restrain; hamper, inhibit, obstruct
DESCEND (dih <u>sehnd</u>) (dee <u>sehnd</u>) *v.* **-ing,-ed.**
  to pass from a higher place to a lower place
    Synonyms: fall, dismount, gravitate

outside, now entered. Joseph was <u>fain</u>, I believe, of the lad's removal; Hareton seemed a thought bothered; though he was more taken up with staring at Catherine than thinking of Linton. But the master bid him get off to bed again: we didn't want his help. He afterwards made Joseph remove the body to his chamber, and told me to return to mine, and Mrs. Heathcliff remained by herself.

"In the morning, he sent me to tell her she must come down to breakfast; she had undressed, and appeared going to sleep, and said she was ill; at which I hardly wondered. I informed Mr. Heathcliff, and he replied:

"'Well, let her be till after the funeral; and go up now and then to get her what is needful; and, as soon as she seems better, tell me.'"

Cathy stayed upstairs a <u>fortnight</u>, according to Zillah, who visited her twice a day, and would have been rather more friendly, but her attempts at increasing kindness were proudly and promptly **repelled**.

Heathcliff went up once, to show her Linton's will. He had **bequeathed** the whole of his, and what had been her, movable property to his father: the poor creature was threatened, or coaxed, into that act during her week's absence, when his uncle died. The lands, being a minor, he could not **meddle** with. However, Mr. Heathcliff has claimed and kept them in his wife's right and his also: I suppose legally: at any rate, Catherine, **destitute** of cash and friends, cannot disturb his possession.

"Nobody," said Zillah, "ever approached her door, except that once, but I; and nobody asked anything about her. The first occasion of her coming down into the house was on a Sunday afternoon. She had cried out, when I carried up her dinner, that she couldn't bear any longer being in the cold: and I told her the master was going to Thrushcross Grange, and Earnshaw and I needn't **hinder** her from **descending**; so, as soon as she heard Heathcliff's horse trot off, she made her appearance donned in black, and her yellow curls combed back behind her ears as plain as a Quaker: she couldn't comb them out.

SULLEN (<u>suh</u> luhn) *adj.*
   brooding, gloomy
      Synonyms: morose, sulky, somber, glum

CIVILITY (sih <u>vihl</u> ih tee) *n.*
   a courteous behavior or politeness
      Synonyms: compliment, pleasantry

"Joseph and I generally go to chapel on Sundays." (The <u>kirk</u>, you know, has no minister now, explained Mrs. Dean, and they call the Methodists' or Baptists' place, I can't say which it is, at Gimmerton, a chapel.) "Joseph had gone," she continued, "but I thought proper to bide at home. Young folks are always the better for an elder's overlooking; and Hareton, with all his bashfulness, isn't a model of nice behaviour. I let him know that his cousin would very likely sit with us, and she had been always used to see the Sabbath respected; so he had as good leave his guns and bits of indoor work alone, while she stayed. He coloured up at the news, and cast his eyes over his hands and clothes. The train-oil and gunpowder were shoved out of sight in a minute. I saw he meant to give her his company; and I guessed, by his way, he wanted to be presentable; so, laughing, as I durst not laugh when the master is by, I offered to help him, if he would, and joked at his confusion. He grew **sullen**, and began to swear."

"Now, Mrs. Dean," Zillah went on, seeing me not pleased by her manner, "you happen think your young lady too fine for Mr. Hareton; and happen you're right: but I own I should love well to bring her pride a peg lower. And what will all her learning and her daintiness do for her, now? She's as poor as you or I: poorer, I'll be bound: you're saving, and I'm doing my little all that road."

Hareton allowed Zillah to give him her aid; and she flattered him into a good humour: so, when Catherine came, half-forgetting her former insults, he tried to make himself agreeable, by the housekeeper's account.

"Missis walked in," she said, "as chill as an icicle, and as high as a princess. I got up and offered her my seat in the arm-chair. No, she turned up her nose at my **civility**. Earnshaw rose, too, and bid her come to the <u>settle</u>, and sit close by the fire: he was sure she was starved.

"'I've been starved a month and more,' she answered, resting on the word as scornful as she could.

"And she got a chair for herself, and placed it at distance from both of us. Having sat till she was warm, she

DAUNT (dawnt) *v.* **-ing,-ed.**
to discourage, intimidate
Synonyms: demoralize, dishearten, consternate, cow

OBLIGED (uh bliejd) *adj.*
grateful, appreciative
Synonyms: thankful, indebted, owing

began to look around, and discovered a number of books in the dresser; she was instantly upon her feet again, stretching to reach them: but they were too high up. Her cousin, after watching her endeavours a while, at last summoned courage to help her; she held her frock, and he filled it with the first that came to hand.

"That was a great advance for the lad. She didn't thank him; still, he felt gratified that she had accepted his assistance, and ventured to stand behind as she examined them, and even to stoop and point out what struck his fancy in certain old pictures which they contained; nor was he **daunted** by the saucy style in which she jerked the page from his finger: he contented himself with going a bit farther back, and looking at her instead of the book. She continued reading, or seeking for something to read. His attention became, by degrees, quite centred in the study of her thick, silky curls: her face he couldn't see, and she couldn't see him. And, perhaps, not quite awake to what he did, but attracted like a child to a candle, at last he proceeded from staring to touching; he put out his hand and stroked one curl, as gently as if it were a bird. He might have struck a knife into her neck, she started round in such a taking.

"'Get away, this moment! How dare you touch me? Why are you stopping there?' she cried, in a tone of disgust. 'I can't endure you! I'll go upstairs again, if you come near me.'

"Mr. Hareton recoiled, looking as foolish as he could do: he sat down in the settle very quiet, and she continued turning over her volumes another half-hour; finally, Earnshaw crossed over, and whispered to me:

"'Will you ask her to read to us, Zillah? I'm stalled of doing naught; and I do like—I could like to hear her! Dunnot say I wanted it, but ask of yourseln.'

"'Mr. Hareton wishes you would read to us, ma'am,' I said immediately. 'He'd take it very kind—he'd be much **obliged**.'

"She frowned; and looking up, answered:

HYPOCRISY (hih <u>pah</u> krih see) *n.*
the practice of claiming beliefs or virtues that one doesn't really possess
Synonyms: fraud, falseness, fakeness, lip service

KINDLE (<u>kihn</u> duhl) *v.* **-ing,-ed.**
to excite or inspire; to set fire to or ignite
Synonyms: arouse, awaken; light, spark

RESTRAIN (rih <u>strayn</u>) *v.* **-ing,-ed.**
to control, repress, restrict, hold back
Synonyms: hamper, bridle, curb, check

CONDESCEND (kahn dih <u>sehnd</u>) *v.* **-ing,-ed.**
to lower oneself below one's level or dignity; to possess an attitude of superiority
Synonyms: stoop, descend; patronize

VENOMOUS (<u>vehn</u> uh muhs) *adj.*
malicious or spiteful; poisonous
Synonyms: harmful; noxious, deadly

"'Mr. Hareton, and the whole set of you, will be good enough to understand that I reject any pretence at kindness you have the **hypocrisy** to offer! I despise you, and will have nothing to say to any of you! When I would have given my life for one kind word, even to see one of your faces, you all kept off. But I won't complain to you! I'm driven down here by the cold; not either to amuse you or enjoy your society.'

"'What could I ha' done?' began Earnshaw. 'How was I to blame?'

"'Oh! You are an exception,' answered Mrs. Heathcliff. 'I never missed such a concern as you.'

"'But I offered more than once, and asked,' he said, **kindling** up at her pertness. 'I asked Mr. Heathcliff to let me wake for you—'

"'Be silent! I'll go out of doors, or anywhere, rather than have your disagreeable voice in my ear!' said my lady.

"Hareton muttered she might go to hell, for him! And unslinging his gun, **restrained** himself from his Sunday occupations no longer. He talked now, freely enough; and she presently saw fit to retreat to her solitude: but the frost had set in, and, in spite of her pride, she was forced to **condescend** to our company, more and more. However, I took care there should be no further scorning at my good-nature: ever since, I've been as stiff as herself; and she has no lover or liker among us: and she does not deserve one; for, let them say the least word to her, and she'll curl back without respect of any one! She'll snap at the master himself, and as good as dares him to thrash her, and the more hurt she gets, the more **venomous** she grows."

At first, on hearing this account from Zillah, I determined to leave my situation, take a cottage, and get Catherine to come and live with me: but Mr. Heathcliff would as soon permit that as he would set up Hareton in an independent house; and I can see no remedy, at present, unless she could marry again: and that scheme it does not come within my province to arrange.

PROPHECY (<u>prah</u> feh see) *n.*
    the foretelling of events, a prediction of the future
        Synonyms: dream, forecast, vision

ENTREAT (ehn <u>treet</u>) *v.* **-ing,-ed.**
    to plead, beg
        Synonyms: beseech, implore, importune, request

INVOKE (ihn <u>vohk</u>) *v.* **-ing,-ed.**
    to call upon, request help
        Synonyms: summon, solicit, conjure, evoke

RUSTIC (<u>ruh</u> stihk) 1. *n.* 2. *adj.*
    1. a rural person with a simplistic character
        Synonyms: bumpkin, hick, clod, countryman
    2. simple and unsophisticated; typical of country life
        Synonyms: unrefined, crude; bucolic, pastoral

Thus ended Mrs. Dean's story. Notwithstanding the doctor's **prophecy**, I am rapidly recovering strength; and though it be only the second week in January, I propose getting out on horseback in a day or two, and riding over to Wuthering Heights, to inform my landlord that I shall spend the next six months in London; and, if he likes, he may look out for another tenant to take the place after October. I would not pass another winter here for much.

Chapter 31

Yesterday was bright, calm, and frosty. I went to the Heights as I proposed; my housekeeper **entreated** me to bear a little note from her to her young lady, and I did not refuse, for the worthy woman was not conscious of anything odd in her request. The front door stood open, but the jealous gate was fastened, as at my last visit; I knocked, and **invoked** Earnshaw from among the garden beds; he unchained it, and I entered. The fellow is as handsome a **rustic** as need be seen. I took particular notice of him this time; but then he does his best, apparently, to make the least of his advantages.

I asked if Mr. Heathcliff were at home? He answered, No; but he would be in at dinner-time. It was eleven o'clock, and I announced my intention of going in and waiting for him, at which he immediately flung down his tools and accompanied me, in the office of watchdog, not as a substitute for the host.

We entered together: Catherine was there, making herself useful in preparing some vegetables for the approaching meal; she looked more sulky and less spirited than when I had seen her first. She hardly raised her eyes to notice me, and continued her employment with the same disregard to common forms of politeness as before; never returning my bow and good-morning by the slightest acknowledgment.

AMIABLE (<u>ay</u> mee uh buhl) *adj.*
  friendly, pleasant, likable
    Synonyms: affable, convivial, amicable, agreeable
SURLILY (<u>suhr</u> lih lee) *adv.*
  rudely, with a bad temper
    Synonyms: gruffly, ungraciously, crossly
PARING (<u>payr</u> ihng) *n.*
  trimming, excess
    Synonyms: clipping, shaving, sliver
ADROITLY (uh <u>droyt</u> lee) *adv.*
  skillfully, competently
    Synonyms: deftly, dexterously, proficiently, adeptly

MISSIVE (<u>mihs</u> ihv) *n.*
  note or letter
    Synonyms: bulletin, dispatch, epistle,
    memorandum, message

STEALTHILY (<u>stehl</u> thuh lee) *adv.*
  quietly and cautiously
    Synonyms: furtively, secretly, surreptitiously,
    covertly
PERUSE (puh <u>roos</u>) *v.* **-ing,-ed.**
  to examine closely
    Synonyms: scrutinize, inspect, study; browse
SOLILOQUY (suh <u>lih</u> luh kwee) *n.*
  literary or dramatic speech by one character, not
  addressed to others
    Synonyms: monologue, solo

She does not seem so **amiable**, I thought, as Mrs. Dean would persuade me to believe. She's a beauty, it is true; but not an angel.

Earnshaw **surlily** bid her remove her things to the kitchen. "Remove them yourself," she said, pushing them from her as soon as she had done; and retiring to a stool by the window, where she began to carve figures of birds and beasts out of the turnip **parings** in her lap. I approached her, pretending to desire a view of the garden; and, as I fancied, **adroitly** dropped Mrs. Dean's note on to her knee, unnoticed by Hareton—but she asked aloud, "What is that?" and chucked it off.

"A letter from your old acquaintance, the housekeeper at the Grange," I answered; annoyed at her exposing my kind deed, and fearful lest it should be imagined a **missive** of my own. She would gladly have gathered it up at this information, but Hareton beat her; he seized and put it in his waistcoat, saying Mr. Heathcliff should look at it first. Thereat, Catherine silently turned her face from us, and, very **stealthily**, drew out her pocket-handkerchief and applied it to her eyes; and her cousin, after struggling a while to keep down his softer feelings, pulled out the letter and flung it on the floor beside her, as ungraciously as he could. Catherine caught and **perused** it eagerly; then she put a few questions to me concerning the inmates, rational and irrational, of her former home; and gazing towards the hills, murmured in **soliloquy**:

"I should like to be riding Minny down there! I should like to be climbing up there! Oh! I'm tired—I'm *stalled*, Hareton!" And she leant her pretty head back against the sill, with half a yawn and half a sigh, and lapsed into an aspect of abstracted sadness: neither caring nor knowing whether we remarked her.

"Mrs. Heathcliff," I said, after sitting some time mute, "you are not aware that I am an acquaintance of yours? So intimate that I think it strange you won't come and speak to me. My housekeeper never wearies of talking about and praising you; and she'll be greatly disappointed

CONTRIVE (kuhn <u>triev</u>) *v.* **-ing,-ed.**
to devise, plan, or manage; to form in an artistic manner
Synonyms: concoct, scheme; create, design

INDIGNANT (ihn <u>dihg</u> nuhnt) *adj.*
angry, incensed, offended
Synonyms: furious, irate, mad, wrathful, ireful

EMULOUS (<u>ehm</u> yoo luhs) *adj.*
ambitious and desirous to equal another
Synonyms: rivalrous, eager, imitative

if I return with no news of or from you, except that you received her letter and said nothing!"

She appeared to wonder at this speech, and asked:

"Does Ellen like you?"

"Yes, very well," I replied hesitatingly.

"You must tell her," she continued, "that I would answer her letter, but I have no materials for writing: not even a book from which I might tear a leaf."

"No books!" I exclaimed. "How do you **contrive** to live here without them, if I may take the liberty to inquire? Though provided with a large library, I'm frequently very dull at the Grange; take my books away, and I should be desperate!"

"I was always reading, when I had them," said Catherine, "and Mr. Heathcliff never reads; so he took it into his head to destroy my books. I have not had a glimpse of one for weeks. Only once, I searched through Joseph's store of <u>theology</u>, to his great irritation; and once, Hareton, I came upon a secret stock in your room— some Latin and Greek, and some tales and poetry: all old friends. I brought the last here—and you gathered them, as a magpie gathers silver spoons, for the mere love of stealing! They are of no use to you; or else you concealed them in the bad spirit that as you cannot enjoy them nobody else shall. Perhaps *your* envy counselled Mr. Heathcliff to rob me of my treasures? But I've most of them written on my brain and printed in my heart, and you cannot deprive me of those!"

Earnshaw blushed crimson when his cousin made this revelation of his private literary accumulations, and stammered an **indignant** denial of her accusations.

"Mr. Hareton is desirous of increasing his amount of knowledge," I said, coming to his rescue. "He is not *envious* but *emulous* of your attainments. He'll be a clever scholar in a few years."

"And he wants me to sink into a dunce, meantime," answered Catherine. "Yes, I hear him trying to spell and read to himself, and pretty blunders he makes! I wish you

ANECDOTE (<u>aa</u> nihk doht) *n.*
   a short, often funny, account of an event
      Synonyms: story, joke
TOTTER (<u>tah</u> tuhr) *v.* **-ing,-ed.**
   to stand with unsteadiness
      Synonyms: wobble, sway, stagger
APPROPRIATE (uh <u>proh</u> pree ayt) *v.* **-ing,-ed.**
   to take possession of; to set aside for a purpose
      Synonyms: usurp, arrogate, commandeer; allocate,
      designate
CONSECRATE (<u>kahn</u> suh krayt) *v.* **-ing,-ed.**
   to declare sacred; dedicate to a worship
      Synonyms: sanctify; devote
DEBASE (dih <u>bays</u>) *v.* **-ing,-ed.**
   to degrade or lower in quality or stature
      Synonyms: demean, denigrate, defile, adulterate
PROFANE (proh <u>fayn</u>) *v.* **-ing,-ed.**
   to treat abusively, to desecrate or defile
      Synonyms: corrupt, deprave, debauch
MALICE (<u>maal</u> ihs) *n.*
   animosity, spite, hatred
      Synonyms: malevolence, cruelty, enmity, rancor,
      hostility
WRATH (raath) *n.*
   anger, rage
      Synonyms: fury, ire, resentment, indignation
SUPPRESS (suh <u>prehs</u>) *v.* **-ing,-ed.**
   to hold back, restrain
      Synonyms: subdue, stifle, muffle, quell, curb

would repeat 'Chevy Chase' as you did yesterday: it was extremely funny. I heard you; and I heard you turning over the dictionary to seek out the hard words, and then cursing because you couldn't read their explanations!"

The young man evidently thought it too bad that he should be laughed at for his ignorance, and then laughed at for trying to remove it. I had a similar notion; and, remembering Mrs. Dean's **anecdote** of his first attempt at enlightening the darkness in which he had been reared, I observed:

"But, Mrs. Heathcliff, we have each had a commencement, and each stumbled and **tottered** on the threshold; had our teachers scorned instead of aiding us, we should stumble and **totter** yet."

"Oh!" she replied, "I don't wish to limit his acquirements: still, he has no right to **appropriate** what is mine, and make it ridiculous to me with his <u>vile</u> mistakes and mispronunciations! Those books, both prose and verse, are **consecrated** to me by other associations; and I hate to have them **debased** and **profaned** in his mouth! Besides, of all, he has selected my favourite pieces that I love the most to repeat, as if out of deliberate **malice**."

Hareton's chest heaved in silence a minute: he laboured under a severe sense of mortification and **wrath**, which it was no easy task to **suppress**. I rose, and, from a gentlemanly idea of relieving his embarrassment, took up my station in the doorway, surveying the external prospect as I stood. He followed my example, and left the room; but presently reappeared, bearing half-a-dozen volumes in his hands, which he threw into Catherine's lap exclaiming: "Take them! I never want to hear, or read, or think of them again!"

"I won't have them now," she answered. "I shall connect them with you, and hate them."

She opened one that had obviously been often turned over, and read a portion in the drawling tone of a beginner, then laughed, and threw it from her. "And listen," she

PROVOKINGLY (proh <u>voh</u> kihng lee) *adv.*
  in a manner that causes a response, e.g., anger or
  disagreement
    Synonyms: aggravatingly, stimulatingly, vexingly
MANUAL (<u>maan</u> yoo uhl) *adj.*
  by hand; hand-operated
    Synonyms: physical; mechanical
COUNTENANCE (<u>kown</u> tuh nuhns) *n.*
  appearance, facial expression
    Synonyms: face, features, visage

IMPART (ihm <u>pahrt</u>) *v.* **-ing,-ed.**
  to give or share, to pass on
    Synonyms: bestow, contribute, reveal, convey
INCITEMENT (ihn <u>siet</u> mehnt) *n.*
  motive, incentive
    Synonyms: urge, impulse, catalyst

CONFLAGRATION (kahn fluh <u>gray</u> shuhn) *n.*
  a big, destructive fire; an intense scene
    Synonyms: blaze, holocaust, inferno; spectacle
INDIGNANT (ihn <u>dihg</u> nuhnt) *adj.*
  angry, incensed, offended
    Synonyms: furious, irate, mad, wrathful, ireful
AGITATION (aa gih <u>tay</u> shuhn) *n.*
  commotion, excitement; uneasiness
    Synonyms: disturbance; restlessness, anxiety
PRECLUDE (prih <u>clood</u>) *v.* **-ing,-ed.**
  to rule out
    Synonyms: prevent, avert, obviate, forestall, deter

THWART (thwahrt) *v.* **-ing,-ed.**
  to block or prevent from happening; to frustrate
    Synonyms: oppose, defeat, foil, balk; hinder, baffle

continued **provokingly**, commencing a verse of an old ballad in the same fashion.

But his self-love would endure no further torment: I heard, and not altogether disapprovingly, a **manual** check given to her saucy tongue. The little wretch had done her utmost to hurt her cousin's sensitive though uncultivated feelings, and a physical argument was the only mode he had of balancing the account, and repaying its effects on the inflictor. He afterwards gathered the books and hurled them on the fire. I read in his **countenance** what anguish it was to offer that sacrifice to spleen. I fancied that as they consumed, he recalled the pleasure they had already **imparted**, and the triumph and ever-increasing pleasure he had anticipated from them; and I fancied I guessed the **incitement** to his secret studies also. He had been content with daily labour and rough animal enjoyments, till Catherine crossed his path. Shame at her scorn, and hope of her approval, were his first prompters to higher pursuits; and, instead of guarding him from one and winning him to the other, his endeavours to raise himself had produced just the contrary result.

"Yes; that's all the good that such a <u>brute</u> as you can get from them!" cried Catherine, sucking her damaged lip, and watching the **conflagration** with **indignant** eyes.

"You'd *better* hold your tongue, now," he answered fiercely.

And his **agitation precluded** further speech; he advanced hastily to the entrance, where I made way for him to pass. But ere he had crossed the door-stones, Mr. Heathcliff, coming up the causeway, encountered him, and laying hold of his shoulder, asked:

"What's to do now, my lad?"

"<u>Naught, naught</u>," he said, and broke away to enjoy his grief and anger in solitude.

Heathcliff gazed after him, and sighed.

"It will be odd if I **thwart** myself," he muttered, unconscious that I was behind him. "But when I look for his

599

COUNTENANCE (<u>kown</u> tuh nuhns) *n.*
appearance, facial expression
Synonyms: face, features, visage

DESOLATION (deh suh <u>lay</u> shuhn) *n.*
barren wasteland; sadness, loneliness
Synonyms: bleakness, devastation, ruin; despair

DISPOSITION (dihs puh <u>zih</u> shuhn) *n.*
mood or temperament
Synonyms: behavior, tendency, inclination, nature

RETAIN (rih <u>tayn</u>) *v.* **-ing,-ed.**
to hold, keep possession of
Synonyms: withhold, reserve, maintain, remember

BANISH (<u>baan</u> ish) *v.* **-ing,-ed.**
to force to leave, to exile
Synonyms: expel, deport

father in his face, I find *her* every day more. How the devil is he so like? I can hardly bear to see him."

He bent his eyes to the ground, and walked moodily in. There was a restless, anxious expression in his **countenance** I had never remarked there before; and he looked sparer in person. His daughter-in-law, on perceiving him through the window, immediately escaped to the kitchen, so that I remained alone.

"I'm glad to see you out of doors again, Mr. Lockwood," he said, in reply to my greeting. "From selfish motives partly, I don't think I could readily supply your loss in this **desolation**. I've wondered more than once what brought you here."

"An idle whim, I fear, sir," was my answer, "or else an idle whim is going to spirit me away. I shall set out for London, next week; and I must give you warning that I feel no **disposition** to **retain** Thrushcross Grange beyond the twelve months I agreed to rent it. I believe I shall not live there any more."

"Oh, indeed; you're tired of being **banished** from the world, are you?" he said. "But if you be coming to plead off paying for a place you won't occupy, your journey is useless. I never relent in exacting my due from any one."

"I'm coming to plead off nothing about it," I exclaimed, considerably irritated. "Should you wish it, I'll settle with you now," and I drew my note-book from my pocket.

"No, no," he replied coolly. "You'll leave sufficient behind to cover your debts, if you fail to return: I'm not in such a hurry. Sit down and take your dinner with us; a guest that is safe from repeating his visit can generally be made welcome. Catherine, bring the things in: where are you?"

Catherine reappeared, bearing a tray of knives and forks.

"You may get your dinner with Joseph," muttered Heathcliff aside, "and remain in the kitchen till he is gone."

TRANSGRESS (traans <u>grehs</u>) *v.* **-ing,-ed.**
    to violate a law or command; to trespass
        Synonyms: sin, disobey, offend; overstep
MISANTHROPIST (mihz <u>aan</u> throh pihst) *n.*
    person who hates human beings
        Synonyms: cynic, loner, curmudgeon

MIGRATE (<u>mie</u> grayt) *v.* **-ing,-ed.**
    to wander or travel from place to place
        Synonyms: roam, move, trek, voyage

IMPULSE (<u>ihm</u> puhls) *n.*
    an unexpected tendency, inclination
        Synonyms: urge, whim

She obeyed his directions very punctually; perhaps she had no temptation to **transgress**. Living among clowns and **misanthropists**, she probably cannot appreciate a better class of people when she meets them.

With Mr. Heathcliff, grim and <u>saturnine</u>, on the one hand, and Hareton, absolutely dumb, on the other, I made a somewhat cheerless meal, and bade <u>adieu</u> early. I would have departed by the back way, to get a last glimpse of Catherine and annoy old Joseph; but Hareton received orders to lead up my horse, and my host himself escorted me to the door, so I could not fulfill my wish.

"How dreary life gets over in that house!" I reflected, while riding down the road. "What a realisation of something more romantic than a fairy tale it would have been for Mrs. Linton Heathcliff, had she and I struck up an attachment, as her good nurse desired, and **migrated** together into the stirring atmosphere of the town!"

Chapter 32

1802—

This September I was invited to devastate the moors of a friend in the north, and on my journey to his <u>abode</u>, I unexpectedly came within fifteen miles of Gimmerton. The 'ostler at a roadside public-house was holding a pail of water to refresh my horses, when a cart of very green oats, newly <u>reaped</u>, passed by, and he remarked:

"Yon's trough Gimmerton, nah! They're allas three wick after other folk wi' ther harvest."

"Gimmerton?" I repeated—my residence in that locality had already grown dim and dreamy. "Ah! I know. How far is it from this?"

"Happen fourteen mile o'er th' hills; and a rough road," he answered.

A sudden **impulse** seized me to visit Thrushcross Grange. It was scarcely noon, and I conceived that I

HINDER (<u>hihn</u> duhr) *v.* **-ing,-ed.**
    to prevent action; to delay or impede
        Synonyms: restrain; hamper, inhibit, obstruct

BUSTLE (<u>buh</u> suhl) *v.* **-ing,-ed.**
    to move quickly and energetically
        Synonyms: scurry, scramble, dash, whirl, fuss

might as well pass the night under my own roof as in an inn. Besides, I could spare a day easily to arrange matters with my landlord, and thus save myself the trouble of invading the neighbourhood again. Having rested awhile, I directed my servant to inquire the way to the village; and, with great fatigue to our beasts, we managed the distance in some three hours.

I left him there, and proceeded down the valley alone. The grey church looked greyer, and the lonely churchyard lonelier. I distinguished a moor sheep cropping the short turf on the graves. It was sweet, warm weather—too warm for travelling; but the heat did not **hinder** me from enjoying the delightful scenery above and below: had I seen it nearer August, I'm sure it would have tempted me to waste a month among its solitudes. In winter nothing more dreary, in summer nothing more divine, than those glens shut in by hills, and those <u>bluff</u>, bold swells of <u>heath</u>.

I reached the Grange before sunset, and knocked for admittance; but the family had retreated into the back premises, I judged, by one thin, blue wreath curling from the kitchen chimney, and they did not hear. I rode into the court. Under the porch, a girl of nine or ten sat knitting, and an old woman reclined on the house-steps, smoking a meditative pipe.

"Is Mrs. Dean within?" I demanded of the dame.

"Mistress Dean? Nay!" she answered. "Shoo doesn't bide here: shoo's up at th' Heights."

"Are you the housekeeper, then?" I continued.

"Eea, aw keep th' house," she replied.

"Well, I'm Mr. Lockwood, the master. Are there any rooms to lodge me in, I wonder? I wish to stay all night."

"T' maister!" she cried in astonishment. "Whet, whoiver knew yah wur coming? Yah sud ha' send word. They's nowt norther dry nor mensful abaht t' place: nowt there isn't!"

She threw down her pipe and **bustled** in, the girl followed, and I entered too; soon perceiving that her report was true, and, moreover, that I had almost upset her wits

APPARITION (aa puh <u>rih</u> shuhn) *n.*
an unexpected or unusual sight or appearance; a
ghostly figure
Synonyms: illusion; spirit, specter

MAL-APPROPRIATE (maal uh <u>proh</u> pree ayt) *v.* **-ing,-ed.**
to set aside for the wrong purpose
Synonyms: misuse, mistake

DERIVE (dih <u>riev</u>) *v.* **-ing,-ed.**
to receive from a source, to originate
Synonyms: infer, descend, deduce, come (from)

by my unwelcome **apparition**, I bade her be composed. I would go out for a walk; and, meantime, she must try to prepare a corner of a sitting-room for me to sup in, and a bedroom to sleep in. No sweeping and dusting, only good fire and dry sheets were necessary. She seemed willing to do her best; though she thrust the hearth-brush into the grates in mistake for the poker, and **mal-appropriated** several other articles of her craft: but I retired, confiding in her energy for a resting-place against my return. Wuthering Heights was the goal of my proposed excursion. An after-thought brought me back, when I had quitted the court.

"All well at the Heights?" I inquired of the woman.

"Eea, f'r owt ee knaw," she answered, scurrying away with a pan of hot cinders.

I would have asked why Mrs. Dean had deserted the Grange, but it was impossible to delay her at such a crisis, so I turned away and made my exit, rambling leisurely along with the glow of a sinking sun behind, and the mild glory of a rising moon in front—one fading, and the other brightening—as I quitted the park, and climbed the stony by-road branching off to Mr. Heathcliff's dwelling. Before I arrived in sight of it, all that remained of day was a beamless amber light along the west: but I could see every pebble on the path, and every blade of grass, by that splendid moon. I had neither to climb the gate nor to knock—it yielded to my hand. That is an improvement, I thought. And I noticed another, by the aid of my nostrils; a fragrance of stocks and wallflowers wafted on the air from amongst the homely fruit-trees.

Both doors and <u>lattices</u> were open; and yet, as is usually the case in a coal district, a fine, red fire illumined the chimney: the comfort which the eye **derives** from it renders the extra heat endurable. But the house of Wuthering Heights is so large, that the inmates have plenty of space for withdrawing out of its influence; and accordingly, what inmates there were had stationed themselves not far from one of the windows. I could both see them and hear

INFERNAL (ihn <u>fuhr</u> nuhl) *adj.*
   relating to the dead or hell; devilish
      Synonyms: damned, accursed; fiendish, awful, malicious
MALIGNANT (muh <u>lihg</u> nehnt) *adj.*
   evil in influence or effect; aggressively malicious;
   tending to produce death
      Synonyms: vindictive, threatening; destructive,
      harmful; lethal, fatal
SKULK (skuhlk) *v.* **-ing,-ed.**
   to move in a stealthy or cautious manner, to sneak
      Synonyms: lurk, shirk, hide, evade, prowl

them talk before I entered, and looked and listened in consequence; being moved thereto by a mingled sense of curiosity and envy, that grew as I lingered.

"Con-*trary*!" said a voice as sweet as a silver bell— "That for the third time, you dunce! I'm not going to tell you again. Recollect, or I'll pull your hair!"

"Contrary, then," answered another, in deep but softened tones. "And now, kiss me, for minding so well."

"No, read it over first correctly, without a single mistake."

The male speaker began to read: he was a young man, respectably dressed and seated at a table, having a book before him. His handsome features glowed with pleasure, and his eyes kept impatiently wandering from the page to a small white hand over his shoulder, which recalled him by a smart slap on the cheek, whenever its owner detected such signs of inattention. Its owner stood behind; her light, shining ringlets blending, at intervals, with his brown locks, as she bent to superintend his studies; and her face—it was lucky he could not see her face, or he would never have been so steady. I could; and I bit my lip in spite, at having thrown away the chance I might have had of doing something besides staring at its smiling beauty.

The task was done, not free from further blunders; but the pupil claimed a reward, and received at least five kisses: which, however, he generously returned. Then they came to the door, and from their conversation I judged they were about to issue out and have a walk on the moors. I supposed I should be condemned in Hareton Earnshaw's heart, if not by his mouth, to the lowest pit in the **infernal** regions, if I showed my unfortunate person in his neighbourhood then; and feeling very mean and **malignant**, I **skulked** round to seek refuge in the kitchen. There was unobstructed admittance on that side also, and at the door sat my old friend Nelly Dean, sewing and singing a song; which was often interrupted from within

by harsh words of scorn and intolerance, uttered in far from musical accents.

"I'd rayther, by th' haulf, hev 'em swearing i' my lugs fro'h morn to neeght, nor hearken ye, hahsiver!" said the tenant of the kitchen, in answer to an unheard speech of Nelly's. "It's a blazing shame, that I cannot oppen t' blessed Book, but yah set up them glories to Sattan, and all t' flaysome wickednesses that iver were born into th' warld! Oh! Ye'er a raight nowt; and shoo's another, and that poor lad'll be lost atween ye. Poor lad!" he added, with a groan. "He's witched: I'm sartin on't! O Lord, judge 'em, for there's norther law nor justice among wer rullers!"

"No! Or we should be sitting in flaming <u>fagots</u>, I suppose," retorted the singer. "But <u>wisht</u>, old man, and read your Bible like a Christian, and never mind me. This is 'Fairy Annie's Wedding'—a <u>bonny</u> tune—it goes to a dance."

Mrs. Dean was about to recommence, when I advanced; and recognising me directly, she jumped to her feet, crying:

"Why, bless you, Mr. Lockwood! How could you think of returning in this way? All's shut up at Thrushcross Grange. You should have given us notice!"

"I've arranged to be accommodated there, for as long as I shall stay," I answered. "I depart again to-morrow. And how are you transplanted here, Mrs. Dean? Tell me that."

"Zillah left, and Mr. Heathcliff wished me to come, soon after you went to London, and stay till you returned. But, step in, pray! Have you walked from Gimmerton this evening?"

"From the Grange," I replied, "and while they make me lodging room there, I want to finish my business with your master, because I don't think of having another opportunity in a hurry."

"What business, sir?" said Nelly, conducting me into the house. "He's gone out at present, and won't return soon."

"About the rent," I answered.

LAUD (lawd) *v.* **-ing,-ed.**
  to honor, to praise
    Synonyms: commend, admire, glorify

OBLIGE (uh bliej) *v.* **-ing,-ed.**
  to be obligated, to require or force someone to obey
    Synonyms: compel, constrain, bind, favor

"Oh! Then it is with Mrs. Heathcliff you must settle," she observed, "or rather with me. She has not learnt to manage her affairs yet, and I act for her: there's nobody else."

I looked surprised.

"Ah! You have not heard of Heathcliff's death, I see," she continued.

"Heathcliff dead!" I exclaimed, astonished. "How long ago?"

"Three months since: but sit down and let me take your hat, and I'll tell you all about it. Stop, you have had nothing to eat, have you?"

"I want nothing: I have ordered supper at home. You sit down too. I never dreamt of his dying! Let me hear how it came to pass. You say you don't expect them back for some time—the young people?"

"No—I have to scold them every evening for their late rambles: but they don't care for me. At least have a drink of our old ale; it will do you good: you seem weary."

She hastened to fetch it before I could refuse, and I heard Joseph asking whether "it warn't a crying scandal that she should have followers at her time of life? And then, to get them jocks put o' t' maister's cellar! He fair shaamed to 'bide still and see it."

She did not stay to retaliate, but re-entered in a minute, bearing a <u>reaming</u> silver pint, whose contents I **lauded** with becoming earnestness. And afterwards she furnished me with the sequel of Heathcliff's history. He had a "queer" end, as she expressed it.

"I was summoned to Wuthering Heights, within a <u>fortnight</u> of your leaving us," she said, "and I obeyed joyfully, for Catherine's sake. My first interview with her grieved and shocked me: she had altered so much since our separation. Mr. Heathcliff did not explain his reasons for taking a new mind about my coming here; he only told me he wanted me, and he was tired of seeing Catherine: I must make the little parlour my sitting-room, and keep her with me. It was enough if he were **obliged** to see her once or twice a day. She seemed pleased at this arrange-

OBLIGE (uh bliej) *v.* **-ing,-ed.**
to be obligated, to require or force someone to obey
Synonyms: compel, constrain, bind, favor

SULLEN (suh luhn) *adj.*
brooding, gloomy
Synonyms: morose, sulky, somber, glum

ment; and, by degrees, I smuggled over a great number of books, and other articles, that had formed her amusement at the Grange; and flattered myself we should get on in tolerable comfort. The delusion did not last long. Catherine, contented at first, in a brief space grew irritable and restless. For one thing, she was forbidden to move out of the garden, and it fretted her sadly to be confined to its narrow bounds as spring drew on; for another, in following the house, I was forced to quit her frequently, and she complained of loneliness: she preferred quarrelling with Joseph in the kitchen to sitting at peace in her solitude. I did not mind their skirmishes: but Hareton was often **obliged** to seek the kitchen also, when the master wanted to have the house to himself; and though in the beginning she either left it at his approach, or quietly joined in my occupations, and shunned remarking or addressing him—and though he was always as **sullen** and silent as possible—after a while she changed her behaviour, and became incapable of letting him alone: talking at him; commenting on his stupidity and idleness; expressing her wonder how he could endure the life he lived—how he could sit a whole evening staring into the fire and dozing.

"He's just like a dog, is he not, Ellen?" she once observed. "Or a cart-horse? He does his work, eats his food and sleeps eternally! What a blank, dreary mind he must have! Do you ever dream, Hareton? And, if you do, what is it about? But you can't speak to me!"

Then she looked at him; but he would neither open his mouth nor look again.

"He's, perhaps, dreaming now," she continued. "He twitched his shoulder as Juno twitches hers. Ask him, Ellen."

"Mr. Hareton will ask the master to send you upstairs, if you don't behave!" I said. He had not only twitched his shoulder but clenched his fist, as if tempted to use it.

"I know why Hareton never speaks, when I am in the kitchen," she exclaimed, on another occasion. "He is

PERUSE (puh <u>roos</u>) *v.* **-ing,-ed.**
   to examine closely
      Synonyms: scrutinize, inspect, study; browse

PERSEVERE (pehr suh <u>veer</u>) *v.* **-ing,-ed.**
   to continue with determination, remain steadfast
      Synonyms: persist, endure, plod

INDOLENCE (<u>ihn</u> duh luhnts) *n.*
   habitual laziness, idleness
      Synonyms: slothfulness, languor, lethargy,
      sluggishness

REPROVE (rih <u>proov</u>) *v.* **-ing,-ed.**
   to criticize or correct
      Synonyms: rebuke, admonish, reprimand, chide,
      reproach

INGENUITY (ihn jeh <u>noo</u> ih tee) *n.*
   cleverness
      Synonyms: inventiveness, imagination, creativity

OBSTINATE (<u>ahb</u> stih nuht) *adj.*
   stubborn
      Synonyms: headstrong, stiff-necked, bullheaded,
      pigheaded, mulish

DISINCLINED (dihs ihn <u>kliend</u>) *adj.*
   opposed, unwilling
      Synonyms: reluctant, afraid, uneager

BANISH (<u>baan</u> ish) *v.* **-ing,-ed.**
   to force to leave, exile
      Synonyms: expel, deport

afraid I shall laugh at him. Ellen, what do you think? He began to teach himself to read once; and because I laughed, he burned his books, and dropped it: was he not a fool?"

"Were not you naughty?" I said. "Answer me that."

"Perhaps I was," she went on, "but I did not expect him to be so silly. Hareton, if I gave you a book, would you take it now? I'll try!"

She placed one she had been **perusing** on his hand; he flung it off, and muttered, if she did not give over, he would break her neck.

"Well, I shall put it here," she said, "in the table drawer, and I'm going to bed."

Then she whispered me to watch whether he touched it, and departed. But he would not come near it; and so I informed her in the morning, to her great disappointment. I saw she was sorry for his **persevering** sulkiness and **indolence**: her conscience **reproved** her for frightening him off improving himself: she had done it effectually. But her **ingenuity** was at work to remedy the injury: while I ironed, or pursued other such stationary employments as I could not well do in the parlour, she would bring some pleasant volume and read it aloud to me. When Hareton was there, she generally paused in an interesting part, and left the book lying about: that she did repeatedly, but he was as **obstinate** as a mule, and, instead of snatching at her bait, in wet weather he took to smoking with Joseph; and they sat like <u>automatons</u>, one on each side of the fire, the elder happily too deaf to understand her wicked nonsense, as he would have called it, the younger doing his best to seem to disregard it. On fine evenings the latter followed his shooting expeditions, and Catherine yawned and sighed, and teased me to talk to her, and ran off into the court or garden, the moment I began; and, as a last resource, cried, and said she was tired of living: her life was useless.

Mr. Heathcliff, who grew more and more **disinclined** to society, had almost **banished** Earnshaw from his

COMPEL (kuhm <u>pehl</u>) *v.* **-ling,-led.**
  to urge or force
    Synonyms: coerce, oblige, constrain

MOROSE (muh <u>rohs</u>) (maw <u>rohs</u>) *adj.*
  gloomy, sullen, surly
    Synonyms: glum, dour, saturnine

BEGUILE (buh <u>giel</u>) *v.* **-ing,-ed.**
  to pass time; to charm; to deceive, mislead
    Synonyms: amuse, occupy; enchant, inveigle; lure,
    coax, cozen

EJACULATION (ih <u>jaak</u> yuh lay shuhn) *n.*
  a sudden exclamation
    Synonyms: chatter, vociferation, expletive

STEADFASTLY (<u>stehd</u> faast lee) *adv.*
  continuously; loyally
    Synonyms: constantly; faithfully, staunchly

BESTOW (bih <u>stoh</u>) *v.* **-ing,-ed.**
  to apply or devote, as in time or effort; to give as a gift
    Synonyms: allocate, dedicate; endow, confer, present

UNCOMPROMISING (uhn <u>kahm</u> pruh miez ihng) *adj.*
  unwilling to concede or to take the middle ground
    Synonyms: stubborn, inflexible, unyielding

apartment. Owing to an accident at the commencement of March, he became for some days a fixture in the kitchen. His gun burst while out on the hills by himself; a splinter cut his arm, and he lost a good deal of blood before he could reach home. The consequence was that, perforce, he was condemned to the fireside and tranquillity, till he made it up again. It suited Catherine to have him there: at any rate, it made her hate her room upstairs more than ever: and she would **compel** me to find out business below, that she might accompany me.

On Easter Monday, Joseph went to Gimmerton fair with some cattle; and, in the afternoon, I was busy getting up linen in the kitchen. Earnshaw sat, **morose** as usual, at the chimney-corner, and my little mistress was **beguiling** an idle hour with drawing pictures on the window panes; varying her amusement by smothered bursts of songs and whispered **ejaculations**, and quick glances of annoyance and impatience in the direction of her cousin, who **steadfastly** smoked, and looked into the grate. At a notice that I could do with her no longer intercepting my light, she removed to the hearthstone. I **bestowed** little attention on her proceedings, but, presently, I heard her begin:

"I've found out, Hareton, that I want—that I'm glad—that I should like you to be my cousin now, if you had not grown so cross to me, and so rough."

Hareton returned no answer.

"Hareton, Hareton, Hareton! Do you hear?" she continued.

"Get off wi' ye!" he growled, with **uncompromising** gruffness.

"Let me take that pipe," she said, cautiously advancing her hand and abstracting it from his mouth.

Before he could attempt to recover it, it was broken, and behind the fire. He swore at her and seized another.

"Stop," she cried, "you must listen to me first; and I can't speak while those clouds are floating in my face."

"Will you go to the devil!" he exclaimed ferociously. "And let me be!"

REPENT (rih pehnt) *v.* **-ing,-ed.**
to regret a past action
Synonyms: rue, atone, apologize

RESOLUTELY (reh suh loot lee) *adv.*
with determination; with a clear purpose
Synonyms: firmly, unwaveringly; intently

DIVINE (dih vien) *v.* **-ing,-ed.**
to foretell or know by inspiration
Synonyms: predict, intuit, auger, foresee, presage

OBDURATE (ahb duhr uht) *adj.*
stubborn
Synonyms: inflexible, inexorable, adamant,
impenitent, intractable

PERVERSITY (puhr vuhr sih tee) *n.*
deliberate misbehavior
Synonyms: disobedience, defiance, opposition

"No," she persisted, "I won't: I can't tell what to do to make you talk to me; and you are determined not to understand. When I call you stupid, I don't mean anything: I don't mean that I despise you. Come, you shall take notice of me, Hareton! You are my cousin, and you shall own me."

"I shall have <u>naught</u> to do wi' you and your mucky pride, and your damned mocking tricks!" he answered. "I'll go to hell, body and soul, before I look sideways after you again. Side out o' t' gate, now; this minute!"

Catherine frowned, and retreated to the window-seat chewing her lip, and endeavouring, by humming an eccentric tune, to conceal a growing tendency to sob.

"You should be friends with your cousin, Mr. Hareton," I interrupted, "since she **repents** of her sauciness. It would do you a great deal of good: it would make you another man to have her for a companion."

"A companion!" he cried. "When she hates me, and does not think me fit to wipe her shoon! Nay! If it made me a king, I'd not be scorned for seeking her good-will any more."

"It is not I who hate you, it is you who hate me!" wept Cathy, no longer disguising her trouble. "You hate me as much as Mr. Heathcliff does, and more."

"You're a damned liar," began Earnshaw. "Why have I made him angry, by taking your part, then, a hundred times? And that when you sneered at and despised me, and— Go on plaguing me, and I'll step in yonder, and say you worried me out of the kitchen!"

"I didn't know you took my part," she answered, drying her eyes, "and I was miserable and bitter at everybody; but now I thank you, and beg you to forgive me: what can I do besides?"

She returned to the hearth, and frankly extended her hand. He blackened and scowled like a thunder-cloud, and kept his fists **resolutely** clenched, and his gaze fixed on the ground. Catherine, by instinct, must have **divined** it was **obdurate perversity**, and not dislike, that prompted

DOGGED (<u>daw</u> guhd) *adj.*
  stubbornly persevering
    Synonyms: tenacious, obstinate, pertinacious,
    determined, mulish
DRAW *v.* **drawing, drew, drawn**
  to pull, drag; to lead, to bring about on purpose;
  to attract
    Synonyms: haul, tow, yank; provoke, elicit; lure, entice
DEMURELY (dih <u>myoor</u> lee) *adv.*
  modestly, sometimes also flirtatiously; in a reserved
  manner
    Synonyms: shyly, bashfully, coyly; seriously,
    reticently
REPROVINGLY (rih <u>proov</u> ihng lee) *adv.*
  disapprovingly
    Synonyms: accusingly, reproachfully

SURLY (<u>suhr</u> lee) *adj.*
  rude and bad-tempered
    Synonyms: gruff, testy, grumpy
INAUDIBLE (ihn <u>aw</u> dih buhl) *adj.*
  not capable of being heard
    Synonyms: faint, muffled, unclear, imperceptible
INTERROGATIVELY (ihn tuhr <u>ahg</u> uh tihv lee) *adv.*
  in the manner or form of a question, inquisitively
    Synonyms: curiously, doubtfully, quizzically

this **dogged** conduct; for, after remaining an instant unde-
cided, she stooped and impressed on his cheek a gentle
kiss. The little <u>rogue</u> thought I had not seen her, and
drawing back, she took her former station by the window,
quite **demurely**. I shook my head **reprovingly**, and then she
blushed and whispered:

"Well! What should I have done, Ellen? He wouldn't
shake hands, and he wouldn't look: I must show him
some way that I like him—that I want to be friends."

Whether the kiss convinced Hareton, I cannot tell: he
was very careful, for some minutes, that his face should
not be seen, and when he did raise it, he was sadly puzzled
where to turn his eyes.

Catherine employed herself in wrapping a handsome
book neatly in white paper, and having tied it with a bit of
ribbon, and addressed it to "Mr. Hareton Earnshaw," she
desired me to be her ambassadress, and convey the present to its destined recipient.

"And tell him, if he'll take it I'll come and teach him to
read it right," she said. "And, if he refuse it, I'll go
upstairs, and never tease him again."

I carried it, and repeated the message; anxiously
watched by my employer. Hareton would not open his
fingers, so I laid it on his knee. He did not strike it off,
either. I returned to my work. Catherine leaned her
head and arms on the table, till she heard the slight rustle of the covering being removed; then she stole away,
and quietly seated herself beside her cousin. He trembled, and his face glowed: all his rudeness and all his
surly harshness had deserted him: he could not summon
courage, at first, to utter a syllable in reply to her questioning look, and her murmured petition.

"Say you forgive me, Hareton, do? You can make
me so happy by speaking that little word."

He muttered something **inaudible**.

"And you'll be my friend?" added Catherine
interrogatively.

COUNTENANCE (<u>kown</u> tuh nuhns) *n.*
  appearance, facial expression
    Synonyms: face, features, visage
RATIFY (<u>raa</u> tih fie) *v.* **-ing,-ed.**
  to approve formally, confirm
    Synonyms: endorse, sanction, certify, accredit
CONFOUND (kuhn <u>fownd</u>) *v.* **-ing,-ed.**
  1. to baffle, perplex; to mistake something for another
    Synonyms: overwhelm, disconcert, entangle,
    muddle; confuse, misidentify
  2. to damn or condemn
    Synonyms: doom, jinx, revile, punish
SOLEMNLY (<u>sah</u> luhm lee) *adv.*
  seriously or somberly
    Synonyms: quietly, earnestly, ceremonially

"Nay, you'll be ashamed of me every day of your life," he answered, "and the more ashamed, the more you know me; and I cannot bide it."

"So you won't be my friend?" she said, smiling as sweet as honey, and creeping close up.

I overheard no further distinguishable talk, but, on looking round again, I perceived two such radiant **countenances** bent over the page of the accepted book, that I did not doubt the treaty had been **ratified** on both sides; and the enemies were, thenceforth, sworn allies.

The work they studied was full of costly pictures; and those and their position had charm enough to keep them unmoved till Joseph came home. He, poor man, was perfectly aghast at the spectacle of Catherine seated on the same bench with Hareton Earnshaw, leaning her hand on his shoulder, and **confounded** at his favourite's endurance of her proximity: it affected him too deeply to allow an observation on the subject that night. His emotion was only revealed by the immense sighs he drew, as he **solemnly** spread his large Bible on the table, and overlaid it with dirty bank-notes from his pocket-book, the produce of the day's transactions. At length, he summoned Hareton from his seat.

"Tak' these in to t' maister, lad," he said, "and bide there. I's gang up to my own rahm. This hoile's neither mensful nor seemly for us: we mun side out and seearch another."

"Come, Catherine," I said, "we must 'side out' too; I've done my ironing, are you ready to go?"

"It is not eight o'clock!" she answered, rising unwillingly. "Hareton, I'll leave this book upon the chimney-piece, and I'll bring some more to-morrow."

"Ony books that yah leave, I shall tak' into the hahse," said Joseph, "and it'll be mitch if yah find em agean; soa, yah may please yerseln!"

Cathy threatened that his library should pay for hers; and, smiling as she passed Hareton, went singing upstairs: lighter of heart, I venture to say, than ever she

625

CIVILISE or CIVILIZE (<u>sih</u> vuhl iez) *v.* **-ing,-ed.**
to educate in cultural matters and manners, to polish
Synonyms: refine, cultivate, humanize
PARAGON (<u>paar</u> uh gon) *n.*
model of excellence or perfection
Synonyms: ideal, nonpareil, paradigm, example
CONTRIVE (kuhn <u>triev</u>) *v.* **-ing,-ed.**
to devise, plan, or manage; to form in an artistic manner
Synonyms: concoct, scheme; create, design

IMPRACTICABLE (ihm <u>praak</u> tih kuh buhl) *adj.*
incapable of being performed by the means employed;
impassable
Synonyms: insane, imprudent, absurd, impossible;
blocked
RETAIN (rih <u>tayn</u>) *v.* **-ing,-ed.**
to hold, keep possession of
Synonyms: withhold, reserve, maintain, remember

had been under that roof before; except, perhaps, during her earliest visits to Linton.

The intimacy thus commenced grew rapidly; though it encountered temporary interruptions. Earnshaw was not to be **civilised** with a wish, and my young lady was no philosopher, and no **paragon** of patience; but both their minds tending to the same point—one loving and desiring to esteem, and the other loving and desiring to be esteemed—they **contrived** in the end to reach it.

You see, Mr. Lockwood, it was easy enough to win Mrs. Heathcliff's heart. But now, I'm glad you did not try. The crown of all my wishes will be the union of those two. I shall envy no one on their wedding-day: there won't be a happier woman than myself in England!

Chapter 33

On the morrow of that Monday, Earnshaw being still unable to follow his ordinary employments, and therefore remaining about the house, I speedily found it would be **impracticable** to **retain** my charge beside me, as heretofore. She got downstairs before me, and out into the garden, where she had seen her cousin performing some easy work; and when I went to bid them come to breakfast, I saw she had persuaded him to clear a large space of ground from currant and gooseberry bushes, and they were busy planning together an importation of plants from the Grange.

I was terrified at the devastation which had been accomplished in a brief half-hour; the black currant trees were the apple of Joseph's eye, and she had just fixed her choice of a flower-bed in the midst of them.

"There! That will be all shown to the master," I exclaimed, "the minute it is discovered. And what excuse have you to offer for taking such liberties with the garden? We shall have a fine explosion on the head of it: see

DISCRETION (dih skrehsh uhn) *n.*
good judgment, judiciousness
Synonyms: thoughtfulness, caution, good sense

PROVOKE (proh vohk) *v.* **-ing,-ed.**
to cause a response, e.g., anger or disagreement
Synonyms: aggravate, stimulate, vex, incite
COUNTENANCE (kown tuh nuhns) *n.*
appearance, facial expression
Synonyms: face, features, visage
EVINCE (ih vihns) *v.* **-ing,-ed.**
to show clearly or display
Synonyms: express, exhibit, demonstrate, manifest
SCRUTINISE or SCRUTINIZE (skroot ihn iez) *v.* **-ing,-ed.**
to observe carefully
Synonyms: examine, study, survey
ABHOR (uhb hohr) *v.* **-ring,-red.**
to loathe, detest, despise
Synonyms: hate, condemn, abominate, execrate
INFERNAL (ihn fuhr nuhl) *adj.*
devilish; relating to the dead or hell
Synonyms: fiendish, awful, malicious; damned, accursed

if we don't! Mr. Hareton, I wonder you should have no more wit, than to go and make that mess at her bidding!"

"I'd forgotten they were Joseph's," answered Earnshaw, rather puzzled, "but I'll tell him I did it."

We always ate our meals with Mr. Heathcliff. I held the mistress's post in making tea and carving; so I was indispensable at table. Catherine usually sat by me, but to-day she stole nearer to Hareton; and I presently saw she would have no more **discretion** in her friendship than she had in her hostility.

"Now, mind you don't talk with and notice your cousin too much," were my whispered instructions as we entered the room. "It will certainly annoy Mr. Heathcliff, and he'll be mad at you both."

"I'm not going to," she answered.

The minute after, she had <u>sidled</u> to him, and was sticking primroses in his plate of porridge.

He dared not speak to her there: he dared hardly look; and yet she went on teasing till he was twice on the point of being **provoked** to laugh. I frowned, and then she glanced toward the master whose mind was occupied on other subjects than his company, as his **countenance evinced**; and she grew serious for an instant, **scrutinising** him with deep gravity. Afterward she turned, and recommenced her nonsense; at last, Hareton uttered a smothered laugh. Mr. Heathcliff started, his eye rapidly surveyed our faces. Catherine met it with her accustomed look of nervousness and yet defiance, which he **abhorred**.

"It is well you are out of my reach," he exclaimed. "What fiend possesses you to stare back at me, continually, with those **infernal** eyes? Down with them! And don't remind me of your existence again. I thought I had cured you of laughing."

"It was me," muttered Hareton.

"What do you say?" demanded the master.

Hareton looked at his plate, and did not repeat the confession. Mr. Heathcliff looked at him a bit, and then silently resumed his breakfast and his interrupted musing.

PRUDENTLY (<u>proo</u> dehnt lee) *adv.*
    carefully, cautiously
        Synonyms: pragmatically, judiciously, sensibly

LAMENT (luh <u>mehnt</u>) *v.* **-ing,-ed.**
    to deplore, grieve
        Synonyms: mourn, sorrow, regret, bewail

We had nearly finished, and the two young people **prudently** shifted wider asunder, so I anticipated no further disturbance during that sitting: when Joseph appeared at the door, revealing by his quivering lip and furious eyes, that the outrage committed on his precious shrubs was detected. He must have seen Cathy and her cousin about the spot before he examined it, for while his jaws worked like those of a cow chewing its cud, and rendered his speech difficult to understand, he began:

"I mun hev my wage, and I mun goa! I *hed* aimed to dee, wheare I'd sarved fur sixty year, and I thowt I'd lug my books up into t' garret, and all my bits o' stuff, and they sud hev t' kitchen to theirseln; for t' sake o' quietness. It were hard to gie up my awn hearthstun, but I thowt I *could* do that! But, nah, shoo's taan my garden fro' me, and by th' heart, maister, I cannot stand it! Yah may bend to th' yoak, and ye will—I noan used to 't, and an old man doesn't sooin get used to new barthens. I rayther arn my bit and my sup wi' a hammer in th' road!"

"Now, now, idiot!" interrupted Heathcliff. "Cut it short! What's your grievance? I'll interfere in no quarrels between you and Nelly. She may thrust you into the coal-hole for anything I care."

"It's noan Nelly!" answered Joseph. "I sudn't shift for Nelly—nasty ill nowt as shoo is. Thank God! *Shoo* cannot stale t' sowl o' nob'dy! Shoo were niver soa handsome, but what a body mud look at her 'bout winking. It's yon flaysome, graceless quean, that's witched our lad, wi' her bold een and her forrard ways—till—Nay! It fair bursts my heart! He's forgotten all I've done for him, and made on him, and goan and riven up a whole row o' t' grandest currant trees, i' t' garden!" And here he **lamented** outright; unmanned by a sense of his bitter injuries, and Earnshaw's ingratitude and dangerous condition.

"Is the old fool drunk?" asked Mr. Heathcliff. "Hareton, is it you he's finding fault with?"

"I've pulled up two or three bushes," replied the young man, "but I'm going to set 'em again."

INSOLENT (<u>ihn</u> suh luhnt) *adj.*
  insulting, arrogant
    Synonyms: audacious, rude, presumptuous,
    impertinent

CONFOUNDED (kuhn <u>fown</u> dihd) *adj.*
  baffled, perplexed
    Synonyms: overwhelmed, confused, disconcerted,
    entangled, muddled

EXECUTE (<u>ehk</u> sih kyoot) *v.* **-ing,-ed.**
  to carry out fully; to make or produce
    Synonyms: accomplish, achieve; perform, effectuate
DETEST (dee <u>tehst</u>) (dih <u>tehst</u>) *v.* **-ing,-ed.**
  to feel intense and violent hatred toward
    Synonyms: dislike, loathe
REPROACHFULLY (rih <u>prohch</u> fuh lee) *adv.*
  disapprovingly or critically; disparagingly
        Synonyms: shamefully; severely

"And why have you pulled them up?" said the master.
Catherine wisely put in her tongue.

"We wanted to plant some flowers there," she cried.
"I'm the only person to blame, for I wished him to do it."

"And who the devil gave *you* leave to touch a stick
about the place?" demanded her father-in-law, much surprised. "And who ordered *you* to obey her?" he added,
turning to Hareton.

The latter was speechless; his cousin replied:

"You shouldn't grudge a few yards of earth for me to
ornament, when you have taken all my land!"

"Your land, **insolent** slut! You never had any," said
Heathcliff.

"And my money," she continued; returning his angry
glare, and meantime biting a piece of crust, the remnant
of her breakfast.

"Silence!" he exclaimed. "Get done, and begone!"

"And Hareton's land, and his money," pursued the
reckless thing. "Hareton and I are friends now; and I
shall tell him all about you!"

The master seemed **confounded** a moment: he grew
pale, and rose up, eyeing her all the while, with an expression of mortal hate.

"If you strike me, Hareton will strike you," she said,
"so you may as well sit down."

"If Hareton does not turn you out of the room, I'll
strike him to hell," thundered Heathcliff. "Damnable
witch! Dare you pretend to rouse him against me? Off
with her! Do you hear? Fling her into the kitchen! I'll kill
her, Ellen Dean, if you let her come into my sight again!"

Hareton tried, under his breath, to persuade her to go.

"Drag her away!" he cried savagely. "Are you staying to
talk?" And he approached to **execute** his own command.

"He'll not obey you, wicked man, any more," said
Catherine, "and he'll soon **detest** you as much as I do."

"Wisht! Wisht!" muttered the young man **reproachfully**.
"I will not hear you speak so to him. Have done."

"But you won't let him strike me?" she cried.

PROVOKE (proh <u>vohk</u>) *v.* **-ing,-ed.**
    to cause a response, e.g., anger or disagreement
        Synonyms: aggravate, stimulate, vex, incite
REPENT (rih <u>pehnt</u>) *v.* **-ing,-ed.**
    to regret a past action
        Synonyms: rue, atone, apologize
ENTREAT (ehn <u>treet</u>) *v.* **-ing,-ed.**
    to plead, beg
        Synonyms: beseech, implore, importune, request

INSOLENCE (<u>ihn</u> suh luhnts) *n.*
    a tendency to be insulting; arrogance
        Synonyms: audacity, rudeness, presumption,
        impertinence; superiority, haughtiness

INTIMATE (<u>ihn</u> tuh mayt) *v.* **-ing,-ed.**
    to hint or suggest obscurely
        Synonyms: implicate, allude, insinuate

DISPARAGEMENT (dih <u>spaar</u> ihj mihnt) *n.*
    belittlement, verbal disrespect
        Synonyms: denigration, derogation, ridicule,
        derision
WAX (waaks) *v.* **-ing,-ed.**
    to begin to be; to increase gradually
        Synonyms: become, grow; enlarge, expand, swell

"Come, then," he whispered earnestly.

It was too late: Heathcliff had caught hold of her.

"Now *you* go!" he said to Earnshaw. "Accursed witch! This time she has **provoked** me when I could not bear it; and I'll make her **repent** it for ever!"

He had his hand in her hair; Hareton attempted to release her locks, **entreating** him not to hurt her that once. Heathcliff's black eyes flashed; he seemed ready to tear Catherine in pieces, and I was just worked up to risk coming to the rescue, when of a sudden his fingers relaxed; he shifted his grasp from her head to her arm, and gazed intently in her face. Then he drew his hand over her eyes, stood a moment to collect himself apparently, and turning anew to Catherine, said, with assumed calmness: "You must learn to avoid putting me in a passion, or I shall really murder you some time! Go with Mrs. Dean, and keep with her; and confine your **insolence** to her ears. As to Hareton Earnshaw, if I see him listen to you, I'll send him seeking his bread where he can get it! Your love will make him an outcast and a beggar. Nelly, take her; and leave me, all of you! Leave me!"

I led my young lady out: she was too glad of her escape to resist; the other followed, and Mr. Heathcliff had the room to himself till dinner. I had counselled Catherine to dine upstairs; but, as soon as he perceived her vacant seat, he sent me to call her. He spoke to none of us, ate very little, and went out directly afterwards, **intimating** that he would not return before evening.

The two new friends established themselves in the house during his absence; when I heard Hareton sternly check his cousin, on her offering a revelation of her father-in-law's conduct to his father. He said he wouldn't suffer a word to be uttered in his **disparagement**: if he were the devil, it didn't signify: he would stand by him; and he'd rather she would abuse himself, as she used to, than to begin on Mr. Heathcliff. Catherine was **waxing** cross at this; but he found means to make her hold her tongue, by asking how she would like *him* to speak ill of

ANTIPATHY (aan <u>tih</u> puh thee) *n.*
  dislike, hostility; extreme opposition or aversion
    Synonyms: antagonism; enmity, malice

DEGRADATION (day greh <u>day</u> shuhn) *n.*
  the act of losing moral or intellectual character; the
  act of falling in rank or status
    Synonyms: abasement, disgrace, shame; demotion
COMMENDATION (kah mehn <u>day</u> shuhn) *n.*
  an act of praise or a show of respect; an award; the
  act of entrusting into someone's care
    Synonyms: acclaim, approval, flattery; tribute,
    reward; relegation, assignment

ANIMATE (<u>aa</u> nih mayt) *v.* **-ing,-ed.**
  to make lively and excited, to fill with spirit
    Synonyms: elate, inspire, stimulate
NOVELTY (<u>nah</u> vuhl tee) *n.*
  something new and original
    Synonyms: surprise, change, innovation

her father? Then she comprehended that Earnshaw took the master's reputation home to himself; and was attached by ties stronger than reason could break—chains, forged by habit, which it would be cruel to attempt to loosen. She showed a good heart, thenceforth, in avoiding both complaints and expressions of **antipathy** concerning Heathcliff; and confessed to me her sorrow that she had endeavoured to raise a bad spirit between him and Hareton: indeed, I don't believe she has ever breathed a syllable, in the latter's hearing, against her oppressor since.

When this slight disagreement was over, they were friends again, and as busy as possible in their several occupations of pupil and teacher. I came in to sit with them, after I had done my work; and I felt so soothed and comforted to watch them, that I did not notice how time got on. You know, they both appeared in a measure my children: I had long been proud of one; and now, I was sure, the other would be a source of equal satisfaction. His honest, warm, and intelligent nature shook off rapidly the clouds of ignorance and **degradation** in which it had been bred; and Catherine's sincere **commendations** acted as a spur to his industry. His brightening mind brightened his features, and added spirit and nobility to their aspect: I could hardly fancy it the same individual I had beheld on the day I discovered my little lady at Wuthering Heights, after her expedition to the Crags. While I admired and they laboured, dusk grew on, and with it returned the master. He came upon us quite unexpectedly, entering by the front way, and had a full view of the whole three, ere we could raise our heads to glance at him. Well, I reflected, there was never a pleasanter, or more harmless sight; and it will be a burning shame to scold them. The red firelight glowed on their two <u>bonny</u> heads, and revealed their faces **animated** with the eager interest of children; for, though he was twenty-three and she eighteen, each had so much of **novelty** to feel and

EVINCE (ih <u>vihns</u>) *v.* **-ing,-ed.**
to show clearly or display
Synonyms: express, exhibit, demonstrate, manifest

SENTIMENT (<u>sehn</u> tuh muhnt) *n.*
an attitude, thought, or judgement prompted by
feeling; a romantic or nostalgic feeling
Synonyms: idea; emotion

SOBER (<u>soh</u> buhr) *adj.*
self-controlled; serious; not intoxicated
Synonyms: subdued, sedate; grave; dry, not drunk

HAUGHTY (<u>haw</u> tee) (<u>hah</u> tee) *adj.*
arrogant and condescending
Synonyms: proud, disdainful, supercilious, scornful,
vainglorious

FACULTY (<u>faa</u> kuhl tee) *n.*
the ability to act or do
Synonyms: aptitude, capability, sense, skill

AGITATION (aa gih <u>tay</u> shuhn) *n.*
uneasiness; commotion, excitement
Synonyms: restlessness, anxiety; disturbance

BROOD *v.* **-ing,-ed.**
to think about in a gloomy or serious way
Synonyms: ponder, worry, obsess

HINDER (<u>hihn</u> duhr) *v.* **-ing,-ed.**
to prevent action; to delay or impede
Synonyms: restrain; hamper, inhibit, obstruct

MAGNANIMITY (maag naan <u>ihm</u> ih tee) *n.*
generosity, nobility of spirit
Synonyms: unselfishness, altruism, goodness

learn, that neither experienced nor **evinced** the **sentiments** of **sober** disenchanted maturity.

They lifted their eyes together, to encounter Mr. Heathcliff: perhaps you have never remarked that their eyes are precisely similar, and they are those of Catherine Earnshaw. The present Catherine has no other likeness to her, except a breadth of forehead, and a certain arch of the nostril that makes her appear rather **haughty**, whether she will or not. With Hareton the resemblance is carried farther: it is singular at all times, *then* it was particularly striking; because his senses were alert, and his mental **faculties** wakened to <u>unwonted</u> activity. I suppose this resemblance disarmed Mr. Heathcliff: he walked to the hearth in evident **agitation**; but it quickly subsided as he looked at the young man: or, I should say, altered its character, for it was there yet. He took the book from his hand, and glanced at the open page, then returned it without any observation; merely signing Catherine away: her companion lingered very little behind her, and I was about to depart also, but he bid me sit still.

"It is a poor conclusion, is it not," he observed, having **brooded** a while on the scene he had just witnessed, "an absurd termination to my violent exertions? I get levers and <u>mattocks</u> to demolish the two houses, and train myself to be capable of working like Hercules, and when everything is ready and in my power, I find the will to lift a slate off either roof has vanished! My old enemies have not beaten me; now would be the precise time to revenge myself on their representatives: I could do it; and none could **hinder** me. But where is the use? I don't care for striking; I can't take the trouble to raise my hand! That sounds as if I had been labouring the whole time only to exhibit a fine trait of **magnanimity**. It is far from being the case: I have lost the **faculty** of enjoying their destruction, and I am too idle to destroy for nothing.

"Nelly, there is a strange change approaching: I'm in its shadow at present. I take so little interest in my daily life, that I hardly remember to eat and drink. Those two

RETAIN (rih <u>tayn</u>) *v.* **-ing,-ed.**
    to hold, keep possession of
        Synonyms: withhold, reserve, maintain, remember
INVOKE (ihn <u>vohk</u>) *v.* **-ing,-ed.**
    to call upon, request help
        Synonyms: summon, solicit, conjure, evoke
INCLINE (ihn <u>klien</u>) *v.* **-ing,-ed.**
    to have a specific tendency, to be predisposed
        Synonyms: lean to, influence, impel, prefer

SECLUDED (sih <u>cloo</u> dihd) *adj.*
    isolated and remote
        Synonyms: solitary, sequestered, out-of-the-way

ACCOST (uh <u>cahst</u>) (uh <u>kawst</u>) *v.* **-ing,-ed.**
    to approach and speak to someone, often in an
    aggressive way
        Synonyms: stop, address, detain, buttonhole

DEGRADATION (day greh <u>day</u> shuhn) *n.*
    the act of losing moral or intellectual character; the
    act of falling in rank or status
        Synonyms: abasement, disgrace, shame; demotion

who have left the room are the only objects which **retain** a distinct material appearance to me; and that appearance causes me pain, amounting to agony. About *her* I won't speak; and I don't desire to think; but I earnestly wish she were invisible: her presence **invokes** only maddening sensations. *He* moves me differently: and yet if I could do it without seeming insane, I'd never see him again. You'll perhaps think me rather **inclined** to become so," he added, making an effort to smile, "if I try to describe the thousand forms of past associations and ideas he awakens or embodies. But you'll not talk of what I tell you; and my mind is so eternally **secluded** in itself, it is tempting at last to turn it out to another.

"Five minutes ago, Hareton seemed a <u>personification</u> of my youth, not a human being: I felt to him in such a variety of ways, that it would have been impossible to have **accosted** him rationally. In the first place, his startling likeness to Catherine connected him fearfully with her. That, however, which you may suppose the most potent to arrest my imagination, is actually the least: for what is not connected with her to me? And what does not recall her? I cannot look down to this floor, but her features are shaped in the flags! Every cloud, in every tree—filling the air at night, and caught by glimpses in every object by day—I am surrounded with her image! The most ordinary faces of men and women—my own features—mock me with a resemblance. The entire world is a dreadful collection of memoranda that she did exist, and that I have lost her! Well, Hareton's aspect was the ghost of my immortal love; of my wild endeavours to hold my right; my **degradation**, my pride, my happiness, and my anguish.

"But it is a frenzy to repeat these thoughts to you: only it will let you know why, with a reluctance to be always alone, his society is no benefit; rather an aggravation of the constant torment I suffer; and it partly contributes to render me regardless how he and his cousin go on together. I can give them no attention, any more."

PRESENTIMENT (prih <u>sehn</u> tih mehnt) *n.*
the anticipation or sense that something may happen
Synonyms: expectation, premonition

CONSTITUTION (kahn stih <u>too</u> shuhn) *n.*
the physical structure or health of something or
someone; the sum of components, composition
Synonyms: disposition, nature, stature; formation,
design, architecture, make-up

TEMPERATE (<u>tehm</u> puhr iht) *adj.*
restrained, moderate, not excessive
Synonyms: conservative, self-controlled, even

UNPERILOUS (uhn <u>pehr</u> uh luhs) *adj.*
safe from danger
Synonyms: harmless, unthreatening, careful

COMPULSION (kuhm <u>puhl</u> shuhn) *n.*
an irresistible urge, an impulsive act
Synonyms: drive, obsession, necessity, preoccupation

FACULTY (<u>faa</u> kuhl tee) *n.*
the ability to act or do
Synonyms: aptitude, capability, sense, skill

INCLINE (ihn <u>klien</u>) *v.* **-ing,-ed.**
to have a specific tendency, to be predisposed
Synonyms: lean to, influence, impel, prefer

"But what do you mean by a *change*, Mr. Heathcliff?" I said, alarmed at his manner though he was neither in danger of losing his senses, nor dying, according to my judgment: he was quite strong and healthy: and, as to his reason, from childhood he had a delight in dwelling on dark things, and entertaining odd fancies. He might have had a <u>monomania</u> on the subject of his departed idol; but on every other point his wits were as sound as mine.

"I shall not know that till it comes," he said, "I'm only half conscious of it now."

"You have no feelings of illness, have you?" I asked.

"No, Nelly, I have not," he answered.

"Then you are not afraid of death?" I pursued.

"Afraid? No!" he replied. "I have neither a fear, nor a **presentiment**, nor a hope of death. Why should I? With my hard **constitution** and **temperate** mode of living, and **unperilous** occupations, I ought to, and probably *shall*, remain above ground till there is scarcely a black hair on my head. And yet, I cannot continue in this condition! I have to remind myself to breathe—almost to remind my heart to beat! And it is like bending back a stiff spring: it is by **compulsion** that I do the slightest act not prompted by one thought; and by **compulsion** that I notice anything alive or dead, which is not associated with one universal idea. I have a single wish, and my whole being and **faculties** are yearning to attain it. They have yearned towards it so long, and so unwaveringly, that I'm convinced it *will* be reached—and *soon*—because it has devoured my existence: I am swallowed up in the anticipation of its fulfilment. My confessions have not relieved me; but they may account for some otherwise unaccountable phases of humour which I show. O God! It is a long fight, I wish it were over!"

He began to pace the room, muttering terrible things to himself, till I was **inclined** to believe, as he said Joseph did, that conscience had turned his heart to an earthly hell. I wondered greatly how it would end. Though he seldom before had revealed this state of mind, even by

CONJECTURE (kuhn <u>jehk</u> shuhr) *v.* **-ing,-ed.**
   to infer, predict, guess
      Synonyms: postulate, hypothesize, suppose, surmise
LACONIC (luh <u>kah</u> nihk) *adj.*
   using few words
      Synonyms: terse, concise, pithy, succinct

AVERSION (uh <u>vuhr</u> zhuhn) *n.*
   intense dislike
      Synonyms: antagonism, antipathy, abhorrence,
      repulsion, repugnance
SUSTENANCE (<u>suh</u> steh nehns) *n.*
   means of living, source of nourishment
      Synonyms: food, provisions, necessities

BEGUILE (buh <u>giel</u>) *v.* **-ing,-ed.**
   to charm; to deceive, mislead; to pass time
      Synonyms: enchant, inveigle; lure, coax, cozen;
      amuse, occupy

PROCURE (proh <u>kyoor</u>) *v.* **-ing,-ed.**
   to obtain
      Synonyms: acquire, secure, get, gain
COUNTENANCE (<u>kown</u> tuh nuhns) *n.*
   appearance, facial expression
      Synonyms: face, features, visage

looks, it was his habitual mood, I had no doubt: he asserted it himself; but not a soul, from his general bearing, would have **conjectured** the fact. You did not when you saw him, Mr. Lockwood: and at the period of which I speak he was just the same as then: only fonder of continued solitude, and perhaps still more **laconic** in company.

Chapter 34

For some days after that evening, Mr. Heathcliff shunned meeting us at meals; yet he would not consent formally to exclude Hareton and Cathy. He had an **aversion** to yielding so completely to his feelings, choosing rather to absent himself; and eating once in twenty-four hours seemed sufficient **sustenance** for him.

One night, after the family were in bed, I heard him go down-stairs, and out at the front door. I did not hear him re-enter, and in the morning I found he was still away. We were in April then: the weather was sweet and warm, the grass as green as showers and sun could make it, and the two dwarf apple-trees near the southern wall in full bloom. After breakfast, Catherine insisted on my bringing a chair and sitting with my work under the fir-trees at the end of the house; and she **beguiled** Hareton, who had perfectly recovered from his accident, to dig and arrange her little garden, which was shifted to that corner by the influence of Joseph's complaints. I was comfortably revelling in the spring fragrance around, and the beautiful soft blue overhead, when my young lady, who had run down near the gate to **procure** some primrose roots for a border, returned only half laden, and informed us that Mr. Heathcliff was coming in. "And he spoke to me," she added with a perplexed **countenance**.

"What did he say?" asked Hareton.

ASCERTAIN (aa suhr <u>tayn</u>) *v.* **-ing,-ed.**
   to determine, discover, make certain of
      Synonyms: verify, calculate, detect

AVERT (uh <u>vuhrt</u>) *v.* **-ing,-ed.**
   to turn away; avoid
      Synonyms: deflect, parry; deter, forestall, preclude
CONTEMPTUOUSLY (kuhn <u>tehmp</u> choo uhs lee) *adv.*
   scornfully
      Synonyms: derisively, disdainfully, superciliously
DIVINE (dih <u>vien</u>) *v.* **-ing,-ed.**
   to foretell or know by inspiration
      Synonyms: predict, intuit, auger, foresee, presage
ADMONITION (aad muh <u>nih</u> shuhn) *n.*
   cautionary words, warning
      Synonyms: reproof, advice

AMENDS (uh <u>mehnds</u>) *n. pl.*
   compensation for a loss or something that caused harm
      Synonyms: reparations, restitutions, apologies

"He told me to begone as fast as I could," she answered. "But he looked so different from his usual look that I stopped a moment to stare at him."

"How?" he inquired.

"Why, almost bright and cheerful. No, *almost* nothing—*very much* excited, and wild and glad!" she replied.

"Night-walking amuses him, then," I remarked, affecting a careless manner. In reality, as surprised as she was and anxious to **ascertain** the truth of her statement—for to see the master looking glad was not to be an everyday spectacle—I framed an excuse to go in. Heathcliff stood at the open door, he was pale, and he trembled: yet, certainly, he had a strange, joyful glitter in his eyes, that altered the aspect of his whole face.

"Will you have some breakfast?" I said. "You must be hungry, rambling about all night!" I wanted to discover where he had been, but I did not like to ask directly.

"No, I'm not hungry," he answered, **averting** his head and speaking rather **contemptuously**, as if he guessed I was trying to **divine** the occasion of his good-humour.

I felt perplexed: I didn't know whether it were not a proper opportunity to offer a bit of **admonition**.

"I don't think it right to wander out of doors," I observed, "instead of being in bed: it is not wise, at any rate, this moist season. I dare say you'll catch a bad cold, or a fever: you have something the matter with you now!"

"Nothing but what I can bear," he replied, "and with the greatest pleasure, provided you'll leave me alone; get in, and don't annoy me."

I obeyed: and, in passing, I noticed he breathed as fast as a cat.

"Yes!" I reflected to myself. "We shall have a fit of illness. I cannot conceive what he has been doing."

That noon he sat down to dinner with us, and received a heaped-up plate from my hands, as if he intended to make **amends** for previous fasting.

ALLUSION (uh loo zhuhn) *n.*
indirect reference
Synonyms: intimation, suggestion
INCLINATION (ihn cluh nay shuhn) *n.*
tendency toward
Synonyms: leaning, trend, preference, disposition, propensity
EXTINCT (ihk stingkt) *adj.*
dead; no longer active
Synonyms: exterminated, eradicated, annihilated, eliminated, destroyed; defunct

ANIMATED (aa nih may tihd) *adj.*
lively, excited, filled with spirit
Synonyms: elated, vivacious, inspired

"I've neither cold nor fever, Nelly," he remarked, in **allusion** to my morning's speech, "and I'm ready to do justice to the food you give me."

He took his knife and fork, and was going to commence eating, when the **inclination** appeared to become suddenly **extinct**. He laid them on the table, looked eagerly towards the window, then rose and went out. We saw him walking to and fro in the garden while we concluded our meal, and Earnshaw said he'd go and ask why he would not dine: he thought we had grieved him some way.

"Well, is he coming?" cried Catherine, when her cousin returned.

"Nay," he answered, "but he's not angry: he seemed rarely pleased indeed; only I made him impatient by speaking to him twice; and then he bid me be off to you: he wondered how I could want the company of anybody else."

I set his plate to keep warm on the fender; and after an hour or two he re-entered, when the room was clear, in no degree calmer: the same unnatural—it was unnatural—appearance of joy under his black brows; the same bloodless hue, and his teeth visible, now and then, in a kind of smile; his frame shivering, not as one shivers with chill or weakness, but as a tight-stretched cord vibrates—a strong thrilling, rather than trembling.

I will ask what is the matter, I thought: or who should? And I exclaimed:

"Have you heard any good news, Mr. Heathcliff? You look uncommonly **animated**."

"Where should good news come from to me?" he said. "I'm **animated** with hunger, and, seemingly, I must not eat."

"Your dinner is here," I returned, "why won't you get it?"

"I don't want it now," he muttered hastily. "I'll wait till supper. And, Nelly, once for all, let me beg you to warn Hareton and the other away from me. I wish to be troubled by nobody: I wish to have this place to myself."

BANISHMENT (<u>baan</u> ish mehnt) *n.*
the act of forcing someone to leave, exile, ostracism
Synonyms: deportment, expatriation, removal

PRY (prie) *v.* **-ing,-ied.**
to intrude into; force open
Synonyms: snoop, nose, spy, eavesdrop; probe

EJACULATION (ih <u>jaak</u> yuh lay shuhn) *n.*
a sudden exclamation
Synonyms: chatter, vociferation, expletive

"Is there some new reason for this **banishment**?" I inquired. "Tell me why you are so queer, Mr. Heathcliff? Where were you last night? I'm not putting the question through idle curiosity, but—"

"You are putting the question through very idle curiosity," he interrupted, with a laugh. "Yet, I'll answer it. Last night I was on the threshold of hell. To-day, I am within sight of my heaven. I have my eyes on it: hardly three feet to sever me! And now you'd better go! You'll neither see nor hear anything to frighten you, if you refrain from **prying**."

Having swept the hearth and wiped the table, I departed; more <u>perplexed</u> than ever.

He did not quit the house again that afternoon, and no one intruded on his solitude; till, at eight o'clock, I deemed it proper, though unsummoned, to carry a candle and his supper to him. He was leaning against the ledge of an open <u>lattice</u>, but not looking out: his face was turned to the interior gloom. The fire had smouldered to ashes; the room was filled with the damp, mild air of the cloudy evening; and so still, that not only the murmur of the <u>beck</u> down Gimmerton was distinguishable, but its ripples and its gurgling over the pebbles, or through the large stones which it could not cover. I uttered an **ejaculation** of discontent at seeing the dismal grate, and commenced shutting the <u>casements</u>, one after another, till I came to his.

"Must I close this?" I asked, in order to rouse him; for he would not stir.

The light flashed on his features as I spoke. Oh, Mr. Lockwood, I cannot express what a terrible start I got by the momentary view! Those deep black eyes! That smile, and ghastly paleness! It appeared to me, not Mr. Heathcliff, but a goblin; and, in my terror, I let the candle bend towards the wall, and it left me in darkness.

"Yes, close it," he replied, in his familiar voice. "There, that is pure awkwardness! Why did you hold the candle horizontally? Be quick, and bring another."

I hurried out in a foolish state of dread, and said to Joseph:

REKINDLE (ree <u>kihn</u> duhl) *v.* **-ing,-ed.**
to set fire to again, or reignite; excite or inspire again
Synonyms: relight; reawaken

INCARNATE (ihn <u>kahr</u> niht) *adj.*
having human or bodily form; personified
Synonyms: embodied, corporal, physical; typefied

BANE (bayn) *n.*
something causing death, destruction, or ruin
Synonyms: destroyer, curse, scourge, poison

VEX (vehks) *v.* **-ing,-ed.**
to irritate, annoy; confuse, puzzle
Synonyms: bother, plague, afflict, irk; perplex, perturb

OBLIGE (uh <u>bliej</u>) *v.* **-ing,-ed.**
to be obligated, to require or force someone to obey
Synonyms: compel, constrain, bind, favor

ASCERTAIN (aa suhr <u>tayn</u>) *v.* **-ing,-ed.**
to determine, discover, make certain of
Synonyms: verify, calculate, detect

"The master wishes you to take him a light and **rekindle** the fire." For I dared not go in myself again just then.

Joseph rattled some fire into the shovel, and went; but he brought it back immediately, with the supper-tray in his other hand, explaining that Mr. Heathcliff was going to bed, and he wanted nothing to eat till morning. We heard him mount the stairs directly: he did not proceed to his ordinary chamber, but turned into that with the panelled bed: its window, as I mentioned before, is wide enough for anybody to get through; and it struck me that he plotted another midnight excursion, of which he had rather we had no suspicion.

"Is he a ghoul or a vampire?" I mused. I had read of such hideous **incarnate** demons. And then I set myself to reflect how I had tended him in infancy, and watched him grow to youth, and followed him almost through his whole course; and what absurd nonsense it was to yield to that sense of horror. "But where did he come from, the little dark thing, harboured by a good man to his **bane**?" muttered Superstition, as I dozed into unconsciousness. And I began, half dreaming, to weary myself with imagining some fit parentage for him; and, repeating my awaking meditations, I tracked his existence over again, with grim variations; at last, picturing his death and funeral: of which, all I can remember is, being exceedingly **vexed** at having the task of dictating an inscription for his monument, and consulting the <u>sexton</u> about it; and, as he had no surname, and we could not tell his age, we were **obliged** to content ourselves with the single word, "Heathcliff." That came true: we were. If you enter the <u>kirkyard</u>, you'll read on his headstone, only that, and the date of his death.

Dawn restored me to common sense. I rose, and went into the garden, as soon as I could see, to **ascertain** if there were any footmarks under his window. There were none. He has stayed at home, I thought, and he'll be all right to-day." I prepared breakfast for the household, as

RAPTURED (<u>raap</u> chuhrd) *adj.*
    ecstatic or extremely joyful; deeply absorbed
        Synonyms: exalted, delighted, elated; transfixed
COUNTENANCE (<u>kown</u> tuh nuhns) *n.*
    appearance, facial expression
        Synonyms: face, features, visage

was my usual custom, but told Hareton and Catherine to get theirs ere the master came down, for he lay late. They preferred taking it out of doors, under the trees, and I set a little table to accommodate them.

On my re-entrance, I found Mr. Heathcliff below. He and Joseph were conversing about some farming business; he gave clear, minute directions concerning the matter discussed, but he spoke rapidly, and turned his head continually aside, and had the same excited expression, even more exaggerated. When Joseph quitted the room he took his seat in the place he generally chose, and I put a basin of coffee before him. He drew it nearer, and then rested his arms on the table, and looked at the opposite wall, as I supposed, surveying one particular portion, up and down, with glittering, restless eyes, and with such eager interest that he stopped breathing during half a minute together.

"Come now," I exclaimed, pushing some bread against his hand, "eat and drink that, while it is hot: it has been waiting near an hour."

He didn't notice me, and yet he smiled. I'd rather have seen him gnash his teeth than smile so.

"Mr. Heathcliff! Master!" I cried. "Don't, for God's sake, stare as if you saw an unearthly vision."

"Don't, for God's sake, shout so loud," he replied. "Turn round, and tell me, are we by ourselves?"

"Of course," was my answer, "of course we are."

Still I involuntarily obeyed him, as if I was not quite sure. With a sweep of his hand he cleared a vacant space in front among the breakfast things, and leant forward to gaze more at his ease.

Now, I perceived he was not looking at the wall; for when I regarded him alone, it seemed exactly that he gazed at something within two yards' distance. And whatever it was, it communicated, apparently, both pleasure and pain in exquisite extremes: at least the anguished, yet **raptured**, expression of his **countenance** suggested that idea. The fancied object was not fixed: either his eyes

DILIGENCE (<u>dihl</u> uh juhns) *n.*
  steady, earnest application of effort
    Synonyms: perseverance, attentiveness
PROTRACTED (proh <u>traak</u> tihd) *adj.*
  prolonged, drawn out, extended
    Synonyms: lengthy, elongated, stretched
ABSTINENCE (<u>aab</u> stih nihnts) *n.*
  the act of refraining from some activity or action
    Synonyms: temperance, self-restraint; fasting
COMPLIANCE (kuhm <u>plie</u> uhnts) *n.*
  submission, yielding
    Synonyms: malleability, complacency, acquiescence
ENTREATY (ehn <u>tree</u> tee) *n.*
  a plea or request
    Synonyms: imploration, prayer, petition
SAUNTER (<u>sawn</u> tuhr) *v.* **-ing,-ed.**
  to walk leisurely or amble
    Synonyms: stroll, ramble, perambulate
DESCEND (dih <u>sehnd</u>) (dee <u>sehnd</u>) *v.* **-ing,-ed.**
  to pass from a higher place to a lower place
    Synonyms: fall, dismount, gravitate
MISGIVING (mihs <u>gihv</u> ihng) *n.*
  a feeling of apprehension, doubt, sense of foreboding
    Synonyms: distrust, presentiment, qualm, disquiet
INSPIRATION (ihn spuhr <u>ay</u> shuhn) *n.*
  a breath
    Synonyms: inhalation, gasp
DIVERT (die <u>vuhrt</u>) *v.* **-ing,-ed.**
  to distract or amuse; to move in different directions
  from a particular point
    Synonyms: deter, occupy, entertain; deviate, separate
REVERIE (<u>rehv</u> uh ree) *n.*
  a daydream
    Synonyms: dream, absorption, muse, meditation

pursued it with unwearied **diligence**, and, even in speaking to me, were never weaned away. I vainly reminded him of his **protracted abstinence** from food: if he stirred to touch anything in **compliance** with my **entreaties**, if he stretched his hand out to get a piece of bread, his fingers clenched before they reached it, and remained on the table, forgetful of their aim.

I sat, a model of patience, trying to attract his absorbed attention from its engrossing speculation; till he grew irritable, and got up, asking why I would not allow him to have his own time in taking his meals? And saying that on the next occasion, I needn't wait: I might set the things down and go. Having uttered these words he left the house; slowly **sauntered** down the garden path, and disappeared through the gate.

The hours crept anxiously by: another evening came. I did not retire to rest till late, and when I did, I could not sleep. He returned after midnight, and, instead of going to bed, shut himself into the room beneath. I listened, and tossed about, and, finally, dressed and **descended**. It was too <u>irksome</u> to lie there, harassing my brain with a hundred idle **misgivings**.

I distinguished Mr. Heathcliff's step, restlessly measuring the floor, and he frequently broke the silence by a deep **inspiration**, resembling a groan. He muttered detached words also; the only one I could catch was the name of Catherine, coupled with some wild term of endearment or suffering; and spoken as one would speak to a person present: low and earnest, and wrung from the depth of his soul. I had not courage to walk straight into the apartment; but I desired to **divert** him from his **reverie**, and therefore fell foul of the kitchen fire, stirred it, and began to scrape the cinders. It drew him forth sooner than I expected. He opened the door immediately, and said:

"Nelly, come here—is it morning? Come in with your light."

"It is striking four," I answered. "You want a candle to take upstairs: you might have lit one at this fire."

KINDLE (<u>kihn</u> duhl) *v.* **-ing,-ed.**
  to set fire to or ignite; to excite or inspire
    Synonyms: light, spark; arouse, awaken

BESTOW (bih <u>stoh</u>) *v.* **-ing,-ed.**
  to apply or devote, as in time or effort; to give as a gift
    Synonyms: allocate, dedicate; endow, confer, present

REPENT (rih <u>pehnt</u>) *v.* **-ing,-ed.**
  to regret a past action
    Synonyms: rue, atone, apologize

REPOSE (rih <u>pohz</u>) *n.*
  relaxation, leisure; a state of peace or tranquility
    Synonyms: rest, ease, idleness; calmness, serenity

"No, I don't wish to go upstairs," he said. "Come in, and **kindle** *me* a fire, and do anything there is to do about the room."

"I must blow the coals red first, before I can carry any," I replied, getting a chair and the bellows.

He roamed to and fro, meantime, in a state approaching distraction; his heavy sighs succeeding each other so thick as to leave no space for common breathing between.

"When day breaks I'll send for Green," he said. "I wish to make some legal inquiries of him while I can **bestow** a thought on those matters, and while I can act calmly. I have not written my will yet; and how to leave my property I cannot determine. I wish I could annihilate it from the face of the earth."

"I would not talk so, Mr. Heathcliff," I <u>interposed</u>. "Let your will be a while: you'll be spared to **repent** of your many injustices yet. I never expected that your nerves would be disordered: they are, at present, marvellously so, however, and almost entirely through your own fault. The way you've passed these three last days might knock up a Titan. Do take some food, and some **repose**. You need only look at yourself in a glass to see how you require both. Your cheeks are hollow, and your eyes bloodshot, like a person starving with hunger and going blind with loss of sleep."

"It is not my fault that I cannot eat or rest," he replied. "I assure you it is through no settled designs. I'll do both as soon as I possibly can. But you might as well bid a man struggling in the water rest within arm's length of the shore! I must reach it first, and then I'll rest. Well, never mind Mr. Green: as to **repenting** of my injustices, I've done no injustice, and I **repent** of nothing. I'm too happy; and yet I'm not happy enough. My soul's bliss kills my body, but does not satisfy itself."

"Happy, master?" I cried. "Strange happiness! If you would hear me without being angry, I might offer some advice that would make you happier."

"What is that?" he asked. "Give it."

PRECEPT (<u>pree</u> sehpt) *n.*
a command or principle intended as a general rule of
action
Synonyms: law, tenet, edict, axiom

OBLIGED (uh <u>bliejd</u>) *adj.*
grateful, appreciative
Synonyms: thankful, indebted, owing

UNCOVETED (uhn <u>kuh</u> vih tihd) *adj.*
unwanted, not desired
Synonyms: disliked, ignored, rejected

PERSEVERE (pehr suh <u>veer</u>) *v.* **-ing,-ed.**
to continue with determination, remain steadfast
Synonyms: persist, endure, plod

OBSTINATE (<u>ahb</u> stih nuht) *adj.*
stubborn
Synonyms: headstrong, stiff-necked, bullheaded,
pigheaded, mulish

"You are aware, Mr. Heathcliff," I said, "that from the time you were thirteen years old, you have lived a selfish, unchristian life; and probably hardly had a Bible in your hands during all that period. You must have forgotten the contents of the Book, and you may not have space to search it now. Could it be hurtful to send for some one—some minister of any denomination, it does not matter which—to explain it, and show you how very far you have erred from its **precepts**; and how unfit you will be for its heaven, unless a change takes place before you die?"

"I'm rather **obliged** than angry, Nelly," he said, "for you remind me of the manner in which I desire to be buried. It is to be carried to the churchyard in the evening. You and Hareton may, if you please, accompany me: and mind, particularly, to notice that the <u>sexton</u> obeys my directions concerning the two coffins! No minister need come; nor need anything be said over me.—I tell you I have nearly attained *my* heaven; and that of others is altogether unvalued and **uncoveted** by me."

"And supposing you **persevered** in your **obstinate** fast, and died by that means, and they refused to bury you in the precincts of the <u>kirk</u>?" I said, shocked at his godless indifference. "How would you like it?"

"They won't do that," he replied. "If they did, you must have me removed secretly: and if you neglect it you shall prove, practically, that the dead are not annihilated!"

As soon as he heard the other members of the family stirring he retired to his den, and I breathed freer. But in the afternoon, while Joseph and Hareton were at their work, he came into the kitchen again, and, with a wild look, bid me come and sit in the house: he wanted somebody with him. I declined: telling him plainly that his strange talk and manner frightened me, and I had neither the nerve nor the will to be his companion alone.

"I believe you think me a fiend," he said, with his dismal laugh, "something too horrible to live under a decent roof." Then turning to Catherine, who was there, and who drew behind me at his approach, he added, half-sneer-

661

SOLICIT (suh <u>lih</u> siht) *v.* **-ing,-ed.**
  to petition persistently, to seek out
    Synonyms: entice, tempt, request, entreat

KEEN *adj.*
  intellectually sharp, perceptive; having a sharp edge
    Synonyms: acute, quick, canny; pointed, razorlike

STARK (stahrk) *adj.*
  bare; empty, vacant
    Synonyms: naked; austere, barren, bleak, grim,
    dismal
EXULTATION (ihg suhl <u>tay</u> shuhn) *n.*
  the act of being extremely joyful
    Synonyms: celebration, delight, jubilation

ingly—"Will *you* come, chuck? I'll not hurt you. No! To you I've made myself worse than the devil. Well, there is *one* who won't shrink from my company! By God! She's relentless. Oh, damn it! It's unutterably too much for flesh and blood to bear—even mine."

He **solicited** the society of no one more. At dusk, he went into his chamber. Through the whole night, and far into the morning, we heard him groaning and murmuring to himself. Hareton was anxious to enter, but I bade him fetch Dr. Kenneth, and he should go in and see him. When he came, and I requested admittance and tried to open the door, I found it locked; and Heathcliff bid us be damned. He was better, and would be left alone; so the doctor went away.

The following evening was very wet: indeed it poured down till day-dawn; and, as I took my morning walk round the house, I observed the master's window swinging open, and the rain driving straight in. He cannot be in bed, I thought: those showers would drench him through. He must either be up or out. But I'll make no more ado, I'll go boldly and look.

Having succeeded in obtaining entrance with another key, I ran to unclose the panels, for the chamber was vacant; quickly pushing them aside, I peeped in. Mr. Heathcliff was there—laid on his back. His eyes met mine so **keen** and fierce, I started; and then he seemed to smile. I could not think him dead: but his face and throat were washed with rain; the bedclothes dripped, and he was perfectly still. The <u>lattice</u>, flapping to and fro, had grazed one hand that rested on the sill; no blood trickled from the broken skin, and when I put my fingers to it, I could doubt no more: he was dead and **stark**!

I <u>hasped</u> the window; I combed his black long hair from his forehead; I tried to close his eyes: to extinguish, if possible, that frightful, life-like gaze of **exultation** before any one else beheld it. They would not shut: they seemed to sneer at my attempts; and his parted lips and sharp white teeth sneered too! Taken with another fit of

RESOLUTELY (reh suh <u>loot</u> lee) *adv.*
   with determination; with a clear purpose
      Synonyms: firmly, unwaveringly; intently
MEDDLE (<u>meh</u> duhl) *v.* **-ing,-ed.**
   to interfere in others' affairs, to impose
      Synonyms: interlope, tamper, snoop, encroach

ABSTAIN (uhb <u>stayn</u>) *v.* **-ing,-ed.**
   to forgo an activity or action
      Synonyms: forbear, refrain

VERDANT (<u>vuhr</u> dnt) *adj.*
   green with vegetation; inexperienced
      Synonyms: grassy, leafy, wooded; immature
AFFIRM (uh <u>fihrm</u>) *v.* **-ing,-ed.**
   to state positively, to assert as valid or confirmed
      Synonyms: declare, avow, maintain

<u>cowardice</u>, I cried out for Joseph. Joseph shuffled up and made a noise; but **resolutely** refused to **meddle** with him.

"Th' divil's harried off his soul," he cried, "and he may hev his carcass into t' bargain, for aught I care! Ech! What a wicked un he looks girning at death!" and the old sinner grinned in mockery. I thought he intended to cut a caper round the bed; but, suddenly composing himself, he fell on his knees, and raised his hands, and returned thanks that the lawful master and the ancient stock were restored to their rights.

I felt stunned by the awful event; and my memory unavoidably recurred to former times with a sort of oppressive sadness. But poor Hareton, the most wronged, was the only one who really suffered much. He sat by the corpse all night, weeping in bitter earnest. He pressed its hand, and kissed the sarcastic savage face that every one else shrank from contemplating; and bemoaned him with that strong grief which springs naturally from a generous heart, though it be tough as tempered steel.

Dr. Kenneth was <u>perplexed</u> to pronounce of what disorder the master died. I concealed the fact of his having swallowed nothing for four days, fearing it might lead to trouble, and then, I am persuaded, he did not **abstain** on purpose: it was the consequence of his strange illness, not the cause.

We buried him, to the scandal of the whole neighbourhood, as he wished. Earnshaw and I, the <u>sexton</u>, and six men to carry the coffin, comprehended the whole attendance. The six men departed when they had let it down into the grave: we stayed to see it covered. Hareton, with a streaming face, dug green sods, and laid them over the brown mound himself: at present it is as smooth and **verdant** as its companion mounds—and I hope its tenant sleeps as soundly. But the country folk, if you ask them, would swear on the Bible that he *walks*: there are those who speak of having met him near the church, and on the moor, and even in this house. Idle tales, you'll say, and so say I. Yet that old man by the kitchen fire **affirms** he has

TRAVERSE (truh <u>vuhrs</u>) (traa <u>vuhrs</u>) *v.* **-ing,-ed.**
    to travel or move across; to turn or move laterally
        Synonyms: cross, intersect, pass through; swivel,
        zigzag

LEVITY (<u>leh</u> vih tee) *n.*
    humor, frivolity, gaiety
        Synonyms: lightness, amusement, humor, cheer

seen two on 'em, looking out of his chamber window, on every rainy night since his death: and an odd thing happened to me about a month ago. I was going to the Grange one evening—a dark evening, threatening thunder—and, just at the turn of the Heights, I encountered a little boy with a sheep and two lambs before him; he was crying terribly; and I supposed the lambs were skittish, and would not be guided.

"What's the matter, my little man?" I asked.

"There's Heathcliff and a woman, yonder, under t' <u>nab</u>," he blubbered, "un' I darnut pass 'em."

I saw nothing; but neither the sheep nor he would go on; so I bid him take the road lower down. He probably raised the phantoms from thinking, as he **traversed** the moors alone, on the nonsense he had heard his parents and companions repeat. Yet, still, I don't like being out in the dark now; and I don't like being left by myself in this grim house: I cannot help it; I shall be glad when they leave it, and shift to the Grange.

"They are going to the Grange, then," I said.

"Yes," answered Mrs. Dean, "as soon as they are married, and that will be on New Year's day."

"And who will live here, then?"

"Why, Joseph will take care of the house, and, perhaps, a lad to keep him company. They will live in the kitchen, and the rest will be shut up."

"For the use of such ghosts as choose to inhabit it," I observed.

"No, Mr. Lockwood," said Nelly, shaking her head. "I believe the dead are at peace: but it is not right to speak of them with **levity**."

At that moment the garden gate swung to; the ramblers were returning.

"They are afraid of nothing," I grumbled, watching their approach through the window. "Together they would brave Satan and all his legions."

As they stepped on to the door-stones, and halted to take a last look at the moon—or, more correctly, at each

SAT Vocabulary

IMPEL (ihm pehl) *v.* **-ling,-led.**
　to urge forward as if driven by a strong moral pressure
　　Synonyms: push, prompt, drive, incite, instigate
EXPOSTULATION (ihk spahs chuh <u>lay</u> shuhn) *n.*
　an expression of opposition; reasoning
　　Synonyms: argument, dissuasion, remonstration;
　　assertion
INDISCRETION (ihn dih <u>skrehsh</u> uhn) *n.*
　lack of good judgment, injudiciousness
　　Synonyms: thoughtlessness, misjudgment
DIVERSION (dih <u>vuhr</u> zhuhn) (die <u>vuhr</u> zhuhn) *n.*
　a distraction; an amusing or relaxing activity
　　Synonyms: deviation; entertainment, recreation

BENIGN (bih <u>nien</u>) *adj.*
　kindly, gentle, or harmless
　　Synonyms: innocuous, mild, safe

other by her light—I felt irresistibly **impelled** to escape them again; and, pressing a remembrance into the hand of Mrs. Dean, and disregarding her **expostulations** at my rudeness, I vanished through the kitchen as they opened the house door; and so should have confirmed Joseph in his opinion of his fellow-servant's gay **indiscretions**, had he not fortunately recognised me for a respectable character by the sweet ring of a <u>sovereign</u> at his feet.

My walk home was lengthened by a **diversion** in the direction of the <u>kirk</u>. When beneath its walls, I perceived decay had made progress, even in seven months: many a window showed black gaps deprived of glass; and slates jutted off, here and there, beyond the right line of the roof, to be gradually worked off in coming autumn storms.

I sought, and soon discovered, the three head-stones on the slope next the moor: the middle one grey, and half buried in <u>heath</u>: Edgar Linton's only harmonised by the turf and moss creeping up its foot: Heathcliff's still bare. I lingered round them, under the **benign** sky; watched the moths fluttering among the <u>heath</u> and harebells, listened to the soft wind breathing through the grass, and wondered how any one could ever imagine unquiet slumbers for the sleepers in that quiet earth.

Glossary

The following words appear <u>underlined</u> throughout the text.

abode (uh <u>bohd</u>) *n.* a home or house; a place to dwell

accursed (uh <u>kuhr</u> sihd) *adj.*
hateful, unwanted; doomed to ruin or misery

adieu (uh <u>dyoo</u>) *n.;* **adieux** (uh <u>dyoos</u>) *n. pl. French.*
an expression of farewell or goodbye

adjourn (uh <u>juhrn</u>) *v.* **-ing,-ed.**
to move from one place to another; to retire for the day

adjuration (aah jeh <u>ray</u> shuhn) *n.*
an earnest appeal or request

advent (<u>aad</u> vehnt) *n.*
an arrival or approach of something

ague (<u>ay</u> gyoo) *n.* a state of chills or shivering

alight (uh <u>liet</u>) *v.* **-ing,-ed.**
to dismount; to settle or come to rest

annum (<u>aa</u> nuhm) *n.* a year

asseverate (uh <u>seh</u> vuhr ayt) *v.* **-ing,-ed.**
to declare positively, to affirm

attempt the coxcomb (<u>cahks</u> cohm) *phrase.* to act foolish

automaton (aw <u>tah</u> mih tuhn) *n.*
someone who acts like a machine; a robot

bairn (bayrn) *n.;* **bairny** (<u>bayr</u> nee) *n. Scottish.* a child

basilisk (<u>baa</u> sih lihsk) *n.*
a serpent or dragon, believed to kill by breath or look

bathos (<u>bay</u> thahs) *n.*
a state of being common

beck (behk) *n. British.* a small creek or brook

besetting (bih <u>seh</u> tihng) *adj.* troubling, harassing

bewail (bih <u>wayl</u>) *v.* **-ing,-ed.**
to cry over, to express unhappiness

bludgeon (<u>bluh</u> jihn) *n.* a short wooden club

671

bluff (bluhf) *adj.* having a steep and flat front; firm

bonnie or bonny (<u>bah</u> nee) *adj. Scottish.* pretty

box (bahks) *n. British.* a gift, usually given at Christmas

brach (braak) *n. British.*
a derogatory expression meaning a female hound dog

brindled (<u>brihn</u> duhld) *adj.*
having patchy coloring, especially of the fur

brute (broot) *n.;* **brutishness** (<u>broo</u> tihsh nehs) *n.*
a mean, crude person; ignorant insensitivity

bugbear (<u>buhg</u> bayr) *adj.* frightening

cant (kaant) *v.* **-ing,-ed.** to whine, to speak nonsensically

cant (kaant) *adj.;* **canty** (<u>kaan</u> tee) *adj. British.*
cheerful, lively, pleasant

capital (<u>kaa</u> pih tuhl) *adj.* excellent, top-notch

carriage (<u>kaa</u> rihj) *n.* posture, manner of carrying oneself

carrion (<u>kaa</u> ree ihn) *n.* dead and rotting flesh

casement (<u>kays</u> mehnt) *n.*
a window with hinged coverings that open outward

catechise or **catechize** (<u>kaa</u> tih chiez) *v.* **-ing,-ed.**
to give religious instruction; to instruct with questions

catechism (<u>kaa</u> tih kih zuhm) *n.*
serious questioning or examination

changeling (<u>chaynj</u> lihng) *n.*
a child secretly exchanged for another at a very
young age

chit (chiht) *n.* a bold and saucy girl or young woman

coalscuttle (<u>kohl</u> skuh tuhl) *n.* a container for holding coal

cockatrice (<u>kahk</u> uh trihs) *n.*
a monster, part serpent and part fowl, whose glance is
deadly

commination (kah mih <u>nay</u> shuhn) *n.*
a prayer to God asking Him to punish sinners

concourse (<u>kahn</u> kohrs) *n.* a large crowd

constable (<u>kahn</u> stuh buhl) *n. British.* a police officer

consumption (kuhn <u>suhmp</u> shuhn) *n.*
a wasting disease or sickness

contrariety (kahn truh <u>rie</u> ih tee) *n.*
disagreement, opposition

cow (kow) *v.* **-ing,-ed.** to scare with threats and force

cowardice (<u>kow</u> uhr dihs) *n.*
fear of danger or pain; lack of courage

cudgel (<u>kuh</u> juhl) *n.* a short club

cur (kuhr) *n.* a dog of inferior quality or breeding

curate (<u>kyoor</u> ayt) *n.*
a person who can lead religious worship

decamp (dih <u>kaamp</u>) *v.* **-ing,-ed.**
to leave suddenly, to run away

delft (dehlft) *n.*
a type of pottery, usually of white and blue colors

denominate (dih <u>nah</u> mih nayt) *v.* **-ing,-ed.**
to name, to designate

despatch (dihs <u>paach</u>) *n.; v.* **-ing,-ed.**
haste; to send, to do something quickly

dree *adj. British.* tiresome, tedious

dunnock (<u>duh</u> nuhk) *n. British.* a small brown sparrow

eft (ehft) *n.* a young newt

elf-bolt (<u>ehlf</u> bohlt) *n.* an arrowhead

Elysium (ih lihz <u>ee</u> uhm) (ih <u>lihz</u> ee uhm) *n.*
a place of perfect happiness, a utopia

embalm (ehm <u>bahlm</u>) *v.* **-ing,-ed.**
to prevent decay with preservatives

ensue (ehn <u>soo</u>) *v.* **-ing,-ed.**
to follow afterward, to happen subsequently

entrails (<u>ehn</u> trayls) *n. pl.* guts, intestines

essay (<u>ehs</u> ay) *n.;* **essay** (eh <u>say</u>) *v.* **-ing,-ed.**
a trial, test, or attempt; to try or attempt

Glossary

fagot (<u>faa</u> giht) *n.* a bundle of sticks

fain (fayn) *adv.; adj.* gladly, rather; glad, content, happy

ferocity (fuhr <u>ahs</u> ih tee) *n.* fierceness, violent wildness

festoon (fehs <u>toon</u>) *n.*
a graceful loop or arc of fabric draped decoratively

flight (fliet) *v.* **-ing,-ed.** to frighten

fold (fohld) *n. British.*
a rolling hill in the countryside; a pen for sheep

fondle (<u>fahn</u> duhl) *v.* **-ing,-ed.** *Obsolete.*
to spoil, to treat with excessive kindness or affection

fondling (<u>fahn</u> dlihng) *n.* a fool, a simple-minded person

fortnight (<u>fohrt</u> niet) *n.* a two-week period of time

frame (fraym) *v.* **-ing,-ed.**
to go; to make up, create, contrive

furze (fuhrz) *n.*
a thorny shrub with yellow flowers found in W. Europe

gad (gaad) *v.* **-ding,-ded.** to wander without a purpose

gaiters (<u>gay</u> tuhrs) *n. pl.*
leather or cloth coverings for the lower legs and ankles

gaoler (<u>jay</u> luhr) *n.* one who guards prisoners; a jailer

garret (<u>gaa</u> reht) *n.* an attic

griffin (<u>grih</u> fihn) *n.*
an imaginary creature that is part lion and part eagle

gripe (griep) *n.* a strong hold or grasp of something

guttural (<u>guh</u> tuhr uhl) *adj.*
relating to a sound formed in the throat

habit (<u>haa</u> biht) *n.* a specific type of dress or costume

hale (hayl) *adj.* healthy, robust

hasp (haasp) *v.* **-ing,-ed.** to close, to fasten shut

heath (heeth) *n.* a low-growing shrub

hector (<u>hehk</u> tuhr) *v.* **-ing,-ed.**
to intimidate or threaten, as a bully does

674

heifer (<u>heh</u> fuhr) *n.*
a young cow, usually one that has not had calves

hem (hehm) *v.* **-ming,-med.**
to cough, in order to fill an uncomfortable silence; to
hesitate while speaking

heterodox (<u>heht</u> uhr uh dahks) *adj.*
having opinions that oppose those of the church or
accepted doctrine

hob (hahb) *n.*
a shelf in a fireplace used to keep food warm

hovel (<u>huh</u> vuhl) *n.* a small, crude hut or dwelling place

imbecile (<u>ihm</u> buh sihl) *adj.* stupid, idiotic

immolation (ih moh <u>lay</u> shuhn) *n.*
an act of sacrifice with the use of fire

imp (ihmp) *n.* a small devil or demon; a mischievous child

insufferable (ihn <u>suhf</u> uhr uh buhl) *adj.*
impossible to handle or endure, not tolerable

interdict (<u>ihn</u> tuhr dihkt) *n.* an order; a prohibition

interpose (ihn tuhr <u>pohz</u>) *v.* **-ing,-ed.**
to come between; to interject or interrupt

irksome (<u>urk</u> suhm) *adj.* annoying or tedious

jade (jayd) *n.* a mean woman, a wench

kirk (kuhrk) *n.;* **kirkyard** (<u>kuhrk</u> yahrd) *n. British.*
a church; a churchyard

Lascar (<u>laas</u> kuhr) *n.*
a sailor or military servant of the East Indies

lattice (<u>laat</u> ihs) *n.*
a window with a criss-crossed pattern of wood or metal

leveret (<u>lehv</u> uhr iht) *n.* a baby rabbit

ling (lihng) *n.*
a short evergreen shrub with pinkish flowers

magisterial (maaj ih <u>steer</u> ee uhl) *adj.*
dominating, arrogant, authoritative

mantle (<u>maan</u> tuhl) *n.* a cloak, a sleeveless coat

mattock (<u>maat</u> ihk) *n.*
a tool with two blades used for digging

maxillary (<u>maak</u> sih laa ree) *adj.* relating to the jaw

mire (mier) *n.* a muddy, wet area; a bog

miscreant (<u>mihs</u> kree ehnt) *n.*
an uncaring person who lacks morals, a scoundrel

monomania (mah noh <u>may</u> nee uh) *n.*
an obsession with one thing or idea

nab (naab) *n.* a rocky hill, peak, knoll

naught or nought (nawt) *n.* nothing; nonexistence

negus (<u>nee</u> gihs) *n.*
beverage of wine, water, lemon juice, sugar, and nutmeg

orison (<u>aw</u> rih sihn) *n.* a prayer

ousel (<u>oo</u> zuhl) *n.* a blackbird

palaver (puh <u>laa</u> vuhr) *n.* chatter; flattery

paroxysm (puh <u>rahk</u> sihz uhm) *n.*
an outburst of passion or emotion; a convulsion

peevish (<u>pee</u> vihsh) *adj.;* **peevishly**, *adv.;* **peevishness**, *n.*
discontented, cranky; in a discontented way; discontent

penetralium (peh nih <u>tray</u> lee uhm) *n.*
the innermost section of a building, a private sanctuary

perplex (puhr <u>pleks</u>) *v.* **-ing,-ed.**; **perplexity**, *n.*
to confuse, trouble, or make complicated; confusion, complication

personification (puhr sahn ih fih <u>kay</u> shuhn)
something that is a perfect example of an idea or quality

pettish (<u>peht</u> ihsh) *adj.;* **pettishly**, *adv.;* **pettishness**, *n.*
irritable, moody, petulant; irritably; irritability

phlegm (flehm) *n.*
indifference, lack of caring; sluggishness

phraseology (fray zee <u>ahl</u> ih jee) *n.* speech or writing style

physiognomy (fih zee <u>ahg</u> nuh mee) *n.*
characteristic facial features; the art of judging one's character from facial features

pitch (pihch) *n.* a level or degree, often used to describe intensity

postern (<u>poh</u> sturn) *n.*
a small gate in the back of a house, a private door

preterhuman (preh tuhr <u>hyoo</u> mehn) *adj.*
superhuman, virtually impossible

psalmody (<u>sahl</u> muh dee) *n.* a collection of psalms

puling (<u>pyoo</u> lihng) *adj.* whimpering, complaining

purgatory (<u>puhr</u> guh tohr ee) *n.*
a condition of suffering; in Catholicism, a place of redemption and purification between death and heaven

qualm (kwahm) *n.* a feeling of nausea; a feeling of doubt

rankle (<u>raang</u> kuhl) *v.* -ing,-ed.
to irritate or inflame; to fester

reaming (<u>ree</u> mihng) *adj.* frothing, overflowing

reap (reep) *v.* -ing,-ed.; **reaper** (<u>reep</u> uhr) *n.*
to harvest or cut a crop; a worker who harvests crops

redound (rih <u>downd</u>) *v.* -ing,-ed.
to contribute, strengthen; to rebound, reverberate

refuse (<u>reh</u> fyoos) *n.* trash, useless items

rent (rehnt) *n.* a ripped hole, a tear

resurrection (rehz uh <u>rehk</u> shuhn) *n.*
a rising from inactivity; a rising from the dead

rheumatism (<u>roo</u> muh tihz uhm) *n.*
painful inflammation of the joints and muscles

rive (riev) *v.* -ing,-ed,-en. to rip apart, tear to pieces

rogue (rohg) *n.*
a mischievous, playful person, a rascal

ruffian, (<u>ruhf</u> ee ihn) *n.;* **ruffianly**, *adj.*
a bully, a cruel person; rough, brutal, cruel

sally (<u>saa</u> lee) *v.* **-ing,-ied.** to set out, to leave for a trip

saturnine (<u>saat</u> uhr nien) *adj.* gloomy, sullen, dark

sceptre or **scepter** (<u>sehp</u> tuhr) *n.*
a staff that symbolizes power, authority, or royalty

settle (<u>seh</u> tuhl) *n.*
a high-backed wooden bench with storage underneath

sexton (<u>sehk</u> stihn) *n.*
a member of the church who digs graves

sheaves (sheevz) *n. pl.* bundles of stalks

sidle (<u>sie</u> duhl) *v.* **-ing,-ed.**
to move near someone or something in a coy manner

signet (<u>sihg</u> niht) *n.*
an impression made by a hard blow; an official seal

sizar (<u>sie</u> zuhr) *n. British.*
a student on scholarship at certain British universities

slattern (<u>slaat</u> uhrn) *n.* a dirty woman, a prostitute

slaver (<u>slah</u> vuhr) *v.* **-ing,-ed.**; **slaver**, *n.*
to drool or slobber; saliva, slobber

slavish (<u>slay</u> vihsh) *adj.*
having the qualities of a slave; subservient, submissive

slough (sluhf) *n.* a deep hole

smite (smiet) *v.* **-ing,-ote.**
to reproach, to attack physically or verbally, to strike

snuff (snuhf) *v.* **-ing,-ed.** to extinguish; to inhale, sniff

snuffers (<u>snuhf</u> uhrs) *n.* a device used to cut a candle wick

sotto voce (<u>soh</u> toh <u>voh</u> cheh) *adv. & adj. Italian.*
in a soft voice [**sotto** = *under*, **voce** = *voice*]

sough (sow) (suhf) *n.* a bog, swamp, or small pool

sovereign (<u>sahv</u> uhr ihn) (<u>sahv</u> rihn) *n.*
a gold coin, once used in Great Britain

spectre (<u>spehk</u> tuhr) *n.*
a ghost; something that haunts the mind

Glossary

stanchion (<u>staan</u> chihn) *n.* a vertical post or support

staunch (stawnch) *adj.;* **staunchly**, *adv.*
firm, constant, steadfast; faithfully

suffuse (suh <u>fyooz</u>) *v.* **-ing,-ed.**
to spread or cover with something, as with color or light

sundry (<u>suhn</u> dree) *adj.* assorted, various, miscellaneous

taper (<u>tay</u> puhr) *n.* a small thin candle

tarry (<u>taa</u> ree) *v.* **-ing,-ied.**
to wait, to loiter, to delay leaving

theology (thee <u>ahl</u> uh jee) *n.* religious study

thible (<u>thih</u> buhl) *n.* a kitchen utensil similar to a spatula

toilette (twah <u>leht</u>) *n. French.*
the act of grooming and dressing

unhasp (uhn <u>haasp</u>) *v.* **-ing,-ed.**
to open, to release the latch

unwonted (uhn <u>wawn</u> tihd) *adj.* uncommon, unusual

vagary (<u>vay</u> guh ree) *n.*
a wild action, a whim, an impulse

victuals (<u>viht</u> uhls) *n. pl.*
food; a collection of necessary supplies

vile (viel) *adj.* wretched, offensive, disgusting

vivisection (<u>vihv</u> ih sehk shuhn) *n.*
the act of cutting or dissecting a living thing, usually
for research purposes

vocation (voh <u>kay</u> shuhn) *n.*
a job, particularly one for which a person is qualified;
a life's calling

whelp (wehlp) *n.;* **whelphood**, *n.*
a puppy; the period of time and growth before adulthood

wicket (<u>wih</u> kiht) *n.* a small gate

wisht (wihsht) *interj.*
an utterance used to urge silence, similar to *hush*

wrest (rehst) *v.* **-ing,-ed.** to obtain using force or violence